Sociology of Aging

Sociology of Aging

Diana K. Harris

UNIVERSITY OF TENNESSEE

William E. Cole

UNIVERSITY OF TENNESSEE

HARPER & ROW, PUBLISHERS, New York
Cambridge, Philadelphia, San Francisco, Washington,
London, Mexico City, São Paulo, Singapore, Sydney
1817

To Aaron Harris and
Gladys Alexander

Printed in the U.S.A.

Library of Congress Catalog Card Number: 79–89742

ISBN: 0–395–28528–3

Cover credit: Peter Arnold, Inc.

Part opening credits: I Jeroboam Inc. Mitchell Payne. II Courtesy of Tennessee Commission on Aging. III Jeroboam Inc. Kent Reno. IV and VI ACTION. V Jeroboam Inc. Karen R. Preuss.

Contents

Preface

This book was written in response to a need—our need to find a suitable textbook for our large lecture sections in social gerontology. Our problem stems from the fact that currently there are few textbooks in the aging field as well as a scarcity of books that can be used as texts. After a long and frustrating search, we finally decided that the solution was simply to write our own text.

Objectives

First of all, we have tried to integrate the subject of aging into a systematic sociological framework. In this sense, our book represents a pioneering effort as being the first true sociology of aging text. A second objective was not only to cover all the traditional topics found in books on aging, but to include some material that might be considered unique. Full chapters, for example, are devoted to cultural values, social groups, and social stratification. In addition, full chapters are given to areas that most aging books only mention or omit entirely, such as socialization, religion, education, and crime. Another objective is that throughout the text, wherever relevant, we have included cross-cultural materials. We feel that this not only captures the students' interest but, and more importantly, it gives them an increased awareness and objectivity toward aging in their own culture, as well as making them more tolerant of cultural differences and deviations. Finally, an underlying theme throughout this book has been to examine recent research and to show how its results disprove many widely held assumptions and "myth-conceptions" regarding aging and the aged.

Organization

The book is organized into six parts. The introduction presents a general overview of the field of aging, some of the research methods that are employed, and a description of the demographic aspects of aging. Part II focuses on culture and socialization. Chapters 3, 4, and 5 emphasize the importance of culture and how it shapes behavior. Socialization is then discussed followed by a chapter on the biological and psychological aspects of aging. Part III looks at older people in social groups. Two types of stratification systems are then discussed: social class and minority relations. Part IV focuses on the elderly in relation to the five major social institutions: the family, economy, political system, religion, and education. A separate chapter is devoted to each institution. Our concern in Part V is with some of the major problems confronting older people: income, health, housing and transportation, crime, and death and dying. Finally, in Part VI one chapter discusses some solutions to the problems posed in Part V, while the final chapter deals with societal trends in the future that pertain to the elderly.

Features

We have tried to produce a book that is clearly written and free of jargon. Our goal has been to communicate in plain, simple English: to be understood, not to impress. All significant terms are italicized and clearly defined and explained when they first appear. They are defined again in a comprehensive glossary at the end of the book for easy reference. At the end of each chapter is a numbered summary that reviews the most important concepts and findings contained in the chapter. Boxed inserts have been included where appropriate to enliven and complement the material in the text. The text includes a number of visual devices to increase its effectiveness. Tables and charts are used to help make the data easier to understand. The photographs and cartoons have been carefully selected to reinforce the material in the text. Each chapter contains extensive notes and an annotated list of books for suggested reading for those students who wish to pursue the subject more deeply. Available for use with the text is an Instructor's Manual prepared by the authors. The Manual includes major concepts and topics for discussion, chapter outlines, and multiple-choice and essay questions for each chapter.

Acknowledgments

We would like to acknowledge our critical readers who took the time to carefully review the entire manuscript: Donald O. Cowgill, University of Missouri at Columbia; Richard G. Dumont, Tennessee Technological University; Robert L. Dunbar, City College of San Francisco; George L. Maddox, Duke University Medical Center; Hallowell Pope, The University of Iowa at Iowa City; and Irving L. Webber, The University of Alabama at University. We are grateful to them for their helpful suggestions and criticisms. Special thanks are due the Houghton Mifflin staff who have made this book possible.

D.K.H.
W.E.C.

I
Introduction

1

The Field and
Its Methods

The aged are frequently seen as infirm, forgetful, isolated, sexually inactive, dependent, irritable, useless, and unhappy. If you think that the preceding sentence presents a distorted view of older people, you are right! Yet thousands of people believe such stereotypes even though much evidence proves that these have little or no basis in fact. Granted there may be some elderly to whom the above adjectives might apply, but they comprise only a small fraction of the elderly population.

Stereotypes and Myth-Conceptions

Stereotypes are oversimplified, exaggerated generalizations about a group or category of people. Stereotypes may be positive or negative, but they are always distortions of fact. For example, we generalize when we say that the English are snobbish and reserved, the Irish are witty and pugnacious, intelligent children have high foreheads, and redheads are quick-tempered. These generalizations are erroneous because they do not take into account the many variations within a group and because they indiscriminately attribute the same characteristics to all the members. Many stereotypes or "myth-conceptions" surround older people and the aging process. The following list includes some of the more common myths, along with the chapters in which these ideas are discussed in this text.

1. All older people are alike. (Chapter 2)
2. Most older people live in institutions. (Chapter 17)
3. The majority of older people are lonely and are isolated from their families. (Chapter 11)
4. Older people have a higher incidence of acute illnesses than younger persons do. (Chapter 17)
5. Retirement is less difficult for women than for men. (Chapter 12)
6. Most older people are in poor health and spend many of their days in bed. (Chapter 17)
7. Older people cannot learn. (Chapters 7 and 15)

8. Most older people are not interested in sex and are incapable of sexual activity. (Chapter 7)
9. Older people are more fearful of death than younger persons. (Chapters 1 and 20)
10. The majority of older people are grouchy and cantankerous. (Chapter 7)
11. Senility is to be expected with old age. (Chapter 7)
12. Retirement brings poor health and an early death. (Chapter 12)
13. Older workers have high accident and absentee rates. (Chapters 7 and 12)
14. Most older people prefer to live with their children. (Chapter 11)
15. Old age begins at 65. (Chapter 2)
16. Older people are inflexible and unable to change. (Chapters 7 and 12)
17. Older workers are less productive than younger ones. (Chapters 7 and 12)
18. Older people vote less frequently than younger persons and show lower levels of political interest. (Chapter 13)
19. Being sick is a necessary part of being old. (Chapter 17)
20. People become increasingly more religious as they reach old age. (Chapters 1 and 14)
21. Older people spend a lot of their time sleeping. (Chapter 1)
22. With the aging process there is a marked decrease in intelligence. (Chapters 1 and 7)
23. As people age, they become more politically conservative. (Chapter 13)
24. At retirement, most persons move to Florida and the other sunshine states. (Chapter 2)
25. The majority of older people have incomes below the poverty level. (Chapter 16)

How did these myths get started? No one really knows. Many studies of aging in the 1940s and 1950s were based on samples of elderly persons who were ill and institutionalized. Those elderly in good health and not in institutions were largely neglected in these studies, so that although these studies have some value, they cannot be used as the basis for generalizations about all older people. Also, some research during this same period contained methodological weaknesses that made the results invalid. Yet many people continue to accept the conclusions drawn from it. For example, in a compendium of findings of the behavioral sciences prior to 1964, the following statement appears: "In terms of absolute, not relative test performance, mental ability grows rapidly from birth through puberty, somewhat more slowly from then until the early twenties, at which point slow but steady decline sets

"Old" people are people who have lived a certain number of years, and that is all. . . . Once an older person comes to be seen, not as old first and provisionally a person second, but as a person who happens also to be old, and who is still as he or she always was, plus experience and minus the consequences of certain physical accidents of time — only then will social gerontology have made its point.

SOURCE: Alex Comfort, *A Good Age*, Crown, New York, 1976, pp. 13, 27.

in, with rather rapid deterioration beginning about age 65."[1] Recent studies reveal that no such pronounced decline in intelligence occurs. In fact, by some measures intelligence actually increases as a person ages.

Myths and stereotypes are perpetuated by the mass media. All too familiar are the "dirty old man" and the "little old lady from Pasadena" stereotypes. A study done by Aronoff in 1974 of prime network television drama found that the incidence of failure tends to increase with age for television characters of both sexes, but for different reasons.[2] Males fail because they are evil, whereas females fail because they are aging. Aging in television drama is "associated with increasing evil, failure, and unhappiness."[3]

Stereotypes of the elderly are also transmitted and reinforced through humor. Palmore analyzed the content of 264 jokes about aging and found that over half the jokes reflected a negative view of aging.[4] Those concerned with physical appearance or ability, age concealment, mental abilities, and old maids appeared to be the most negative. Jokes about older women tended to be more negative than jokes about older men; in fact, more than three-fourths of the jokes about women were negative. Palmore suggests that we may have a double standard about aging in our society, which views older women more negatively than older men.

Some ideas about older people stem from so-called common-sense observations. These are often expressed in the form of vague, glib generalizations that many people, both young and old, unquestioningly accept as obvious truths about human behavior. Although some common-sense maxims may be in accord with scientific knowledge, others — such as "there's no fool like an old fool," or "old age is a second childhood" — are completely false and quite negative. Sometimes these expressions contradict one another as well as the facts. Common-sense maxims tell us, for example, that "old dogs can't learn new tricks," but "you're never too old to learn." Scientific evidence reveals that the primary ability to learn changes little as one ages. Thus, one aim of sociological research is to separate fact from fallacy and myth from reality.

The Development of Gerontology

Gerontology, the scientific study of aging, began to emerge as a scientific field about 1940. The rapidly increasing number of older people in the population gave impetus to this new science. Research in gerontology began first with the biological and then with the psychological process of aging. Later the social aspects of aging were studied. In the 1950s a subfield of gerontology was created called *social gerontology*, which deals with the behavioral aspects of aging and contains specialities in such other disciplines as, economics, political science, anthropology, and sociology.

Themes in Literature

Interest in aging is not new. It had its recorded beginnings over three thousand years ago when people began seeking ways to prolong life and youth. The early literature generally emphasized one of these major themes: (1) the antediluvian; (2) the hyperborean; and (3) the rejuvenation.[5]

The antediluvian theme is found in many religions and mythologies. This theme refers to the belief that people in ancient times lived much longer than they do today. In Sumerian mythology Larek, the god-king, lived 28,800 years, and the god Dumuzi, even longer. Examples of this theme in the Old Testament include Methuselah, who lived to be 969, Noah, who died at age 950, and Adam who lived to be 930.

The hyperborean theme refers to the belief that people in some faraway places have extremely long lives. Originating with the ancient Greeks, this idea in modern times has reappeared in James Hilton's imaginary Shangri-La. Today three places in the world approximate a kind of Shangri-La to some people: the Caucasus region of the U.S.S.R., Hunza in the Pakistani region of Kashmir, and the village of Vilcabamba in Ecuador. Many people in these areas claim they live to be well over a hundred years old.

The rejuvenation theme has recurred many times in history. Long before Ponce de León's search for the Fountain of Youth in the early 1500s, Chinese physicians were administering dried animal organs to their patients in an attempt to restore the lost vigor of youth. Today some modern Ponce de Leóns travel to Switzerland for lamb fetus injections, while others go to Rumania for shots of Gerovital. Both treatments are supposed to retard or even reverse the aging process, but so far, medical research has failed to substantiate these claims. We will explore this search more fully in Chapter 2 when we discuss longevity.

Early Gerontologists

Lambert A. Quételet, a Belgian scientist and statistician, is considered to be the first gerontologist. His principal work, which he published in 1835, contains a summary of his statistical research on the average man — both intellectual and physical statistics. In that volume he compares the productivity and age of British and French playwrights. He concludes:

> We shall perceive that, both in England and France, dramatic talent scarcely begins to be developed before the 21st year; between 25 and 30, it manifests itself very decidedly; it continues to increase, and continues vigorous, until towards the 50th or 55th year; then it gradually declines, especially if we consider the value of the works produced.[6]

Another early researcher in this field was Sir Francis Galton, who in 1884 measured 9,337 males and females on such characteristics as their visual acuity and reaction time. From these measurements, Galton was able to show that certain abilities vary with age.

Early in this century, three noted biologists began research in the field of aging. Charles S. Minot compiled his investigations in cytology in *The Problems of Age, Growth, and Death,* published in 1908. That same year Elie Metchnikoff published *The Prolongation of Life,* and in 1922 Raymond Pearl published *The Biology of Death.* In 1926 Pearl did research into the lives of over 5,000 people and showed that alcohol used in moderation did not shorten a person's life.[7] In a later study he analyzed and compared the ancestry of two groups of people in regard to length of life, and he concluded that heredity was an important factor in longevity.[8] Gerontologists today support the conclusion that genetic factors are important in longevity, but they also recognize that no single factor determines longevity and that it results from the interplay of many factors.

Metchnikoff's interest centered on senescence, death, and specifically the relationship between intestinal flora and aging.[9] According to his hypothesis, toxins that arise from intestinal putrefaction are one of the principal causes of aging. To destroy these toxins and to reduce the onset of aging, Metchnikoff advocated drinking sour milk. He reasoned that sour milk contained acid-producing bacteria that when intro-duced into the intestine would prevent the breeding of "noxious microbes," which need an alkaline medium. He pointed to such populations as the Bulgarians who drank large amounts of fermented milk and who were thought to live a long time.

Metchnikoff failed to consider many organisms that age and die without possessing large intestines in which putrefaction can take place.

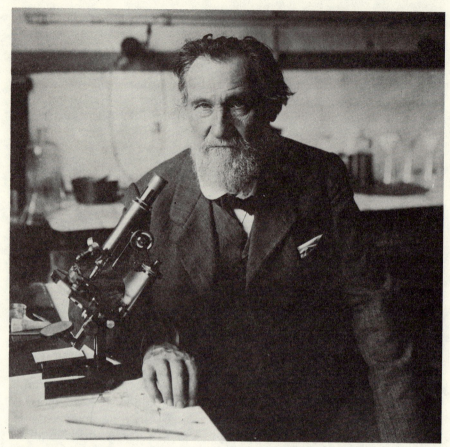

Elie Metchnikoff (1845–1916), a Russian-born biologist, who made a special study of bacteria in the intestines of human beings, is shown in his laboratory in Paris. (Brown Brothers)

His theory, despite its naiveté, has been revived many times. Recently, much has been written about the long-living people in the Caucasus Mountains of the Soviet Union who drink large amounts of a yogurt-like milk. A food manufacturer in the United States, who specializes in milk products, has cleverly capitalized on this by producing a series of television commercials and magazine advertisements showing old people in Soviet Georgia eating his brand of yogurt.

Later Developments

Great strides in the field of gerontology were made in the late 1930s as biologists began studying the changes that take place in cells and tissues

Persons in the Caucasus Mountain region of the Soviet Union have a reputation for good health and longevity. This advertisement shows an 89-year-old Abkhasian man eating a cup of yogurt, while his 114-year-old mother stands beside him with an approving smile. (Courtesy of Dannon Dairy Products)

as they age and the mechanisms that cause these changes. Cowdry's summarizing volume, *Problems of Aging,* which appeared in 1939, gave further impetus to research in this area. Finally, the formation of the Gerontological Society in 1945 added to the interest in research.

Scientific investigation into the psychological aspects of aging was officially launched around 1930 by the Stanford Later Maturity Research Project, conducted by Walter Miles and his associates. Before this time, little work had been done in the area of aging by psychologists, except for G. Stanley Hall, who wrote a book on senescence in 1922 and later did some research in this field.[10] Hall studied religious beliefs and attitudes toward death among older people. His research revealed that as people grow older, they do not necessarily become more religious, nor do they become fearful of death. His findings are still valid today. Many older people worry more about finances than they do about death. Actually, it has been found that younger people fear death more than do the elderly. Since 1946, when the American Psychological Association set up a Division of Later Maturity and Old Age, research into the psychological aspects of aging has grown rapidly.

A pioneering effort in the social sciences was Judson T. Landis's study of the *Attitudes and Adjustments of Aged Rural People in Iowa*, which appeared in 1940, and in 1945 Leo W. Simmons published his classic work, *The Role of the Aged in Primitive Society*. Besides these, there were at this time only a few scattered studies on the social aspects of aging. But in 1943 Ernest W. Burgess, while serving as chairperson of the Social Science Research Council's Committee on Social Adjustment, helped to form the Committee on Social Adjustment in Old Age.[11] The task of this group was to develop an orientation for the study of adjustment problems in old age and to provide suggestions for social research. The report of this committee's work was published in 1948 and laid the foundation for, and gave direction to the study of the sociological aspects of aging.

Perspectives on Aging

Aging may be defined as all the regular changes that take place in biologically mature individuals as they advance through the life cycle.* Aging involves a pattern of changes not only in the structure and functioning of the body, but also in the adjustment and behavior of the person. In addition, aging can be viewed as "a sequence of events that take place or are expected to take place during an individual's life course."[12] From these definitions you can see that the study of aging encompasses a wide range of subjects and can be viewed from many perspectives. For our purposes we will attempt to single out three approaches to the study of aging: the biological, the psychological, and the sociological.

Biological Approach

Research on the biological aspects of aging focuses on the processes that limit the length of life of species and individuals. Or, put another way, such research investigates why species and individuals within a species have fixed life spans. Although opinions differ as to which factors limit the length of life of various species, there is consensus that these factors are genetically programmed.[13] The goal of biological research is twofold: first, to increase longevity, and second, and more important, to make the added years vigorous and productive ones.

---

*Terms set in italics are defined in the Glossary.

"To . . .hell . . . with . . . yogurt." (drawing by Charles Addams; © 1979. The New Yorker Magazine, Inc.)

Psychological Approach

The subject matter of the psychological aspects of aging includes the study of the effects of aging upon sensory function, psychomotor skills, personality, learning, perception, and the emotions and needs of the aging individual. The psychologist is interested in studying the adjustments that the older person makes to the aging process and to its problems.

Sociological Approach

A third approach, the one that we will use throughout this book, focuses on the sociological aspects of aging or the sociology of aging. The sociology of aging is an area of specialization within the broader field of sociology; it focuses mainly on one segment of the population — older people.* *Sociology* may be defined as the scientific study of human interaction; likewise, we might define the *sociology of aging* as the scientific study of the interaction of older people in society. The key word in both definitions is interaction. *Interaction* involves acting toward someone who interprets the act and responds to it. For example, suppose an elderly man is walking down one side of the street and an attractive elderly woman is walking down the other. The man sees the woman and whistles at her. By whistling, he is acting toward her. She must then interpret this act before she can respond to it. For instance, she might think that the man is whistling because he has lost his dog, or that he is whistling because he wants to become better acquainted with her. If she interprets his whistling as a search for a dog, she might offer to help him look for it. On the other hand, if she interprets his whistling as an overture, she might smile at him or even cross to his side of the street.[14]

Interaction is simply social behavior between people. People interact in various ways, by means of language, both written and spoken, and by gestures and symbols. The field of aging from the perspective of sociology focuses not on the older individual as a single unit, but on his or her interaction with other people. The sociology of aging emphasizes how roles and statuses change with age in relation to the major social institutions, and examines the adjustments that individuals make to these changes and the consequences of these actions. This field is interested in the impact that the rapidly increasing number of older people have on society, as well as the effect of society on older people.

Basic Research Methods

When we defined the sociology of aging, we referred to it as a *scientific* study. This qualification rests on the assumption that the body of knowledge pertaining to the sociology of aging has been developed through scientific methods of investigation. What are these methods and how is research done in the field of aging? In the broadest sense there are three basic methods used in sociological research: the sample survey, the experiment, and the case study.

The Sample Survey

A *sample survey*, as the name implies, consists of two elements: a sample and a survey. The group that the researcher plans to study is called a

---

*Although some social scientists study the aging process over the entire life cycle, most sociologists in the field of aging limit their study to the latter half of the cycle.

population. This population may consist of college students, voters, housewives, or retirees. Because researchers cannot study all the members in a population, they select a *sample* from the population. The sample must be *representative* of the population, that is, it must contain basically the same distribution of pertinent characteristics as the population from which it was drawn. In this way, findings from the study can be generalized to the population as a whole. The researchers then collect the data on the characteristics of the population being studied by having informants fill out questionnaires, or by asking them questions from interview schedules.

A landmark study of aging presents an example of how a sample survey was employed. In the late spring and summer of 1974 the National Council on the Aging commissioned Louis Harris and Associates to conduct a major in-depth survey to examine the public's expectations of what it is like to be old and to document the views and experiences of older people themselves.[15] Trained interviewers conducted 4,254 in-person household interviews. The sample included a representative cross-section of the American public, 18 years of age and over, selected by a random sampling method. In a *random sample*, each member of the population, or in this case each household, has an equal chance of being chosen. Because older people, especially older blacks, make up a small proportion of the population, a weighted cross-section design was employed to insure that adequate numbers would be included in the sample. This design involved the oversampling of three subgroups: those over 65, those between the ages of 55 and 64, and blacks 65 and over. These subgroups were weighted back to their true proportions when the data were analyzed.

The study shows large discrepancies between the public's expectations of how the elderly feel and their actual reactions. For instance, 60 percent of the public believe that "loneliness is a very serious problem" for older people. Yet, only 12 percent of the elderly said loneliness was "very serious," while 7 percent of those under 65 reported the same problem. Fifty-four percent of the public think that "not feeling needed" is a very serious problem for older people. But only 7 percent of the elderly complained about not being needed compared to 5 percent of the younger people who felt they were not needed. (See Table 1.1.)

In addition, the results reveal that many Americans have misconceptions about how the elderly spend their time. For example, 67 percent of the public believe that most older people "watch T.V. a lot." But only 36 percent of the elderly said that they watch T.V. frequently, compared to 23 percent of the younger group queried. Thirty-nine percent of the public believe that older people spend their time "sleeping a lot." Only 16 percent of the elderly, however, reported that they do indeed sleep a lot, while almost the same percentage of younger people reported that they spend much of their time sleeping. The findings from this study

Table 1.1 Problems that people 65 and over experience compared with problems attributed to them by the public

	"Very serious" problems that the elderly experience	"Very serious" problems attributed to most elderly by the public	Net difference
Fear of crime	23%	50%	+27%
Poor health	21	51	+30
Not having enough money to live on	15	62	+47
Loneliness	12	60	+48
Not having enough medical care	10	44	+34
Not having enough education	8	20	+12
Not feeling needed	7	54	+47
Not having enough to do to keep busy	6	37	+31
Not having enough friends	5	28	+23
Not having enough job opportunities	5	45	+40
Poor housing	4	35	+31
Not having enough clothing	3	16	+13

SOURCE: Reprinted from *The Myth and Reality of Aging in America,* a study prepared by Louis Harris and Associates, Inc. for The National Council on the Aging, Inc., Washington, D.C. © 1975, p. 31.

suggest that people 65 and over do not differ much from those under 65. The similarities between the two groups seem more numerous than the differences.

The Harris study also found that the self-image that older people have of themselves is far more positive than the public's view of them. Two sets of figures illustrate this difference in viewpoint. Sixty-eight percent of the elderly feel that they are "very bright and alert," while only 29 percent of the public consider them to have these characteristics. Again, 63 percent of the older population believe themselves to be very "open-minded and adaptable," while only 21 percent of the public believe this to be the case.

Lastly, the study indicates the existence of a negative stereotype about being old, which is reflected in the way people resist the fact that they are old. When asked how they liked to be referred to, the majority of those 65 and over said that they preferred to be called *senior citizens,* followed by *mature Americans*, and *retired persons*. The most disliked names were *old man* and *old woman*.

A great advantage of the sample survey as a research tool is shown by the Harris study. Certain important questions can only be answered by asking people. Finding out what Americans believe about older people, as well as how the elderly feel about themselves, can be determined only through the sample survey. No experimental study, no matter how well designed, can do this. This method does have disadvantages: sometimes people purposely conceal their true feelings, or express opinions on subjects they know nothing about; also, what people say may not always coincide with how they act.

The Experiment

In the *experiment* the investigator controls or manipulates at least one variable being studied and then makes precise measurements or observations of the results. For example, Jack Botwinick and his associates were interested in finding out whether people become more cautious as they grow older.[16] They wanted to know if older people needed a high degree of certainty before committing themselves to a response. For the experiment, two groups were selected — one old and one young. Ages in the old group ranged from 65 to 71; the young group ranged from 18 to 35 years old. The subjects were shown sets of vertical bars, and they were to judge in each instance which of the two bars was the shorter. Sometimes the difference between the bars was great, making discrimination easy, while at other times the difference between the two bars was quite small, making discrimination difficult. Both groups were asked to respond as quickly as possible. The time limit for each judgment was set at two seconds, but the judgments were all made in less time. The older persons responded much slower than the younger persons, especially when the bars were nearly the same length.

The experimenter then told both groups that their time for viewing the two bars would be reduced to 0.15 seconds. Both groups made their judgments in less time than before, but the older subjects greatly increased their speed even in cases where discrimination was difficult.

The results of the study showed that the speed of response of the older persons tended to vary with the amount of time they were given. In the first instance, when they had more time to respond, they took it. Later, when they were told they had less time and were pushed by the experimenter to make faster responses, their speed greatly improved.

The investigators concluded that the extra time taken by the older group reflected the increased level of confidence that was required by older persons before giving a response, and not their inability to make correct discriminations in the length of the bars. One reason for this insecurity may be that our society devalues old age. We expect old people to fail; we brand them as inadequate. Because of these societal expectations, older people require more certainty from a situation in order to minimize the chances for their expected failure and in order to avoid being labelled as deficient.

The *independent variables* in an experiment are those variables directly manipulated by the investigator. In this experiment the investigator manipulated both the amount of viewing time and the length of the vertical bars that the subjects were to view, making these the independent variables.

Dependent variables are what is measured during the experiment; they are affected by the actual process of the experiment. In this illustration, the dependent variable is the response time of the subjects. We can say, then, that the response time (the dependent variable) is a function of the amount of viewing time allowed and the difficulty of the discriminations to be made (the independent variables).

In sociological research, experiments generally take place with small groups of people in limited settings. To do otherwise is not practical because of the expense and time that would be involved. Another point to be considered is that when people know that they are being watched and studied, this may influence the way they behave or respond. Because of these two factors — the small size of the sample and the behavioral change that may take place with the subjects — an experimental group cannot be said to be representative of the larger population. As a result, findings from experiments are limited in their degree of generalization. A great advantage of laboratory experiments is that we can learn from them exactly how a certain variable affects behavior under a specific condition; this situation would be difficult to control or duplicate in a real-life situation.

The Case Study

The *case study* method focuses on a single case in considerable depth and detail, usually over a long period of time. A case may be the life history of a person or a detailed account of some social process or event. With this method we can also study a work group, a family, or a retirement community.

Participant observation is a technique commonly used by sociologists in case studies. The investigator takes part in whatever group is being studied. For example, William F. Whyte wanted to study an Italian slum gang in Boston, so he joined the gang and participated in all its activities over a period of several years. John Loftland's interest in radical religious groups led him to become a member of the Divine Precepts cult in order to observe and study this group as an insider.

One problem encountered in using this technique is the possible influence or effect on the people that the presence of the observer might have. Also, participant observers must be on guard against getting too involved in the group being investigated and thus losing their objectivity. The participant observer method is an excellent way to get information about groups about which so little is known that other research methods cannot be effectively utilized. The main advantage of participant observation lies in the rich insights and intimate, first-hand knowledge that the investigator gains — information hardly possible to come by through other research methods.

The following account shows how a sociologist, Arlie Hochschild, used the participant observation method in studying 43 residents of Merrill Court, a small public-housing apartment building near the shore of San Francisco Bay.[17] Of the 43 residents, 37 were elderly, widowed females. In the summer of 1966 Hochschild secured a job as an assistant recreation director of Merrill Court, where she worked for the better part of three years. After the first few months, she told the residents that she was a sociologist doing a study, but this fact did not seem to matter to them. During the course of her job at Merrill Court she took part in many activities with the residents and worked with them on recreational projects.

> Initially, my watching went on in the Recreation Room, where I sat and did handiwork at a table with five or six others. As I drove residents to the doctor, to the housing office, to church, and occasionally to funerals, joined them on visits to relatives, shopped with them, kept bowling scores, visited their apartments and took them to mine, I gradually came to know and to like them. Through sharing their lives I came to see how others treated them and how their own behavior changed as their audience did.[18]

Hochschild felt that the most outstanding feature of Merrill Court was that it was a vibrant, thriving community, not just an apartment house of old people. She was interested in finding out the reasons for this cohesiveness. Her study suggests that the communal feeling manifested by Merrill Court residents can be largely attributed to two factors: the homogeneity of the residents and the social arrangements under which they lived.

First of all, the majority of the residents had similar interests and needs. They shared a "we are in the same boat" feeling. Most were white Anglo-Saxon Protestant widowed females in their late sixties who were rural-born and had working-class backgrounds. Nearly all were living on welfare payments, except for a few who received social security benefits. They sometimes jokingly referred to themselves as "us poor pensioners." All but one person had been born in the United States, and the majority of them came from either the Midwest or Southwest.

The second factor that contributed to making Merrill Court a community was the social patterns of the residents. These patterns revolved around upstairs and downstairs roles. Downstairs roles mainly took place in the recreation room and were more formal, whereas upstairs roles involved an informal network of neighboring among residents. The residents enjoyed a particular type of relationship among themselves — a sibling bond. The term *sibling bond* is used by Hochschild to denote a relationship in which there is a reciprocity and sharing among members. Reciprocity results in an almost equal exchange of favors and mutual aid:

> Most residents of Merrill Court are social siblings. The customs of exchanging cups of coffee, lunches, potted plants, and curtain checking suggest reciprocity. Upstairs, one widow usually visited as much as she was visited. In deciding who visits whom, they often remarked, "Well, I came over last time. You come over this time." They traded, in even measure, slips from house plants, kitchen utensils, and food of all sorts. They watched one another's apartments when someone was away on a visit, and they called and took calls for one another.[19]

Hochschild concludes that the family unit, which has held generations together in the past, is declining in strength, and as a result, she predicts that the sibling bond will grow in importance. This bond, she believes, will allow more flexibility in relationships between generations by forging solidarity within generations. She feels that the time is right for sibling-bond interaction and age-segregated communities like Merrill Court.

Because Hochschild's work involved one specific group of older people, we cannot generalize and say that her findings apply to all similar groups. Her in-depth study of Merrill Court does, however, provide much insight, many descriptive examples, and suggestions for perceptive hypotheses.

Cross-sectional and Longitudinal Studies

Much research on aging is based on the *cross-sectional* design, which examines the characteristics of a population at one point in time. The previously cited sample survey by Harris illustrates this method. Because the cross-sectional method is conducted in a brief time period, it has the obvious advantages of saving time, money, and effort. Another method, *longitudinal* research, studies the same person, group, or population over a period of time, usually with a certain number of years between examinations.[20]

With the longitudinal method we can identify individual patterns of aging and development that cannot be detected with the cross-sectional design. The investigator often encounters serious problems in using the cross-sectional design to compare characteristics of older and younger groups in order to shed light on the aging process. For example, we must ask, what amount, if any, of the differences between the groups is due to the passage of time?

Research on the intellectual capacity of the aged was for many years cross-sectional in nature. The investigator would administer intelligence tests to a group of young people and a group of old people and then compare the performance levels of the two groups. The older persons scored consistently lower than the younger ones, so the conclusion was drawn that as people age, their intellectual level declines. This type of interpretation suggests an anecdote by Robert Kastenbaum concerning a researcher studying a Boston neighborhood.

> The old residents often spoke English with an Italian accent, while their children and grandchildren did not. After much thought and field work, the investigator reached the following conclusion: "As people grow older they develop Italian accents. This surely must be one of the prime manifestations of aging on the psychological level."[21]

The disparity between the scores of the young and the old on intelligence tests is due mainly to generational and cultural differences, not to the aging process. By using longitudinal studies that involve testing the same individual over a period of years by examining his or her performance at different ages, researchers are finding that intelligence does not rapidly decline with age, as was once assumed.

Though the longitudinal studies are the ideal way to study changes over time within the individual, they are not always the most practical method to use. For one thing, it is difficult, if not impossible, to keep the same professional research team together for a five- or ten-year period. In addition, there is always some loss of the subjects that are being studied, as some move away, drop out of the study, become ill, or die. Also, longitudinal studies are expensive and require long-term financial support. Even the matter of storing the data can be a problem, especially when large amounts have been collected over a period of years. The merits of such a study, however, certainly outweigh the disadvantages.

Why Study Aging?

What does studying the subject of aging do for you? Becoming old is something that happens to us all — if we live long enough. What you learn now about this subject will give you a perspective on the problems of aging earlier in your life-cycle, will help you plan for a more successful retirement, and will give you a better understanding of the aging process within yourself. Studying aging will also help you to dispel some false beliefs and myths about growing older and, in doing so, may give you a more positive attitude toward getting older, as well as allay some fears associated with aging.

Lastly, studying the sociology of aging may help you in relating to your parents and grandparents and give you a better understanding of some problems that they, as well as other older Americans, face. Helping our nation and its communities to provide a more satisfactory life for the elderly should improve conditions not only for today's older people, but for those who will be old tomorrow.

Summary

1. Many stereotypes about older people are inaccurate and untrue. A stereotype is an oversimplified generalization that is applied indiscriminately to all members of a group or category.

2. Gerontology is defined as the scientific study of aging. A subfield of gerontology that deals with the behavioral aspects of aging is called social gerontology.

3. Early literature on aging can be classified according to three major types of themes: the antedeluvian, the belief that people used to live longer; the hyperborean, the notion that people in some faraway place are living long lives; the rejuvenation, the ways to prolong life and youth.

4. The earliest work on aging was done by Quetelet and Galton. Scientific research in the biological sciences began with such men as Minot, Pearl, and Metchnikoff. Studies on the psychological aspects of aging can be traced back to the work of Hall and Miles, and research on the sociological aspects of aging originated with the works of Landis, Simmons, and Pollak.

5. Aging refers to the changes that take place in an individual after maturation. The study of aging can be viewed from three main perspectives: the biological, the psychological, and the sociological. The sociological perspective, or the sociology of aging, may be defined as the scientific study of interaction of older people in society.

6. The three basic methods for doing sociological research are the sample survey, the experiment, and the case study. Each of these studies takes place in either a cross-sectional or longitudinal time setting. In a cross-sectional design, the characteristics of a population are studied at one point in time, whereas in a longitudinal design the study takes place over a period of time.

Notes

1. Bernard Berelson and Gary A. Steiner, *Human Behavior: An Inventory of Scientific Findings*, Harcourt, Brace & World, New York, 1964, p. 220.

2. Craig Aronoff, "Old Age in Prime Time," *Journal of Communication*, 24 (Autumn 1974) 86–87.

3. Ibid., p. 87.

4. Erdman Palmore, "Attitudes Toward Aging as Shown by Humor," *The Gerontologist*, 2, no. 3 (1971), Pt. I, 181–186.

5. James E. Birren and Vivian Clayton, "History of Gerontology," in *Aging: Scientific Perspectives and Social Issues*, ed. Diana S. Woodruff and James E. Birren, D. Van Nostrand, New York, 1975, pp. 15–20.

6. Lambert A. J. Quetelet, *A Treatise on Man and the Development of His Faculties* (a facsimile reproduction of the English translation of 1842), Scholars' Facsimiles and Reprints, Gainesville, Fla., 1969, p. 75.

7. Raymond Pearl, *Alcohol and Longevity*, Alfred A. Knopf, New York, 1926.

8. Raymond Pearl, *The Ancestry of the Long-lived*, Johns Hopkins University Press, Baltimore, 1934.

9. Olga Metchnikoff, *Life of Elie Metchnikoff*, Houghton Mifflin, Boston, 1921.

10. G. Stanley Hall, *Senescence: The Last Half of Life*, Appleton, New York, 1922.

11. See Otto Pollak, *Social Adjustment in Old Age: A Research Planning Report*, Social Science Research Council, Bulletin 59, 1948.

12. Vern L. Bengtson and David A. Haber, "Sociological Approaches to Aging," in *Aging: Scientific Perspectives and Social Issues*, ed. Diana S. Woodruff and James E. Birren, D. Van Nostrand, New York, 1975, p. 70.

13. James E. Birren, "Aging: Psychological Aspects," *International Encyclopedia of the Social Sciences*, ed. David L. Sills, Macmillan, New York, 1968, p. 177.

14. Diana K. Harris and William E. Cole, *Study Guide and Readings for Sociology: The Study of Human Interaction*, Alfred A. Knopf, New York, 1977, p. 7.

15. Louis Harris and Associates, *The Myth and Reality of Aging in America*, The National Council on the Aging, Washington, D.C., 1975.

16. Jack Botwinick, *Aging and Behavior: A Comprehensive Interpretation of Research Findings*, Springer, New York, 1973, p. 97.

17. Arlie Russell Hochschild, *The Unexpected Community*, Prentice-Hall, Englewood Cliffs, N.J., 1973.

18. Arlie Russell Hochschild, *The Unexpected Community*, © 1973, p. 5. Reprinted by permission of Prentice-Hall, Inc., Englewood Cliffs, New Jersey.

19. Ibid., pp. 65–66.

20. For an excellent example of this type of design see Erdman Palmore, ed., *Normal Aging: Reports from the Duke Longitudinal Studies, 1955–1969*, Duke University Press, Durham, N.C., 1970, and Erdman Palmore, ed., *Normal Aging II: Reports from the Duke Longitudinal Studies, 1970–1973*, Duke University Press, Durham, N.C., 1974.

21. James D. Manney, Jr., *Aging in American Society: An Examination of Concepts and Issues*, The Institute of Gerontology, University of Michigan–Wayne State University, Ann Arbor, 1975, p. 5.

For Further Study

Butler, Robert N. *Why Survive? Being Old in America*. Harper & Row, New York, 1975. This excellent book is based on public policy and research material that realistically portrays the experience of older people in the United States.

Cole, William E., and Diana K. Harris. *The Elderly in America*. Allyn & Bacon, Boston, 1977. A concise overview of aging and the aged.

Comfort, Alex. *A Good Age*. Crown, New York, 1976. This well-written, highly readable book gives the basic facts about aging.

Hendricks, Jon, and C. Davis Hendricks. *Aging in Mass Society: Myths and Realities*. Winthrop, Cambridge, Mass., 1977. Chapter 2 contains a good discussion of aging in its historical context.

Kalish, Richard A. *Late Adulthood: Perspectives on Human Development*. Brooks/Cole, Monterey, Calif., 1975. Written from a psychological perspective, this short but comprehensive book provides a good introduction to human aging.

Labovitz, Sanford, and Robert Hagedorn. *Introduction to Social Research*. McGraw-Hill, New York, 1971. A concise, clearly written explanation of sociological research methods.

Maddox, George L., and James Wiley. "Scope, Concepts and Methods in the Study of Aging." In *Handbook of Aging and the Social Sciences*, edited by Robert H. Binstock, and Ethel Shanas. Van Nostrand Reinhold, New York, 1976. This chapter discusses the origins and scope of interest in aging as a social phenomenon.

2

The Older Population and Longevity

John Lamb was a college teacher. He was a bachelor and lived alone. His health problems became an increasingly important concern to him as he passed the 40-year-old mark. Around age 45, John developed arthritis. By age 50, his arthritis had worsened, and he had developed hypertension. At 59, he decided to give up teaching and to apply for disability retirement. After a long series of conferences and consultations, he was finally granted retirement on the grounds that he was disabled. Now age 65, Lamb, who has suffered a stroke, lives in a nursing home.

Lucille Rogers is 85 years old. She was 65 when she retired as city librarian. At age 75, she made the initial study that formed the basis for many programs and activities of the council on aging in her home city. Lucille is still much in demand as a speaker by groups and organizations concerned with the elderly. She serves as a consultant to local public officials on the needs of the elderly. Although chronologically aged, Lucille enjoys good health, is energetic, and has youthful attitudes.

Lucille and John illustrate the diversity of conditions found in the category of people we designate as *aged* or *retired*. Some people retire at 55, while others work until 70 or later. For some individuals, physical decline occurs early; for others it happens much later. Older people vary as much in health, vigor, performance, and mental outlook as do young or middle-aged people.

The Aging Population

Identifying the Elderly

There is no fixed time in a person's life when he or she becomes old. Aging is a gradual and sometimes almost imperceptible process. Because of this lack of a clearly defined time, different societies use various criteria for determining when someone has reached the status of an elderly person. Some societies define old age in functional terms, such as physical decline. Among the Kikuya of Kenya a man is considered old when he must stop and rest by the side of the road while others pass him by, and when the odor of food no longer awakens him from sleep. The Kikuya consider a woman old when she can no longer work in the garden, when she cannot carry a small load on her back, and when she keeps dropping the cooking pot.[1]

Other societies view the beginning of old age in formal terms related to external events. For instance, the Maricopa Indians of Arizona consider a person old if he or she has a grandchild. In Western society, particularly in the United States, old age is defined in terms of a temporal or chronological definition of how many years a person has lived. In our society we use the age of 65 as the point at which a person is thought to be old. It is commonly believed that at this age a person is physically over the hill and is ready for retirement. The basis for this belief may be traced back to the Social Security Act of 1935, which was passed under the administration of Franklin D. Roosevelt. The Act set 65 as the age of eligibility for social security payments. American employers then began using 65 as the age for mandatory retirement in order to coincide retirement with the time that social security benefits would begin. So the age of 65 was arbitrary and had no basis in reality as the point at which a person actually becomes old. Primarily as a result of social security legislation, most studies use 65 as the earliest age at which people are considered to be old. Much statistical data often group those aged 65 and over into a single broad category. For the sake of convenience and clarity, therefore, throughout this book we will refer to those age 65 and over as *older people* or *the elderly*.

The Number and Proportion of Older People in the United States

The number of elderly people in the United States has rapidly increased since the beginning of this century when they totaled three million. Thirty years later the older population had more than doubled (Figure 2.1). By 1975 there were 22.4 million elderly, and at present they number nearly 25 million (Table 2.1). The phenomenal growth of the older population stems from these factors: the high immigration rate before World War I, the high birthrate during the late nineteenth and early twentieth centuries, and the dramatic increase in life expectancy during the first half of this century.

The fastest growing segment in the older population, as well as in the total population, is the 75-and-over group. In 1900 the proportion aged

Figure 2.1   The growth of the older population in the twentieth century

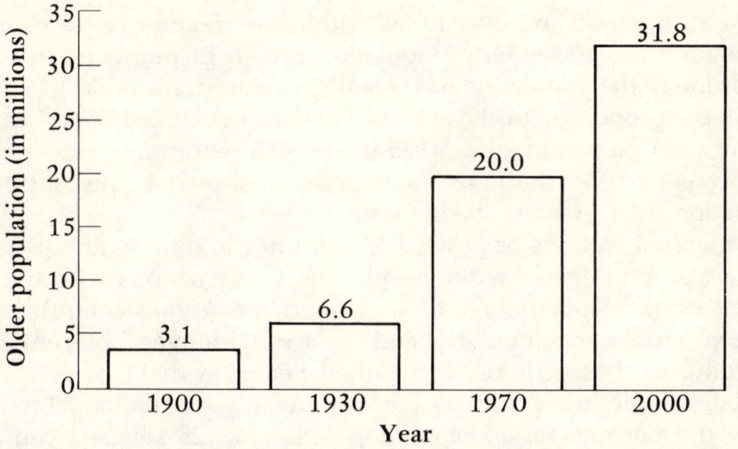

SOURCE: National Clearing House on Aging, *Facts About Older Americans, 1978*, U.S. Government Printing Office, Washington, D.C., 1979.

Table 2.1   Population 65 and over in the United States, 1900–1975, with projections to 2000

Year	Number (in thousands)	Percentage of total population
1900	3,099	4.1%
1910	3,986	4.3
1920	4,929	4.6
1930	6,705	5.4
1940	9,031	6.8
1950	12,397	8.1
1960	16,675	9.2
1970	20,085	9.8
1975	22,400	10.5
1980[a]	24,927	11.2
1990[a]	29,824	12.3
2000[a]	31,822	12.2

[a]From U.S. Senate, *Developments in Aging: 1978*, A Report of the Special Committee on Aging, U.S. Government Printing Office, Washington, D.C., 1979, p. xxiv.
SOURCES: Adapted from U.S. Bureau of the Census, *Current Population Reports*, Special Studies, Series P-23, No. 59, U.S. Government Printing Office, Washington, D.C. (May 1976), pp. 3, 9.

75 and over was 29 percent of the 65-plus group, and by 1975 it had climbed to 38 percent, or 8.5 million people. This trend is expected to continue at least to the year 2000. At that time, we may expect about 44 percent of those 65 and over to fall within the 75-and-over category.[2]

Not only has the elderly population grown in numbers, but their proportion in the population has steadily increased. As Table 2.1 shows, in 1900 the proportion of those 65 and over in the United States was 4.1 percent, or 1 person in 25; in 1975 it was 10.5 percent, or 1 in every 10 Americans. In 1979 the elderly comprised just over 11 percent of the population, or 1 in every 9 Americans.*

The United Nations has classified countries into three groups based on their proportions of older people: the *young* nations with under 4 percent of their population 65 and over; the *mature* countries with between 4 to 7 percent elderly; and the *aged* with over 7 percent aged. According to these criteria, the United States, with 11 percent of its population elderly, would be considered an aged nation. Table 2.2 shows the percentages of older populations in 25 selected countries between .1968 and 1976. Of these, the German Democratic Republic, Sweden, and Austria have the highest proportion of older people with 16.3, 15.1, and 15.0 percent, respectively. According to this table, nearly all the aged nations are among the more developed countries.

Where Older People Live

Despite what is touted in the press as a large movement of older persons to Florida and the other sunshine states, over two-thirds of the elderly continue to live in the same community and often in the same house where they have spent most of their adult lives. The states with the largest populations also have the largest numbers of older people: New York and California each have about two million persons aged 65 and over. Five other states having over a million older residents are Illinois, Ohio, Pennsylvania, Texas, and Florida. These seven states account for about 45 percent of the older population in the United States.

Although California and New York have the largest numbers of older people, Florida leads all the states with the largest proportion of older people — 17.6 percent (Table 2.3). This high percentage is mainly due to the in-migration of older people because of the favorable climate in Florida. Five agricultural states — Arkansas, Iowa, Missouri, Nebraska and South Dakota — also have a high proportion of elderly residents, but for a different reason — the high out-migration of younger people. Older people are left behind as the younger people move to more

*It is estimated that in 1790, when the first United States Census was taken, about 2 percent of the population, or every fiftieth American, was 65 or over.

Table 2.2   Proportion of population 65 and over in 25
countries, 1968–1976

Country	Year	Percentage of total population[a]
German Democratic Republic	1976	16.3%
Sweden	1975	15.1
Austria	1975	15.0
England/Wales	1975	14.2
Denmark	1973	12.9
France	1972	12.6
Italy	1974	11.8
United States	1976	10.7
Canada	1975	8.5
Japan	1975	7.9
Israel	1975	7.8
Cuba	1975	6.5
Lebanon	1970	5.0
Turkey	1975	4.5
Union of South Africa	1970	4.1
Pakistan	1968	3.9
Ecuador	1974	3.8
Syrian Arab Republic	1976	3.5
Mexico	1976	3.4
Jordan	1971	3.4
Brazil	1975	3.3
India	1974	3.2
Iran	1971	3.1
Philippines	1976	2.9
Greenland	1974	2.9

[a]Numbers are rounded to the nearest tenth.
SOURCE: United Nations, *Demographic Yearbook 1976* (28th ed.) United Nations, New York, 1977.
Copyright, United Nations, 1977. Reproduced by permission.

industrial and urban sections of the nation in their search for better
economic opportunities.

The last decennial census giving the rural and urban distribution of
the elderly was conducted in 1970. These data are shown in Table 2.4. Of
the 20 million persons 65 and over in 1970, over half (55 percent) lived in
urbanized areas.* About a third (34.1 percent) of all elderly persons

*An urbanized area contains at least one city of 50,000 or more inhabitants (central city)
plus the surrounding densely settled incorporated and unincorporated areas.

resided in central cities, and slightly over a fourth (27.1 percent) had rural homes. A higher proportion of older persons lived in central cities or in towns and cities with over 2,500 inhabitants, whereas a lower proportion of older persons were found in the urban fringe, the area beyond the established suburbs of a city.

In 1970, 32 percent of the white elderly lived in central cities, compared to 47 percent of the black elderly. By 1977 the proportion of black elderly living in central cities had increased to 55 percent, while the proportion of white elderly had dropped to 29 percent. Stephen Golant believes that this trend will continue so that by the year 2000 the white aged will become more dispersed through suburban areas, while the black elderly will be increasingly concentrated in central cities.[3] At the same time, there will be more black communities with higher proportions of elderly persons in the areas immediately outside the central city and in the older suburbs.

Table 2.3   Proportion of population 65 and over by state, 1978

Rank	State	Percentage of total population	Rank	State	Percentage of total population
1	Florida	17.6%	26	Tennessee	11.0%
2	Arkansas	13.4	27	Alabama	10.9
3	Iowa	13.1	28	Illinois	10.7
4	Missouri	13.0	29	Washington	10.6
5	South Dakota	13.0	30	Indiana	10.5
6	Nebraska	12.9	31	Ohio	10.5
7	Rhode Island	12.9	32	Montana	10.3
8	Kansas	12.6	33	California	10.1
9	Oklahoma	12.4	34	Idaho	9.9
10	Pennsylvania	12.4	35	North Carolina	9.9
11	Maine	12.2	36	Texas	9.7
12	Massachusetts	12.1	37	Delaware	9.5
13	West Virginia	12.0	38	Michigan	9.4
14	North Dakota	12.0	39	Louisiana	9.3
15	New York	11.8	40	Georgia	9.3
16	Oregon	11.7	41	Virginia	9.1
17	Wisconsin	11.7	42	Maryland	8.9
18	Minnesota	11.6	43	South Carolina	8.8
19	Arizona	11.4	44	Colorado	8.7
20	Vermont	11.3	45	New Mexico	8.5
21	New Jersey	11.3	46	Wyoming	8.4
22	Mississippi	11.2	47	Nevada	8.4
23	Connecticut	11.2	48	Utah	7.8
24	Kentucky	11.1	49	Hawaii	7.4
25	New Hampshire	11.0	50	Alaska	2.5
	United States			11.0	

SOURCE: Adapted from U.S. Senate, *Developments in Aging: 1978*, A Report of the Special Committee on Aging, U.S. Government Printing Office, Washington, D.C., 1979, pp. xxvii–xxviii.

Life Expectancy

All species of animals have fixed *life spans*, although individual lives vary within these spans. The mayfly lives for only one day, whereas humans have a biological age limit of around 100 years. Although the human life span has changed very little, if any, since ancient times, life expectancy at birth has changed dramatically. *Life expectancy* refers to the average number of years of life that a person has remaining to him or her at a specified age. For example, at birth, life expectancy in the United States

Table 2.4 Distribution of population 65 and over by size of place, United States, 1970

Size of place	Number (in thousands)	Percentage of 65 and over population
Urban	14,631	72.9%
Urbanized areas	11,106	55.3
Central cities	6,842	34.1
Urban fringe areas	4,264	21.2
Other urban		
Places of 10,000 to 50,000 persons	1,788	8.9
Places of 2,500 to 10,000 persons	1,737	8.7
Rural	5,434	27.1
Places of 1,000 to 2,500 persons	903	4.5
Other rural areas	4,532	22.6
Total population	20,066	100.0

SOURCE: Adapted from U.S. Bureau of the Census, *Current Population Reports,* Special Studies, Series P-23, No. 59, U.S. Government Printing Office, Washington, D.C., 1976, p. 24.

in 1967 was about 70 years, whereas at age 60, life expectancy was 18 years. The data on expectation of life prior to the eighteenth century are sketchy. It is estimated that about 500 B.C. in ancient Greece life expectancy at birth was around 18 years, and that in 100 A.D. in Rome it rose to 25 years (Figure 2.2). Life expectancy had no significant increase from the late Roman Empire to the eighteenth century.

The earliest data on life expectancy in the United States date back to 1789; in that year, persons in Massachusetts had a life expectation of approximately 35 years at birth. By 1900, life expectancy for people in the entire nation had increased to 47 years, and by mid-century, to 68 years. Life expectancy in 1976 was 72.8 years (Table 2.5). Several reasons account for the dramatic increase in this century: (1) a reduction of infant and child mortality rates; (2) advances in the prevention and cure of most contagious diseases; (3) some decline in death rates during the adult years; and (4) general improvement in the standard of living for the nation.

As the overall life expectation at birth has increased, a difference in life expectancy between the sexes has become progressively greater. For example, in 1920 life expectation was 53.6 years for males and 54.6 for females, a one-year difference. By 1976 life expectation for females exceeded that of males by 7.7 years (Table 2.5).

Figure 2.2 Life expectancy through the ages

Table 2.5 Life expectancy at birth in the United States, 1900–1976

| | Life expectancy (in years) | | |
Year	Total population	Male population	Female population
1900	47.3	46.3	48.3
1910	50.0	48.4	51.8
1920	54.1	53.6	54.6
1930	59.7	58.1	61.6
1940	62.9	60.8	65.2
1950	68.2	65.6	71.1
1960	69.7	66.6	73.1
1970	70.9	67.1	74.8
1976	72.8	69.0	76.7

SOURCE: U.S. Bureau of the Census, *Statistical Abstract of the United States: 1978*, U.S. Government Printing Office, Washington, D.C., 1978, p. 69; and National Center for Health Statistics, *Vital Statistics of the United States*, vol. 2, U.S. Government Printing Office, Washington, D.C., 1973.

An archeologist who has studied the ages of prehistoric skeletons has found that 95 percent of the populations died before they reached 40, and that 75 percent failed to reach 30. The length of life in prehistoric populations has been calculated as follows:

Population	Percentage dead by age:		
	30	40	50
Neanderthal (90,000 to 40,000 years ago)	80.0%	95.0%	100.0%
Cro-Magnon (35,000 to 10,000 years ago)	61.7	88.2	90.0
Mesolithic (around 12,000 years ago)	86.3	95.5	97.0

SOURCE: David H. Fischer, *Growing Old in America* (expanded ed.), Oxford University Press, New York, 1978, pp. 6–7.

Why do females now outlive males? No one really knows. Some people argue that women live longer because they take better care of themselves than men do, and because women are more likely to secure earlier diagnosis and treatment for health problems than men. Others claim that males are generally engaged in more strenuous and dangerous occupations than women are. In the U.S.S.R., however, where men and women work at similar occupations, the difference in life expectation between the sexes is even greater in favor of women than it is in the United States. In fact, in all the developed countries throughout the world, women have a greater life expectancy than men (Table 2.6).

There is strong evidence that the difference in life expectation between the sexes has a biological basis. Several authorities point out that females outlive males not only in the human species, but in most other species as well, including such varied organisms as spiders, rats, fish, and fruit flies. Some attempts have been made to explain the longer life of the females in genetic terms. One theory is that females have an additional X-chromosome that gives them a biological advantage over males. Females are also believed to have a better immunization system against disease than males possess. Morris Rockstein points out that "with only a few exceptions, whatever the specific disease causing death, the female fares better at every adult age level.[4] Another explanation for the difference in life expectation between the sexes is that women have superior vitality. With the decrease in contagious diseases, maternal mortality, and degenerative diseases, this vital superiority is becoming more apparent.[5]

Table 2.6 Life expectancy at birth for selected countries

| | | Life expectancy (in years) | |
| | | Male population | Female population |
Country	Year(s)		
Australia	1965–1967	67.6	74.1
Austria	1974	67.7	74.9
Belgium	1968–1972	67.7	74.2
Canada	1970–1972	69.3	76.3
Denmark	1974–1975	71.1	76.8
England/Wales	1973	69.1	75.3
France	1974	69.0	76.9
German Democratic Republic	1969–1970	68.8	74.1
Greece	1960–1962	67.4	70.7
Italy	1970–1972	68.9	74.8
Japan	1976	72.1	77.3
Netherlands	1971–1975	71.2	77.2
Norway	1973–1974	71.5	77.8
Scotland	1971–1973	67.2	73.6
Spain	1970	69.6	74.9
Sweden	1971–1975	72.0	77.6
Switzerland	1968–1973	70.2	76.2
United States	1975	68.7	76.5
U.S.S.R.	1971–1972	64.0	74.0
Yugoslavia	1970–1972	65.4	70.2

SOURCE: United Nations, *Statistical Yearbook*, 1977, 29th ed., United Nations, New York, 1978, pp. 80–84. Copyright, United Nations 1978. Reproduced by permission.

Because women live longer than men and tend to marry men older than themselves, a large percentage of married women must eventually cope with the problem of widowhood. The number of widows in the population is five times that of widowers. As of 1977, 52 percent of females aged 65 and over were widows, while only 14 percent of males the same age were widowers (Figure 2.3). (For a life expectancy self-test, see Table 2.7.)

Life expectation varies not only with sex, but also with race. In fact, a sizable disparity in life expectation occurs between the black and white races: in 1976 life expectancy at birth for white males was 69.7 years, while for blacks it was 64.1 years. For females, the difference was less: expectancy at birth was 77.3 years for whites and 72.6 years for blacks. Some of this discrepancy between the races is due to the lower

Figure 2.3 Distribution of older persons by marital status, 1977

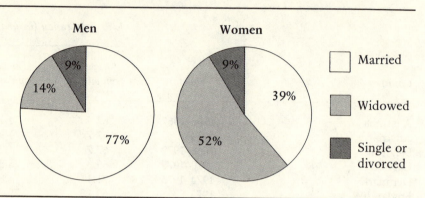

SOURCE: National Clearing House on Aging, *Facts About Older Americans*, 1978, U.S. Government Printing Office, Washington, D.C., 1979.

socioeconomic status of the blacks. Because their income as a whole falls below that of whites, the blacks' medical care and living conditions are poorer than the whites', and these factors contribute to the shorter life expectancy of blacks. At age 65, however, the life expectancies of blacks and whites almost become equal. In 1976, the average life expectancy of white men at age 65 was 13.7 years and for older black men 13.8 years By the same token, in 1976 the life expectancy of white women at age 65 was 18.1 years and for elderly black women 17.6 years.

No discussion of longevity would be complete without looking at some ways people have used to attempt to outwit old age. Legends and stories abound that describe such efforts. Not content with wishing for a longer life and for ways to reverse the aging process, many individuals and groups have devised some ingenious and unusual methods of combating old age.

The Extension of Life and Youth

From time immemorial, people have yearned for long life and at the same time have wished to remain youthful. This theme underlies many stories, even ancient ones. The following example is contained in the *Homeric Hymn to Aphrodite:*

Eos, the goddess of dawn, fell in love with Tithonus, a handsome Trojan youth. She went to Zeus and asked that Tithonus be given immortality, and Zeus granted her request. But Eos neglected to ask Zeus to allow Tithonus to retain his youthfulness. All went well between the happy pair until Tithonus began to age. In time he became

Table 2.7 The odds for a long life

NOTE: The figures are unscientific and extremely imprecise—merely sketchy indicators of some characteristics and practices that may contribute to long life. Furthermore, the predictions here are geared to the mythical average man and woman; they will predict for any one of us only in terms of very rough odds. As a result, anybody past middle age may find that the "prediction" for him or her is death several years ago.

	Life expectancy at birth (in years & months)	
Year of birth	*Men*	*Women*
1880–1900	35–40	37–42
1901–1904	46 & 2 mos.	48 & 8 mos.
1905–1908	48 & 8	51 & 5
1909–1912	50 & 7	54 & 4
1913–1916	51 & 8	55 & 5
1917–1920	52 & 6	56 & 5
1921–1924	58 & 2	61 & 2
1925–1928	58 & 5	61 & 10
1929–1932	58 & 10	63 & 2
1933–1936	60 & 6	65 & 5
1937–1940	62	66
1941–1944	64 & 6	68
1945–1948	65	70 & 4
1949–1952	65 & 11	71 & 6
1953–1956	67	74
1957–1961	67 & 6	74 & 2
1962–	67 & 8	74 & 4

Write down your basic expectancy: _____ years _____ months

Present age

Age	*Add*	*Age*	*Add*	*Age*	*Add*
1–4 yrs.	1 yr.	31–35 yrs.	3 yrs.	61–65 yrs.	8 yrs.
5–10	2 yrs.	36–40	3½	66–70	9½
11–15	2	41–45	4	71–75	11½
16–20	2	46–50	4½	76–80	12
21–25	2½	51–55	5½	81–85	6½
26–30	3	56–60	6½	85 plus	4½

New total: _____ years _____ months

Table 2.7 (cont.)

Family history

Add 1 year for each 5-year period your father has lived past 70. Do the same for your mother.

New total _____ years _____ months

Marital status

If you are married, add 5 years. If you are over 25 and not married, deduct 1 year for every unwedded decade.

New total _____ years _____ months

Where you live

Small town—add 3–5 years. City—subtract 2 years.

New total _____ years _____ months

Economic status

If wealthy or poor for greater part of life, deduct 3 years.

New total _____ years _____ months

Your shape

If you are over 40, deduct 1 year for every 5 pounds you are overweight. For each inch your girth measurement exceeds your chest measurement, deduct 2 years.

New total _____ years _____ months

Exercise

Regular and moderate—add 3 years. Regular and vigorous—add 5 years.

New total _____ years _____ months

Disposition

Good natured and placid—add 1–5 years. Tense and nervous—subtract 1–5 years.

New total _____ years _____ months

Alcohol

Heavy drinker—subtract 5 years. Very heavy drinker—subtract 10 years.

New total _____ years _____ months

Smoking

½ to 1 pack per day—subtract 3 years
1 to 1½ packs per day—subtract 5 years
1½ to 2 packs per day—subtract 10 years
Pipe or cigar—subtract 2 years

New total _____ years _____ months

Family environment

Regular medical checkups and regular dental care—add 3 years.
Frequently ill—subtract 2 years.

Final total _____ years _____ months

SOURCE: "Report on Longevity: Ah, to Be Young While Old." Copyright © 1973 by *Harper's Magazine.* All rights reserved. Reprinted from the June 1973 issue by special permission.

so old and feeble that he could not move or raise his limbs. Denied death, he was doomed to suffer the infirmities of old age forever.[6]

As this legend illustrates, a long life is not enough. It is the quality of the added years that is important. The search for ways to increase longevity and to retain youth and vigor is reflected in literature, where nostrums and treatments to effect these goals abound.

Techniques used to forestall aging and prolong life vary widely among different cultures. Some of the earliest attempts at rejuvenation were based on the practice of *gerocomy*, the belief that an old man may absorb youth from young women. This custom was widely practiced in many Near Eastern and Far Eastern countries.[7] For example, in the Old Testament, King David's servants secured a young maiden to sleep in his bed to revitalize the aging king with the heat from her body. Both the Yukaghirs of Siberia and the Navaho Indians advocated keeping vermin or lice on the body to ward off old age. According to the Hopi Indians (also from the Southwest), bathing in icy water and rubbing the body with snow helped to keep the skin from getting wrinkled. The Kwakiutl people of Vancouver Island believed that bathing one's face in urine and one's body in salt water would accomplish the same purpose. To retard aging, the Xosa of Africa advocated that men remove all gray hairs and frequently marry young women. Among the Labrador Eskimos, wishing for a long life and being brave were two ways to achieve longevity. And finally, the secret of long life according to the Dieri, an Australian aborigine tribe, was simply to avoid one's mother-in-law.[8]

A common source for rejuvenation potions and treatments over the centuries has been the sex organs of animals. This use was probably due to the linking of sexual vigor to the prolongation of youth. Many early physicians, including Hippocrates, the Father of Medicine, administered dried animal organs to their patients, or even advised that they eat the testicles of tigers. Around 1890, the idea of sex organ therapy reappeared. Charles E. Brown-Séquard, a noted French professor of physiology, advocated injections of an extract prepared from animal testicles. Following in Dr. Brown-Séquard's footsteps, Serge Voronoff, a Russian-born French surgeon, achieved fame in the 1920s by grafting pieces of testicles from chimpanzees into male patients.

In recent years, two of the more popular techniques used to try to retard the aging process are cell therapy and the drug called Gerovital. Cell therapy, developed in Switzerland by Dr. Paul Niehans, consists of a series of injections. The solution is derived from lamb fetuses taken from specially bred black sheep; certain organs are removed from the fetuses and ground up, and then the material is suspended in an injectable solution. The theory is that the cells from certain organs of the unborn lamb will revitalize the corresponding organs of the person receiving the injections. The second technique is the drug, Gerovital;

this is essentially a form of procaine, which is widely used in dentistry as a local anesthetic. According to Dr. Ana Aslan, the drug's developer, Gerovital is successful in combating arthritis, arteriosclerosis, and a number of problems associated with old age.*

America's Centenarians

People who remain vigorous and healthy while living to extreme old age have always been regarded with great fascination. They are usually asked the inevitable question: "What is the secret of your longevity?" A social security worker asks it in the following interview:

> When I asked 112-year-old Mrs. DuPea the secret of her longevity, she said, "I don't plan for tomorrow. I live today. I don't count on being here tomorrow." Then she went on to say that her philosophy of life was "to think right, do right and don't worry." I questioned her as to the secret of her good health. She said, "I eat proper food. In food is your medicine. I eat everything fresh, not from cans." Mrs. DuPea told me that she never seems to require a doctor's care. However, she does have a doctor anyway. The doctor said, "Well, as far as I can see you're in good health," and wondered why she had come to see him. She replied, "In case I drop dead, you can sign my death certificate.[9]

As in the case of Mrs. DuPea, most centenarians† have a pet theory to explain their longevity. Some offer such explanations as: "I never drink whiskey," "I eat sunflower seeds each day," "I drink goat's milk," "I eat only fresh foods," and "Each day I take a vitamin pill and a glass of wine."[10] Other centenarians maintain that their long life is due to heredity, hard work, and exercise. According to Belle Beard's study of 270 American centenarians, "Demonstrated Human Ability After 100," the majority exercise daily, some walking as much as a mile or more each day.[11] Additional reasons cited by centenarians for their longevity include: "I behave myself," "I take life as it comes," "My belief in God," and "I've stayed away from doctors."[12]

Charlie Smith claimed to have celebrated his 137th birthday and appeared to be the oldest living American until his death in 1979. When he was 12 years old, he came to this country from Liberia aboard a slave ship. He was purchased by a Texas cattleman in the New Orleans slave

---

*At the present time the Food and Drug Administration (FDA) will not permit the practice of cell therapy in the United States or license Gerovital for use in this country. The FDA, however, can only regulate drugs involved in interstate commerce. In May 1977, in an effort to sidestep the need for FDA approval, a measure was passed in Nevada to legalize the manufacture and use of Gerovital in that state only.

†A centenarian is a person who is 100 years old or over.

Charlie Smith was recognized as being the oldest person in the United States. He was made to retire from his work on an orange grove because he was considered too old to climb trees. He then operated a small store until he moved into a nursing home at the age of 133. (New Times Publishing Company. Sam Merrill—Photographer)

market. In 1955 Smith's age was presumed to have been authenticated when his original bill of sale was located in New Orleans by *Life Magazine*. At that time he was working in an orange grove in Florida and was said to be, at 113 years of age, the oldest working American.[13]

The actual number of centenarians in the United States is not known. This inaccuracy stems from systematic errors in the 1970 census made in recording and processing responses, as well as age misstatements by the respondents themselves. Out of the 106,000 persons reported as centenarians in 1970, Jacob Seigel and Jeffrey Passel estimate that only about 5 percent, or 4,800, were actually over 100 years of age.[14] People tend to reduce their age during their middle years, but to exaggerate it in the later years. The following anecdote illustrates this tendency:

Take the history of one Bessie Singletree. . . . On her twenty-seventh birthday Miss Singletree became twenty-four years of age and was married.

At thirty-five she was thirty. At forty she was thirty-nine until she was close to fifty. At fifty Bessie was forty; at sixty, fifty-five. At sixty-five she was sixty-eight and on her seventieth birthday everyone said Grandmother Singletree was pretty chipper for an octogenarian. At seventy-five she had her picture in the paper as the oldest woman in the county, aged ninety-three. Ten years later she passed away at the ripe old age of one hundred and nine.[15]

Seigel and Passel indicate that until a country's vital registration system or population register has been in existence for at least a century, the exact number of those over the age of 100 cannot be determined. They feel that it will be 75 more years before this condition will occur in the United States. At that time, census reports of centenarians can be checked against their birth certificates.

Centenarians in Three Societies

In his famous novel, *Lost Horizon*, James Hilton describes a mythical utopia called Shangri-La, in which life is extended indefinitely. In this utopia people are "granted the best of both worlds, a long and pleasant youth . . . and an equally long and pleasant old age."[16] As we mentioned earlier, many people today believe that at least three places are comparable to Shangri-La: the village of Vilcabamba in Ecuador, the principality of Hunza in Pakistan, and the Caucasus region of the Soviet Union (especially Abkhasia). Reports indicate that in each of these three areas exist large proportions of centenarians who are amazingly fit and lead vigorous, productive lives.[17] In addition, many of the centenarians claim to be 120, 140, or even older. Before his death in 1973, Shirali Mislimov, an Azerbaijani farmer in the U.S.S.R., claimed to be the world's oldest living person at the age of 168; Khfaf Lasuria celebrated her 140th birthday in the Soviet village of Kutol in 1975. Miguel Carpio in the Ecuadorian village of Vilcabamba says that he is over 129 years old.

Soviet centenarians *(Opposite page)*

Top left: Shirali Mislimov, a farmer from the Soviet village of Barzavu, was touted as the world's oldest man. At the time of his death in 1973, he claimed to be 168 years old. (UPI)

Top right: Zibeida Sheidayeva, said to be 114 years old, received an award for 100 years of employment at a rug factory. The Novosti Press Agency said that her productivity equalled that of younger workers. (UPI)

Bottom: Khfaf Lasuria, from the village of Kutol in the Soviet Union, claimed to have been born in 1835. She is pictured with her son, said to be 100 years old. Until her death in 1975, it was reported that she could thread a needle without eyeglasses. (*Tass* from Sovfoto)

The claims of these people are extraordinary when compared with the much lower number of centenarians in the populations of other parts of the world. In general, there are only two to three centenarians in every 100,000 persons, only one person in a million lives to the age of 105, and only one in 40 million reaches the age of 110.[18] But according to the 1970 census, the total number of centenarians in the Caucasus region was between 4,500 and 5,000. The Soviet republic of Azerbaijan had the greatest concentration of centenarians, with 63 per 100,000, followed by the republic of Georgia, with 39 per 100,000. In the 1971 census, the village of Vilcabamba in Ecuador had 9 centenarians out of a population of 819. This extrapolates to 1,100 centenarians per 100,000 population! No official Pakistani census data is available for Hunza.[19]

In all three areas, however, there is no adequate scientific proof to validate the claims of longevity that are made. As Hayflick points out:

> The gullibility of scientifically trained observers who have reported these claims without sufficiently emphasizing the meager evidence for the allegations does a disservice to biology generally and to gerontology specifically. Reliance on anything short of biological proof of age is suspect in view of the fact that birth and death records were not even legally required in highly developed countries until the early part of this century. The veneration of the aged in these villages has established a competition between them such that their wild, unsubstantiated claims of longevity have increased to stretch the limits of credibility. . . . Surely claims of super-longevity should be taken with as much skepticism as any claim unsupported by proof.[20]

After studying longevity in many areas of the U.S.S.R., Zhores Medvedev, the distinguished Russian gerontologist, now living in London, concludes that the exceptional longevity claimed by the aged in many areas of the Soviet Union does not exist.[21] He suggests several reasons behind these claims. First, old people in these areas enjoy high social status; the older a person gets, the more honor, respect, and authority he or she receives from both family and community. Status alone would be motive enough to exaggerate one's age, but another incentive for exaggerated age is the national and international publicity given these centenarians. Pictures and stories about them frequently appear in magazines and newspapers; they are regarded as celebrities and in some cases as national heroes. And for purposes of political propaganda, the government considers these long-lived people to be a special achievement of the Soviet Union.

Medvedev offers still another explanation for the phenomenon of longevity in the U.S.S.R. During World War I and also the Russian Revolution, thousands of men falsified their ages, often using their fathers' documents, to avoid conscription or to mask their desertion from the army. Afterward, many continued the pretense because of the benefits mentioned above. An example is a man from Yahutia, who was found to be 130 years old in the 1959 census. His picture and an article about him were published in the government newspaper, *Isvestia*. Later, a letter arrived from a group of Ukrainian villagers; they recognized him as a fellow villager who had deserted from the army during World War I. It was discovered that this man was only 78 years old, and that he had falsified his age in order to escape further military service.

Summary

1. Different societies have different ways of determining when a person is old. Our society uses 65, the age set for eligibility for social security benefits, to define old age.

2. The number and the proportion of older people in the population have been rapidly increasing during this century. In 1900 in the United States there were 3 million persons 65 and over, or 4.1 percent of the total population. By 1975 the elderly population had increased to 22.4 million, or 10.5 percent. Today there are nearly 25 million elderly, and their proportion in the American population is about 11 percent.

3. California and New York, the two states with the largest populations, also have the largest number of older people. The state with the largest proportion of elderly is Florida. Agricultural states such as Arkansas, Iowa, and Missouri also have high concentrations of older people.

4. In the 1970 U.S. census, over half the elderly lived in urbanized areas. Of these about a third lived in central cities. An increasing proportion of elderly are expected to be concentrated in metropolitan areas in the future.

5. In the United States, life expectancy at birth has increased from 47 years in 1900 to 72.8 years in 1976. Life expectancy varies, according to sex and race. Expectation of life for females exceeds that of males by over seven years. Blacks have a shorter life expectancy than whites up to the age of 65; after that point, blacks tend to outlive whites.

6. For centuries, most people have dreamed of prolonging life and remaining youthful. Many methods have been tried in order to achieve these goals. The two most recent techniques are cellular therapy and Gerovital.

7. There are about 4,800 centenarians in the United States. The oldest was Charlie Smith who was reputed to be 137 years old at the time of his death. Three areas in the world have large concentrations of centenarians: the Caucasus region of the Soviet Union, Hunza in Pakistan, and Vilcabamba in Ecuador. But no adequate scientific proof validates the ages of these people, and many of their claims of longevity stretch the limits of credibility.

Notes

1. Frances M. Cox with Ndung'u Mberia, *Aging in a Changing Village Society: A Kenyan Experience*, International Federation on Ageing, Washington, D.C., 1977, p. 8.

2. U.S. Bureau of the Census, *Current Population Reports,* Special Studies, Series P-23, No. 59, U.S. Government Printing Office, Washington, D.C. (May 1976), p. 9.

3. Stephen M. Golant, "Residential Concentrations of the Future Elderly," *The Gerontologist,* 15, no. 1 (1975), Pt. II, 16–23.

4. Jack Botwinick, *Aging and Behavior,* Springer, New York, 1973, p. 9.

5. U.S. Bureau of the Census, *Current Population Reports,* Special Studies, Series P-23, No. 59, U.S. Government Printing Office, Washington, D.C. (May 1976), pp. 29–30.

6. Mark P. Morford and Robert J. Lenardon, *Classical Mythology,* David McKay, New York, 1971, p. 25.

7. Ewald W. Busse, "Theories of Aging," in *Behavior and Adaptation in Late Life,* ed. Ewald W. Busse and Eric Pfeiffer, Little, Brown, Boston, 1977, pp. 8–9.

8. Leo W. Simmons, *The Role of the Aged in Primitive Society,* Yale University Press, New Haven, 1945, pp. 220–223.

9. Tatzumble DuPea, *America's Centenarians,* vol. 1, Social Security Administration, 1963, unpaged.

10. Ibid., vols. 1–13.

11. Belle Boone Beard, *Aging,* February 1968, p. 8.

12. *America's Centenarians,* vols. 1–13.

13. Sam Merrill, "The Oldest Living American at 133," *New Times Magazine,* February 6, 1976.

14. Jacob S. Seigel and Jeffrey S. Passel, "New Estimates of the Number of Centenarians in the United States," *Journal of the American Statistical Association,* 71 (September 1976), 559–566.

15. Ibid., p. 560.

16. James Hilton, *Lost Horizon,* William Morrow, New York, 1936, p. 152.

17. For example, see Alexander Leaf, *Youth in Old Age,* McGraw-Hill, New York, 1975.

18. Zhores A. Medvedev, "Caucasus and Altay Longevity: A Biological or Social Problem?" *The Gerontologist,* 14, no. 5 (1974), Pt. I, 381.

19. Alexander Leaf, "Getting Old," *Scientific American,* 229 (September 1973), 44–52.

20. Leonard Hayflick, "The Strategy of Senescence," *The Gerontologist,* 14, no. 1 (1974), 43.

21. Medvedev, "Caucasus and Altay Longevity," pp. 381–387.

For Further Study

Beard, Belle Boone. *Social Competence of Centenarians.* Social Science Institute, University of Georgia, Athens, Ga., 1967. A collection of papers dealing with the author's research on centenarians.

Benet, Sula. *How to Live to Be 100*. Dial, New York, 1976. An interesting account of the people of the Caucasus and their way of life.

Cole, William E. *Urban Society*. Houghton Mifflin, Boston, 1958. See Chapter 26 for a good discussion of the demographic aspects of the older population.

Cutler, Neal E., and Robert A. Harootyn. "Demography of the Aged." In *Aging: Scientific Perspectives and Issues*, edited by Diana S. Woodruff and James E. Birren. D. Van Nostrand, New York, 1975. An excellent source of demographic data relevant to the issues of gerontology.

Hauser, Phillip M. "Aging and World-Wide Population Change," in *Handbook of Aging and the Social Sciences*, edited by Robert H. Binstock and Ethel Shanas. Van Nostrand Reinhold, New York, 1976. A comprehensive discussion of aging and the extension of life in developed and less developed countries throughout the world.

Leaf, Alexander, *Youth in Old Age*. McGraw-Hill, New York, 1975. The author describes his visits to Vilcabamba, Hunza, and the Caucasus and speculates on some reasons for the health and the vigor of elderly persons in these places.

United States Bureau of the Census. *Current Population Reports*. Special Studies, Series P-23, No. 59, May 1976. A wide range of data on the older population, including age, sex, racial composition, and certain social and economic characteristics.

II

Culture and Adult Socialization

3

Age Norms and Age Status

Among the Todas of Southern India, thumbing one's nose at another person is a sign of respect. Certain Eskimo tribes offer their wives for the night to a visitor to show hospitality, and in some villages in New Guinea, old persons sleep with pigs for warmth. Why do these people adhere to such practices and customs? The answer is simple: that is the way they were taught. It is their way of life, or more specifically, their culture. *Culture*, in the sociological sense, refers to the social heritage of a society that is transmitted to each generation; it is learned behavior that is shared with others. Culture includes all the beliefs, customs, knowledge, and products of a society. Culture guides the life's activities of a people and may be likened to a blueprint or map for everyday living.

The Meaning of Culture

Sociologists give *culture* a much broader meaning than is used in everyday speech. Popularly, the term is used to denote good taste and refinement. We think of a cultured person as one who drinks wine with meals, is well read, and enjoys opera and the ballet, rather than one who drinks beer, reads comic books, and shoots craps. To sociologists, however, all human beings and all societies have culture. All people are considered "cultured" in the sense that they are participants in the culture of the society in which they live.

It has been said that the last thing a person who lived under water all his life would discover would be water. We spend our lives so immersed in the culture of the society in which we live that we are often completely unaware of its influence on us. We follow the habits, beliefs, and customs of our culture automatically and unthinkingly. According to Kluckhohn, "Culture regulates our lives at every turn. From the moment we are born until we die there is, whether we are conscious of it or not, constant pressure upon us to follow certain types of behavior."[1] The fact that we prefer steak to fresh worms or caterpillars, that we eat

Life in the ASU

When people in this society* reach a certain age, a large feast is prepared in their honor, and they are presented with an apparatus made from a precious metal in which to mark the passage of time. They are then relieved of all their official duties and are expected to remain in their quarters most of the day and to sit on a large piece of wood that is molded to the shape of their body. It is curved at the bottom in order to permit them to move back and forth with the slightest motion.

Sometimes they venture out to a large grassy area where there are long flat pieces of wood to sit on. Here they observe a peculiar type of rite that takes place between two people. Each moves little discs on a small surface covered with squares until all of the discs of one color are gone.

Other times they may attend a ceremony for people of their own age. They all sit together at large rectangular surfaces watching small pieces of paper. One person chants strange sounds while the others place small pellets on the papers from time to time. After a while someone will jump up and yell the name of the ceremony.

*Reverse the letters in ASU.

sitting down and not squatting or standing up, or that we believe that a man should have only one wife and not two or more at the same time are all patterns of our culture.

To understand the concept of culture more fully, look at the anthropological account of some of the unusual customs and practices that occur in a well known contemporary society, which appears in the box on this page. With so many interesting activities to occupy their time, it is hard to understand why old people in this society sometimes complain of being bored and want to resume their official duties.

Norms

Our culture defines for us what is proper and improper behavior, what is right and wrong, and what we are expected to do and not do. These standards or rules of behavior are called *norms*.* Norms help us to predict the behavior of others, and in turn, allow others to know what to expect of us. In our society the expected pattern of behavior, or norm, on being introduced to someone is to extend the right hand. This seems natural to us, but it is not so natural to people in some other societies,

*The term *norm* is not used here in the statistical sense.

who may misinterpret our behavior as being aggressive or even nonsensical.

A woman from another culture, after having an American male shake her hand, remarked that she was glad he decided to shake her hand and not her head. The normative behavior for greeting varies from culture to culture. Among some Eskimos, you lick your hands and then draw them first over your own face and then over the face of the stranger whom you are greeting. The Burmese and Mongols greet one another by smelling each other's cheeks. Polynesians embrace and rub each other's back, and in some places they greet by placing one arm around the neck of the other person and tickling him or her under the chin.

Some norms, such as shaking hands, apply to all members of our society, whereas others apply only to certain groups. Such factors as sex and age may determine whether or not a specific norm applies to a group or category of people. For example, in our society norms about bathing attire are determined by sex. A female must cover both the upper and lower part of the body, whereas a male is required only to cover the lower part. Similarly, males are expected to open doors for females, but females are not expected to do the same for males.

People also have expectations about what is considered proper behavior at different ages. These expectations are called *age norms*. We can understand a five-year-old boy kicking and crying when his mother refuses him an ice-cream cone. But imagine a 21-year-old man exhibiting the same type of behavior. We would not expect a teenager to dress in the style of a grandmother, nor would we expect to see a 65-year-old man and woman dressed as flower children.

Age norms also define when major life events should occur. They define the proper age for a man or woman to marry, to finish school, to become a grandparent, or to retire. In other words, there exists what Bernice Neugarten calls a "prescriptive timetable."[2] Most people use this as a criterion for judging either their conformity or deviance to the timing of family and occupational events. Table 3.1 illustrates the high degree of consensus that exists regarding such age-appropriate or expected behavior.

Sociologists distinguish among norms by their degree of importance and by the type of sanctions applied when they are violated. Norms may be grouped into three types: folkways, mores, and laws.

Folkways

Most of the rules that govern the conventions and routines of everyday life, and define what is socially correct consist of *folkways*. These range from using the proper fork to keeping your grass cut. Folkways are

Table 3.1 Consensus in a middle-class, middle-aged sample regarding various age-related characteristics

	Age range designated as appropriate or expected	Percentage who concur	
		Men (N = 50)	Women (N = 43)
Best age for a man to marry	20–25	80%	90%
Best age for a woman to marry	19–24	85	90
When most people should become grandparents	45–50	84	79
Best age for most people to finish school and go to work	20–22	86	82
When most men should be settled on a career	24–26	74	64
When most men hold their top jobs	45–50	71	58
When most people should be ready to retire	60–65	83	86
A young man	18–22	84	83
A middle-aged man	40–50	86	75
An old man	65–75	75	57
A young woman	18–24	89	88
A middle-aged woman	40–50	87	77
An old woman	60–75	83	87
When a man has the most responsibilities	35–50	79	75
When a man accomplishes most	40–50	82	71
The prime of life for a man	35–50	86	80
When a woman has the most responsibilities	25–40	93	91
When a woman accomplishes most	30–45	94	92
A good-looking woman	20–35	92	82

SOURCE: Bernice L. Neugarten, Joan W. Moore, and John C. Lowe, "Age Norms, Age Constraints, and Adult Socialization," *American Journal of Sociology*, 70 (May 1965), 712. Reprinted with permission of the publisher, The University of Chicago Press.

enforced informally, but effectively, by such means of social control as gossip, raised eyebrows, or ridicule. Because folkways are not considered important to the well-being of the group, only mild disapproval results when they are violated.

Many age norms fall into this category. Appropriate behavior for older people is often specified in the folkways. We expect older people not to be interested in sex or in subjects having to do with sex. An older man who makes suggestive remarks or jokes may be dubbed as a "dirty old man." ("He shouldn't think about sex at his age.") We expect older people to wear conservative styles of clothing. ("She's too old to dress like that.") An elderly woman wearing a bikini on the beach would definitely raise eyebrows and be subjected to uncomplimentary remarks. We expect older people not to do strenuous work. ("He shouldn't be doing that type of work at his age.")

Folkways also define the proper etiquette toward the elderly. The following are expectations regarding behavior toward the elderly, some of which are gradually disappearing today. For example, a Boy Scout is expected to help an elderly lady across the street. A young person is supposed to offer a seat to an older person on a crowded bus or subway. A younger person is expected to allow an elderly person to go first through a doorway and is supposed to pick up an object dropped by an older person. In other situations, a younger individual is supposed to offer to carry a heavy parcel or suitcase for an elderly person.

Certain folkways govern housing, intergenerational obligations, and finances. The preferred residence pattern is for older persons to live in their own homes, but to be near their children and relatives. Older people expect their children and relatives to maintain frequent contact with them. Grandparents are expected to show an interest in their grandchildren; some grandparents even overconform to this expectation. People are expected to save money while they are young in order to support themselves when they stop working. Adults are supposed to give financial aid to their aged parents in need. By the same token, the aged parents are expected to help their children if circumstances permit.

Mores

In contrast to folkways, *mores* relate to the basic needs of a society and are considered extremely important for the welfare of the group. Violations of the mores, unlike the folkways, are considered very serious and carry with them strong negative sanctions. When they are violated, people react with disgust, shock, or horror. Mores define what is morally right or wrong.

When mores are expressed in the negative form of "must not" and "thou shalt not," they are called taboos. Many of the Ten Commandments fall into this category. What are some of the mores of our society? We must not murder, steal, or eat human flesh. Americans are expected to be sexually faithful to their spouses, loyal to their country, and have only one spouse at a time.

Some age norms can be classified as mores. For example, an old woman dating a young man violates our mores. We believe that an elderly woman should not date and certainly should not marry a man who is much younger than herself. A divorce between an elderly couple who have been married for 40 or 50 years is much more severely censured than a divorce between a younger couple. Some older couples violate the mores when they live together without being married in order to avoid losing financial benefits through remarriage.

The mores of some cultures prescribe that old people should be killed outright or abandoned when they become feeble and infirm. To us these are shocking practices that offend our sense of decency and morality. One reason why the concept of euthanasia is a difficult one for us is that it involves the violation of a deeply engrained norm.

The dividing line between folkways and mores is not always sharp. They can best be viewed as being on a continuum ranging from those norms that elicit mild disapproval to those that elicit strong disapproval. Both folkways and mores regulate human behavior and are enforced by informal social controls.

Laws

Informal social controls alone are not sufficient to guarantee that a complex society functions in an orderly manner. A more formalized type of control is needed — namely, laws. *Laws* are rules enacted by those who exert political power and are enforced by the police and other officials who have been given the authority to do so. They maintain social order through force or the threat of force.

Some laws, such as those against bigamy and murder, are supported by the mores. The violation of these laws is considered to be both immoral and illegal. Laws firmly rooted in our mores are the most effective because most people want to conform to them and exert informal pressure on others to do likewise. At times, laws may conflict with the folkways and mores; these laws are difficult, if not impossible, to enforce. A classic example was the prohibition amendment to the Constitution, which did not express the beliefs of the majority of our population and was repealed after 15 years. Most traffic laws are not backed by folkways or mores and are widely violated. The 55-mile-an-hour speed limit is a case in point.

Just as there are folkways and mores associated with age, there are also laws related to certain ages in a society. At 18 an individual is considered eligible to vote, at 30 generally eligible for public office, and from ages 62 to 65 one may begin receiving social security benefits. In 1965 the Older Americans Act outlining a national policy to improve the situation of older persons was passed. Some objectives included in this statute are adequate income, housing, and employment for the elderly. The Age Discrimination in Employment Act, passed in 1967, barred employers from denying job opportunities or dismissing employees

Living in Sin

Old people complain that for them, the social security system invites living in sin.* Louis Marathon, 80, and Madeline Clarke, 81, met in a Miami nursing home last year and lived together for several months, between his hospital stays. . . . Last June, they got married and Madeline may now lose her benefits. . . . Even if their money is reduced, however, the Marathons are glad they married. "There's more respect," says Madeline, who is almost blind. "If we live together, it's just common-law, and with that anyone could get disgusted and walk out."

*Under recent amendments to the Social Security Act, widows and widowers aged 60 and over who remarry will no longer have their benefits reduced.
SOURCE: "Living Together," *Newsweek*, August 1, 1977, p. 48.

between the ages of 40 and 65 solely on the basis of age. In 1978 the law was amended to include persons up to age 70. One of the most controversial issues today is whether or not denying a person the chance to work through mandatory retirement policies is constitutional. According to opinion polls, the majority of Americans are opposed to inflexible, mandatory retirement systems; they feel that a person should be allowed to work as long as he or she wants. This topic will be discussed more fully in Chapter 14.

Norms for Older People

An early study of the social aspects of aging done by Robert Havighurst and Ruth Albrecht in 1949 and 1951 in Prairie City, a small midwestern town, still contains much relevant data on age norms.[3] One part of their study consisted of a questionnaire in which persons of various ages were interviewed to determine their approval or disapproval of certain types of behavior for older persons. For example, the respondents were asked to register approval, disapproval, or indifference to such items as: "Joins an organization limited to older people," "Lives alone after the death of wife or husband," and "Spends a lot of time in a tavern with some old friends."

The findings of Havighurst and Albrecht revealed that there are few norms that apply specifically to older people. Most norms apply to all age groups. Of the norms they found that did exist for the elderly, the ones most strongly approved focused on family, church, and work and income maintenance. For example, older persons should be greatly interested in their grandchildren and great-grandchildren. They should visit grown children at regular intervals, especially holidays, but otherwise they should lead a separate life from them. As persons age, they should become more interested in church and religion. They should go to church regularly, be active leaders in church and, in general, keep up or increase church activities. As far as work and income are concerned, older persons should retire between the ages of 65 and 70, they should cut down on their work loads and only do as much work as they feel comfortable doing. They should continue to hold on to their business, profession, or land for as long as possible. Persons should accept old age pensions when they have used up their savings.

Havighurst and Albrecht found that the norms which were strongly disapproved, generally, applied to persons of all ages and not just the elderly. For instance, sitting around and doing nothing was censured as was not visiting friends or not keeping in touch with relatives. Also disapproved was lack of interest in politics, having nothing to do with the church, and dropping out of all clubs. They conclude that: "American society desires and expects a good deal of activity and independence from its older people, tolerates a wide variety of roles on their part, and wishes them to slow down gradually as they grow older."[4]

Irving Rosow argues that not only are there fewer significant norms for older people to follow, but they tend to be more ambiguous and less clear-cut than norms for younger persons.[5] The activities that older people should pursue, how they should utilize their time, or in what way they should pattern their lives are for the most part without guidelines and structure. With fewer and less specific norms to guide their behavior in old age, older people are left in an ambiguous position, uncertain what to do or what is expected of them. Rosow comments, "Indeed, this is precisely why so many older people are consumed by inactivity and boredom. The culture does not provide them with definitions and meaningful norms as it does all previous life stages."[6] Furthermore, the uncertainty about what is proper and preferred conduct can be a source of anxiety and alienation for older people.

While Rosow emphasizes the negative aspects of the decrease in normative expectations with age, Vern Bengtson argues that this decrease can have positive consequences, such as increase in personal freedom.[7] The very lack of definite, prescribed norms for older people to follow allows them more flexibility and freedom in their behavior and permits them a wide range of options in their lives. He indicates that the decrease in specific norms "represents a potential opportunity to pick and choose among alternative behaviors — a degree of freedom from societal restraints that is perhaps greater than at any other period of the life cycle . . . to those who choose (and have the capability) to exploit it."[8]

The Double Standard of Aging

Since ancient times, people have believed that the onset of old age takes place earlier for women than for men. According to Hippocrates, old age began at about 55–60 years for men and at 45–55 years for women. Plato set the prime of life for a man at 30 and for a woman at 20. Today in our society, people still believe that women age sooner than men. Table 3.1 gives the age for an old man at 65–75 years, whereas old age for a woman begins five years earlier and occurs between 60 and 75 years. What is being reflected here are sex norms associated with aging, or a double standard of aging.

Women can expect to live longer than men, and they also tend to be healthier through their life spans. Yet, why does our society picture them as aging much more rapidly than their male counterparts? One reason is that women in our society are more dependent on their physical appearance for status and self-concept than men. Femininity is associated with sexual attractiveness, while masculinity is associated with power and position. Men derive their status and self-concept from their earning ability, their occupation, and leadership. These abilities not only diminish more slowly than does physical appearance, but they actually increase throughout middle age. As a woman nears middle age, she often begins to feel some loss in her sexual attractiveness and with it a decline in self-esteem and self-concept.

Our culture, then, defines women as growing old much sooner than men. This may explain in part why women are more evasive than men in telling their age. Remember all the old maid jokes you've heard? Now think for a minute about old bachelor jokes. The chances are that you have not heard one. Erdman Palmore, in his study of humor and the aging, discusses jokes about old maids, but reports there are no old bachelor jokes.[9] According to Palmore, "While the term 'old maid' generally has negative connotations, there is no corresponding negative term for men such as 'old bachelor'."[10] Obviously, being old and unmarried is acceptable for a man in our society, but is not acceptable for a woman. Our norms prescribe that a woman should be married by a certain age, otherwise, she is to be pitied. The same norm does not hold true for a man.

Norms governing the age of marital partners also differ. A woman is supposed to marry a man her own age or older, and certainly no more than a few years her junior. A man, however, may marry a woman 25 or 30 years younger than himself and this act is not only acceptable but is sometimes even laudable. Romantic involvements between an older man and a younger woman have been reinforced by novels, plays, television, and movies.

The mass media glamorize and legitimate the older man–younger woman

Growing old is particularly difficult for women in our society. Unlike men, much of their self-concept and status is derived from their physical appearance. (Suzanne Opton)

relationship. Successful actors continue to play romantic leads well into their fifties and sometimes sixties. Frequently, they are cast opposite actresses at least half their age, and the story line rarely even acknowledges the difference. They are simply an average romantic couple. The question of whether the 20-year-old heroine is out of her mind to marry the greying 55-year-old hero is not even raised.[11]

As we mentioned earlier, the situation of an older woman marrying a

---

Middle-Age Is the Thing
to Be—If You're Male

CHICAGO (UPI) — Middle-aged men are the most attractive males of any age group, a study presented in Chicago concludes.

Carol Nowak, assistant professor of psychology at Wayne State University in Michigan, said she made the study by showing slides to a variety of persons.

All groups, including young women, agreed that the middle-aged men were most attractive, she said.

The magic didn't transmit to middle-aged women, though.

Miss Nowak said her viewers found middle-aged women the least attractive of any age group. Even middle-aged women agreed with the general consensus, she said.

SOURCE: *Knoxville News-Sentinel*, May 8, 1976, p. 1. Reprinted by permission of United Press International.

younger man is met with strong disapproval in our culture. Some may argue how illogical this kind of normative behavior is. After all, since women live on the average about eight years longer than men, would it not be more rational for a woman to marry a younger man instead of an older one and avoid a long period of widowhood? But our culture defines what are approved and disapproved standards for our behavior, and we judge behavior not by its being logical or reasonable but by its conformity to the norms.

Age Status System

Status

Status is like a calling card: it identifies who we are and defines our position. As we move from one group to another, we occupy a different status.* In the classroom we have the status of student, in the dormitory the status of roommate, and at home the status of son or daughter, or wife or husband. Each individual then has many statuses, and with each status go certain rights and obligations. When people put these rights and obligations into effect, they are performing their roles. A *role* is the expected behavior of one who holds a certain status. Just as a person has

---

*Status as used in this sense does not refer to rank or a position in a hierarchy.

many statuses, he or she also has many roles. Usually a person's occupation is considered the key status.

Statuses may be classified into two types: ascribed and achieved. *Ascribed statuses* are those assigned to us by society; we don't have to earn them. *Achieved statuses* are those, as the name implies, achieved by our own efforts. Being a doctor, a wife, or a teacher are achieved statuses. Sex is an ascribed status; you are born male or female. This status is assigned at birth without regard to individual ability. Basic to all societies is the ascription of statuses with regard to sex. All groups specify different attitudes, behavior, and activities for men and women. We discussed earlier how these differences are reflected in the norms of our society.

Age Status

Another important way of establishing status is by the use of age. Like sex, our age is ascribed. All societies have at least three or four age categories (infant and/or child, adult, and old), and some have delineated many more. Poets and writers have long described the succession of age statuses that individuals pass through in the course of their life spans. Ancient writers divided the life cycle into five or ten stages. For example, Solon, an Athenian poet of the seventh century B.C., suggested a ten-stage life cycle, each stage lasting seven years. The idea of seven ages of man, originally proposed by Hippocrates, was popularized by Shakespeare in *As You Like It*. Modern scholars, such as Erik Erikson, view the life cycle in terms of eight categories, and Rosow has suggested a series of nine age statuses that most people may normally expect to occupy.[12]

The term *age status* refers to the differential rights and obligations awarded to individuals on the basis of age. All members of society move from one age category to the next as they progress through the life cycle. Each new category represents a new status and requires the learning of new roles and culturally defined patterns of behavior. All societies are faced with the tasks of preparing members for their new statuses and making the transition as smooth as possible. To accomplish this, they employ what are called *rites-of-passage* ceremonies. These ceremonies mark the transition from one status to the next and publicly announce the new status.

Rites of Passage

Arnold Van Gennep in his classic work, *Rites of Passage*, distinguished three phases of such a ceremony: separation or removal from a former

"I used to be old, too, but it wasn't my cup of tea." (Drawing by Weber; © 1977. The New Yorker Magazine, Inc.)

status, transition, and incorporation of the person into a new status.[13] He noted that the person who moves to a new status may often find the change disturbing and that rites of passage ease the adjustment and help to incorporate the individual into a new status in the group. Van Gennep said:

> The life of an individual in any society is a series of passages from one age to another and from one occupation to another. . . . [These passages all have]

similar ends and beginnings: birth, social puberty, marriage, fatherhood, advancement to a higher class, occupational specialization, and death. For every one of these events there are ceremonies whose essential purpose is to enable the individual to pass from one defined position to another which is equally well defined.[14]

According to Ralph Linton, one of the most universally observed status changes is the transition to adulthood, which in most societies occurs with the marriage ceremony.[15] In some societies, although the husband is given adult status at marriage, the wife does not receive it until the birth of her first child. Another ceremonial observance involves puberty rites, which mark the transition of the child to the adolescent or adult category, depending on the society. In primitive societies, this observance is usually marked by hazing, physical ordeals, and instruction in the history, skills, and crafts of the tribe. The closest ceremonies to puberty rites in our society would be confirmations, bar mitzvahs, and debuts.

Transition to Old Age

The change from adult status to aged status receives little social recognition in most societies. One reason for this lack is because the onset of old age is so gradual and almost imperceptible that we cannot pinpoint when it occurs. In addition, the transition from adult to old-age status is often accompanied by feelings of regret and reluctance, and the individuals concerned are not eager for public acknowledgment of the change.

A few societies have what may be called retirement ceremonies. In these instances a man gives his successor the powers that he formerly possessed, or he may relinquish some prerogatives of his adult male status. Formerly among the Comanche Indians when a man became too old to actively participate in war, he was expected to give up his "medicines," at which time he was then eligible for the position of peace chief. In modern Japan there is a special retirement celebration in which families honor individuals who have reached 61 years of age.

On the sixty-first birthday the elder dons a bright kimono, such as those worn by children, to symbolize that he or she is no longer bound by the somber duties of middleage. Traditionally, all the children and close relatives gather to celebrate this transition. On this day also, or whenever the woman formally retires as mistress of the house, the woman traditionally presents her daughter-in-law with the family rice ladle as the baton of domestic authority. The elder couple then literally retire to a separate room; if possible, a separate retirement cottage may be built for them, and they are referred to as "those living in retirement." (inkyo).[16]

The nearest equivalent in our society to a retirement rite would be a dinner given by a company or organization for an employee or group of employees who have reached the age of 65 or thereabouts and are being retired. After the meal, some speeches and a few jokes, the retirees are presented with a gift (often the traditional gold watch), in recognition of their years of service.

Compared to other age passages, the transition to old age is the most difficult to make. Whereas younger members of a society look forward to moving on to the next age status, most people are not eager to achieve the status of an elderly person. In fact, in all societies the individual who enjoys the prospect of getting old is atypical.[17] In order to induce people to assume this status, some societies accord the aged much power and prestige. In certain societies, as women age, their freedom and authority increase; they may then be exempt from the social and ceremonial restrictions that were once imposed on them. In our society the entry into old-age status is associated with retirement and the relinquishing of many adult responsibilities. Many individuals, depending on their personality, are glad to be relieved of their obligations, while others are reluctant to let go of them and may miss the power they wielded.

Summary

1. The term *culture* has a specific meaning in sociology that differs from the popular usage of the word. Culture is the social heritage of a society that is transmitted to each generation. It is learned behavior that is shared with others. Often we are completely unaware of the extent to which our lives and behavior are influenced by our culture.

2. *Norms* are standards or rules of behavior. Norms help us to predict the behavior of others, as well as to permit others to know what to expect of us. Not all norms apply to all members in a society. Such factors as sex and age may determine the application of some norms.

3. Norms may be divided into three broad types: *folkways, mores,* and *laws.* Folkways are not considered too important, but mores are considered essential to the group's welfare. Both folkways and mores are informally enforced, whereas laws are backed by the coercive power of the government.

4. Age norms that apply to older people tend to be fewer and less definite than those that apply to younger persons. Our society has what may be termed a double standard of aging. Culturally, women tend to age earlier than men. Our society censures women who do not marry — but not men. Age norms closely regulate the choice of a marital partner for women, whereas men have greater freedom in their selection.

5. *Status* identifies who we are and generally defines our position, whereas a *role* is the behavior expected of a person who holds a certain status. Statuses may be

classified into two kinds: achieved and ascribed. Age and sex are two types of ascribed statuses.

6. All societies are divided into different age-status levels. An individual moves from one level to the next as he or she progresses from infancy to old age. Ceremonies marking these transitions are called *rites of passage*. In our society the entry into the status of old age receives the least ritual observance and is the most difficult transition to make.

Notes

1. Clyde Kluckhohn, *Mirror for Man*, Fawcett, Greenwich, Conn. 1944, p. 31.

2. Bernice L. Neugarten, Joan W. Moore, and John C. Lowe, "Age Norms, Age Constraints, and Adult Socialization," *American Journal of Sociology*, 70 (May 1965), 711.

3. Robert J. Havighurst and Ruth Albrecht, *Older People*, Longmans, Green, New York, 1953.

4. Ibid., p. 37.

5. Irving Rosow, *Socialization to Old Age*, University of California Press, Berkeley, Calif., 1974, pp. 68–69.

6. Irving Rosow, *Social Integration of the Aged*, Free Press, New York, 1967, p. 31.

7. Vern L. Bengtson, *The Social Psychology of Aging*, Bobbs-Merrill, Indianapolis, 1976.

8. Ibid., p. 25.

9. Erdman Palmore, "Attitudes Toward Aging as Shown by Humor," *The Gerontologist*, 12, no. 3 (1971), 184–185.

10. Ibid., p. 185.

11. Inge Powell Bell, "The Double Standard," *Growing Old in America*, ed. Beth B. Hess, Transaction Books, New Brunswick, N.J., 1976, p. 154.

12. Erik H. Erikson, *Identity: Youth and Crisis*, W. W. Norton, New York, 1968, and Rosow, *Socialization to Old Age*.

13. Arnold Van Gennep, *Rites of Passage*, trans. M. Vizedom and G. Caffee, Routledge & Kegan Paul, London, 1960.

14. Ibid., pp. 2–3.

15. Ralph Linton, "Age and Sex Categories," *American Sociological Review*, 7 (October 1942), 589–603.

16. Reprinted from *The Honorable Elders* by Erdman Palmore, p. 95, by permission of Duke University Press. Copyright 1975 by Duke University Press.

17. Ralph Linton, *The Study of Man*, D. Appleton-Century, New York, 1936, p. 119.

For Further Study

Cain, Leonard. "Life Course and Social Structure." In *Handbook of Modern Sociology*, edited by Robert E. Faris. Rand McNally, Chicago, 1964, pp. 272–309. A comprehensive discussion of age status.

Davis, Kingsley. *Human Society*. Macmillan, New York, 1949. See Chapter 3 for a classic statement on norms.

Kluckhohn, Clyde. *Mirror for Man*. Fawcett, Greenwich, Conn., 1944. A readable and excellent introduction to anthropology.

Linton, Ralph. *The Study of Man*. D. Appleton-Century, New York, 1936. See especially Chapter 8, which contains a discussion of the concepts of *status* and *role* as they were first introduced into sociology and anthropology by Linton.

Neugarten, Bernice L. *Middle Age and Aging: A Reader in Social Psychology*. The University of Chicago Press, Chicago, 1968. Part I contains a collection of papers dealing with age status and age norms in American society.

Sumner, William Graham. *Folkways*. Ginn, Boston, 1906. A source book on folkways and mores.

4

Cultural Values

By today's standards an American male would probably not be impressed with the figure of Venus de Milo, nor would he find the nudes painted by Goya very desirable. He might even consider them candidates for Weight Watchers! Our ideas of beauty and desirability are defined by the values of our culture. *Values* are socially learned and shared conceptions of what is desirable, good, or right; values serve as criteria for judging ideas, behavior, events, people, and things. For example, most Americans believe that honesty is good, that prejudice is wrong, that Abe Lincoln was a great man, and that communism is bad. Americans believe in freedom, fair play, equality, democracy, and patriotism. These values are culturally approved sentiments that people support and feel strongly about. But sometimes there are significant contradictions between people's beliefs and their behavior.

Dominant American Value Themes

Every society has certain dominant values that give it a distinctive character and differentiate it from other cultures. The following lists show the striking difference between the values of modern American society and those of preindustrial Japan:[1]

Twentieth-Century American Values	Old World Japanese Values
Democracy	Aristocracy
Youth	Age
Individualism	Familism
Change	Stability
Future orientation	Past orientation
Status by achievement	Status by birth
Progress	Tradition
Equality	Elitism
Science	Intuition

These concepts represent some of the major value orientations found in these two cultures.

One approach to studying the aged and aging is analyzing some dominant values in our own culture. For this purpose we will single out only a few major value orientations: (1) youth-orientation; (2) the work ethic; (3) independence and self-reliance; (4) education; and (5) progress. After discussing each value, we will examine how it affects the elderly.

Youth-Orientation

Americans live in a youth-oriented society. Young people and the virtues of youth are extolled. We believe that youth is a time of energy and enthusiasm. The young are thought to be inventive, resourceful, and resilient — qualities that were highly valued in the development of this country and are still considered to be characteristic of most Americans.

In early America, during the seventeenth century, young people behaved with deference, respect, and veneration toward the elderly. Youth were told to venerate the elderly, and in turn the elderly were expected to condescend toward the young. This behavior was especially predominant among the Puritans, who made a cult of old age. The pattern of exalting old age was manifested in such customs as reserving the choice seats in New England meeting houses for the oldest men and women. Old men held high offices until they died, fathers waited until their sixties to turn over their land to their sons, and the elderly maintained a position of authority within the family.[2]

According to David Fischer, the devaluation of old age and the exaltation of youth began during the French and American revolutions — also a time of social revolution in attitudes toward the elderly. "On the surface it introduced a spirit of age equality. . . . But beneath that surface a new sort of inequality was being born, a new hierarchy of generations in which youth acquired the moral advantage that age had lost."[3]

In the nineteenth century a youth cult began to develop in the United States. This emphasis on youth has grown rapidly since World War II. The young have influenced American society in recent years in the areas of our domestic and foreign policy and in our culture, especially music, fashions, recreation, even language.

The power of the young consumers is keenly felt in the marketplace. In fact, some American marketeers have gone to extremes to try to gain their share of the youth market. One adman indicates this emphasis:

As I watch television and read magazines and attend movies these days, I sometimes wonder if anybody besides myself is over 30. There seems to be a conscious denial of middle age — and certainly of old age. TV ads continue to feature shaggy-haired surfers and long-limbed, golden blondes swigging Pepsi or dashing around in Detroit's latest scat-abouts. Seldom does an older face show up, except in those stultifying ads for laxatives and denture adhesives.[4]

A common belief that permeates American life is that the best years of life are those of youth, and that after this period, maturity and old age are largely downhill. We tell our young people to enjoy themselves while they can because later they will be tied down with responsibilities. In a Harris Poll, 69 percent of the general public considered the teens, twenties, and thirties as the best years of a person's life. Only 2 percent of the public felt that way about the sixties.[5] In contrast, both old and young Samoans consider old age as the best years of a person's life. For them, it is a time of great personal freedom, fewer demands, and maximum security. If old people so desire, they may relax while their relatives and children support them, or they may continue to work and contribute to the group.

Most Americans feel that adventure, excitement, and opportunity belong to youth. Science fiction writer Isaac Asimov wryly remarks:

It is generally accepted that past a certain age, what is worthwhile in life is gone. Creative thought is for the young only; beauty and charm are for the young only; sexual activity is for the young only. Make the mistake of growing old and all the world will tell you that you cannot learn new tricks, that you are either sexually neutral or perverted, that you can do nothing more useful than remain out of the way.[6]

Because of the above beliefs, many people experience fear and panic as they age. Advertisers prey on this fear and help reinforce the desire to remain young looking as long as possible; they make us feel that we must get rid of the signs of the aging process. We are told to keep our hair its "natural" color and not to let it get gray. We are urged to eliminate bald spots through having hair transplants, or by wearing wigs or toupees. Claims are made for many creams, ranging from turtle oil to hormone cream, that they help defy the skin's aging process. The face-lift is being popularized, and plastic surgery is also available for other parts of the body. Erdman Palmore observes a major difference between American and Japanese attitudes regarding aging:

Most Japanese over 60 do not try to hide their age. In fact, they are usually proud of it. It is considered polite and proper to ask an older Japanese his age and to congratulate him on it. Most Americans know it is impolite to ask an older American his age. . . . The popularity of hair dyes and cosmetics to conceal wrinkles attest to the prevalence of age concealment among older Americans. Some middle-aged Japanese also dye their greying hair, but most older Japanese do not. It is probably not an exaggeration to say that most Japanese believe "grey is beautiful" and that most Americans do not.[7]

Peter Stearns points out that leisure-time activities and sports reflect our society's emphasis on the youth culture. For example, if a 40-year-old professional football player kicks the ball or sometimes plays the quarterback position, we consider his performance amazing. We think such a person exceptional, although he is not really old. "But in spending so much time watching the young excel in sports, and yearning with jealous amazement when someone around 40 can even stay in the game, we seem to confirm the hold of youth upon us."[8]

Looking for a job after age 40, or even at 35, can be a disheartening experience. Many employers consider a person of 40 to be an older worker. And then there is mandatory retirement at age 70; by this time, most workers are looked on as worn-out models that are ready to be traded in.

It is difficult to grow old in a society that values youth and devalues old age. Older people are made to feel that they are useless, out-of-date, and incapable of adapting to new and changing conditions. In this environment, no wonder people clutch frantically to youth and try to deny and postpone old age as long as possible.

The Work Ethic

A second major orientation in American culture is the work ethic. Americans place a high value on work and believe staying busy is important. "Americans are not merely optimistic believers that 'work counts'," notes Kluckhohn, but adds "Their creed insists that anyone, anywhere in the social structure, can and should 'make the effort.' "[9]

Robin Williams cites three reasons why work has become an inherent part of the American value system. First, in early America, work was necessary for group survival along the frontier. If people did not work, they were told that they could not eat. Secondly, the early settlers were mostly people of the working class from Great Britain and Europe, and hard work was part of their way of life. Lastly, the strong influence of the Protestant ethic emphasized dedication to work as a means of serving God.[10]

The *Protestant ethic* refers to a cluster of values and attitudes embodied in certain religious groups, particularly seventeenth-century Calvinists. The underlying basis for the ethic stems from the Calvinist doctrine of predestination. According to this doctrine, God has foreordained the salvation of individual souls, and nothing done during one's lifetime can achieve salvation if one is not already chosen. Believers in the doctrine became anxious to find out whether or not they were among the elect, and they sought some outward sign to let them know. To reduce their uncertainty, the Puritans began to interpret success in an individual's occupation or calling as such a sign. They believed that if a person worked hard at an occupation and accumulated wealth in this world, this success would mean that he or she had hopes of salvation.

The Puritans regarded work as one of the highest forms of moral activity. It was considered a defense against temptations, including religious doubts. And no matter how successful Puritans were in their occupations, they could not relax, but continued to work even harder because they had no guarantee of divine favor. They also needed to convince themselves of their worth. Their values are clearly expressed in the maxims of Benjamin Franklin: "Early to bed and early to rise, makes a man healthy, wealthy, and wise"; "Plough deep while sluggards sleep"; "God gives all things to industry"; and "Remember that time is money." Almost two centuries later, President Calvin Coolidge also talked about the work ethic. He said at his inaugural address in 1924: "The business of America is business. The man who builds a factory builds a temple. The man who works there, worships there."

Over the years, there has been a gradual shift away from the Protestant ethic and its religious overtones, but the work ethic endures and is perhaps strongest in older people. Indeed, work continues to be of central interest and importance in the lives of most individuals, and no dramatic change is likely in the near future. In a nationwide survey of young people, Daniel Yankelovich found that a majority accept the necessity of hard work and are seeking challenging careers. Seventy-nine percent of college youth believe that commitment to a meaningful career is important.[11]

In our society, at about the age of 65 a person generally retires and loses his or her customary work role. Many older people feel that without a work role their lives are meaningless. Our elderly have grown up in a work-centered society and have been told all their lives that hard work pays, that they should stay busy, and that it is bad to be idle. Retirees often feel guilty about not working and uncomfortable about having too much unstructured time. (Forced retirement in many ways is a contradiction in cultural values.)

At retirement, a person not only gives up a productive role, but loses occupational status and prestige as well. In place of work, an individual is offered leisure, but our society has not yet legitimized leisure as a full-time pursuit. This lack of legitimacy only adds further to the loss experienced by older people. People, especially those gainfully employed, too often view those who engage only in leisure-time activities as idle or lazy. And once more the values of our culture place the elderly in a dilemma.

Independence and Self-reliance

Independence and self-reliance are highly praised values in our society. These characteristics are reflected in such phrases as: "People should stand on their own two feet"; "He's a self-made man"; "I've never asked anyone for anything." We point with pride to such cultural heroes as Andrew Carnegie and Abraham Lincoln who "pulled themselves up by their own bootstraps." Parents stress the importance of being independent and often deride their children for lack of independence. A child's peers reinforce the need for independence by disapproving certain dependent types of behavior.

We are taught that dependency is a sign of weakness, a lack of character, or even a sickness. A dependent person is frequently the object of ridicule and hostility and is sometimes called derogatory terms, such as *moocher, good-for-nothing, sponge, leech,* or *bum.*

Margaret Mead argues that we pay a high price for our emphasis on independence and self-reliance:

> Old people in this country have been influenced by an American ideal of independence and autonomy. The most important thing in the world is to be independent. So old people live alone, perhaps on the verge of starvation, in time without friends — but we are independent. . . . It is a poor ideal and pursuing it does a great deal of harm.
>
> The ideal of independence also contains a tremendous amount of selfishness. In talking to today's young mothers, I have asked them what kind of grandmothers they are going to be. I have heard devoted, loving mothers say that when they are through raising their children, they have no intention of becoming grandmothers. They are astonished to hear that in most of the world, throughout most of its history, families have three- or four-generation families living under the same roof. We have emphasized the small family unit — father, mother, small children. We think it is wonderful if Grandma and Grandpa, if he's still alive, can live alone.
>
> We have reached the point where we think the only thing we can do for our children is to stay out of their hair, and the only thing we can do for our daughters-in-law is to see as little of them as possible. Old people's homes, even the best, are filled with older people who believe the only thing they can do for their children is to look cheerful when they come to visit. So in the end older people have to devote their energies to "not being a burden."[12]

Other cultures do not have the American ideal of independence and self-reliance; they neither promote it nor take pride in it. Francis Hsu notes that in traditional China, aged parents would be happy and proud if their children could support them in a lifestyle better than the parents had been accustomed to.[13] They would tell everyone what good children they were. If a similar situation occurred in our society, not only would the parent not brag about it, but the parent might even be ashamed of such support. In fact, the desire for independence is so strong in our culture that a parent would probably resent being supported by his or her children and would seek to become independent at the first opportunity.

In a study of 435 men and women (aged 62 to 94 years) in San Francisco, Margaret Clark and Barbara Anderson found the most frequently cited source of self-esteem was independence. They noted that one of the striking findings of their research is the singularity of the subjects in it. "This singularity is interpreted by these subjects in many ways: it is proud independence; it is an autonomy prized as befitting 'a good, upstanding American,' or it is shrinking from others for fear of rejection, . . . or the offering of unwanted 'charity.' "[14] The importance of preserving independence, self-reliance, and autonomy in order to maintain self-esteem was expressed in such statements as:

> I hope to always be able to take care of myself and continue in good health.
>
> I wouldn't want to get on welfare. I just wouldn't go to see them. I wouldn't want to do that.
>
> The most important things my parents did for me was that they . . . taught me how to be independent and self-reliant.
>
> It's very important that I do not become a burden on somebody.[15]

When these people were asked to express their sources of depression or dissatisfaction, dependency (either financial or physical) ranked first on the list. Other sources of dissatisfaction in order of rank were: physical discomfort, loneliness, and boredom. Although other losses can be tolerated, it appears that the loss of independence is the hardest to bear. Clark and Anderson point out the extremes that some older people will go to to avoid dependence:

> Such people will draw their curtains to avoid critical appraisals for their helplessness; they will not get enough to eat; they will stay away from the doctor and forego even vital drugs; they will shiver with the cold; they will live in filth and squalor — but pride they will relinquish only as a last resort.[16]

Two sets of reasons for wanting to avoid dependence were given by the subjects in this study. One set Clark and Anderson called *adaptive*, and the other, *maladaptive*. Taking pride in being independent and not wanting to be an inconvenience or burden to others are adaptive reasons. By not impinging on the freedom of loved ones, the elderly feel that they can maintain their own self-respect, as well as the respect of others. Maladaptive reasons center on fears and mistrust of others. Independence is seen as a defense against the possibility of bad treatment and neglect. By isolating themselves, these persons avoid any potential rejection and manipulation. As Clark and Anderson emphasize:

> In America, one must simply not admit that, when one grows old, one will need to lean more and more upon others. In America *no adult* has any *right* to do this. At all costs, the major work must be done, the major values must be acted out. Those who cannot do these things are either "children" or fools, useless or obsolete. It is the central values of American culture which lay down such cruel alternatives.[17]

If the self-esteem of older people in our society tends to rest heavily on the cultural values of independence and self-reliance, then what happens when we reach the point where we are no longer able to maintain our autonomy and need the assistance and support of others? Here lies the crux of the problem. We socialize people in our society to believe that independence is good and that dependence is bad. If we live long enough, eventually we all become dependent on others.

Education

A British professor once predicted that, given the way Americans emphasize mass education, soon after an American baby is born, they will simply hang a bachelor's degree around its neck. Most foreign observers are struck by the faith and high value that most Americans place on education. Many Americans believe that, no matter what the problem — poverty, crime, or discrimination — education is the cure-all for social ills. Robin Williams notes: "To some Americans education is a magic panacea, the prime agency of progress; and America's faith in universal public education is its greatest asset."[18] We believe that everyone is entitled to some formal education, and great resources are directed toward achieving this goal.

This American value of education has existed for a long time and is based on several perceptions. First, in a democracy, people need to be educated in order to be responsible citizens. Secondly, to have a unified country, despite differences in language and culture brought by immigrants, then most of American society must acquire the same language and values. Finally, part of the American ideology is that talents are to be rewarded on the basis of ability alone, so all must have equal educational opportunities. For the individual, education affords one the best opportunities to improve his or her economic and social position in society.

The system of public education as we know it today was not achieved until the middle of the nineteenth century. At that time, public elementary schools began appearing in large numbers in most states. In

Many of today's elderly attended elementary school in a one-room schoolhouse. Although mass secondary education grew rapidly during the early part of the twentieth century, higher education was still the privilege of a small minority. (Courtesy of Tennessee Valley Authority)

1852 Massachusetts was the first state to pass a law requiring compulsory attendance at school, and by 1918 all states had enacted a similar statute. By the time of the Civil War, many states started establishing free public high schools, and the movement for higher education expanded rapidly. The expansion of mass education in the United States since the end of the nineteenth century has been unparalleled. In 1900 about 7 percent of American students graduated from high school. Today, over 80 percent do. Four percent of the high school graduates attended college in 1900, compared to the current enrollment of about 40 percent.

Despite the great increase in persons with higher education, many older Americans have had little or no formal schooling. In addition, in a technological society like ours, change occurs so rapidly that even those elderly whose education or training was adequate when they were young find that their knowledge is often considered obsolete and outmoded.

The educational attainment of older persons as a group is much lower than that of the whole adult population. About 10 percent of the

Americans 65 and over are classified as being functionally illiterate, that is, they have had less than 5 years of schooling. In 1975 half of those 65 and over had completed less than 9 years of school, whereas half of those between the ages of 25 and 64 had completed 12 years of school. Thirty-five percent of the elderly graduated from high school, compared to 62 percent of the younger population. But the levels of educational attainment have been rising for both young and old groups (Table 4.1).

The elderly who lack formal schooling in a society that values education find their prestige further diminished. In contrast, in preliterate societies the elderly derive much authority from possessing superior knowledge through experience. In a society without books, schools, and other specialized educational institutions, the older person's role as the source of knowledge becomes indispensable. Older people in our society have lost their teaching function because many of their skills are considered obsolete and useless, whereas in preliterate societies the old are the chief instructors of the young.

A common activity of the aged in many societies is story telling, which both instructs and entertains. Leo Simmons observes how the old people among the Hopi, as is the case in many preliterate societies, are the repositories of knowledge, traditions, and skills:

> Often they alone knew the old land boundaries, the sites of distant shrines, and the complicated rituals. . . . Aged women were technicians in pottery and basketry, and old men were skilled instructors in weaving and the tanning of hides. Old men watched the sun, kept the calendar, and supervised dates for crop-planting katchina dances, rain-making ceremonies, and harvest regulations.[19]

Table 4.1 Educational attainment of the population 65 years and over and 25 years and over, 1952–1975

Year	Median school years completed		Percentage of high school graduates	
	65 years and over	25 years and over	65 years and over	25 years and over
1952	8.2	10.1	18.4%	38.4%
1965	8.5	11.8	23.5	49.0
1970	8.7	12.2	28.3	55.2
1975	9.0	12.3	35.2	62.6

Source: Adapted from United States Bureau of the Census, *Current Population Reports*, Special Studies, Series P-23, No. 59, U.S. Printing Office, Washington, D.C. (May 1976), p. 50.

Still another factor operates in American society to work against older people: the concept of *human investment* in education. Instead of viewing the cost of education as a necessary expense like food or clothing, education is now regarded as a capital investment, in much the same way as buildings, machines, or materials are. People will invest money to train and educate young persons with a view to a future payoff, but they are not willing to do the same for older people. The obvious reason for this reluctance is that an older person's remaining years are limited, and the return would not be enough to justify such an investment. Robert Butler observes that "we create 'old fogies' if we continue to dispose of non-reusable human beings rather than recycle people through retraining."[20]

Progress

The American emphasis on youth and education relates to our belief in progress. We stress the future, rather than the past or present. "Throughout their history Americans have insisted that the best was yet to be. . . . The American knew nothing was impossible in his brave new world. . . . Progress was not, to him, a mere philosophical ideal but a commonplace of experience."[21] Such words as *outmoded, out-of-date, old-fashioned, backward,* and *stagnant* have taken on negative connotations. We assume that the new is better than the old, that it is better to move forward than backward, and that by standing still we stagnate.

Belief in progress is based on the idea that we are moving in a definite, desirable direction. The belief that progress will go on indefinitely, and that things will continue to get better as we progress toward an ever-increasing enlightenment and perfection, has been a driving force throughout our history. The idea of progress and an optimistic view of the future reached its peak during the nineteenth and early part of the twentieth century. Many disillusioning events, beginning with the Depression of the thirties and World War II, have caused some to seriously question the American faith in progress.

Progress is social change of a desirable nature and implies a value judgment that the change taking place is for the better. In a certain population some people may view various changes as progressive,

Opposite, top: Much of the information and skills that the aged once passed on to younger generations is often ignored or considered obsolete and useless today. This grandmother is spinning wool yarn, an art that is being lost in industrial societies like ours. (Courtesy of the Tennessee Valley Authority)

Opposite, bottom: A popular pastime of the elderly in many societies is storytelling. The Navaho man is narrating a legend to the children about their forefathers. (Life Magazine © Time Inc. Leonard McCombe—Photographer)

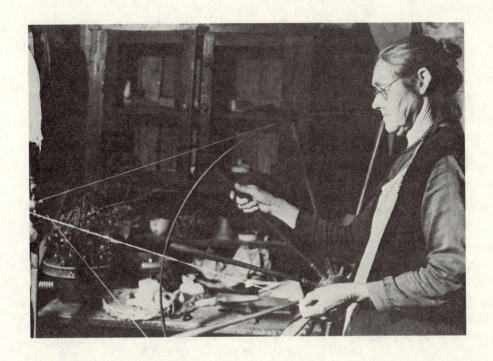

while others may consider them to be retrogressive. Progress is thus a subjective, not a scientific, concept.

A society's rate of social change greatly affects the status and role of the elderly. In those traditional societies in which change proceeds slowly, the elderly seem to be more highly regarded. Simmons comments on this tendency:

> There is a pattern of participation for the aged that becomes relatively fixed in stable societies but suffers disruption with rapid social change. . . . The general principle seems to be: In the long and steady strides of the social order, the aging get themselves fixed and favored in positions, power, and performance. They have what we call seniority rights. But when social conditions become unstable and the rate of change reaches a galloping pace, the aged are riding for an early fall and the more youthful associates take their seats in the saddle.[22]

Gordon Streib notes that in Ireland there is a shift now taking place from a traditional society, oriented to slow change, to one that emphasizes rapid change, youth orientation, and technological development. "If Ireland decides to take her place along with the other nations of Europe, some of the traditional ways of thinking and behaving will have to be left behind. The veneration of the old may be one of the casualties of progress."[23]

In a future-oriented society like our own where social change is occurring at a rapid pace, the elderly have been stripped of an important social function. James Manney describes this situation: "Progressive American society also deprives the old person of the one role he has had in most traditional cultures: the role of elder statesman who epitomizes social stability and continuity with the past. A society which treasures the . . . future has little need for someone to embody the past."[24]

Urbanization, residential mobility, and changes in technology and occupational systems have adversely affected the lives of older Americans. For a case in point, let us look briefly at occupational specialization. In the last few decades, occupational specialties have increased enormously. Their growth has resulted in an even greater level of technological progress. As technology becomes more complex, skills become outdated more rapidly. This condition may leave the older worker in a state of occupational obsolescence.

Automation has caused many older workers to lose their jobs to computerized operations and to younger employees. Often older people find it difficult to get other jobs. Many job opportunities lie in specialities for which older persons have no training, and employers are reluctant to train them. Another outgrowth of our expanding technology has been the lowering of the retirement age. This change has occurred partly because technical ability is considered more important than seniority, because some workers prefer early retirement, and because in some cases this lower retirement age has been used to get rid of older workers, who have been dubbed "dead wood." "An emphasis on youth and newness has replaced the older stress on continuity and experience. Young people are valued partly because of their superior technical education, but also simply because they are young."[25]

The accelerated rate of social and technological change in our society has served to further undermine the position of older people. They have lost some functions that they performed in the past and, because of this, have also experienced diminished status and prestige. In a country that equates the latest, the newest, and the most modern with the finest and the best, experience and continuity with the past and its traditions have little value. With epithets like *old-fashioned*, *out-of-date*, and *over the hill*, old people are made to feel like anachronisms and superannuated members of a progress-oriented society.

This simplified view of five major value orientations in American society is bound to be imprecise, subject to many exceptions, and controversial. Nevertheless, these abstracted patterns are useful because they provide a greater understanding of our culture and insight into the problems and conflicts of America's elderly.

Value Similarities and Differences Between Generations

The Youth and the Elderly

Some values that create problems for older people in our society may do the same for younger people. Richard Kalish argues that some of the same values that discriminate against the elderly also tend to discriminate against the young, specifically college students.[26] These values include: productivity, achievement, material gain, independence, and hard work. He maintains that in many ways the old and young are both caught in the same bind, and makes the following comparisons between the two generations:

1. *The youth and the elderly belong to somewhat segregated groups.* They are both stereotyped in ways that the middle-aged group seldom faces.

2. *Both generations are continually reminded of their nonproductive roles in society.* Both are taking out of the system rather than putting into it, and because of this circumstance, they are discriminated against by the working-age group.

3. *Both young and old persons have a lot of unstructured time.* Working-age adults structure their time around their jobs. But college youth and older people have less routine and more free time.

4. *Both groups desire to be financially independent.* The young want to be

independent of their parents, whereas the elderly want to be independent of their children. Both the elderly and the young receive a large
share of their money and maintenance from sources not related to what
they are doing.

5. *Both generations are poor.* This condition makes them weak and
vulnerable. They are looked upon as living on a kind of charity offered
by the working group.[27]

Kalish concludes that the young and old have much in common; in
fact, he sees them as "generation-gap allies." Other observers have also
noted a closeness between the first and third generations. Maggie Kuhn,
leader of the Gray Panthers, remarks: "Our society is age-ist . . .
age-ism goes both ways — hurting both the young and the old —
depriving both groups of the right to control their own lives. The same
issues oppress us both . . . the first and third generations get along fine.
The gaps are between the middle-aged and both groups."[28] Arthur
Flemming echoes her sentiments: "There may be a generation gap
between youth and the middle-aged, but . . . There's a real affinity
between the aged and youth . . . because they face a common
enemy — the middle-aged. The middle-aged tell youth, 'You're too
young to deal with the problems,' and they tell the old people, 'You're
over the hill.' "[29]

The Generation Gap

So much has been written in the last decade about the relations between
generations along with the differences between them, that the term
generation gap has become commonplace. Social scientists who have
examined this area usually take one of three approaches: the *great-gap*
position, the *gap-is-an-illusion* position, or the *selective-continuity-and-
difference* position.[30]

THE GREAT-GAP POSITION   Social scientists with this perspective argue
that profound differences exist between today's young people and
adults with respect to values, interaction, communication, power, and
authority. Some researchers maintain that a social revolution between
generations is occurring, while others view the problem as a psychological disease that is pulling age groups in our society apart. The great-gap
position stresses that certain basic differences between age groups in our
society cannot be resolved, and that these differences supply the
impetus for a cultural transformation. Old responses and adaptations no
longer suit a rapidly changing society.

THE GAP-IS-AN-ILLUSION POSITION   In contrast to the great-gap position,
this perspective stresses continuity, rather than discontinuity, between

generations. Proponents of this view argue that the differences between age groups are greatly exaggerated and offer historical documentation to show that conflict between age groups is inevitable and recurrent.

THE SELECTIVE-CONTINUITY-AND-DIFFERENCE POSITION This perspective combines the two preceding positions. It maintains that, in most respects, generational conflict is marginal, and that there is substantial solidarity and continuity of values between all age groups. Like the first position, this one stresses that the rapid rate of change in our society requires new adaptations and modes of behavior.

Studies Comparing Three Generations

Most work in the area of the generation gap has concentrated on the relation between youth and their parents. Vern Bengtson and his co-authors note that, with a few exceptions, little attention has been given to analyzing the generation gap with regard to older people.[31] These authors see the generation gap affecting older persons in two ways, the first being at their cohort level, which refers to the differences in standards of behavior between their own age group and those younger. The second, and the position that we will discuss, is at the lineage level, which refers to the differences between generations in the same family.

Lineage studies investigate similarities, as well as differences, in values between, say, a 72-year-old woman, her 48-year-old daughter, and her 21-year-old granddaughter. Richard Kalish and Ann Johnson made such a study and found that the grandmothers and the mothers appeared to be the furthest apart, whereas the mothers and the daughters were the closest in their values.[32] A similar finding was made by Joan Aldous and Reuben Hill in an earlier study.[33]

The middle-aged group had more fear of aging and less regard for older people than either the daughters or the grandmothers, according to Kalish and Johnson. Older people were found to be less afraid of death and dying than were the other two generations. Although old people may discuss death frequently, contrary to popular belief they do not seem to be fearful of it. Perhaps the elderly feel that they have lived their lives and that, unlike those who die young, they have had their share of time and experience. Kalish and Johnson note that "values held by the young women in our sample were substantially related to values held by their mothers and their grandmothers. And, even though substantial differences were found between children and their parents, equally substantial differences were found between parents and grand-parents."[34]

In a similar study, Alfred Fengler and Vivian Wood focused on value

Some scholars contend that there is a closeness between youth and the elderly and that if a generation gap exists, it is between youth and the middle-aged, not between the old and the young. (Courtesy of Tennessee Commission on Aging)

differences among three generations.[35] The sample studied consisted of college students, together with both parents and one grandparent of each student; these subjects were asked how they felt on six issues. Each generation was found to be twice as liberal as the generation preceding it on such issues as drugs, race relations, and religion. In the area of sexual norms, the gap was far wider between the middle-aged group and their elderly parents than it was between students and their parents. Again, this result points out that generational differences are not limited to today's young people and their parents. However, on the issue of "distribution of political and economic power," there was more agreement between the students and their grandparents than between students and their parents. "The relatively powerless state of both students and grandparents suggests a situational alliance on this issue."[36]

Bengtson's study of three-generational families explored two value dimensions: humanism versus materialism, and collectivism versus individualism.[37] He found two main differences in values between generations. First, the young and the old generations rated humanism and materialism similarly, and the middle-aged were found to be the most materialistic of the three. Secondly, the young generation seemed the most individualistic, and the elderly, the most collectivistic or traditionally oriented. But overall, Bengtson's study suggests no marked differences between generations nor any great gaps in values.

The findings from three-generational studies indicate the following:

1. Generational differences in values occur not only between the second and third generations, but also between the first and second.
2. Differences between generations often depend on which issues or values are involved.
3. Differences tend to be greater between the middle and the oldest generations than between the youngest generation and their parents.
4. There is a similarity in certain values between parents, children, and grandchildren.
5. People often feel there is a greater generation gap in the larger society than exists in their own family.

Summary

1. Values are socially learned and shared conceptions of what is desirable, good, or right. One approach toward interpreting and understanding the problems of older people is through an examination of some of our society's basic values. Among these values are youth-orientation, the work ethic, independence, education, and progress.

2. Americans place a high value on youth and feel that this period is the best time in one's life. Many people fear old age because they see it as a time when a person is devalued and cast aside by society. As a result, many aging persons frantically try to stay young and to deny their old age as long as possible.

3. Another value emphasized is hard work, an attitude that stems in part from the Protestant ethic. Although some of its influence has faded, the work ethic continues to occupy a central place in most Americans' lives. When the work role is lost after retirement, many older people feel their lives are meaningless and useless.

4. Independence and self-reliance are values highly promoted and praised in America. One dilemma confronting its older people is the desire for independence, coupled with the fact that often in old age they unavoidably become dependent and need others.

5. Americans have a strong faith in education and a belief that everyone is entitled to formal schooling. The high percentage of students finishing high school and attending college in recent years reflects this emphasis. In a society

where the young are better educated than their elders, this situation tends to further undermine the power of old people and strips them of roles as instructors.

6. Another dominant value in American society is progress. Americans have always believed in moving ahead and have always looked optimistically toward the future. In doing so, they tend to devalue traditions and continuity with the past. The elderly have lost some of their previous roles because of our rapidly changing society, and are made to feel that they have become outmoded.

7. Many observers feel that there is a great affinity between the first and third generations, and Kalish has pointed out some parallels in their situations. In recent years, much has been written about the generation gap, the bulk of the research centering on the relationships between young people and their parents. But only a few studies have investigated the generation gap by considering three generations, including older people; these studies have explored the similarities and differences in values that exist between generations.

Notes

1. Adapted from Harold M. Hodges, Jr., *Conflict and Consensus: An Introduction to Sociology*, Harper & Row, New York, 1974, p. 54.

2. David Hackett Fischer, *Growing Old in America* (expanded ed.), Oxford University Press, New York, 1978.

3. Ibid., p. 78.

4. Charles F. Adams, "The Power of the Aging in the Marketplace," *Business Week*, November 20, 1971, p. 52.

5. Louis Harris and Associates, *The Myth and Reality of Aging in America*, The National Council on the Aging, Washington, D.C., 1975, p. 2.

6. Isaac Asimov, "The Pursuit of Youth," *Ladies Home Journal*, June 1974, p. 154.

7. Reprinted from *The Honorable Elders* by Erdman Palmore, pp. 104–105, by permission of Duke University Press. Copyright 1975 by Duke University Press.

8. Peter N. Stearns, *Old Age in European Society*, Holmes & Meir, New York, 1976, p. 156.

9. Clyde Kluckhohn, *Mirror for Man*, Fawcett, Greenwich, Conn., 1944, p. 200.

10. Robin Williams, *American Society: A Sociological Interpretation*, Alfred A. Knopf, New York, 1970, p. 459.

11. Donald Light, Jr., and Suzanne Keller, *Sociology*, Alfred A. Knopf, New York, 1975, p. 85.

12. Margaret Mead, "A New Style of Aging," p. 44. Reprinted from the Nov. 15, 1971 issue of *Christianity and Crisis*, copyright © 1971 by Christianity and Crisis, Inc..

13. Francis L. K. Hsu, "American Core Value and National Character," in *Psychological Anthropology*, ed. Francis L. K. Hsu, Schenkman, Cambridge, Mass., 1972, p. 250.

14. From Margaret Clark and Barbara G. Anderson, *Culture and Aging*, 1967, p. 425. Courtesy of Charles C Thomas, Publisher, Springfield, Illinois.

15. Ibid., pp. 177–178.

16. Ibid., p. 391.

17. Ibid., p. 425.

18. Williams, *American Society*, p. 313.

19. Leo W. Simmons, *The Role of the Aged in Primitive Society*, Yale University Press, New Haven, 1945, p. 133.

20. Robert N. Butler, *Why Survive? Being Old in America*, Harper & Row, New York, 1975, p. 89.

21. Henry Steele Commager, quoted in Williams, *American Society*, p. 468.

22. Leo W. Simmons, "Aging in Modern Society," in *Toward Better Understanding of the Aging*, Council on Social Work Education, New York, 1959, p. 4.

23. Gordon F. Streib, "Old Age in Ireland: Demographic and Sociological Aspects," in *Aging and Modernization*, ed. Donald O. Cowgill and Lowell D. Holmes, Appleton-Century-Crofts, New York, 1972, p. 181.

24. James D. Manney, Jr., *Aging in American Society*, The Institute of Gerontology, University of Michigan-Wayne State University, Ann Arbor, Mich., 1975, p. 56.

25. Ibid., p. 57.

26. Richard A. Kalish, "The Old and the New as Generation Gap Allies," *The Gerontologist*, 9, no. 2 (1969), 83–89.

27. Ibid., pp. 87–88.

28. Maggie Kuhn, "The Grey Panthers," *Parade*, January 28, 1973.

29. Arthur S. Flemming, "The Power of the Aging in the Marketplace," *Business Week*, November 20, 1971, p. 54.

30. The following discussion on generation-gap positions is drawn from Vern L. Bengtson, "The Generation Gap: A Review and Typology of Social-Psychological Perspectives," *Youth and Society*, 2 (September 1970), 16–25.

31. Vern L. Bengtson, Edward B. Olander, and Anees A. Haddad, "The 'Generation Gap' and Aging Family Members: Toward a Conceptual Model," in *Time, Roles, and Self in Old Age*, Human Sciences Press, New York, 1976, p. 239.

32. Richard A. Kalish and Ann I. Johnson, "Value Similarities and Differences in Three Generations of Women," *Journal of Marriage and the Family*, 34 (February 1972), 49–54.

33. Joan Aldous and Reuben Hill, "Social Cohesion, Lineage Type and Intergenerational Transmission," *Social Forces*, 43 (1965), 471–482.

34. Kalish and Johnson, "Value Similarities and Differences," p. 54.

35. Alfred P. Fengler and Vivian Wood, "The Generation Gap: An Analysis of Attitudes on Contemporary Issues," *The Gerontologist*, 12, no. 2 (1972), Pt. I, 124–128.

36. Ibid., p. 126.

37. Vern L. Bengtson, "Generation and Family Effects in Value Socialization," *American Sociological Review*, 40, no. 3 (1975), 358–371.

For Further Study

Achenbaum, W. Andrew. *Old Age in the New Land*. John Hopkins University Press, Baltimore, 1978. A detailed study of the history of old age in the United States since 1790.

Bengtson, Vern L., Edward B. Olander, and Anees A. Haddad. "The 'Generation Gap' and Aging Family Members: Toward a Conceptual Model." In *Time, Roles, and Self in Old Age*, edited by Jaber F. Gubrium. Human Sciences Press, New York, 1976. An exploration of the similarities and differences between generations.

Bengtson, Vern L., and Neal E. Cutler. "Generations and Intergenerational Relations: Perspectives on Age Groups and Social Change." In *Handbook of Aging and the Social Sciences*, edited by Robert H. Binstock and Ethel Shanas. Van Nostrand Reinhold, New York, 1976. An examination of some major issues in current generational analysis.

Clark, Margaret, and Barbara Anderson. *Culture and Aging: An Anthropological Study of Older Americans*. Charles C Thomas, Springfield, Ill., 1967. An application of the concepts of anthropology to the problems of the elderly in American society.

Cowgill, Donald O., and Lowell D. Holmes, eds. *Aging and Modernization*. Appleton-Century-Crofts, New York, 1972. A survey of aging in a wide range of cultural groups and national societies.

Mead, Margaret. *Culture and Commitment: A Study of the Generation Gap*. National History Press, Doubleday, Garden City, N.Y., 1970. A good discussion of some significant discontinuities between primitive, historical, and contemporary cultures.

Reich, Charles A. *The Greening of America*. Random House, New York, 1970. A popular book predicting some changes in values that will constitute social revolution.

Williams, Robin A. *American Society: A Sociological Interpretation*. Alfred A. Knopf, New York, 1970. See Chapter 11 for the most comprehensive analysis of American values to date.

5

Cultural Diversity

Cultural Universals

Every society has some characteristics that are unique, some that it shares with certain other societies, and some that it has in common with all societies. The general traits or characteristics that all societies have are called *cultural universals*. Some years ago, anthropologist George Murdock compiled a list of these features. Among them are: age-grading,* athletic sports, bodily adornment, calendar, cleanliness training, courtship, dancing, decorative art, division of labor, education, ethics, etiquette, family, feasting, folklore, funeral rites, games, gift-giving, greetings, hospitality, incest taboos, inheritance rules, joking, marriage, mourning, obstetrics, residence rules, status differentiation, toolmaking, and weather control.[1]

Cultural universals represent general categories and not specific content of particular cultures. For example, *the family* is a universal category: no known society exists or can exist without some type of family organization. Family organization, however, may and does take many different forms. In some societies a man can have only one wife *(monogamy)*, in others he can have two or more wives *(polygyny)*, and in a few places he may be one among several husbands of the same woman *(polyandry)*. All societies, then, address themselves to the same general questions, but each devises its own solutions.

After studying older persons in primitive and historical settings, Leo Simmons found certain recurrent and persistent interests among the elderly in all societies:[2]

1. To live as long as possible, or at least until life's satisfactions no longer compensate for its privations, or until the advantages of death seem to outweigh the burdens of life.

2. To get more rest, or . . . to get some release from the necessity of wearisome exertion at humdrum tasks and to have protection from too great

---

*Age-grading means the arranging of people in a society into levels based on age groupings. At each age level, members of a society are expected to conform to certain roles and norms.

exposure to physical hazards — opportunities, in short, to safeguard and preserve the waning physical energies. Old people have to hoard their diminished resources.

3. To safeguard or even strengthen any prerogatives acquired in mid-life such as skills, possessions, rights, authority, and prestige. The aged want to hold on to whatever they have. Thus seniority rights are zealously guarded.

4. To remain active participants in the affairs of life, in either operational or supervisory roles. Any sharing in group interests being preferred to idleness and indifference. . . .

5. Finally, to withdraw from life when necessity requires it, as timely, honorably, and comfortably as possible and with maximal prospects for an attractive hereafter.[3]

Simmons maintains that the above five interests of the elderly can be summed up in two words, *influence* and *security*. The goals of aging involve a reciprocal relationship between the individual and his or her group. On the one hand are the attitudes and obligations of the group toward elderly people; on the other hand is their desire to be assured of care, support, and a place in the group.

In their book, *Aging and Modernization*, Donald Cowgill and Lowell Holmes identified the following demographic principles that they consider to be universal and to affect the social conditions under which aging occurs:

1. The aged always constitute a minority within the total population.
2. In an older population, females outnumber males.
3. Widows comprise a high proportion of an older population.
4. In all societies, some people are classified as old and are treated differently because they are so classified.
5. There is a widespread tendency for people defined as old to shift to more sedentary, advisory, or supervisory roles involving less physical exertion and more concerned with group maintenance than with economic production.
6. In all societies, some old persons continue to act as political, judicial and civic leaders.
7. In all societies, the mores prescribe some mutual responsibility between old people and their adult children.
8. All societies value life and seek to prolong it, even in old age.[4]

Cultural Variations

Although the similarities between societies are impressive, the immense diversity among them is equally great. For instance, in many societies the old are given tedious, monotonous tasks requiring little physical strength. In other places, older people are expected to take things easy while their children and relatives support them. In some societies when the elderly become feeble and can no longer work or be useful, they are neglected or abandoned.

Ethnocentrism

Foods that people eat differ enormously from society to society. Some relish dog meat, some mosquito or ant larvae, and others rodents. Among the Aranda of Central Australia, older men and women of the tribe exercise their authority by reserving the choicest delicacies, such as lizards and emu fat, for themselves. These foods sound unpalatable to Americans, but by the same token, many foods that we enjoy are defined as inedible by others. A Hindu may be sickened by beef, or a Muslim by pork. We consider milk not only healthful but pleasant to drink, yet many people in the world — for example, those of southeastern Asia — regard it as disgusting and harmful. Irving Hallowell relates the following account: "Once I offered an old Indian and his wife some oatmeal with milk on it. They refused it, although I know they were hungry. The Saulteaux Indians that I know do not like milk. . . . To adapt themselves to milk as a food would require a very strong incentive indeed."[5] Having grown up in our society, we find it difficult to understand that some people believe that milk and steak are unfit for human consumption, and yet they eat insect grubs as a delicacy.

Marriage and other practices vary among societies. We think monogamy is more desirable than polyandry or polygyny. The thought of being one of many wives of the same man at the same time is hard for an American female to accept. But in many societies where this form of marriage prevails, women welcome the additional wives acquired by their husbands because the extra hands lighten the workload. These women would no doubt pity the poor Western woman who has no other wives to help with domestic chores. Again, wife purchase seems like a strange and barbaric custom to us; we cannot understand how a father could sell his daughter to another man. Yet, in societies where this is the custom, the people find it strange that a woman could give herself away. Finally, the Eskimo practice of leaving their aged parents in igloos to freeze to death seems detestable to us. But our practice of placing old people in nursing homes and leaving them there until they die would probably seem abhorrent to the Eskimo.

These examples show that we believe that the values, norms, and tastes of our culture are preferable to all others, and that at the same time people in other societies feel the same preference for their own. The tendency to regard one's own culture as superior to all others is called *ethnocentrism,* a universal phenomenon found in every known society. Our own culture becomes the standard by which we evaluate all other cultures. Those societies with values and norms very different from our own are judged to be greatly inferior, whereas those societies that most resemble ours are considered to be more progressive and civilized.

Cultural Relativism

Part of being ethnocentric is not understanding what a particular pattern of behavior in another culture means to the people who practice it. Therefore, to understand other cultures, we must examine the actions of their people in terms of their values and beliefs and not in terms of our own. Let us return to Eskimo geronticide (killing of the old) and look at it from the Eskimo point of view. Eskimos live in a harsh, demanding environment, which means that all must do their share of the work in order for the group to survive. When an old person becomes so feeble that he or she cannot contribute to the group's welfare or cannot travel great distances in search of food, then the lives of some others or even of the entire community may be placed in jeopardy. Thus, to understand other societies, we must take the position of *cultural relativism*, which implies that all patterns of behavior should be analyzed in the cultural context in which they are found and not by the standards of another culture. There are no universal standards of right and wrong, good and bad, moral and immoral. Standards are relative to the culture in which they occur.

Abandonment of the elderly is not unique to the Eskimo society. As a matter of custom it has been a recurrent theme in Japanese literature since the sixth century. The following modern-day version of the so-called *Obasute* theme clearly demonstrates that an act we consider unthinkably immoral can be moral in another cultural setting:

> [Old] Rin, a woman nearly seventy years old, of outstanding piety and abnegation, and much beloved by her son Tappei, hears the Narayama* song in the street; this song says that when three years have passed one is three years older, and its intention is to make the old people understand that the time for the "pilgrimage" is coming near. The day before the Feast of the Dead those who must "go to the mountain" invite the villagers who have already taken their parents up; this is the only great feast of the year — they eat white rice, the most valued food, and they drink rice-wine. [Old] Rin determines to celebrate the feast this very year. She has made all her preparations, and what is more her son is about to marry again; there will be a woman to look after the house. She is still strong, she can work, and she has all her teeth; this indeed is a source of anxiety for her, for in a village that is so near starvation it is disgraceful still to be able to eat every kind of food at her

Narayama, meaning "Oak Mountain," is the place where old people were supposed to be abandoned.

IN SOME SOCIETIES, THE AGED
ARE HIGHLY ESTEEMED.

age. One of her grandsons has made up a song in which he mocks her, calling her the old woman with thirty-two teeth, and all the children hum it. She manages to break two with a stone, but the mockery does not stop. The eldest of her grandsons marries; now that there are two young women in the house she feels useless and she thinks about the pilgrimage more and more. Her son and her daughter-in-law weep when she tells them of her decision. The feast takes place. She hopes that it will snow up there, for snow would mean that she will be welcomed in the next world. At dawn she sets herself upon a plank and Tappei carries it on his shoulders. In the customary way they steal silently out of the village, no longer exchanging so much as a word. They climb the mountain. As they get near the top they see dead bodies and skeletons beneath the rocks. Watchful crows are flying about. The top itself is covered with bones. The son puts the old woman down on the ground; under a rock she spreads a mat that she has brought with her, sets a bowl of rice upon it, and sits down. She does not utter a word, but she makes violent gestures to send her son away. He goes, weeping. While he is making his way down the mountain the snow begins to fall. He comes back to tell his mother. It is snowing on the mountain-top as well; she is quite covered with white flakes and she is chanting a prayer. He calls out, "It is snowing; the omen is good." Once again she waves him away and he goes. He loves his mother dearly, but his filial love has evolved within the frame of reference provided by the society he belongs to, and since necessity has dictated this custom, it is by carrying [Old] Rin to the top of the mountain that he proves himself to be an affectionate, dutiful son.[6]

As this story illustrates, the mother does not think that being abandoned on the mountain is a sign of cruelty or ingratitude on the part of her son. On the contrary, abandonment in this situation shows love and respect. Both mother and son are merely following the normative behavior prescribed by their culture. This way of life was worked out by the group to adapt to the environment, as was also the case of the Eskimos.

The status of the aged varies from time to time and from place to place. In some societies the aged are powerful, and in others they are powerless. In some societies the aged are highly esteemed, and in others they are merely tolerated. As we will see, the status and the role of the aged in primitive societies are quite different from their status and role in modern industrial societies.

Primitive Societies

In most primitive societies the elderly are accorded considerable respect.[7] This respect is generally based on some special asset that the elderly possess, or on some functions that they perform. Often they are able to render a useful service by assisting others at various economic and household chores. The elderly are highly regarded for their knowledge, skills, and experience, which they utilize to their advantage in such roles as priests and political leaders. In addition, they command much respect and authority through their control of property and the exercising of their family prerogatives.*

Old men tend to possess greater prestige in primitive societies than do old women. In general, aged men receive more prestige in societies based on herding or agriculture, whereas women fare better in societies where food gathering, hunting, and fishing are the main means of subsistence. In societies where old women are highly regarded, in all but rare cases the same regard is also held for old men. But in societies where old men are respected, the same is not necessarily true for women.

Agrarian societies afford the elderly the greatest opportunity to keep

---

*The present tense is used for convenience in this section, but many social and cultural changes have occurred in these societies since these ethnological data were collected.

working. As people age in these societies, they are given less strenuous tasks to perform — usually helping others to garden, to farm, or to do household tasks. In this way the elderly can continue to be useful as long as they live. The Hopi Indians of northeastern Arizona, still mainly a herding and farming people, illustrate this point:

> Old men tend their flocks until feeble and nearly blind. When they can no longer follow the herd, they work on in their fields and orchards, frequently lying down on the ground to rest. They also make shorter and shorter trips to gather herbs, roots, and fuel. When unable to go to the fields any longer, they sit in the house or kiva where they card and spin, knit, weave blankets, carve wood or make sandals. Some continue to spin when they are blind or unable to walk, and it is a common saying that "an old man can spin to the end of his life." Corn shelling is woman's work, but men will do it, especially in their dotage. Old women will cultivate their garden patches until very old and feeble and "carry wood and water as long as they are able to move their legs." They prepare milling stones, weave baskets and plaques out of rabbit weed, make pots and bowls from clay, grind corn, darn old clothes, care for children, and guard the house; and, when there is nothing else to do, they will sit out in the sun and watch the drying fruit. The old frequently express the desire to "keep on working" until they die.[8]

Besides performing menial tasks in the field and home, the elderly often find other, more prestigious ways to utilize their talents and abilities in primitive societies. These ways require brains, not brawn, and are well-suited to an older person's declining physical strength.

Knowledge, Magic, and Religion

In primitive societies where information must be transmitted orally and retained in the memory, the aged person is the custodian of knowledge, wisdom, traditions, and customs. In this way the elderly perform an invaluable function for the group. They use their knowledge not only in assisting and teaching others but also in enacting their roles as *shamans* and priests. In these roles they provide comfort to the distraught, diagnose illnesses, and serve as mediators between the individual and the unknown. During times of crisis, they are the ones to whom people turn for advice and guidance. Because of their advanced age, it is believed that the older persons will soon be spirits, and people attribute a supernatural power to them, an advantage in their roles as shamans or priests.

Among the Polar Eskimos some old shamans are believed to be so powerful that they can perform many miraculous feats:

> Certain old men among the Polar Eskimo were reputedly able to raise storms, produce calms, call up or drive off birds and seals, steal men's souls out of

their bodies, and cripple anyone for life. They could fly up to heaven or dive down to the bottom of the sea, remove their skins like dirty garments and put them on again. Old women often made "soul flights" to the realm of the dead in order to save the lives of very sick persons. All these mighty works were said to be wrought by magic words.[9]

On one occasion, after a heavy snowstorm a group of Eskimos became terrified when the ice underneath their camp began to split. They gave presents to the shaman and begged him to stop the oncoming catastrophe. He went into a deep trance and communicated with a young caribou spirit, which helped uncover the fact that a young girl had violated a sewing taboo by repairing a hole in her boot. Once she confessed, the ice stopped cracking, and the whole camp was saved.

Religious and ceremonial functions, like magic, give the elderly an opportunity to use their knowledge and wisdom, as well as to hold a prestigious position in the community. Many old people serve as keepers of shrines and temples and are leaders in performing prayers, ceremonies, and sacrifices.

Government

Other effective and important roles for the elderly lie in political, civil, and judicial affairs. The position of chief is found in nearly all primitive societies, and often it is occupied by an old man. Among the Dahomeans of West Africa the chief of each clan is always the oldest living male member regardless of his wealth, reputation, or ability. He cannot be replaced unless he becomes senile, and in that event the next oldest clan member may govern in his name. The tremendous power and respect enjoyed by the chief is reflected in the way the Dahomeans must approach him: they must bare their heads and torsos and kneel until their foreheads touch the ground. The oldest living women are treated with similar respect.[10]

Some primitive societies have a *gerontocratic* type of government in which a group of old men rule by virtue of the superior knowledge they are supposed to possess because of their age. The Sidamo of Ethiopia are ruled by an assembly of old men who make the important decisions for the group and settle disputes. The aged also hold such positions as advisors and councilmen. In Australia, the Aranda have a council of elders that consists of the oldest and most respected men of the group, who act as advisors to the totem chief. They are called on for such matters as conducting ceremonies, dealing with strangers, and organizing groups to avenge crimes.

In agricultural societies, the elderly have their best opportunity for continued employment. In this setting, they maintain useful and productive roles until very near the end of life. (Courtesy of Tennessee Valley Authority)

Property Rights

Property rights have always been an important source of authority and respect for the elderly. The power that comes from holding property has afforded the elderly with a means to control others, despite declining strength. Aged persons with property are assured better treatment and command more respect than those without property. The authority that old men derive from owning property is vividly illustrated by the Chukchi and Yakut peoples of northeastern Siberia. Adult sons let their old fathers beat them with sticks or whips, and they dare not retaliate or repel their fathers' blows for fear that it would affect their inheritance.

The question of timing is also important in maintaining control and authority through property rights. Aged Laplanders of northern Europe hide their wealth from their heirs by burying it. When an elderly man is about to die, he will tell his heirs where the secret hiding place is. Sometimes a dying man refuses to reveal where his wealth is buried, and it is lost. Perhaps this custom allows an elderly father to use his possessions to reward or to punish his children, depending on the type of treatment he receives from them. This usage seems to be the case among the Banks Islanders of Oceania, where an old man buries a portion of his wealth and only reveals its hiding place if he feels his son has taken good care of him in his old age. When an aged Hopi Indian has property, he receives better care in life and death because the kin who buried him were entitled to extra shares of his possessions.

Family

Old people can also acquire power and exercise their prerogatives through family relationships. Elderly people in primitive societies often gain advantage through such relationships by marrying younger mates. An old woman will often urge her husband to marry a strong, young woman to help lighten her work. Often the young wife is relegated to the position of maid and does all the household chores for the old couple. Elderly men and women both maintain considerable authority and prestige within the family circle and through kinship ties. In some societies the old men exercise supreme authority over their wives and children.

An old person's prestige in a family often lasts not only into extreme old age, but sometimes until death. Among Samoans the old men, especially chiefs, were once honored and esteemed by being buried alive. Furthermore, if this honorific burial was not performed, the chief's family was disgraced. George Turner gives the following account of such a burial:

> When an old man felt sick and infirm, and thought he was dying, he deliberately told his children and friends to get all ready and bury him. They yielded to his wishes, dug a round deep pit, wound a number of fine mats around his body, and lowered down the poor old man into his grave in a sitting posture. Live pigs were then brought, and tied, each with a separate cord, the one end of the cord to the pig, and the other end to the arm of the old man. The cords were cut in the middle, leaving the one half hanging at the arm of the old man, and the pigs were taken to be killed and baked for the burial feast; the old man, however, was supposed still to take the pigs with him to the world of spirits. . . . His grave was filled up, and his dying groans drowned amid the weeping and wailing of the living.[11]

By attending his own funeral the elderly Samoan could appreciate the high regard in which he was held by the community as evidenced by the large number of people attending his funeral, the many gifts of food, and the speeches extolling his virtues.

Prestige and respect for the aged is a dominant characteristic in nearly all primitive societies. The reasons for this, as we have discussed, are the opportunities that they have to make full use of their talents and abilities. They are able to utilize the knowledge gained through years of experience to acquire important roles in religious, magical, and political affairs of the community. The positions of the elderly are further reinforced by their control and exercise of property rights and their authority and power within the family unit.

Industrial Societies

In their major cross-cultural study, Cowgill and Holmes advance the theory that industrialization results in a relatively lower status* for older people in society.[12] With industrialization land's importance as a source of authority and power decreases, changes occur in technology and cultural values, residential mobility increases, and mass education prevails, all of which cause a decline in the status of the aged. To demonstrate the validity of their thesis, Cowgill and Holmes point to such industrialized nations as the United States, Austria, and Norway where the status of the elderly appears to be declining and "is at best ambiguous; perhaps it is not so much low status as it is no status."[13]

Norway

Work done by C. T. Pihlblad, Eva Beverfelt, and Haktor Helland on status and role of the aged in Norwegian society lends support to Cowgill and Holmes's theory that industrialization leads to a progressive decline in status.[14] Without definite roles to perform, the Norwegian elderly feel useless and uncertain of their status. The authors attribute this feeling of uselessness, in part, to two factors: change in the family structure and mandatory retirement.

In the past, land was handed down from a Norwegian father to his eldest son. On receiving the land, the son was responsible for the care and support of his aged parents; he would provide them with a nearby cottage or with a room in his home. Then, as young people began moving to the cities, they left large concentrations of the elderly behind,

*Social status used in this sense denotes high or low rank.

Industrialization has dramatically changed the way of life of societies by freeing the bulk of the population from work on the land and by permitting them to engage in other specialized roles. (Courtesy of the Tennessee Commission on Aging)

and the nuclear family replaced the three-generation or extended family of the past. Pihlblad and his associates note that with the change in family structure, contact between generations has lost much significance, and increase in intergenerational mobility has tended to create a gap between generations. As a result, the status of the elderly has been undermined.

Though the traditional age of retirement in Norway is 70, many Norwegians are reluctant and sometimes even adamant about retiring at this time. "Most elderly, especially men, rather bitterly resent the loss of the work role. A few have managed to retain it beyond age 70. An investigation in Oslo in 1966 reports about 10 percent of the population over 70 are still gainfully employed."[15] Although Pihlblad, Beverfelt, and Helland have no data on the number of retired people who still want to work, they believe the percentage is probably much higher than the 10 percent still working.

Retirement to the older Norwegian not only means giving up one's usual occupational role, but also means living with the fact that there are few significant roles to replace a job. Opportunities and options open to the elderly are limited; they are expected to use their time for rest and leisure. The general attitude of most younger Norwegians is that the old have earned the right to "rest on their oars."[16] After all, they helped build the present welfare society, and they are now entitled to be supported by it. But the elderly feel differently. To them, rest and leisure carry with them little prestige and only serve to lessen their self-esteem and reduce their status.

Japan

Erdman Palmore takes exception to the theory advanced by Cowgill and Holmes and argues that a marked decline in the status of the elderly is not a necessary result of industrialization.[17] He points to Japan where he feels the elderly continue to enjoy a relatively high status, despite Japan's remarkable rate of industrialization. Palmore cites the following marks of respect shown the aged:

> Respect and affection for the elders are shown on a daily basis by honorific language; bowing; priority for the elders in seating, serving, bathing, and going through doors. It is also reflected in popular sayings, special celebrations of the sixty-first birthday, the national observance of Respect for Elders Day, and the National Law for Welfare of the Aged.[18]

He attributes this respect to two traditions in the Japanese culture. First, a vertical system of relationships exists in Japan, which makes seniority and age the two most important factors in determining rank in their society. Second, the Japanese believe, in accordance with the teachings of Confucius, that filial piety and duty are among the most important virtues that a person may possess.

Other writers, however, contend that Japan, like many other highly industrialized nations, has experienced a decline in the status of its elderly. Douglass Sparks, for example, reports that times have changed in Japan, as has the role of the elders:

> The traditional ideal for old age — being the respected recipient of filial piety, freed from responsibilities and constraints, living in the midst of descendants and supported by the eldest son — still has a good deal of force for the retirees, but it is mainly the force of nostalgia . . . the cultural consensus has been undermined.[19]

By the same token, David Plath notes an increasing ambivalence toward the elderly:

> Today's older Japanese lives in a predominately horizontal society where all ages are presumed to have roughly equal cognitive value, and where children care for their elders more from a grudging sense of decency than from "natural" filial love.[20]

In contrast to Norway and the United States, the family structure in Japan is largely one of a three-generation household, which is rare in industrial societies. This living arrangement reflects the cultural values of the Japanese, who until recently did not regard independence as important and allowed the elderly to be economically and socially dependent on their eldest son. In fact, most elderly felt that it was

Table 5.1   Retirement age for 29 selected countries, as defined by public policy

Country	Age in years	
	Men	Women
Norway	70	70
Ireland	70	70
United States	70[a]	70[a]
Denmark	67	67
Sweden	67	67
Iceland	67	67
Canada	65	65
Luxembourg	65	65
Spain	65	65
Portugal	65	65
Netherlands	65	65
France	65	65
Finland	65	65
Switzerland	65	63
Israel	65	60
United Kingdom	65	60
German Democratic Republic	65	60
Germany, Federal Republic of	65	60
Austria	65	60
Poland	65	60
Australia	65	60
Belgium	65	60
Greece	62	57
U.S.S.R.	60	55
Czechoslovakia	60	55
Japan	60	55
Italy	60	55
Hungary	60	55
Yugoslavia	60	55

[a]Since 1978.

SOURCE: Adapted from United Nations, *The Aging: Trends and Policies,* United Nations, New York, 1975, p. 33. Copyright, United Nations 1975. Reproduced by permission.

shameful to live apart from their children.[21] Most Americans take the opposite view and prefer to remain independent, many voicing the sentiment that they want to live near their children, but not with them.

Although the retirement age for men in Japan is 55, public policy defines 60 as the retirement age, when the public pension begins. This age is much lower than the retirement age in many other countries (Table 5.1). But to the Japanese, retirement does not mean withdrawal from work; it means changing jobs, going to another company to work, or becoming self-employed. Each of these alternatives, however, involves a considerable reduction in wages and responsibilities. Because of this, even though Japanese over 60 often work as many hours as younger workers, they earn less.[22]

Despite lower pay, 70 percent of the Japanese men in their late sixties continue to work, and about one-third over the age of 70 express a desire to work.[23] In the United States, on the other hand, only 20 percent of those 65 and over remain in the labor force. Charles Stewart cites forced retirement at an early age, low incomes or low pensions, and loss of income in the case of workers in the large modern firms as reasons why such a large percentage of Japanese men continue to work in later life.[24] In addition to economic reasons, many elderly Japanese desire work for its own sake. As one retiree remarked, "Whether I receive income or not, I still want to work."[25] The end of the work career in Japan is considered to be the start of old age. No role in society exists to fill the gap between being a worker and being an old person. In fact, the Japanese do not have a single word meaning *retiree*.[26] The role of the retiree is an ambiguous one at best, and most Japanese are anxious to defer it as long as possible.

When we look at the position of the elderly in both primitive and industrial societies, one thing becomes clear — the status and respect for the aged tends to be higher in those societies in which the elderly continue to perform meaningful, clear-cut roles. The lack of a definite functional role appears to be a fundamental problem for the aged in most industrial societies. In Chapter 4, we noted how the values in American society often stripped the elderly of useful roles. Again in this chapter we see how industrialization has a similar effect.

Summary

1. All societies share a number of general traits or characteristics called *cultural universals*. These universals represent only broad categories found in all cultures and do not include specific patterns or content of a culture.

2. In a survey of primitive societies, Simmons found the following interests of older people to be universal: having a longer life, getting more rest, retaining

seniority rights, remaining an active participant in the social group, and experiencing an easy and dignified release.

3. Societies vary tremendously. Most people are habituated to the patterns of their culture, and they consider them preferable to those of other societies. The tendency to regard one's own culture as superior to all others is called *ethnocentrism*.

4. *Cultural relativism* refers to the fact that if we are to understand the behavioral patterns of other groups, we must analyze these patterns in terms of the cultural setting in which they appear.

5. The aged are highly regarded in most primitive societies. This respect is often accorded the elderly because of their knowledge and experience, their property rights, and the important roles that they perform. The aged fill many important positions in primitive societies as shamans, priests, and political leaders.

6. Cowgill and Holmes assert that industrialization causes a decline in the status of the elderly. Their situations in such countries as the United States and Norway lend support to this theory. In Norway the elderly complain of feeling useless and of being without a meaningful role. Palmore argues, however, that although Japan has a highly industrialized economy, the elderly Japanese continue to enjoy a high status. But other writers contend that the status of Japanese old people, like the elderly's status in most other industrialized countries, shows a marked decline.

Notes

1. George Peter Murdock, "The Common Denominator of Culture," in *The Science of Man in the World Crisis*, ed. Ralph Linton, Columbia University Press, New York, 1945, p. 124.

2. Leo W. Simmons, "Aging in Preindustrial Societies," in *Handbook of Social Gerontology*, ed. Clark Tibbitts, The University of Chicago Press, Chicago, 1960, pp. 65–66.

3. Ibid., p. 66.

4. Donald O. Cowgill and Lowell D. Holmes, "Summary and Conclusions: The Theory in Review," in *Aging and Modernization*, ed. Donald O. Cowgill and Lowell D. Holmes, Appleton-Century-Crofts, New York, 1972, p. 321.

5. Irving Hallowell, "Sociopsychological Aspects of Acculturation," in *The Science of Man in the World Crisis*, ed. Ralph Linton, Columbia University Press, New York, 1945, p. 184.

6. Reprinted by permission of G.P. Putnam's Sons from *The Coming of Age* by Simone de Beauvoir, pp. 54–55. English translation copyright © 1972 by André Deutsch, Weidenfeld & Nicolson and G.P. Putnam's Sons.

7. The following discussion is based largely on Leo W. Simmons, *The Role of the Aged in Primitive Society*, Yale University Press, New Haven, 1945.

8. Simmons, "Aging in Preindustrial Societies," p. 73.

9. Simmons, *The Role of the Aged in Primitive Society*, p. 142.

10. George Peter Murdock, *Our Primitive Contemporaries*. Macmillan, New York, 1934, p. 565.

11. George Turner, *Samoa, A Hundred Years Ago and Before*, Macmillan, London, 1884, pp. 335–336.

12. Cowgill and Holmes, *Aging and Modernization*.

13. Ibid., p. 311.

14. C. T. Pihlblad, Eva Beverfelt, and Haktor Helland, "Status and Role of the Aged in Norwegian Society," in *Aged and Modernization*, ed. Donald O. Cowgill and Lowell D. Holmes, Appleton-Century-Crofts, New York, 1972, pp. 227–242.

15. Ibid., p. 234.

16. Ibid., p. 232.

17. Reprinted from *The Honorable Elders* by Erdman Palmore, p. 128, by permission of Duke University Press. Copyright 1975 by Duke University Press.

18. Ibid., p. 128.

19. Douglass E. Sparks, "The Still Rebirth: Retirement and Role Discontinuity," in *Adult Episodes in Japan*, ed. David W. Plath, E. J. Brill, Leiden, The Netherlands, 1975, p. 67.

20. David W. Plath, "Japan: The After Years," in *Aging and Modernization*, ed. Donald O. Cowgill and Lowell D. Holmes, Appleton-Century-Crofts, New York, 1972, p. 141.

21. Daisku Maeda, "Growth of Old People's Clubs in Japan," *The Gerontologist*, 15, no. 3 (1975), 254.

22. Palmore, *The Honorable Elders*, p. 59.

23. Aaron Lipman, "Conference on the Potential for Japanese American Cross-National Research on Aging, *The Gerontologist*, 15, no. 3 (1975), 252.

24. Charles D. Stewart, "The Older Worker in Japan: Realities and Possibilities", *Industrial Gerontology*, 1, no. 1 (1974), 61.

25. Sparks, "The Still Rebirth," p. 67.

26. Ibid.

For Further Study

Beauvoir, Simone de. *The Coming of Age*. G. P. Putnam's Sons, New York, 1972. Chapters 2 and 4 deal with primitive and present-day societies, respectively.

Burgess, Ernest W., ed. *Aging in Western Societies*. The University of Chicago Press, Chicago, 1960. A survey of the major trends and developments in aging in selected countries of Western culture.

Cowgill, Donald O., and Lowell D. Holmes, eds. *Aging and Modernization*. Appleton-Century-Crofts, New York, 1972. A survey of aging in a wide range of cultural groups and national societies.

Goody, Jack. "Aging in Nonindustrial Societies." In *Handbook of Aging and the Social Sciences*, edited by Robert H. Binstock and Ethel Shanas. Van Nostrand Reinhold, New York, 1976, pp. 117–129. The economic, kinship, political, and religious roles of the elderly in nonindustrial societies.

Gubrium, Jaber F. *Late Life: Communities and Environmental Policy*. Charles C Thomas, Springfield, Ill., 1974. Part III contains a collection of papers dealing with the status of the aged and with the impact of change and cross-cultural experiences on the elderly.

Murdock, George P. *Our Primitive Contemporaries*. Macmillan, New York, 1934. A classic in the field of anthropology.

Shanas, Ethel, et al. *Old People in Three Industrial Societies*. Atherton Press, New York, 1968. A good cross-national study of the social and behavioral aspects of aging in Great Britain, Denmark, and the United States.

6

Continued Socialization

In the preceding three chapters we have seen how important culture is in the shaping of human behavior. Now let us turn to the process through which an individual learns his or her culture — *socialization*. Through socialization people acquire the skills, attitudes, values, and roles that make it possible for them to become members of their society. "Without this process of molding which we call 'socialization,' the society could not perpetuate itself beyond a single generation and culture could not exist. Nor could the individual become a person; for without the ever-repeated renewal of culture within him [or her] there could be no human mentality, no human personality."[1]

Socialization as a Lifelong Process

The most obvious phase of socialization takes place during childhood, but the process does not stop there. Socialization gained in childhood cannot fully prepare us for the multiplicity of roles that we perform as adults. Socialization occurs throughout the life span and is a continuing, never-ending process. Each new social position that one attains — such as entering college, beginning a new job, getting married, becoming a parent or a grandparent — requires the learning of a new social role. Socialization, then, may be defined as a lifelong process through which individuals learn and internalize the culture and social roles of their society.

Alex Inkeles divides the life cycle into these stages: infancy and early childhood, late childhood and adolescence, adulthood, and old age.[2] He identifies four elements in socialization that occur at each stage: (1) the *main issue* of socialization that dominates the attention of the one being socialized, as well as that of those doing the socializing; (2) the *agents* of socialization that play the most significant roles in the socialization process; (3) the *objectives* that these agents set as goals for successful socialization; and (4) the *main task* of the one being socialized, such as the skill to be learned or the problem to be solved (Table 6.1).

The main issue of infancy and early childhood is the total helplessness and dependency of the child. The central objective is to help the

Table 6.1 Individual socialization through the life cycle

Elements	Stages			
	Infancy and early childhood	Late childhood and adolescence	Adulthood	Old age
1. Main issue	Helplessness	Adjustment to changes in physical and mental capacity	Acceptance and performance of multiple roles	Acquisition of new skills and changes in habits
2. Agent of socialization	Family and adult kin	School, teachers, peers, etc.	Formal organizational agencies	Peer group
3. Objective of agent	To move child to next stage of development	To help adolescent assume adult roles	To motivate adults to attain highly specific and defined objectives	To help elderly to accept new status
4. Task of the one being socialized	To gain mastery over one's own body	To manage the changes in oneself	To fit in in the large set of new statuses	To give up previously held positions

SOURCE: Adapted from discussion in Alex Inkeles, "Social Structure and Socialization," in *Handbook of Socialization Theory and Research*, ed. David A. Goslin, Rand McNally, Chicago. 1969, pp. 618–629.

child move on to the next stage of development. For the child, the main task is mastering control over his or her body, which includes becoming toilet trained and learning how to walk and talk, and to feed and dress himself or herself.

In late childhood and adolescence, the significant issues revolve around the capacity of the individual to adjust to physical and mental changes, and society's adaptation to the impact of these adjustments. The individual begins to acquire roles that precede or fall within the scope of adult roles. The objective of the agents of socialization at this period is to help train the adolescent for his or her adult roles as effectively as possible. The family is replaced as socializing agent by a diverse group, including teachers, the school, peer groups, religious specialists, public and local heroes, and so on.

The key issue in adulthood is the degree to which the individual accepts and performs the multiplicity of roles that accompany the statuses of adulthood. The task of the one being socialized is to take over these new roles and statuses and to accept adult responsibilities. In old age, one adjusts to physical changes that necessitate learning new skills and changing patterns of behavior. An important part of the older person's task is to relinquish previously held statuses and roles, along with the prestige, power, and economic rewards accompanying them. Learning new roles and skills may be required, especially those suitable to full-time leisure. In old age, one's peer group again becomes an agent of socialization. Children and others whom the elderly had previously socialized also act as socializing agents during this period and encourage the older person to accept the new status.

The most significant aspect of adult socialization is the acquisition of social roles. As individuals move through adulthood into old age, they must constantly learn to perform new or altered roles and give up old ones. As we mentioned earlier, a role is the expected behavior of one who holds a certain status. A single status may involve a number of associated roles. For example, the status of college professor not only involves the role of teacher in relation to students, but also includes a cluster of other roles in relation to colleagues, secretaries, and administrators. All these roles constitute a *role set*, which may be defined as the entire array of related roles associated with a particular status that an individual occupies.

Socialization and Old Age

Role Loss

A person's role sets change during the stages of the life cycle. New roles are added to the sets and old ones discarded. An individual discards the role of a single person in taking on the new role of husband or wife. When one is graduated from college and gets a full-time job, the role of student is exchanged for that of employee. In each instance, the individual relinquishes one role and is given a new role in return. The single person may look forward to marriage, and the college student to a job. But old age differs from other stages in the life cycle because, while roles continue to be discarded, new roles often do not take their place. Eventually the role sets of the elderly begin to shrink.

The major role losses that characterize old age come with retirement and widowhood. The loss of the work role and the marital role differ from role losses in earlier years because one's participation in the occupational structure and the nuclear family, respectively, are ended. Usually there are no new roles to replace them or to look forward to. These events represent points at which the central tasks of men and women are terminated. In old age, most widows do not remarry, and the majority of retired persons never return to the labor force as full-time workers.

Zena Blau finds that "retirement has more detrimental effects than widowhood on the associational life, morale, and self-concept of older people, particularly men."[3] Widowhood differs from retirement because it is a natural event and does not result from the loss of capacity or the failure of the individual to perform the function of the role. Nor does widowhood have the same isolating effect or threaten one's self-esteem and self-concept in the way that retirement does. Thus, for many people, bereavement may be easier to bear.[4]

In a study of 280 persons aged 60 and over, Marjorie Lowenthal and Clayton Haven found that persons having a close relationship with particular individuals in whom they can confide possessed a buffer against the loss of roles.[5] Despite role loss, persons with confidants were more likely to be satisfied and less likely to be depressed than persons without confidants (Table 6.2). This finding held true even with those who suffered such significant role losses as widowhood and retirement. The study also revealed that an individual who had been widowed within seven years but who had a confidant had a higher morale than a person who, though married, had no confidant. Similarly, the morale of retired persons having confidants was the same as the morale of those still working but without confidants.

Other role losses in old age are suffered through the death of friends and relatives, decreasing mobility, and income limitations. Also, the physical decline that often occurs in later years places further restrictions on the social world of the elderly.

Irving Rosow notes that the role loss of the elderly deprives them of vital functions as well as their social identity.[6] The loss of roles bars the elderly from social participation and undermines their sense of self-worth and their feeling of self-esteem. They are likely to feel devalued

Table 6.2   Effect of confidant on morale in the contexts of
widowhood, retirement, and physical illness

	Satisfied	*Depressed*
Widowed within 7 years		
Has confidant	55%	45%
No confidant	(27)[a]	(73)
Married		
Has confidant	65	35
No confidant	(47)	(53)
Retired within 7 years		
Has confidant	50	50
No confidant	(36)	(64)
Not retired		
Has confidant	70	30
No confidant	50	50
Serious physical illness within 2 years		
Has confidant	(16)	(84)
No confidant	(13)	(87)
No serious illness		
Has confidant	64	36
No confidant	42	58

[a]Percentages are placed in parentheses when the numbers on which they are based are less than 20.
SOURCE: Marjorie Fiske Lowenthal and Clayton Haven, "Interaction and Adaptation: Intimacy as a Critical Variable," *American Sociological Review*, 33, no. 1 (1968), 27.

and become alienated from the rest of society. Our society rewards people on the basis of economic usefulness, and the elderly are discredited for their lack not only of economic utility but of social utility. They are often patronized or merely tolerated; other times they are simply disregarded or rejected. "They are first excluded from the mainstream of social existence, and because of this nonparticipation, they are penalized and denied the rewards that earlier came to them routinely."[7] A person's roles identify and describe him or her as a social being; they are the basis of the person's self-conception. Role loss results in an erosion of conception and social identity.

The type of role losses experienced by the elderly underlies the basis for two theories of successful aging — the disengagement theory and the activity theory.

THE DISENGAGEMENT THEORY   This social psychological theory of aging was advanced by Elaine Cumming and William Henry in their book *Growing Old*,[8] a study of 275 men and women between the ages of 50 and

Major role losses characterize the period of later life. The retired person often suffers the loss of occupational identity and a functional role in society. (Black Star. Richard Laurence Stack—Photographer)

Work Offers an Identity

It is by no accident that — when someone meets someone for the first time — "How do you do?" is usually followed by "What do you do?" Since most working people describe themselves by the company or organization to which they belong, work makes them "somebody"; unemployed people become "nobodies." The importance of this job-related identification shows up when a person retires. Scientists attribute much of the trauma associated with retirement to a sudden loss of identity.

SOURCE: *The National Observer*, June 8, 1974. © 1974 Dow Jones & Co. Inc. All rights reserved.

90, who were in good health and reasonable economic circumstances. Their theory is based on the observed fact that aging involves a gradual relinquishment of social roles and a decrease in social interaction. Cumming and Henry maintain that both the individual and society prepare in advance for the ultimate disengagement (death) through a gradual, mutually beneficial process during which the individual and society withdraw from one another. Their statement follows:

> In our theory, aging is an inevitable mutual withdrawal or disengagement, resulting in decreased interaction between the aging person and others in the social system he [or she] belongs to. The process may be initiated by the individual or by others in the situation. The aging person may withdraw more markedly from some classes of people while remaining relatively close in others. His withdrawal may be accompanied from the outset by an increased preoccupation with himself; certain institutions in society may make this withdrawal easy for him. When the aging process is complete, the equilibrium which existed in middle life between the individual and his society has given way to a new equilibrium characterized by a greater distance and an altered type of relationship.[9]

To Cumming and Henry, disengagement is inevitable because death is inevitable. Old people prepare for their deaths by divesting themselves of social relationships and social functions. Society, in turn, encourages its members to do this so their deaths will not be disruptive to its equilibrium. In other words, disengagement is a two-way process whereby the individual withdraws from society and society withdraws from the individual. When the process is complete, the individual has shifted from being preoccupied with society to self-preoccupation.

These authors believe that their theory of disengagement applies to all societies, though they acknowledge that cultural variations occur in the initiation of the process. For instance, in our society old persons may resist the process until it is forced upon them, while in traditional societies the elderly may initiate the process.

On the other hand, Arnold Rose argues that the disengagement process is not inevitable. The lack of involvement in later life may be a continuation of a lifelong pattern for some people.[10] By the same token, many people never disengage and continue to be socially involved all their lives. Rose also maintains that disengagement is not beneficial to the individual. Much empirical evidence suggests that the elderly who are engaged tend to be, in most cases, the happiest and to have the greatest life satisfaction. Also, although Cumming and Henry see disengagement as universal, Rose contends that in many cultures there is little or no disengagement and that the elderly are either shifted into new roles or given much prestige and power. Lastly, Rose asserts that many trends in our society serve to counteract the forces leading to disengagement of the elderly. These trends include: (1) advances in medical care and services, which have led to better health and increased vigor of older people today; (2) more economic security for the elderly through pension plans, social security, and annuities; (3) development of social movements among older people to raise their prestige and to increase their privileges; (4) the trend toward earlier retirement, which may become a factor in motivating re-engagement; and (5) the expansion of activities and hobbies for the elderly, which will afford them more roles and options.

THE ACTIVITY THEORY   In contrast to the disengagement theory is the activity theory, often referred to as the "common-sense theory" of aging. While the disengagement theory emphasizes withdrawal from roles, the activity theory stresses a continuation of role performances. In this view, when roles are lost, such as in retirement and widowhood, the individual is expected to find substitutes. Bernice Neugarten and her associates sum up the main premise of the activity theory:

> The older person who ages optimally is the person who stays active and who manages to resist the shrinkage of his social world. He maintains the activities of middle age as long as possible and then finds substitutes for those activities he is forced to relinquish: substitutes for work when he is forced to retire; substitutes for friends and loved ones whom he loses by death.[11]

Although withdrawal is considered mutual in the disengagement theory, in the activity theory it is not. The activity theory holds that society withdraws from the aging person, but this is against the person's will or desire. To minimize this withdrawal, the person must try to be active, keep busy, and stay "young." The underlying theme seems to be that "it is better to wear out than rust out," or better still, "to die with one's boots on." Many old and young people subscribe to this

Disengagement in our culture is often, alas, sludge language for being ejected, excluded or demeaned, and liking it — an attribute wished on the newly created old to plaster our guilt and provide a piece of jargon to excuse our conduct.

SOURCE: Alex Comfort, *A Good Age*, Crown Publishers, New York, 1976, p. 65.

philosophy, as do most of the practical workers in gerontology. This theory is certainly more in keeping with the American value system than the disengagement theory is.

Despite all the bromides on keeping active, many people have no desire to sustain the high levels of activity and the attitudes of middle age as they grow older. They seek to curtail many activities and social involvements; keeping busy is not their idea of happiness or fulfillment. For some, then, activity may be positively related to life satisfaction, whereas for others, this is not the case. Robert Havighurst notes that "a person with an active, achieving and outward-directed way of life style will be best satisfied to continue this into old age with only slight diminution. Other people with a passive, dependent, home-centered way of life will be best satisfied with disengagement."[12] It seems reasonable to assume that whether persons gradually disengage or whether they maintain a high level of activity, depends on unique lifelong patterns, experiences, and specific needs. Both disengagement and activity theories have their limitations, and neither offers an adequate explanation of the aging process.

Role Ambiguity

Orville Brim and Stanton Wheeler state that the three main purposes of socialization are to help an individual acquire knowledge, ability, and motivation.[13] Before a person can perform a role adequately, that person must know what the normative expectations of the role are, must have the ability to meet the requirements of the role, and must possess the desire or motivation to fulfill the role. These three basic conditions are necessary for successful socialization. Of these conditions, in most cases, the elderly have the ability to perform their roles, but they are seriously hampered by the other two requirements, knowledge and motivation.

For learning to take place efficiently and effectively, the knowledge that one is expected to acquire should be explicit and clearly stated. Students are well aware of this in the classroom. They are often confused and bewildered by instructors who speak in vague generalities and who cannot express their thoughts clearly. A similar situation

occurs in learning a role when the content of the role is vague and ambiguous.

Role ambiguity occurs, therefore, when there are no clearly defined guidelines or expectations concerning requirements of a given role. Role ambiguity is not uncommon. For example, today a lack of consensus exists on what the role of a woman in our society should involve. Should she get married, have children, and remain in the home, or pursue an independent career? Role ambiguity also exists for parents and their adolescent children because there is no clearly defined time in our society when an adolescent becomes an adult. At some point we expect young people to stop being children, and yet we do not view them as adults. In some situations they are treated as children, while in others they are given the responsibilities of adults. Thus, many adolescents become confused about their role and its inconsistencies. In certain states — Tennessee, for example — at 16 persons are considered mature enough to drive, can marry with the permission of parents, but must wait until 19 before being legally of age to buy a bottle of beer.

Many primitive societies have rites of passage ceremonies that mark the transition into adult status, thus eliminating any confusion. Such ceremonies perform the function of letting a person know where he or she stands and of announcing the new status publicly.

The transition into old age and retirement is often characterized by role ambiguity, as there are few established norms regarding these roles. Not only the elderly themselves, but others are uncertain about the proper role for the aged and retired. For instance, when we think of persons who are doctors, plumbers, teachers, or police officers, we have a fairly good idea of what each role entails. But think for a moment of retired persons. What is their role? Do we expect them to sit and watch TV, play bingo, or go fishing? Our expectations are uncertain and vague (see Chapter 3's section on norms). There are few guidelines to give structure and direction to their lives.

Nearly three decades ago, Burgess referred to the ambiguous position of older people in our society at retirement as being an essentially "roleless role."

> The retired older man and his wife are imprisoned in a roleless role. They have no vital function to perform. . . . Nor are they offered a ceremonial role by society to make up in part for their lost functional role. This roleless role is thrust by society upon the older person at retirement, and to a greater or less degree he has accepted it or become resigned to it.[14]

Opposite page: Few norms exist that define the role of the retired, and expectations of what retirees should do with their time and energy are often vague and ambiguous. (Top photo by Allen Green Visual Departures; Bottom photo courtesy of Tennessee Commission on Aging)

Without clear-cut norms to measure conformity or deviation from a role, there can be no positive sanctions or rewards for performing a role successfully. This lack deprives the older person of motivation, which in turn impedes the socialization process. Clearly, two of Brim's necessary conditions for socialization, knowledge and motivation, have not been met in the retirement role.

Role Discontinuity

For many roles in our society, we often prepare ahead. For example, a college student studying to be an engineer, besides taking the necessary courses, gets a summer job working for an engineering firm, begins reading the engineering journals, and joins an engineering society. Or, a mother returns to school to finish her degree when her children are nearing high-school age, so that she may become certified as a teacher. In both cases, there is a continuity of socialization for a new role. Role continuity refers to the learning of new skills, norms, and attitudes that prepare one for the next stage. Such socialization facilitates the movement and adjustment to a new status.

Ruth Benedict describes continuity in the socialization process among the Cheyenne Indians:

> At birth the little boy was presented with a toy bow, and from the time he could run about serviceable bows suited to his stature were specially made for him by the man of the family. Animals and birds were taught him in a graded series beginning with those most easily taken, and as he brought in his first of each species his family duly made a feast of it, accepting his contribution as gravely as the buffalo his father brought. When he finally killed a buffalo, it was only the final step of his childhood conditioning, not a new adult role with which his childhood experience had been at variance.[15]

This description shows how Cheyenne youths are systematically trained from childhood for their adult role. In most societies, people are trained, formally or informally, for their future roles by learning expected behavior and values. In this way, transition from one status to the next is made easy and smooth.

But a lack of preparation and consistency in training for a role that one will take on at the next consecutive stage results in *role discontinuity*. In our society, some serious discontinuities occur in the socialization process. Transitions from the dating role to the marriage role and from the work role to the retirement role are situations involving role discontinuity. What is learned in socialization at one age level may be useless at the next, or may conflict with what has previously been learned, necessitating unlearning. An example of how discontinuity in the socialization process can provide a difficult transition into old age is described by Ralph Linton.

> In certain societies the change from the adult to the old status is made more difficult for the individual by the fact that the patterns for these statuses ascribe different types of personality to each. This was the case among the Comanche, as it seems to have been among most of the Plains tribes. The adult male was a warrior, vigorous, self-reliant, and pushing. Most of his social relationships were phrased in terms of competition. . . . Any willingness to arbitrate differences or to ignore slights was a sign of weakness resulting in loss of prestige. The old man, on the other hand, was expected to be wise and gentle, willing to overlook slights, and, if need be, to endure abuse. . . . Young men strove for war and honor, old men strove for peace and tranquility. There is abundant evidence that among the Comanche the transition was often a difficult one for the individual. Warriors did not prepare for old age, thinking it a better fate to be killed in action. When waning physical power forced them to assume the new role, many of them did so grudgingly. . . .[16]

After being socialized from childhood to be fierce, competitive, and aggressive, then in old age the Comanche suddenly had to become peaceful and passive, making transition from adulthood to old age status extremely difficult for them. Paul Horton and Chester Hunt note that our society demands an equally abrupt transition into old age.

> To be successful in the active adult role, one must develop independence and self-reliance, must learn to find satisfaction in useful work, and in being advisor and protector of the young. As an aged person, one must become dependent and submissive, able to respect oneself with no useful work to do, and must learn to keep advice to oneself while being ignored or patronized by the young.[17]

The transition to old age is characterized by serious role discontinuity in our society. There is little or no advance preparation for becoming old and adapting to a new lifestyle and the status changes that occur. The closest equivalent we have to anticipatory socialization for old age is through preretirement preparation programs.

Anticipatory Socialization

Anticipatory socialization refers to advance preparation for a new status and role. Such socialization, as in the case of preretirement preparation programs, tends to facilitate the transition and the adjustment to retirement. To do this, these programs provide the preretiree with some knowledge about retirement: what to expect, what problems to anticipate, and how to prepare for them.

Generally two approaches are used — individual counseling and group sessions. Individual counseling consists of scheduling interviews with an employee and often his wife to discuss financial planning for retirement. Beside the financial aspect of retirement, other areas dealing with adjustment to retirement may also be included. Interviews are usually conducted by a trained member of the personnel staff and often begin three to five years prior to retirement.

Group sessions are considered by many to be the most effective method of retirement preparation. They give employees the opportunity to exchange ideas and information freely and to discuss retirement problems with one another. Each session, which usually lasts about two hours, focuses on one major topic involved in retirement preparation. These topics generally include finances, health, the sociological and psychological aspects of retirement, living arrangements and locale, the legal aspects of retirement, and the use of leisure time. Most group programs schedule weekly meetings, ranging anywhere over a period of from 6 to 12 weeks; employees are given time off during working hours to attend the sessions. Some firms hold their meetings in the evenings to enable the employee's spouse to attend.

Preretirement programs have been growing rapidly in popularity during the past two decades, not only among business and industrial firms, but also in labor unions and in federal, state, and local governments. In recent years, preparation for retirement has been adopted by many universities, community colleges, and public schools as part of their instructional offerings. Such groups as senior citizen centers, community centers, churches, and libraries also sponsor preretirement programs.

Some companies offer their employees the option of gradual retirement, which involves giving an employee increasing amounts of time away from the job in the form of extended vacations or shorter working hours. Gradual retirement is a type of *role rehearsal* that enables individuals to act out behavior required in their future role. Although the opportunity to rehearse future roles fosters the socialization process, in the case of the ambiguous retirement role a person is limited in what to rehearse. Probably the greatest advantage of gradual retirement is that it allows individuals to experience retirement in small doses. In this way, they gain insight into the adjustments and problems that they will experience later in retirement, and they can use this knowledge to plan accordingly. Also by gradually getting used to being away from the job, persons find that the transition from full-time employment to full-time leisure tends to be less traumatic.

Role Models

The late Elvis Presley served as a role model for many aspiring young singers during the last two decades. His innovative style of strumming a guitar and gyrating his hips while singing were and still are emulated. A *role model* is an individual whose behavior in a certain role provides a pattern for another individual to follow in performing the same role. By having appropriate role models with which to identify, an individual can learn a new role with greater ease. Parents generally act as role models to socialize their children for age, sex, or occupational roles. Role models may range from a public figure to a legendary hero. Beth Hess notes:

> In a society in which youthfulness is the valued state of being, in which wrinkles, gray hair, lack of zap, and irregularity must be eradicated along with spotty glassware, grimy sinks, and dirty floors . . . where are role models who can demonstrate successful aging? This question becomes crucial when we remember that today's old people are the first to survive in large numbers into an old age of retirement from work and family roles, in fair health, and with a good deal of confidence in their capacities for coping. Because this is a new stage in life, there are few models to follow and few institutionalized norms to guide them.[18]

Irving Rosow argues that older people have role models, but these models are often inappropriate because they are youthful.[19] For older persons to judge themselves according to youthful standards seriously hampers their socialization to old age. The elderly who are most admired and serve as role models tend to be those who act youthful, look well preserved, and maintain middle-age lifestyles. Any deviations from these models are regarded as undesirable and negative. The pages of *Modern Maturity*, a magazine published for those 55 and over, are filled with such models. These are headlines in a recent issue: "Still Scouting at 85," "She Has the Secret of Eternal Youth," and "They Wouldn't Give Up."[20]

Much documented evidence shows that most people in their sixties deny their age and continue to think of themselves as middle-aged, although they are considered old by society's standards. Older people maintain they are middle-aged as long as possible mainly because old age is devalued in a youth-oriented society. Often an old person recognizes that others are old, but somehow exempts himself or herself from that category — like the woman who went to her high-school reunion and was amazed at how everyone had aged but herself.

Rosow succinctly sums up the socialization dilemma of old age:

> . . . The elderly want to remain relatively young, but the society will not let them. In this impasse, older people refuse to acknowledge and accept their

social age. With no incentive or compelling pressures from the culture to embrace their age and no meaningful norms by which to live, they simply are not socialized to an aged role.[21]

Summary

1. Socialization, the learning of one's culture, makes it possible for people to become members of their society. The process is not limited to the childhood years, but continues throughout life. Socialization may be defined as a lifelong process whereby individuals become integrated into their society by learning the culture and roles of their society.

2. At each stage of the life cycle, there are four principal elements in the socialization process: the main issue, the agents, the objectives, and the central task. In adulthood the person's task is taking over new roles and statuses and accepting adult responsibilities.

3. Acquiring social roles is the most important single aspect of adult socialization. Each person performs many roles that constitute his or her role sets. A role set is the entire array of related roles associated with a particular status held by an individual. In old age, the individual discards old roles without acquiring new ones, making the role sets fewer in number.

4. The major role losses that occur in later life are caused by the events of retirement and widowhood. The roles of widow/widower and retiree are largely irreversible, and they are seldom adequately offset by substitutes. Some studies show that retirement can have a more devastating effect on an individual than widowhood. Lowenthal and Haven in their research on role loss found that having a close friend in whom to confide helps to soften the loss of major roles. Those persons with confidants were found to be less depressed and better satisfied than those without confidants. Role loss in old age can deprive a person of social participation, social identity, and a sense of self-esteem.

5. Two major theories in gerontology are the disengagement theory and the activity theory. The disengagement theory maintains that aging results in a loss of roles because of the inevitable and mutual withdrawal of the individual and society from one another. The activity theory stresses a continuation of the individual's role performance through substitutes for the roles relinquished. Neither theory adequately explains the aging process.

6. Role ambiguity occurs when there are no clearly defined expectations governing a role, and there is considerable role ambiguity in the transition to retirement and old age. Without definite expectations to determine role conformity or deviation, there can be no rewards for the individual in successfully performing a role.

7. Role discontinuity results from lack of preparation for the new roles acquired at each stage of life. In our society there is a serious discontinuity in the socialization process for old age. The closest equivalent we have to anticipatory socialization for the later years is through preretirement preparation programs.

8. A role model is an individual whose behavior in a certain role provides a

pattern for others. Rosow argues that older people have role models, but that they are youthful ones. Most older people think of themselves as middle-aged and measure themselves by youthful standards. The use of such role models hinders their socialization to old age.

Notes

1. Kingsley Davis, *Human Society*, Macmillan, New York, 1949, p. 195.

2. Alex Inkeles, "Social Structure and Socialization," in *Handbook of Socialization Theory and Research*, ed. David A. Goslin, Rand McNally, Chicago, 1969.

3. Zena Smith Blau, *Old Age in a Changing Society*, New Viewpoints, New York, 1973, p. 213.

4. Matilda White Riley, Anne Foner, Beth Hess, and Marcia L. Toby, "Socialization for Middle and Later Years," in *Handbook of Socialization Theory and Research*, ed. David A. Goslin, Rand McNally, Chicago, 1969, p. 968.

5. Marjorie Fiske Lowenthal and Clayton Haven, "Interaction and Adaptation: Intimacy as a Critical Variable," *American Sociological Review*, 33, no. 1 (1968).

6. Irving Rosow, "Status and Role Change Through the Life Span," in *Handbook of Aging and the Social Sciences*, ed. Robert H. Binstock and Ethel Shanas, Van Nostrand Reinhold, New York, 1976, pp. 457–481.

7. Ibid., p. 466.

8. Elaine Cumming and William E. Henry, *Growing Old*, Basic Books, New York, 1961.

9. Ibid., pp. 14–15.

10. Arnold M. Rose, "A Current Theoretical Issue in Social Gerontology," in *Older People and Their Social World*, ed. Arnold M. Rose and Warren A. Peterson, F. A. Davis, Philadelphia, 1965.

11. Robert J. Havighurst, Bernice L. Neugarten, and Sheldon S. Tobin, "Disengagement and Patterns of Aging," *Middle Age and Aging*, ed. Bernice L. Neugarten, The University of Chicago Press, Chicago, 1968, p. 161.

12. Robert J. Havighurst, "Successful Aging," *Process of Aging*, vol. I, ed. Richard H. Williams, Clark Tibbitts, and Wilma Donahue, Atherton Press, New York, 1963, p. 311.

13. Orville G. Brim, Jr., and Stanton Wheeler, *Socialization After Childhood: Two Essays*, John Wiley, New York, 1966, p. 25.

14. Ernest W. Burgess, *Aging in Western Societies*, The University of Chicago Press, Chicago, 1960, p. 20.

15. Ruth Benedict, "Continuities and Discontinuities in Cultural Conditioning," *Psychiatry*, 1 (1938), 161–167.

16. Ralph Linton, *The Study of Man*, Appleton-Century-Crofts, New York, 1936, pp. 120–121.

17. Paul B. Horton and Chester L. Hunt, *Sociology* (4th ed.), McGraw-Hill, New York, 1976, pp. 109–110.

18. Reprinted from "Stereotypes of the Aged," by Beth B. Hess in the *Journal of Communication*, 24 (Autumn 1974), 80–81. © 1974 Journal of Communication.

19. Irving Rosow, *Socialization to Old Age*, University of California Press, Berkeley, 1974.

20. *Modern Maturity*, June–July 1977.

21. Rosow, *Socialization to Old Age*, p. 148.

For Further Study

Blau, Zena Smith. *Old Age in a Changing Society*. New Viewpoints, New York, 1973. Stresses the exits from adult social roles that occur in later life.

Bredemeier, Harry C., and Richard M. Stephenson. *The Analysis of Social Systems*. Holt, Rinehart & Winston, New York, 1962. Chapter 4 provides a good discussion on the different ways in which social structure may facilitate socialization.

Brim, Orville G., and Stanton Wheeler. *Socialization After Childhood: Two Essays*. John Wiley, New York, 1966. See especially the first essay, which provides a broad overview of socialization and the many problems posed by the study of later-life socialization.

Kimmel, Douglass C. *Adulthood and Aging*. John Wiley, New York, 1974. A developmental approach from young adulthood to old age.

Riley, Matilda White, Anne Foner, Beth Hess, and Marcia L. Toby. "Socialization for the Middle and Later Years." In *Handbook of Socialization Theory and Research*, edited by David A. Goslin. Rand McNally, Chicago, 1969. A comprehensive discussion of socialization dealing with the individual's progress through the life cycle.

Rosow, Irving. *Socialization to Old Age*. University of California Press, Berkeley, 1974. An excellent book on adult socialization theory.

7

Changes and Adaptations in Later Life

Why do people age? What causes the changes that take place in the body? How might these changes be delayed? These questions have posed a fascinating puzzle for scientists. Much research has been done in this area, and many theories have been advanced to try to explain the enigma of aging. It has been estimated that there are over 20 theories of biological aging. Nathan Shock classifies these theories into three principal categories. The first group, genetic theories, explains aging in terms of defects that occur in the transmission of information from the DNA molecules to the cells.* The second group, nongenetic theories, focuses on changes that take place in the cells that interfere with their performance. The third group, physiological theories, explains aging on the basis of the malfunction of a single organ system or some impairment to the regulatory and control mechanism of the body.

Biological Theories of Aging

Genetic Theories

DNA DAMAGE THEORY For a cell to function and reproduce, it must receive the necessary genetic information. Every cell has a nucleus in which the genetic information is stored in the molecules of an amino acid called DNA (deoxyribonucleic acid). The cell then follows the instructions from some of this stored information to manufacture specific enzymes and other proteins that promote chemical reactions within the cell and allow it to function properly. The *DNA damage theory* holds that when the DNA molecules become damaged, the cell cannot receive the genetic information it needs. The cell then loses its ability to

*This discussion on biological theories of aging is based largely on Nathan W. Shock, "Biological Theories of Aging," in *Handbook of the Psychology of Aging*, ed. James E. Birren and K. Warner Schaie, Van Nostrand Reinhold, New York, 1977, pp. 103–113.

produce the proper kind of enzymes necessary for it to function, and eventually the death of the cell results.

SOMATIC MUTATION THEORY   When cells become injured from radiation or from other causes, they undergo mutations or changes in their inherited characteristics. These mutations are usually harmful, and once developed, they tend to persist. According to this theory, aging results from an increase in the number of somatic cell mutations.

ERROR CATASTROPHE THEORY   The error catastrophe theory holds that errors may occur during the transfer of genetic information to the cell. These errors may cause the production of an enzyme that is not an exact copy, and thus the cell cannot function properly and ultimately dies.

Nongenetic Theories

WEAR-AND-TEAR THEORY   The wear-and-tear theory, which dates back to Aristotle, assumes that the living organism is like a machine: from extended usage, its parts wear out and the machine breaks down. Similarly, aging is seen as a product of the gradual deterioration of the organs of the body.

WASTE-ACCUMULATION THEORY   According to the waste-accumulation theory, harmful substances and waste products that cannot be eliminated build up within the various cells. In time, these wastes interfere with the normal functioning of the cells.

CROSS-LINKING THEORY   Cross-linking refers to the attachment of any two large molecules to one another inside or outside the cell. When this coupling occurs, these large molecules become immobilized. The result, according to the cross-linking theory, is an accumulation of a "frozen metabolic pool," which clogs the tissues and cells and impairs their function.

Physiological Theories

THE STRESS THEORY   According to the stress theory, aging comes from a gradual build-up of stresses caused from living. These stresses leave residuals that persist, accumulate, and eventually exhaust the reserve capacities of the organism.

Scientists Say They're near Answer to Reverse Aging, Extend Lifetime

SAN FRANCISCO (AP) — Scientists studying tiny "hooks" that tie up genetic material within cells and make people grow old said yesterday they are close to finding a chemical that will dissolve the bonds and reverse the aging process.

"I'm not interested in gaining five years here and five years there," said Dr. John Bjorksten of Madison, Wis., a pioneer in the study of aging. "I'm shooting for the whole pot."

The "whole pot," he figures, is an average life expectancy of 800 years — the lifespan he said was projected by the life insurance industry if everyone could stay as healthy as they are at 16.

He added that scientists realistically could hope for only 10 percent success, adding 80 years to everyone's lifetime.

Bjorksten told a news conference at the American Chemical Society that aging occurs when two molecules in a gene, the basic unit of heredity, become hooked together by a process called cross-linking.

"If you put handcuffs on two large men, they are hampered by it and they don't do the work they have to do so well," he explained. "Then if a third man comes along and you handcuff him to the other two, it's going to be even more upsetting."

It is the same when molecules are linked together in this way, he said — the cells that contain the molecules do not function as well.

What scientists need to find, he said, is an enzyme — a special kind of chemical — that will dissolve the bonds that link the molecules together. When they find that, he said, they will have found a formula to reverse the process of aging.

SOURCE: *Knoxville News-Sentinel*, September 3, 1976. Reprinted with permission of the Associated Press.

SINGLE-ORGAN THEORIES   The most popular of the single-organ theories attempts to explain aging in terms of the failure of the cardiovascular system. This failure is caused by arteriosclerosis, a disease in which the blood vessels deteriorate.

THE AUTOIMMUNE THEORY   Some scientists postulate that errors in the body's immune system, which is normally directed toward fighting disease, occur with age. The immune system produces antibodies that destroy the very cells that it is supposed to protect. In other words, the system loses the ability to distinguish friend from foe. The autoimmune theory is based on the premise that with advancing age certain body cells become slightly altered. Because of this alteration, the body either overreacts to these changed cells, or is unable to recognize them.

Shock notes that the two theories that hold the greatest promise for the future are the cross-linking and autoimmune theories. Much of the research on studies of extracellular proteins, such as collagen, shows that the cross-links they form over time contribute to the decline in elasticity of the tissues of the body. It has been assumed that a similar situation occurs inside the cells with the DNA molecules. Scientists postulate that prevention of the cross-linking of DNA molecules in the cells or the ability to dissolve the cross-links once they are formed, would slow down or even reverse the aging process.

Substantial evidence shows that with age the autoimmune antibodies increase in the blood. Also such "immune type" diseases as rheumatoid arthritis, anemia, and diabetes tend to be age-related. Takashi Makinodan experimented with old mice by injecting them with cells from young mice. He found that their resistance to disease increased so dramatically that they survived large doses of disease-producing bacteria that previously would have been deadly.[1] Some scientists speculate that in the future, people could have their white blood cells frozen and stored away during youth, and then could use them in old age to revitalize their immune systems.

The fact that each species has a fixed life span has led scientists to conclude that the major factors setting the upper limits of the life span must be genetically programmed. Work done by Leonard Hayflick shows that certain cells of the body are capable of only a limited number of divisions, after which the cells die.[2] Hayflick put human embryo cells in a culture; they doubled approximately 50 times and then stopped. In contrast, cells taken from old animals only undergo from 20 to 25 cell divisions. The finite capacity for cells to divide is now called the "Hayflick limit." His work suggests that there is a cellular clock within us that runs down at a certain predetermined time.

At present, no single theory explains the complexities of the aging process. Most theories do not view aging in terms of the total organism and fail to take into account the relationships and interdependence between tissues, cells, and organs. Perhaps, instead of a single theory, a combination of theories is needed to explain the various aspects of aging. Some theories hold more promise than others, but a great deal of experimental work still needs to be done.

Physiological Changes with Aging

Although we are not exactly sure why people age, we do know that practically no one dies of old age. Aging is not a disease. Aging simply increases the chances that a person may die of any one of a host of

Many persons continue to be active and enjoy good health all their lives. This 91-year-old Vermont woman dispels the myth that physical disability is inevitable with age. (Suzanne Opton)

diseases. We also know that aging is a universal phenomenon. Animals such as mice, horses, dogs, and rabbits all grow old in ways similar to human beings. Furthermore, different organs of the body age at various rates. Because of this fact, it is possible for a 65-year-old person to have a 55-year-old heart and 70-year-old lungs.

Not only are there variations within people as far as aging is concerned, but there are variations among people. Individuals age at such varying rates that it is hard to determine what the "average" physical changes in old age are. Not all of the physical changes described in the following discussion will happen to everyone. Also the degree to which people are affected by these changes will vary (Figure 7.1).

Skin

The first tell-tale signs of aging affect skin and hair. The skin may become dry and lose its elasticity; there is a lessening of the fat and

Figure 7.1   How the body changes with age.

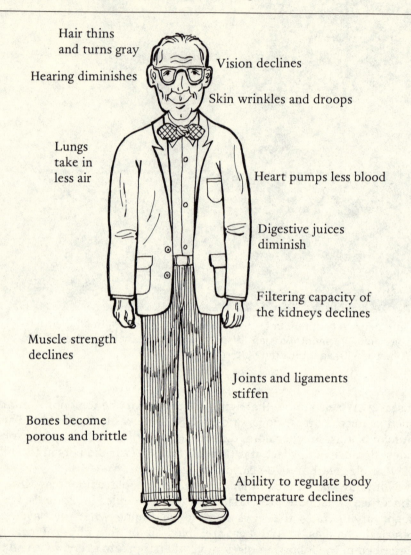

Hair thins
and turns gray

Vision declines

Hearing diminishes

Skin wrinkles and droops

Lungs
take in
less air

Heart pumps less blood

Digestive juices
diminish

Filtering capacity of
the kidneys declines

Muscle strength
declines

Joints and ligaments
stiffen

Bones become
porous and brittle

Ability to regulate body
temperature declines

supportive tissue. These conditions cause the skin to wrinkle. About middle age or sometimes even sooner, the hair begins to gray and then later turns white. Besides inherited baldness in males, there is a thinning of the hair in both men and women due to the atrophy of hair follicles. The loss of subcutaneous tissue and the decrease in the number of nerve cells of the skin, often referred to as heat and cold receptors, are in part responsible for older people's diminished ability to maintain a constant body temperature. This is why older people often complain of being cold, while younger people in the room find the temperature quite comfortable.

Skeletal System

Although a slight reduction in height occurs with age, some of this shrinkage is due to a bent posture. An older person may walk slightly stooped, with hips and knees partially bent and the neck flexed. Much of this postural change is due to the thinning of the cartilage between the spinal discs, which causes the spine to compress and bend. Bones become lighter, increasingly porous, and brittle as calcium is depleted; elasticity in joints and joint cartilage is lost to a varying degree.

Strength and size of muscles decrease with age. For instance, at age 50 the strength of the biceps is only about half of what it was at age 25 to 30. Although the total mass of muscle fibers progressively reduce, the size of the muscles appears to decline much more slowly in those persons who are physically active.

Heart

The size of the heart does not generally change with age, but the amount of blood that it pumps decreases. The capability of the heart rate to compensate in response to stress also diminishes. With advancing age, the resistance of the flow of blood progressively increases and systolic blood pressure tends to be higher.

Lungs

The vital capacity of the lungs, which is the total amount of air one can breathe in and out in a single breath, reduces with age. At age 70, this vital capacity is reduced to less than 50 percent of what it was at age 30. The change is related to the weakening of the muscles in the rib cage and the decreased elasticity of the lungs.

Gastrointestinal Tract

The great preoccupation of older people with food intake and elimination stems from several factors. Difficulties in eating may be related to poorly fitting dentures, loss of teeth, or a decrease in the production of digestive juices. The decline in the activity of peristalsis throughout the intestines, along with the weakened muscles, may contribute to constipation, a common ailment of the elderly.

Urinary Tract

The filtering rate of the kidneys, as well as the actual flow of blood through the kidneys, of persons in their eighties is about half that of persons in their twenties. Excessive urination is common among the aged, and in males it may be due to enlargement of the prostate gland, which occurs in about three-fourths of males over age 55.

Reproductive Organs

Most age-related changes in the reproductive organs occur very gradually except for menopause, which may begin rather abruptly. The change of life usually occurs between ages 46 and 50 in the female, accompanied by an atrophy of the reproductive organs. Some maintain that a similar, though less dramatic, condition occurs in the male somewhere between the fifties and sixties. Often following menopause, a woman's sexual desire may increase because she is freed from the fear of pregnancy. Much research shows that probably two-thirds of elderly people maintain sexual interest and activity well into their seventies. Many people are sexually active in their eighties and beyond. If an elderly person is in good health and has a suitable partner, he or she is as capable of having sex as a younger person.

Senses

A familiar complaint of people as they age is that their arms have gotten too short for them to hold a newspaper or a book so they can read it. One of the most common visual problems associated with aging is *presbyopia*, or farsightedness, which is the loss of the ability to focus on close objects. This condition generally occurs between 40 and 50 years of age. Opacity of the eye lens, known as a *cataract*, is also common among elderly people. The condition necessitates surgery only when it interferes with useful vision. With age, more light is required for maximum vision as the pupil becomes smaller in size. For example, people past 60 need twice as much light as when they were 40. Changes in hearing begin around age 30 and affect men more often than women. The most common source of auditory decline is a gradual loss of the ability to hear high frequencies. This condition is due to the loss of the eardrum's elasticity. Although some people develop hearing impairments with age, the majority of persons retain an adequate hearing ability throughout their lives.

Research about the senses of smell and taste is somewhat inconclusive and at times contradictory. Though many researchers have observed a decline in taste and smell sensitivity with age, not all the evidence supports this conclusion. More research is needed in this area.

Psychological Aspects of Aging

Intelligence

Although there is some general agreement on many biological changes occurring with advanced age — such as the skin wrinkles or the lungs take in less air — the same agreement does not exist regarding the psychological changes associated with aging, such as intellectual functioning. Psychological changes are not as clear cut and are more difficult to measure and assess. The question of whether or not intelligence declines in old age is a controversial one. Some reasons for this controversy relate to the type of research methods used to measure intelligence.

The Army-Alpha test, an early intelligence test developed during World War I, was administered to soldiers between the ages of 18 and 60. The findings showed that intelligence peaked at early adulthood and then began to decline. Similar results were obtained in the early 1930s when the test was given to residents of a New England community. Later, David Wechsler, whose intelligence tests have been among the most widely used in the United States, developed the Wechsler Adult Intelligence Scale (WAIS), which was adjusted for different age groups. The results from the 1955 standardized version of this test also showed a drop in intelligence with age. Wechsler found that mental abilities peaked at about age 24, with a decline beginning after age 30 and continuing into old age.[3]

A major methodological issue of these studies was that they were cross-sectional, in that each subject was tested at a given point in time and the results then compared with other age groups (see Chapter 1). But people of different ages differ in generations and life experiences. Therefore, differences in test scores from a cross-sectional study could be due to age, or generation differences, or both. Longitudinal studies attempt to overcome this problem by comparing the same individual at several points in time. Though some weaknesses are associated with the longitudinal design (such as differentiating age-related changes from those changes due to events in the environment, and dealing with the problem of selective subject dropout), overall the longitudinal method is far superior to the cross-sectional design in investigating age changes within the individual.

In 1956, K. Warner Schaie and his associates gave intelligence tests to

500 subjects ranging in age from 21 to 70. In 1963, 301 of the same subjects were retested, and in 1970, 161 of these subjects were again tested.[4] On the basis of these longitudinal data collected over a 14-year period, Schaie says, "From these studies we can now conclude that on the crystallized abilities there is very little change in intellectual function for an individual throughout adulthood."[5] *Crystallized intelligence* refers to the skills one acquires through education and the socialization process, such as verbal comprehension, inductive reasoning, and numerical skills.

In a three- to four-year follow-up of the Duke longitudinal sample, Carl Eisdorfer found no apparent intellectual decline in a group of relatively normal persons between 60 and 94 years of age.[6] In a 10-year follow-up study of the Duke group, Eisdorfer and Frances Wilkie reported that a group of subjects aged 60 to 69 showed no intellectual decline over the 10-year interval.[7] Their findings along with Schaie's and others suggest that there is little or no loss of intellectual function with age.

James Birren notes that not only is there no decrease with age in general mental ability, but in some areas, such as knowledge and information, there is an increase.

> There appears to be a continual increase in the amount of information that we have stored within us. All things being equal, if you have good health, you will continue to store information as you age. Your vocabulary is going to be significantly larger at age sixty-five than it was at forty, or even than it was when you graduated from college. Your vocabulary may double, in fact, over these years. As a college graduate you may have known 20,000 words and at sixty-five you may know over 40,000 words. This means that intellectual functioning defined as stored information, is increasing as you age.[8]

In general, much of the evidence today points to very little decline in intellectual abilities and skills with age, provided the person remains in reasonably good health. The one aspect of mental performance that does appear to change in most cases, however, is a slowing down in the speed of response.

Motor Performance

The time an older person takes to cross a street is longer than the time for a younger person to do the same thing. Older people are slower in sizing up situations regarding oncoming cars and traffic lights. When they step off the curb, they do so more cautiously and often monitor their movements visually to avoid losing their balance and falling. By watching their feet, they slow down, and some of their attention to the environment is reduced. They then walk across the street at a slow pace, often following younger people.

This slowness of behavior, one of the most distinguishing characteristics of older persons, is due to processes within the central nervous system. These processes involve such factors as the loss of nerve cells, limitation of transmission speed, and a decline in neural excitability. As a result, the elderly are limited to the number of behaviors they can emit per unit of time. This slowness of response with age is found in animals as well.

An elderly person adapts to slowness of response by avoiding situations with unusual time pressures. This avoidance is clearly demonstrated in work situations. Older workers are seldom found in jobs that require continuous activity under paced conditions. An interesting finding, confirmed by several studies, is that the men engaged in moderately heavy work tended to be older than those doing lighter work. The performance of heavy work is usually slower and more self-paced, which in the long run is easier for an older person than light work carried out under pressure.[9]

Most studies show that performance and productivity of older workers are the same or better than those of younger workers in most cases. What older workers lose in speed, they tend to make up in accuracy, experience, and commitment. Contrary to popular opinion, accident rates are usually higher for younger workers than for older workers, which may be explained, in part, by the fact that the older workers exert more caution, take fewer chances, and exercise better judgment on the job. Other research indicates that, in general, older workers have fewer absences because of illness than do younger workers. When older workers do become ill, however, the time off required for recovery tends to be longer than that for younger workers.

The worker over 65, it should be remembered, is a highly select sample of the total population. Workers who could not perform well or who were less skilled or in poor health have left their jobs earlier. Those who continue to work beyond 65 exemplify the survival of the fittest. Birren notes: "If total job behavior is considered, the older worker is sometimes found to be better in comparison with the young worker, particularly if such characteristics as accuracy, absenteeism, and motivation are considered."[10]

Learning

Evidence suggests that under most circumstances the primary capacity to learn undergoes very little change with age. When differences in the ability to learn do appear, they seem to be due more to such problems as perception, attention, motivation, and health than from the ability to learn. Alex Comfort cites an experiment conducted in Australia in which a class of 70-year-olds, with no special motivation, were able to learn German at the same rate as a class of 15-year-olds using the same books and classroom situation.[11] The older pupils made the same grades as the younger ones.

A major problem related to learning is the attitude and expectation of society toward older people. Society expects old people to be incompetent and to fail. Because of this, many older people become anxious in learning situations and avoid any chance of failure by not answering even when they know the correct responses. If they do respond, they proceed cautiously and slowly to minimize error. Many older people accept the negative conception that society has of them. This acceptance in turn undermines their self-confidence and their ability to learn. It is much like a self-fulfilling prophesy. One begins with a false definition of the situation that elicits a new behavior that makes the originally false conception come true.

Creative Productivity

In the early 1950s, Harvey Lehman reported that the outstanding achievements of creative men occurred early in life, before the age of 40 in science, and before the age of 45 in the arts and literature.[12] But his sample included many short-lived persons, which caused the average age of greatest notable achievement to be lower and exaggerated the declines with aging.

Wayne Dennis studied only people who lived to the age of 79 or older and focused on their rates of creative output.[13] He classified their fields of work into three major categories — scholarship, the sciences, and the arts. His work shows that, in almost all the fields, the years between 40 to 49 were either the most productive or only slightly below those that were higher in productivity. In all cases in which the forties were not the

---

There is a wicked inclination in most people to suppose an old man decayed in his intellect. If a young or middle-aged man, when leaving a company, does not recollect where he laid his hat, it is nothing; but if the same inattention is discovered in an old man, people will shrug their shoulders and say, "His memory is going."

— *Samuel Johnson*

Table 7.1 Output of each decade stated as a percentage of the output of the most productive decade, by occupation

			Age decade					
	Number of men	*Number of works*	*20–29*	*30–39*	*40–49*	*50–59*	*60–69*	*70–79*
Scholarship								
Historians	46	615	11	50	76	89	100	84
Philosophers	42	225	14	76	90	82	100	88
Scholars	43	326	26	78	100	100	73	90
Sciences								
Biologists	32	3,456	22	90	100	81	69	55
Botanists	49	1,889	17	67	100	98	100	70
Chemists	24	2,420	45	87	100	80	49	53
Geologists	40	2,672	12	47	81	100	70	53
Inventors	44	616	11	35	51	55	100	65
Mathematicians	36	3,104	43	100	100	95	100	75
Arts								
Architects	44	1,148	24	82	100	84	36	12
Chamber music	35	109	70	100	78	96	87	43
Dramatists	25	803	31	93	100	73	29	9
Librettists	28	164	26	70	100	72	48	12
Novelists	32	494	20	69	64	100	80	24
Opera composers	176	476	26	97	100	50	30	16
Poets	46	402	46	87	100	65	65	40

SOURCE: Wayne Dennis, "Creative Productivity Between the Ages of 20 and 80 Years," *Journal of Gerontology*, 21 (1966), 3. Reprinted with permission of *Journal of Gerontology*.

most productive years (with the exception of chamber music), the highest output occurred at an older age.

In Table 7.1, the decade in which output was the highest is given the value of 100 percent, and the output for all other decades is stated proportionately. In the category of scholarship, productivity remained high in the seventies, while in the sciences there were significant decrements. But the sharpest decline occurred in the arts. For example, between the ages of 70 to 79, dramatists produced only 9 percent as much as in their years of highest output. On the other hand, the output of scholars for that decade was 90 percent of their peak rate. Overall, it appears that productivity does not necessarily decline as one ages, but tends to vary according to the type of creative activity involved. In some fields, productivity remains high into the sixties, seventies, and beyond.

Adaptation and Maladaptation to Aging

Though we have been discussing physiological and psychological changes that occur with aging separately, the two are closely interrelated. Aging is a process that involves not only physiological and psychological factors but social factors as well. All are interdependent. Physical changes affect social behavior, while at the same time social behavior influences physical condition. As Robert Butler and Myrna Lewis emphasize:

> An elderly person who is socially lonely may not eat well and therefore may develop physical symptoms of malnourishment, which in turn cloud intellectual functioning. Hearing loss can lead to a suspiciousness that irritates people and causes them to shun the person's company, leaving him [or her] isolated. A widower, grieving the loss of his wife, may develop psychosomatic symptoms and lose his job.[14]

The physical, psychological, and social changes that accompany aging often place the older person under stress. While some people tend to tolerate changes with minimal stress, changes can have a devastating effect on others. Generally, stress is much harder on older persons because they do not have the physical resiliency and the reserve capacity of a younger person. Consequently, they require a longer recovery time from a stressful situation.

T. S. Holmes and T. H. Holmes have postulated that any type of

---

Some Examples of Creativity in Old Age

Sophocles wrote *Oedipus Rex* at 75.

Goethe completed the last part of *Faust* shortly before he died at 83.

Freud wrote *Moses and Monotheism* at age 83.

Verdi completed the opera *Falstaff* at 80.

Picasso painted until his death at 91.

Pablo Casals continued to play, conduct, and teach until his death at 96.

Tolstoy wrote *Resurrection* at age 71.

Grandma Moses painted until she died at 101.

---

change, whether it is pleasant or unpleasant, can be stressful and make a person more susceptible to disease.[15] Studies have shown the death rate of widows and widowers is higher during the first year of bereavement than at any other time. W. D. Rees and S. G. Lutkins in their study of 4,486 widowers, 55 years of age and older, found that 213 died within the first six months of bereavement.[16] This represents a 40 percent higher mortality rate than would be normally expected for men of that age.

To evaluate empirically how stress from major changes in one's daily life may affect susceptibility to an illness or precede the onset of disease, Thomas Holmes and Richard Rahe developed "The Social Readjustment Rating Scale."[17] They ranked 43 commonly occurring life events that cause stress and assigned mean values to them to coincide with the impact of each specific event on one's life. The items range from the death of a spouse, with a mean value of 100, to a minor traffic violation, with a value of 11 (Table 7.2). Though the death of a spouse carries the highest mean value, other stressful experiences likely in the life of an older person rate fairly high. For example, death of a close family member rates 63; personal injury or illness, 53; retirement, 45; change in financial state, 38; death of a close friend, 37; and change in living conditions, 23. According to the mean values Holmes and Rahe assigned to life events, some of the most stressful changes in life occur in old age and at a time when stress can have the most adverse effect.

Most older people, then, must constantly adapt to changes within themselves as well as to changes in their social world. Many changes result from loss in one form or another and place great stress on emotions. They may be physiological or psychological losses, such as losses in sensory acuities, decline in physical health and strength, changes in bodily appearance, or a slowing down in reaction time. Or they may be social or extrinsic losses, such as loss of significant others, a decline in standard of living, and losses of prestige, occupational status, and social roles.

Adaptation to these losses, along with the problems and crises that accompany them, are a main part of the tasks that confront the elderly. But how does one adapt to these losses? Eric Pfeiffer notes that adaptation involves replacing some social losses with new relationships, acquiring new roles to take the place of those relinquished, and retraining lost capacities, such as receiving speech or physical therapy after a stroke.[18]

Besides adapting to loss, Pfeiffer suggests another task facing older people: the life or identity review. This is characterized by looking back at one's life and reassessing and evaluating successes and failures, resolving conflicts, and seeking to delineate a final identity that may psychologically prepare one for death. While to some the life review may be one of regret, in which they feel that they have wasted their

Table 7.2 The social readjustment rating scale

Rank	Life event	Mean value
1	Death of spouse	100
2	Divorce	73
3	Marital separation	65
4	Jail term	63
5	Death of close family member	63
6	Personal injury or illness	53
7	Marriage	50
8	Fired at work	47
9	Marital reconciliation	45
10	Retirement	45
11	Change in health of family member	44
12	Pregnancy	40
13	Sex difficulties	39
14	Gain of new family member	39
15	Business readjustment	39
16	Change in financial state	38
17	Death of a close friend	37
18	Change to different line of work	36
19	Change in number of arguments with spouse	35
20	Mortgage over $10,000	31
21	Foreclosure of mortgage or loan	30
22	Change in responsibilities at work	29
23	Son or daughter leaving home	29
24	Trouble with in-laws	29
25	Outstanding personal achievement	28
26	Wife begin or stop work	26
27	Begin or end school	26
28	Change in living conditions	25
29	Revision of personal habits	24
30	Trouble with boss	23
31	Change in work hours or conditions	20
32	Change in residence	20
33	Change in schools	20
34	Change in recreation	19
35	Change in church activities	19
36	Change in social activities	18
37	Mortgage or loan less than $10,000	17
38	Change in sleeping habits	16
39	Change in number of family get-togethers	15
40	Change in eating habits	15
41	Vacation	13
42	Christmas	12
43	Minor violations of the law	11

SOURCE: Reprinted with permission from *Journal of Psychosomatic Research*, 11 (1967), 216, Thomas H. Holmes and Richard Rahe, ''The Social Readjustment Rating Scale.'' Copyright 1967 Pergamon Press, Ltd.

lives, to others it can give satisfaction, significance, and meaning to their lives. Robert Butler and Myrna Lewis indicate this:

> Some of the positive results of reviewing one's life can be a righting of old wrongs, making up with enemies, coming to acceptance of mortal life, a sense of serenity, pride in accomplishment, and feeling of having done one's best. It gives people an opportunity to decide what to do with the time left to them and work out emotional and material legacies. People become ready but in no hurry to die. Possibly the qualities of serenity, philosophical development, and wisdom observable in some older people reflect a state of resolution of their life conflicts.[19]

All persons at one time or another use various defense mechanisms to respond to inner conflicts and frustrations. With age, they continue to use some of the adaptive techniques of earlier years, or may add some new ones. The following discussion includes some defense mechanism (outlined by Butler and Lewis) most often utilized by older people to respond to frustrating situations and the anxieties generated by social and physical losses.

1. One type of adaptation is *denial*. Many elderly people refuse to accept the fact that they are old. They continue to think of themselves as middle-aged or younger. Denial of old age and death manifests itself in what Butler and Lewis refer to as the "Peter Pan" syndrome, an older person pretending to be young.

2. Another adaptive mechanism is *projection*, in which some older persons, in an effort to relieve their anxieties, attribute their own undesirable feelings and attitudes to others. They may accuse merchants of cheating them, neighbors of stealing from them, or their children of neglecting them. Some of their complaints may be legitimate, but many are not. Nevertheless, projection does occur, and at times older persons may manifest fears and suspicions to the point of being paranoid.

3. Still another defense mechanism is *displacement*. Older persons may adjust to situations by shifting the blame from the real causes of difficulties to other persons, objects, or situations. For example, an older person may blame physical decline on the fact that "things are not the same today as they used to be," or "the terrible state that the nation or the world is in."

4. Adaptive mechanisms sometimes take the form of *counterphobia*. Counterphobia occurs when individuals ignore reality and face danger to try to overcome their limitations through sheer will power. For example, an elderly man who is experiencing dizzy spells may climb a ladder to paint his house. Or an elderly woman may ignore her doctor's advice.

A 69-year-old woman hospitalized with a severe heart attack, refused to face reality and accept the doctor's diagnosis. She steadfastly maintained that it was only an attack of indigestion. The woman continued to climb the three flights of stairs to her apartment and do all of the heavy household chores.

5. A person may adapt to a situation by the technique of *selective memory*. It is a common belief that when elderly people can remember distant events with greater clarity than recent events, this is a sign of a senile brain disorder or cerebral arteriosclerosis. But often there may be a psychological, instead of a physical, basis for this. Many older persons try to forget unhappy and painful present situations and events by talking about the past when they were happier and more content. Selective memory also occurs when older people screen out the unpleasant events of the past, often referring to the past as the "good old days." Actually a more accurate description would probably be the "good and bad old days."[20]

Emotional and Mental Disorders

Sometimes when losses occur in rapid succession in the life of an older person, the emotional stress becomes too great and the individual may find that the adaptive mechanisms previously used in coping with situations are no longer adequate. This lack of ability to cope may result in a serious mental disorder. Mental disorders in later life fall into two major categories: *functional disorders*, which have an emotional origin; and *organic disorders*, which have a physical basis. Determining the incidence of mental disorders among the older population is difficult because of the lack of reliable statistics. It has been estimated that approximately 15 percent of the older population, or about one in six, suffers from some type of psychological disturbance.

There are many popular misconceptions about the term *senility*. The public believes that as one ages, senility is more or less inevitable. When an older person appears forgetful or rambles on during a conversation, people are likely to assume that the person is senile. Middle-aged and older people are constantly worrying that they may become senile or that others will label them as such. Just what exactly is senility? *Senility* is commonly used by the medical profession and by laypersons to describe the many varied conditions and behaviors of older people, such as confusion, forgetfulness, disturbed concentration, and withdrawal. *Senility* is such a catch-all term that it has lost much of its meaning. The following list of some physical, psychological, and social factors that may lead to senility will illustrate this point: arteriosclerosis, brain disease, radiation, worry, anemia, malnutrition, drugs, alcoholism, loneliness, and bereavement.

Most people become old without suffering brain damage. Not everyone who is bereaved or lonely develops a mental disorder. Senility, then, is not a normal, inevitable accompaniment of aging.[21]

Depression

The most frequent functional disorder of old age is depression. It occurs with varying degrees of intensity and duration. Some periods of depression last for only a few minutes, while others may last for several days or longer. Depressive periods are often a pathological response to the loss of a significant person or object. Guilt, unresolved grief, anger, and loneliness may be the underlying causes for depressive reactions. Psychological characteristics of depression include discouragement, a sense of uselessness, a loss of self-esteem, apathy, and pessimism about the present and future. Depression can interfere with thought processes and can slow down speech and physical movements. Such symptoms as

Depression is a frequent disorder of later life. It is primarily a pathological response to significant losses. (Black Star. Charles Moore—Photographer)

loss of appetite, insomnia, and fatigue frequently accompany depression.

Suicide

Severe depression is the most common cause of suicide. The suicide rate for the white male is highest of any group; this is true throughout the life span, and the rate steadily increases with age (Table 7.3). In the United States, suicide rates for white males 65 years of age and over are nearly five times higher than the rates for white elderly females. The reason

Table 7.3 Suicide rates in the United States (per 100,000), by age, sex, and race, 1976

Age range	White males	White females	Nonwhite males	Nonwhite females
5–14	0.7	0.2	0.3	0.4
15–24	19.2	4.9	14.7	4.0
25–34	23.7	8.6	22.8	6.5
35–44	23.6	11.0	16.8	4.7
45–54	27.7	13.8	13.5	4.3
55–64	31.6	12.1	12.3	2.8
65 and over	39.7	8.3	14.5	3.2

SOURCE: U.S. Bureau of the Census, *Statistical Abstract of the United States: 1978*, U.S. Government Printing Office, Washington, D.C., 1978, p. 183.

why older men are more prone to commit suicide is not clear. Depression is usually given as the main reason, but this state evidently occurs as frequently among older women. Perhaps, decline in status and the loss of physical capacity, employment, and income are more difficult for the older male to bear than for the female. Also, women are less successful in their suicide attempts than are men, and many women expect or want to be stopped in the act. Men are more violent in their attempts and leave little doubt about their intention.

Suicide rates are lower among blacks and other minority groups than among whites. One tentative explanation is that the minority aged have long been accustomed to lesser status, greater dependency, and more poverty; thus, they do not suffer such drastic changes in old age as most whites do. Though depression is the reason given for the majority of suicides, the next largest suicide groups include those who have used alcohol excessively and those who have organic brain syndromes. Only a small percentage of suicides suffer from an untreatable terminal illness.

The suicide rate for older persons is probably much higher than the statistics show. Many older people commit suicide by slow, indirect means such as not eating, refusing medication, or not seeking needed medical help. Such suicides never make the official statistics.

One elderly man who was confined to a wheel chair became deeply depressed because of his dependent state and the fact that he was a burden to his wife. He lost all will to live and one day he suddenly stopped eating. Despite the pleadings of his wife and his adult children, he stubbornly refused all food. Within a short time he was dead.

Personality and Adaptation

Personality markedly influences how a person adapts to aging. Different personality types age differently. A study done by Suzanne Reichard, Florine Livson, and Paul Petersen investigated types of personalities of 87 elderly men.[22] The researchers outlined three types that adapted well to aging and two types that adapted poorly. The first group that adapted well was identified as the "mature": they felt that their lives had been rewarding, and they faced aging without regret. These men continued to participate in many satisfying activities and social relationships, and moved easily into aging and made the most of it. A second group, the "rocking-chair men," also adapted successfully to aging, but in another way: they welcomed the opportunity to be free of responsibilities and were content to take it easy. The third group that adapted well was called the "armored"; they had strong defenses against growing old, and fought off the fear of aging by staying active and keeping busy. To them, activity was a compulsion instead of a source of enjoyment.

Among the poorly adapting men were two groups: the "angry men" and the "self-haters." The angry men felt that they had failed in life and blamed others for their failures; they found aging difficult. The self-haters looked back on their lives with much regret, and they blamed themselves, instead of others, for their misfortunes and failures. These men felt depressed, worthless, and inferior.

Reichard and her associates note that the histories of both the armored and rocking-chair types suggest that their personalities showed very little change throughout their lives. Furthermore, the rocking-chair type shows that disengagement can be a satisfactory adaptation for some older people, although the popularly accepted view is that people who are the happiest continue to maintain a high level of activity. Also, the researchers found that the poor adaptations made by the angry men and self-haters were a continuation of lifelong personality problems. By the same token, the mature group suggests that the same factors that led to a good adaptation in the earlier years continue to exert their influence in the later years.

Another study relating personality type and adaptation to aging was done by Bernice Neugarten and her associates.[23] They studied 59 men and women aged 70–79 and made assessments in three areas: personality type, amount of role activity, and degree of life satisfaction. From these data they derived four major personality types, which they called the "integrated," the "defended," the "passive dependent," and the "unintegrated." These four groups were then further divided into patterns.

The first type, the integrated, was composed of persons who functioned well, whose abilities had not declined, and who had feelings of high regard for themselves. All scored high in life satisfaction, they were in control of their impulses, they were flexible and mature. Three patterns of aging emerged from this type. Those in the pattern called the "reorganizers" engaged in a wide variety of activities and tried to keep active. As one activity was lost, they found another to replace it. Another pattern was the "focused"; this group was selective in their activities and concentrated only on a few activities that were important to them. The third pattern was the "disengaged," made up of persons who had voluntarily moved away from many of their social contacts and role commitments. Their approach to aging was one of calmness, contentment, and withdrawal. They epitomized the rocking-chair type of aging.

The second major type of personality was the armored or the defended. These persons were ambitious, striving, and oriented toward success and achievement, and they maintained strong defenses against aging. This group was divided into two patterns of aging: the "holding-on" and the "constricted." The holding-on pattern consisted of persons who embodied the "I'll die with my boots on" philosophy. To them old age was a threat, and they believed that keeping busy would help ward off anxieties about aging. Their life satisfaction ranged from medium to high. The second pattern, constricted, included people who tried to defend themselves against aging by limiting their social contacts and conserving their energies to fend off "what they seem to regard as imminent collapse."[24] Their life satisfaction was high to medium.

The third type of personality, the passive dependent, yielded two patterns of aging. The "succorance-seeking" included those persons who were very dependent on others for emotional support and managed well as long as they had one or two persons to lean on. The second pattern, the "apathetic," was composed of very passive and submissive individuals who were low in role activity.

The last type, the unintegrated personality, showed a "disorganized" pattern of aging and consisted of persons who suffered deterioration in their thought processes and experienced loss of control over their emotions. They barely managed to maintain themselves in their communities. Table 7.4 gives a summary of the personality types that we have been discussing.

Neugarten and her associates conclude that personality type is the central factor in predicting which individuals will age successfully and which ones will not. These eight patterns are probably predictable and well established by middle age. The key concept appears to be adaptation. Furthermore, they note that there are no dramatic changes or sharp discontinuities of personality with age, but rather a trend toward increasing consistency. In other words, unhappy, complaining middle-aged people are likely to become unhappy, complaining old people. And contrary to what many believe, old people do not get grouchy; grouchy people get old.

Table 7.4 Personality patterns in aging

Personality type	Characteristics of the type	Role activity	Life satisfaction
1. Integrated	Well-adjusted persons with high self-regard, mature; maintain comfortable degree of control over life's impulses		
a. Reorganizer	Competent people, engaged in many activities, who substitute new activities for lost ones	High	High
b. Focused	Persons selective in their activities and who concentrate on one or two roles	Medium	High
c. Disengaged	Those who voluntarily move away from role commitments and social relations; they are calm, contented, and withdrawn	Low	High
2. Armored-Defended	Striving and ambitious persons with high defenses against anxieties associated with aging		
a. Holding-on	Those who try to maintain patterns of middle age as long as possible; to them old age is a threat	High or medium	High
b. Constricted	Persons who defend themselves against aging by limiting their social contacts and trying to conserve their energies	Low or medium	High or medium
3. Passive-Dependent			
a. Succorance-seeking	Those people who are dependent on others for emotional support	High or medium	High or medium
b. Apathetic	Persons who are passive and submissive	Low	Medium or low
4. Unintegrated			
a. Disorganized	Persons with defects in psychological functions	Low	Medium or low

SOURCE: Adapted from Bernice L. Neugarten, Robert J. Havighurst, and Sheldon S. Tobin, "Personality and Patterns of Aging," in *Middle Age and Aging*, ed. Bernice L. Neugarten, The University of Chicago Press, Chicago, 1968, pp. 173–177.

The Positive Side of Aging

Most research and writing about the elderly appears to concentrate on the negative aspects of aging, stressing mental and physical decline, with little or no attention being given to the positive side of growing old. In fact, having just read this sentence, you are probably asking yourself whether there are any positive aspects to aging. We need to change the popular, negative concept of aging and achieve a more balanced view of both its positive and negative aspects.

Among the plus factors of later maturity is, first of all, an increase in general knowledge. The longer a person lives, the more facts and information that person is likely to accumulate. As we pointed out earlier, people know more words and have a larger vocabulary when they get older.

Secondly, through experience a person develops better judgment and what is frequently referred to as wisdom. With maturity, an individual can meet new situations with greater deliberation and poise, which are the basis of good judgment. Busse and Pfeiffer note that "wisdom and judgment . . . come to full flower in old age, at least in some [persons]. Certain qualities, such as statesmanship, seem to be found more often in those of advanced years."[25] Also an older person is likely to have a higher level of occupational skill; this has been gained through long years of experience and practice, which no young person can possess.

Learning becomes more efficient with age. Young people deal with bits and pieces of information because they have not acquired the filing system that older people possess because of their ability to assimilate and organize knowledge into conceptual compartments. Birren explains:

> With maturation comes a greater conceptual grasp so that we can size up the situation and then look to the relevant items in our store. This is what I call the race between the chunks and the bits. While younger people, say those between 18 and 22, can process more bits per second, and even though by age sixty the number may be halved, the older person may process bigger chunks. The race may go to the tortoise because he is chunking, and not to the hare because he is just bitting along.[26]

With age, a person has achieved a real identity and is a "completed" being. The young person is still trying to find out who he or she is and to establish a sense of identity. With age, many potentials of earlier years have been realized: an established place in an occupation, in a family, with friends, and in a community. The individual has become a known entity. Only through the passage of time does one become a "real person"; time also makes one a more interesting person because over the years an individual has seen many things, met many people, and

I must get into a topic . . . that I think has been overlooked by many, and it is easy to see why. I want to discuss the advantages of growing old. For one thing, it is a great satisfaction to be around fewer and fewer people who can say "You are too young to remember . . ." Or "That was before your time." Or "When I was your age . . ." I myself now know the pleasure of saying such things, effectively putting down the young, including those who are only in their early sixties.

SOURCE: Richard Armour, *Going Like Sixty: A Light-hearted Look at the Later Years,* McGraw-Hill, New York, 1974, p. 49.

had many experiences. These give a person more to talk about and make the person more interesting to talk to.[27]

Another positive consequence of aging is the increase in personal freedom. After retirement, a person's time is no longer structured around an eight-hour working day. A person becomes his or her own boss. As children have reached adulthood, the parents' responsibilities are considerably diminished. Though income is likely to be less, obligations are fewer. Although the elderly have lost many roles at this point in the life cycle, they have gained greater freedom and an opportunity to do as they please.[28]

Lastly, Butler notes that older people experience a personal sense of the life cycle, something that younger people cannot have. "An inner sense of the life cycle . . . produces a profound awareness of change and evolution . . . and therefore a profound but nonmorbid realization of the precious and limited quantity of life. For older people it is not the same as 'feeling old'; it is instead a deep understanding of what it means to be human."[29]

Summary

1. There are many theories regarding why people age. These theories fall primarily into three major categories: genetic, nongenetic, and physiological. The two theories that seem to hold the greatest promise are the cross-linking and autoimmune theories.

2. Aging varies not only among persons but also within a person. Different systems of the body age at different rates. Though many physiological changes occur as one ages, not all of these changes happen to everyone or in the same degree. With advancing age, the skin loses some of its elasticity and begins to wrinkle; the hair is likely to gray and begin to thin; bones become porous and brittle; and muscle strength declines.

3. As one ages, the heart pumps less blood and the lungs take in less air. There is a decrease in the production of digestive juices in the intestines, and the filtering rate of the kidneys is often reduced by half. After menopause, there is an atrophy of the female reproductive organs.

4. Changes also occur in sensory acuities with age. Farsightedness is common, as are cataracts. Hearing ability declines with a gradual loss of the ability to hear high frequencies. Although some researchers concur that the senses of smell and taste diminish, the evidence is not conclusive.

5. With age there is little change in mental ability. While most older workers do not do well in fast-paced tasks — a distinguishing characteristic of aging being the slowness of behavior — in other ways their performance and productivity is equal to, or better than younger workers. Under most circumstances the ability to learn does not change with age. Studies focusing on creative productivity in old age reveal that, in general, there is not necessarily a decline with aging. Whether there is a decline depends on what types of creative activity are involved.

6. Physiological, psychological, and sociological aspects of aging are closely interrelated. Many changes in later years result from physical, psychological, or social losses. Adapting to these losses and to the stresses that accompany them is a major task for older people. Some adaptive mechanisms often employed by older people to respond to losses and frustrating situations include: denial, projection, displacement, counterphobia, and selective memory.

7. Mental disorders in later life fall into two major categories: functional and organic. Senility is not a normal, inevitable consequence of aging. The most common functional disorder of old age is depression; severe depression may often lead to suicide. Suicide rates for older white males are the highest of any age group in the population.

8. How one adapts to aging depends to a great extent on his or her personality. Reichard and her associates studied a group of elderly men and found three types of personalities that aged well: the mature, the rocking-chair men, and the armored type. Two types aged poorly: the angry men, and the self-haters. Neugarten and her associates, studying both men and women, derived eight patterns of aging: reorganizers, focused, disengaged, holding-on, constricted, succorance-seeking, apathetic, and disorganized. They concluded that there is no sharp change in personality with age, but instead an increasing consistency.

9. Most research with older people concentrates only on the negative aspects of aging. Some more positive aspects of aging include: an increase in general knowledge, judgment, wisdom, skill, and more efficiency in learning. With age, one has established a real identity, and experiences a personal sense of the life cycle.

Notes

1. Takashi Makinodan, in *The Handbook of the Biology of Aging*, ed. Caleb B. Finch and Leonard Hayflick, Van Nostrand Reinhold, New York, 1977, pp. 401–402.

2. Leonard Hayflick, "The Limited in Vitro Lifetime of Human Diploid Cell Strains," *Experimental Cell Research*, 37 (1965), 614–636.

3. David Wechsler, *The Measurement and Appraisal of Adult Intelligence*, Williams & Wilkins, Baltimore, 1958.

4. K. Warner Schaie, "Age Changes in Adult Intelligence," in *Aging: Scientific Perspectives and Social Issues,* ed. Diana S. Woodruff and James E. Birren, D. Van Nostrand, New York, 1975, pp. 111–124.

5. Ibid., p. 120.

6. Carl Eisdorfer, "Intelligence and Cognition in the Aged," in *Behavior and Adaptation in Late Life,* ed. Ewald W. Busse and Eric Pfeiffer, Little, Brown, Boston, 1977, p. 217.

7. Ibid.

8. James E. Birren, "Aging: The Psychologist's Perspective," in *Aging: Prospects and Issues,* ed. Richard H. Davis, Ethel Percy Andrus Gerontology Center, University of Southern California, 1976, p. 17.

9. A. T. Welford, "Motor Performance," in *Handbook of the Psychology of Aging,* ed. James E. Birren and K. Warner Schaie, Van Nostrand Reinhold, New York, 1977, p. 488.

10. James E. Birren, *The Psychology of Aging,* Prentice-Hall, Englewood Cliffs, N.J., 1964, p. 143.

11. Alex Comfort, *A Good Age,* Crown, New York, 1976, p. 120.

12. Harvey C. Lehman, *Age and Achievement,* Princeton University Press, Princeton, N.J., 1953.

13. Wayne Dennis, "Creative Productivity Between the Ages of 20 and 80 Years," *Journal of Gerontology,* 21 (1966), 1–8.

14. Robert N. Butler and Myrna I. Lewis, *Aging and Mental Health,* C. V. Mosby, St. Louis, Mo., 1977, p. 24.

15. T. Stephenson Holmes and Thomas H. Holmes, "Short-term Intrusions into the Life Style Routine," *Journal of Psychosomatic Research,* 14 (1970), 121–132.

16. W. D. Rees and S. G. Lutkins, "Mortality and Bereavement," *British Medical Journal,* 4 (1967), 13–16.

17. Thomas H. Holmes and Richard H. Rahe, "The Social Readjustment Rating Scale," *Journal of Psychosomatic Research,* 11 (1967), 213–218.

18. Eric Pfeiffer, "Psychopathology and Social Pathology," in *Handbook of the Psychology of Aging,* ed. James Birren and K. Warner Schaie, Van Nostrand Reinhold, New York, 1977, p. 651.

19. Butler and Lewis, *Aging and Mental Health,* p. 50.

20. Ibid., pp. 45–47.

21. See Robert N. Butler, *Why Survive? Being Old in America,* Harper & Row, New York, 1975, esp. chap. 8, "They Are Only Senile."

22. Suzanne Reichard, Florine Livson, and Paul G. Petersen, *Aging and Personality,* John Wiley, New York, 1962, pp. 170–172.

23. Bernice L. Neugarten, Robert J. Havighurst, and Sheldon S. Tobin, "Personality and Patterns of Aging," in *Middle Age and Aging,* ed. Bernice L. Neugarten, The University of Chicago Press, Chicago, 1968, pp. 173–177.

24. Ibid., p. 176.

25. Ewald W. Busse and Eric Pfeiffer, "Functional Psychiatric Disorders in Old

Age," in *Behavior and Adaptation in Late Life,* eds. Ewald W. Busse and Eric Pfeiffer, Little, Brown, Boston, 1977, p. 158.

26. Birren, "The Psychologist's Perspective," p. 18.

27. Robert Tyson, "Have You Discovered the Pluses of Being Over 30?" *Home and Garden,* March 1975, pp. 75, 156.

28. Vern L. Bengtson and Ron C. Manuel, "The Sociology of Aging, in *Aging: Prospects and Issues,* ed. Richard H. Davis, Ethel Percy Andrus Gerontology Center, University of Southern California, 1976, pp. 50–51.

29. Butler and Lewis, *Aging and Mental Health,* p. 138. For some additional advantages of aging, see Erdman Palmore, "Advantages of Aging," *The Gerontologist,* 19, no. 2 (1979), 220–223.

For Further Study

Birren, James E. *The Psychology of Aging.* Prentice-Hall, Englewood Cliffs, N.J., 1964. Deals with the social and physiological as well as the psychological changes that take place as one ages.

Butler, Robert N., and Myrna I. Lewis. *Aging and Mental Health.* C. V. Mosby, St. Louis, Mo., 1973. Emphasizes the emotional and mental disorders of old age and the principles that apply in their treatment and prevention.

Kart, Cary S., Eileen S. Metress, and James F. Metress. *Aging and Health: Biologic and Social Perspectives.* Addison-Wesley, Reading, Mass., 1978. Chapters 3 to 10 deal with the biomedical changes associated with the various body systems as they age.

Neugarten, Bernice L., ed. *Personality in Middle and Late Life.* Atherton Press, New York, 1964. A book of readings with emphasis on the sociological and psychological processes that occur as one moves from middle age into old age.

Riley, Matilda, and Anne Foner. *Aging and Society.* Vol. 1: An Inventory of Research Findings. Russell Sage Foundation, New York, 1968. See Parts 2 and 3 for a good condensation of research findings on the physical and behavioral changes that occur with age.

Rockstein, Morris, and Marvin Sussman. *Biology of Aging.* Wadsworth, Belmont, Calif., 1979. A good introduction to the physiological changes that occur with the aging process.

Working with Older People: Biological, Psychological, and Sociological Aspects of Aging, vol. 2. U.S. Government Printing Office, Washington, D.C., 1972. Clear, concise resource materials for those who work with the elderly.

III

Social Groups and Groupings

8

Social Groups and
the Elderly

For nearly five years, Tommy Seddon, a former 61-year-old machinist in Manchester, England, was shunned by his fellow workers because he refused to join a one-day union walk-out. After that, not one of his co-workers would talk to him. Commenting on the wall of silence, Seddon said: "It upset me at first but it doesn't hurt now. I seem to have found a strength to endure the isolation just as long as it is imposed upon me. Initially, it did come hard. These were the men that I drank with, talked to, laughed with." But all that ended after the strike. Seddon felt that it would have been harder if he had not known that he was right. He said that the work stoppage was politically motivated and that he could not be a party to it. Tommy Seddon's ostracism by his work group ended when his and his co-workers' jobs were eliminated in a factory cutback.[1]

Whether extended isolation is social, as in Tommy's case, or physical, such as solitary confinement in a prison cell, for most people it is intolerable. Human beings are social animals and as such are interdependent on one another. Our interaction with others is necessary for our survival and the satisfaction of our needs.

Social Groups and Social Categories

We spend our lives in the company of others and in the context of such groups as the family, peer groups, occupational groups, religious groups, and the community. Sociologists define a *group* as two or more people who interact with one another in a standardized pattern and who share a sense of common identity. An individual who is a member of a group has a sense of belonging to it. By the same token, the individual belongs to a group when others who consider themselves members accept that individual as part of the group.

People who have some characteristic in common, such as the same occupation, hobby, or age, do not constitute a social group; they are best classified as a *social category*. But if members of a social category begin to interact and develop a sense of identification with one another, then the category may be transformed into a group. One task of the sociologist is to study the conditions under which a category becomes a group. Leonard Broom and Phillip Selznick note:

> The aged are a significant social category, and there is considerable interest today in the kinds of groups older people are likely to form or accept. Is there an old-age style of life that can be the natural basis for separate housing? Or do older people feel little sense of identity with each other despite their similar age and dependency? There have been some old-age political pressure groups, such as the Townsend movement of the 1930s. Should more and increasingly powerful groups of this sort be expected as the number of older people in the population rises? What effect would this have on the political order? These questions indicate the problems raised when the group potential of a social category is explored.[2]

Arnold Rose argues that older Americans are now in the process of changing from a category to a group.[3] He maintains that this is due to the group consciousness forming among those older people who are beginning to feel a sense of positive identification with other elderly people and who see themselves as members of an aging group. Rose cites the growing number of senior citizen centers and golden age clubs as evidence of this trend. Such clubs and organizations give the elderly a place to interact almost exclusively with persons their own age. Through their common concern with issues and problems that affect older people comes a sense of group identification. This occurs when the elderly begin to see their problems, not on an individual basis, but from the perspective of the group. Rose states:

> For the growing minority that has reacted against the negative self-conception characteristic of the aging in our society and has seen the problems of aging in a group context, there are all the signs of group identification. There is a desire to associate with fellow-agers, especially in formal associations, and to exclude younger adults from these associations. There are expressions of group pride. . . . With this group pride has come self-acceptance as a member of an esteemed group. . . . There are manifestations of a feeling of resentment at "the way older people are being mistreated," and indications of their taking social action to remove the sources of their resentment. There are the signs of group-identification that previous sociological studies have found in ethnic minority groups.[4]

Rose not only argues that the elderly are in the process of being transformed from a social category into a group, but he sees a subculture of the aging also developing. He points out that the elderly tend to interact more with one another as they grow older, and less with younger persons, because of the common interests and concerns that the elderly share, and, to some extent, because they are excluded from interacting with other age groups. This segregation results in the development of an aging subculture, similar to the adolescent subculture in our society. A *subculture,* though part of the total culture, usually contains some of its own distinctive lifestyles, values, norms, and language. For example, a subculture based on age, such as the adolescent one in our society, has its own special clothing, style of life, music, behavior, and vocabulary. Subcultures may also be based on occupations, ethnic groups, social classes, or regions.

Rose claims that certain demographic and social trends, favorable for the emergence of an aging subculture, are occurring. These trends include: (1) the growing number and proportion of older people; (2) the trend toward self-segregating retirement communities; (3) the institutionalization of retirement, which has resulted in a decreased amount of interaction with younger workers; (4) the increasing number of older people with more money, education, and leisure time; and (5) the emergence of organizations and groups that are exclusively for older people.

Gordon Bultena tested two hypotheses drawn from Rose's theory of an emergent aging subculture through data obtained from interviews with 434 retired men in Wisconsin.[5] The first hypothesis is that older people interact more with each other than with the younger generation; the second is that advancing age is associated with increased social ties among one's age peers in family, kinship, and community groups. The first hypothesis is supported by his findings. The second hypothesis, that social ties with one's age group increase with age, is not supported by the data. Instead, he found that with advancing age there tends to be a decreased amount of social interaction with one's age peers. "The respondents aged eighty and older had both a greater number of contacts with younger persons and a higher proportion of their total interaction within the younger age categories than did their counterparts aged sixty-five to seventy-nine years."[6]

The number of clubs and organizations that cater exclusively to older people must increase in order for an aging subculture to develop. Yet Bultena and other researchers have found that the proportion of older persons participating in formal groups declines with age. Furthermore, Rose notes that "the aging subculture is a general one that cuts across other subcultures — those based on occupation, religion, sex, and possibly even ethnic identification."[7] But there is little evidence of this taking place. James Manney reports that no investigator so far has found any significant interaction among the elderly that crosses social class lines.[8]

Reference Groups

People may be influenced not only by the groups to which they belong, but also by groups to which they do not belong. Any group or social category that we use as a standard of comparison and by which we measure our accomplishments and failures is called a *reference group*. Such groups or categories may include friends, immediate family members, occupational group, or social class. A reference group may also provide a person with a set of norms, attitudes, and values. For example, a person who aspires to move ahead socially may begin to pattern behavior after a higher status group and acquire its tastes.

Gordon Bultena and Edward Powers state that the aged as yet have no reference groups to provide a specific set of age norms;[9] however, they feel that the social category of the aged constitutes an important reference group to which the elderly can compare themselves. The fact that our society has many negative stereotypes regarding the aged as a social category may work to the advantage of the elderly in one respect: when older people make comparisons of their personal situation, they are likely to judge themselves against these negative stereotypes and feel that their personal situation is not different from, or not as bad as that of other elderly.

In a study of 235 older people in Iowa, Bultena and Powers sought to determine the relationship between reference-group comparisons and the adjustment made to aging.[10] Their data indicates that a large majority of the respondents felt that they were in a comparable or better position than others their age regarding health, income, physical mobility, and social interaction. Also, the respondents who assessed themselves favorably in comparison with others tended to have high levels of life satisfaction and morale.

With advancing age, the elderly lose friends along with reference groups. Vern Bengtson and Ron Manuel recount the following incident:

> So, what happens when the individual reaches the age of seventy and his friends begin to die? One of the authors once interviewed a man who had just celebrated his 104th birthday. He said as he talked about the problems of growing old, "You know, I haven't had a friend since I was 77. That's when my last friend died." It is difficult to imagine living for 27 years without someone who is regarded as a friend! This represents not only loss of a confidant, of contact with an intimate, but also loss of reference group. To what group can this man who is 104 years old refer so he can judge the appropriateness of his behavior, or reinforce his identity? Many older people judge themselves by the standards of middle age, a criterion by which they invariably are at a disadvantage.[11]

Primary and Secondary Groups

Another approach to analyzing groups is to look at the type of relationship that exists between members. A group in which the members have an intimate, personal relationship is called a *primary group*. In a primary group — because communication is deep, free, and extensive — individuals come to know all facets of one another — their personality, their aspirations, desires, fears, and often their innermost thoughts. Primary relationships are valued solely for themselves and are not considered as a means to some specific end. Relationships in a primary group are "personal, spontaneous, sentimental, and inclusive."[12]

Primary groups are of necessity small in size. It is not possible for large numbers of people to interact on a close, intimate basis. For intimacy to arise and be maintained, face-to-face contact is usually necessary and so is the persistence of the group relationship over time. Examples of primary groups include the family, a circle of close friends, and a work team.

Primary groups fulfill many functions for the individual, including the following:

1. *Primary groups help to support and sustain the individual.* All human beings need the emotional support and intimate companionship of others. Lowenthal and Haven, cited earlier, have shown that older people who have one or more primary relationships seem to be happier and in better mental health than those without confidants. The presence of intimate relationships is essential to personal adjustment and emotional sustenance. They serve as a buffer against the age-linked losses of retirement and widowhood. Zena Blau suggests that close friendships are an effective way to help forestall demoralization in old age.[13]

2. *Primary groups function as important instruments of social control.* Many studies illustrate this fact. One of the most famous was the bank-wiring room study conducted at the Hawthorne plant of Western Electric Company in the early 1930s. The bank-wiring room group consisted of 14 men whose job was to wire telephone switchboards. In this group the workers evolved their own production norm as to what they considered to be a "fair day's work" — two completed equipments per man. If a man was working too fast and it was felt he might go over his quota, he was ridiculed and called a "ratebuster" or a "speed king." By the same token, if a man was working too slow and producing too little, he was called a "chiseler." Ridicule was not the only penalty for violating the production norm. Sometimes when a man was thought to be working either too fast or too slow, one of the workers would go up and hit him on the upper arm as hard as he could; this was called "binging." Those workers who still did not conform after being ridiculed or binged ran the risk of being ostracized and socially isolated from the work group. By these means, the group pressured most of its members into conforming to its expectations.[14]

Primary relationships are characterized by close, personal ties. (Jeroboam Inc. Kent Reno)

In her study of the residents of Merrill Court, a small apartment house composed of older people who were mostly widows, Arlie Hochschild observed a similar pressure toward conformity.[15] One resident named Daisy wanted to keep to herself. The group chastised her and made her feel uncomfortable about this desire. The residents felt it was their duty to try and help her to be more sociable and to get involved in their activities. She was the topic of much discussion and gossip.

"There was not only social pressure to keep active and involved, but social pressure to be 'proper'."[16] Another resident, Beatrice, like Daisy, was also considered a deviant, but for a different reason. Beatrice flagrantly disregarded the group's conventions. Everyone disapproved of her behavior and gossiped about her. Many wanted to ostracize her from their service club for her actions. The case of Tommy, the English machinist, mentioned earlier, is still another illustration of how a group penalizes those who do not conform to its expectations.

3. *In a primary group, interaction is more relaxed, more informal, and freer than in a secondary group.* In such a setting people can be themselves. They do not have to prove anything or worry about the impression they make. Hochschild points out that when no younger people were

around, the elderly widows of Merrill Court sang and danced without fear of what others would think. She also notes that their topics of conversation were different.

> When the old people were together alone, everyone was a representative of the past, and no one had to instruct or interpret. They felt free mentally to move back a generation and speak of themselves less as grandmothers and mothers and more as sisters and children of their own deceased parents.[17]

In contrast to primary groups, *secondary group* relationships are relatively impersonal, superficial, and segmental. Secondary relationships do not involve an individual's whole personality, but only that part specifically relevant to the situation. Secondary relationships lack emotional content and are considered only as means to specific ends. For example, when you go into a department store to buy a sweater, the personal qualities of the salesperson are unimportant to you. You are really interested in that segment of the clerk's total personality involved in assisting you in making your purchase. The salesperson serves a limited purpose and is only a means to a specific end. Because the transaction is so impersonal, it would make little difference if another salesperson were to perform the same role. Many relationships in modern industrial societies are of this type.

Formal Organizations

Groups vary in their degree of organization. A small, loosely organized work team such as the one in the bank-wiring room, in which the relationships and normative expectations of the workers were spontaneous and occurred without deliberate planning, is a good example of an *informal organization.* On the other hand, the Western Electric Company, for whom those in the bank-wiring room worked, is an example of a *formal organization;* it is highly organized and impersonal, and its policies and procedures are formally stated. In addition, a formal organization is created to fulfill a specific objective, as in this case, Western Electric's purpose is to manufacture telephone equipment.

A formal organization, then, differs from an informal organization in that formal organizations are highly organized with very specific objectives. Examples of formal organizations include corporations, government agencies, trade unions, and universities. Within every formal organization, informal groups like the bank-wiring room group emerge. Usually formal organizations are considered to be secondary groups, whereas informal organizations are primary groups.

Voluntary Associations

Formal organizations also include *voluntary associations*, in which membership is based on choice. Our society is characterized by a vast array of associations, ranging from the American Red Cross and the National Rifle Association, to the American Association of Retired Persons. Some associations have a religious orientation, such as the National Conference of Christians and Jews; some are recreational, such as the National Contest Association; and others are occupational, such as the American Association of University Professors. Other associations are charitable, political, social, or service groups.

Older people belong to three main categories of voluntary associations: (1) ones in which elderly persons participate, but which are not particularly geared to their specific needs; (2) associations that are organized by and for older people to meet their needs and interests; and (3) those in which others provide services for older people. [18]

Voluntary Associations in Which Older People Participate

Many studies have been made of the membership of older people in voluntary associations. A study by Robert Havighurst and Ruth Albrecht found that the elderly tended to drop out or to become inactive in associations. "In all kinds of associations, older people report themselves as having reduced their activity as they grew older by giving up offices, decreasing attendance, and dropping out of certain organizations." [19] Havighurst and Albrecht noted that practically no older person joined an association as a new member. They found that membership in associations usually began in the thirties, peaked at middle age, and began to decline in later life.

This decline in membership is due to several factors. First, many meetings are held at night when older people do not like to go out. In addition, many elderly have physical disabilities that limit their activities. Also, the cost of dues or other expenses in an organization becomes a hardship for many older people living on fixed, low incomes. Finally, many older people lose interest in group activities appealing to younger people; they may feel out of place and that their ideas and suggestions are being ignored.

Havighurst and Albrecht found that a decline in membership was not only associated with age, but also with social status and sex. A decreasing social status was related to a decrease in associational memberships. Older men of lower status were the most likely to be unaffiliated. More women than men belonged to voluntary associations. A partial reason is that in many communities, such as Prairie City, there are more opportunities for women to belong to organizations than for

The 1977 edition of the *Encyclopedia of Associations* lists over 13,000 associations that Americans belong to. These range from such organizations as the American Association of Sheriff Posses and Riding Clubs, the National Button Society of America, Sons and Daughters of the Pilgrims, to the Flying Senior Citizens of the U.S.A.

SOURCE: *Encyclopedia of Associations* (11th ed.), Gale Research, Detroit, Mich., 1977.

men. Also, older women have more friends and are more active in organizations than older men. Havighurst and Albrecht attribute this situation, in part, to the large number of women who are widowed in their sixties and who try to create social opportunities for themselves. But even before widowhood, Blau notes that women have a greater capacity and need for friendships than men do. Men tend to satisfy their need for a close confidant within marriage, whereas married women fulfill this need with members of their own sex.[20]

The majority of studies on the membership of older people in voluntary associations suggest that:

1. The average rates of membership are higher at middle age and then begin to drop in later life.
2. The drop in membership is more pronounced with older men than older women.
3. Membership rates increase with higher levels of income and educational attainment.
4. If a person participated in voluntary associations when young, this pattern tends to persist in later life.

Voluntary Associations Organized for and by Older People

The Townsend Movement was one of the first associations of older people in this country. Originally called the Old Age and Revolving Pensions, Ltd., it was organized in 1934 by Francis E. Townsend, a retired physician. The goal of the organization was to get Congress to pass a law giving all retired persons over the age of 60 a pension of $200 per month. The movement, largely composed of persons from the lower socioeconomic levels, grew rapidly, and by 1936 there were several thousand local clubs attracting about one and a half million members. Arnold Rose comments about the movement:

> The thousands of local clubs affected their elderly members in various ways. Participants in the clubs were given some hope that their economic needs

Through groups such as the NRTA-AARP, older Americans have become aware of the advantages of concerted social action. (Courtesy of NRTA-AARP)

would be amply met and were brought together in sociable groups. Moreover, the clubs created their first insights of themselves as a social group with common problems.[21]

With the implementation of social security legislation, the main thrust of the Townsend Movement was blunted. The organization then shifted its purpose to promote recreational and social activities for older people. By 1953 the membership had dropped to 23,000 and since then the movement has gradually disappeared.

Today, several voluntary associations link their purposes to the needs, problems, and interests of older people. The largest of these is the American Association of Retired Persons (AARP), which is composed of persons 55 years of age or older. The AARP and its affiliates, the National Retired Teachers Association (NRTA) and Action for Independent Maturity (AIM), have a combined membership of about 13 million, with the AARP alone accounting for over 11 million. The AARP, which was founded in 1958 by Ethel Percy Andrus, a 72-year-old retired high school principal, is a spin-off from the National Retired Teachers Association started by her about 10 years earlier.

The AARP gets much of its financial support from the insurance programs that it offers to its members. It provides many benefits and services for its membership, including adult education, temporary employment, pharmacy service, preretirement programs, and travel service. In addition, the AARP and each of its affiliates publish bimonthly magazines. The AARP works closely with members of Congress and state legislatures to represent the interests of retired persons. Information on legislation of particular interest to AARP members is sent to the officers of its more than 1,300 local chapters throughout the country and directly to its membership through a news bulletin.

Next to AARP in size and power is the National Council of Senior Citizens (NCSC), which was originally organized and strongly supported by labor unions to help push for the passage of Medicare. Their present membership of 3.5 million comes from organizations of older people like senior citizen clubs and councils, as well as from labor unions. The NCSC provides many services similar to the AARP's and encourages its members to take part in political and social action activities. Many of its present policies and concerns reflect its strong ties to organized labor. "A better life for *all* Americans" is its stated goal.

In contrast to these two associations is an intergenerational, militant movement of about 30,000 social activists called the Gray Panthers — a name that a television program director gave them.* Loosely structured and lacking the organization of AARP and NCSC, the Gray Panthers until recently had no dues and were solely dependent on donations. They are a coalition of both young and old, whose primary objective is to change society's outdated concept of age and to fight against age discrimination. About 25 percent of their membership is under the age of 30.

The leader of the group is charismatic, 73-year-old Maggie Kuhn, who started the association in 1970 when she was forced into mandatory retirement after 25 years of service with the Presbyterian Church. Kuhn, who has been described as the "feisty old lady from Philadelphia," seeks to liberate the elderly from the many injustices perpetrated against them and to dispel the negative myths about old age. The Panthers have a steering committee of nine people and have adopted a statement of purpose, which they call the Panther Manifesto, part of which follows:

> We are a group of people — of all ages — drawn together by deeply felt common concerns for human liberation and social change. The old and

*Officially they are called the Coalition of Older and Younger Adults.

Maggie Kuhn, leader of the Gray Panthers, a national organization of social activists. (Courtesy of Maggie Kuhn)

young, in particular, live outside the mainstream of society. Ageism — discrimination against persons on the basis of chronological age — deprives both groups of power and influence.

We believe that the old and the young in our society have much to contribute to make our society more just and human, and that we need to reinforce each other in our goals, our strategy, and our action.[22]

Old people should not be treated as wrinkled babies. . . . Old folks have plenty to offer this country — if only they are given a chance. . . . America is caught up in the Detroit syndrome, and we scrap-pile our old people like wornout car hulks. . . . We warehouse away our so-called senior citizens in senior high-rises and nursing homes — or, as I prefer to call them, "glorified playpens."

Maggie Kuhn

SOURCE: George Michaelson, "Maggie Kuhn: Gray Panther on the Prowl," *Parade*, December 18, 1977, pp. 7–8.

The AARP has a legislative staff that works within the existing political system, but the Panthers believe that many problems of aging stem from defects in the system itself, and that the system should be changed. The Panthers emphasize the importance of involvement in the political process at the grass-roots level. Each of the approximately 100 local groups is given autonomy to pursue those problems and issues that it feels are most important in its own community.

Voluntary Associations that Provide Services for Older People

Probably the most prevalent type of voluntary association providing services for the elderly is the senior citizen center. In the 1940s, the center movement started in New York City to reduce the isolation and loneliness of older people. At first, the programs were largely recreational in character. Today, the scope of the centers has been broadened to include many educational, cultural, health, and social services. The growth of senior centers has been phenomenal: in 1966 there were 340 listed in a national directory of centers, and by 1974 the number had increased to 5,000. Gordon Streib notes:

> The senior centers are important because of the new role opportunities that they provide and also because they provide a meeting place to discuss a variety of community ideas and issues, particularly those involving older Americans. Further they may serve as recruiting sites at which older persons can be contacted and trained to engage in new roles in the area of community service.[23]

The services that senior citizen centers provide vary greatly. David Guttman and Phyllis Miller surveyed 70 senior centers with a total membership of over 150,000 regarding the provision of four major social services.[24] They found that 54 percent of the centers played some role in providing housing services for their members. Forty percent offered financial assistance and consumer education, while 63 percent provided health services by professionals within the center. Sixty-two percent helped in securing paid employment both in the center and in the community.

In addition to these four services, many centers serve as a neighborhood or community social agency. Often representatives from community agencies are on hand to offer counseling to the elderly with personal problems and other assistance in obtaining needed services. Most centers provide some form of transportation for members and low cost, well-balanced meals in a communal dining room. Also instruction in language skills, crafts, and various hobbies is common. Field trips and camping are also part of many center programs, as are plays, musicals, dances, and other forms of entertainment.

Communities

Thus far we have been discussing the various types of groups in which we participate and of which we are members. These groups function within a larger territorial group in which people pursue their daily needs and activities. When we speak of this larger, more inclusive territorial group, we are referring to the community. The community differs from other groups in that membership is based on the sharing of the same general locality. A *community* refers to a grouping of people who live in a limited territorial area where they have a sense of belonging and fulfill most of their daily needs and activities.

The various types of communities, such as rural, urban, and suburban, can be categorized in many ways. One analysis includes these criteria to classify communities: (1) the size and density of the population; (2) the specialized functions of the community within the whole society; and (3) the kind of organization the community has.[25] To these we will add a fourth criterion — age. Although the concept of having whole communities composed of an aged population is not new, only in recent years have retirement communities emerged in this country.

Retirement Communities

Ernest Burgess classified retirement communities according to the following variations:

1. By sponsorship — fraternal lodges, labor unions, religious groups, or private builders.
2. By location — in the open country, adjacent to shopping centers, or in communities but distant from services.
3. By services — complete community facilities with medical care, partial services, or few or no services other than housing.
4. By provision for residents — lifetime right of the residence only, or complete lifetime care.
5. By design of the housing — residence halls, detached apartments, single dwellings, multi-type units, or trailer units.[26]

The term *retirement community* has been used in many ways. To some, it simply means older residents living in age-segregated housing, such as hotels, mobile home parks, condominiums, or apartment buildings. To others, retirement community refers to a planned community

"The break is set for eleven. Pass it on." (Drawing by B. Tobey; © 1973. The New Yorker Magazine, Inc.)

complete with its own shopping, recreational, and medical facilities. For our purposes, we will define a *retirement community* as a planned, relatively self-sufficient entity, which is partially separated from the larger community and whose residents are retired or semi-retired persons.

The rapid growth of retirement communities following World War II has provoked much controversy about whether or not they are desirable alternatives for older people. Some people argue that the retirement community is an unnatural environment and can only lead to stagnation and boredom, while others criticize it for being a pleasure-seeking community dominated by a "fun morality." Another view is that age-segregated communities put undue stress on their residents because of their lack of privacy and the pressure on members to be active and sociable. On the other hand, others claim that retirement communities are beneficial because they afford the elderly a higher degree of social interaction and in this way alleviate the problems of loneliness and isolation. Some feel that adjustment to retirement is made easier in such communities.

Studies of Retirement Communities

One of the earliest studies of retirement communities was made by James Peterson and Aili Larson. They studied the reasons that residents gave for moving to Leisure World, a retirement community in Laguna Beach, California. On the whole, most people said that they had selected Leisure World because of its activities and conveniences.[27] Gordon Bultena and Vivian Wood studied the role of the planned retirement community in American life.[28] Their sample consisted of 521 retired men who had moved from the Midwest to either age-integrated (regular) communities or age-segregated (planned retirement) communities in Arizona. They found that those who settled in retirement communities had higher levels of satisfaction and morale than those who moved to age-integrated communities. Fifty-seven percent of the residents in the retirement community obtained a high score on a life satisfaction scale, compared to 27 percent of those in regular communities (Table 8.1). While both groups indicated that they were satisfied with their move to Arizona, the percentage expressing satisfaction was significantly higher for the residents of the retirement community (75 percent) than for the regular community residents (51 percent).

Bultena and Wood attribute these higher levels of morale in the retirement community to several factors. First, the persons in the retirement community had higher incomes, as well as higher educational and occupational levels; in addition, they perceived their health as being better than those in the regular communities. Secondly, the features of the retirement community contribute positively to the adaptation of the retirement role. Those persons in the retirement community were found to be similar not only in age but in socioeconomic status and background. This homogeneity promotes a high degree of social interaction and facilitates the formation of new friendships. Compared to those in regular communities, a smaller proportion of the migrants to retirement communities reported a decline in close friends as a result of the move, and there was less dissatisfaction with the number of friends they had made. Furthermore, the retirement community has a strong orientation to full-time leisure pursuits as opposed to the orientation to productivity and the work ethic in a regular community. Persons oriented toward leisure-time activities find support for this from other residents in the retirement community, whereas in a regular community setting, they might be criticized for a leisure lifestyle.

In comparing communities, an important point to consider is the factor of selective migration. Many persons who choose retirement communities come from backgrounds characterized by high levels of social participation, and they are attracted to these communities because of the social and recreational activities provided. Those persons who are not predisposed to such activities and have lifelong patterns of minimal

Table 8.1 Percentage distribution on life satisfaction scores of aged migrants in retirement and regular communities in Arizona

Life satisfaction	Retirement communities N = 322	Regular communities N = 199
Low morale	3%	10%
Medium morale	40	63
High morale	57	27

SOURCE: Gordon L. Bultena and Vivian Wood, "The American Retirement Community: Bane or Blessing?" *Journal of Gerontology*, 24 no. 2 (1969), p. 211. Reprinted with the permission of *Journal of Gerontology*.

social participation might be unhappy and demoralized in such a setting. Seventy-five percent of the respondents from the regular community in Arizona expressed negative attitudes toward retirement communities. Bultena and Wood point out that "older persons just as those of other ages, have a diversity of social-interaction styles and that these require differential social structures to maintain morale."[29] It seems evident that retirement communities are not suited to everyone's needs, but for some people they can have a beneficial effect on morale and satisfaction with retirement.

Age-segregated communities are often criticized for being unnatural environments. In his case study of Fun City, a planned retirement community in the West, Jerry Jacobs observed older persons' adjustment to this environment:

> Fun City had no children, young adults, or ethnic minorities. . . . the complete lack of children and/or young adults in Fun City led many new residents to consider their environment unnatural even if they were glad or at least ambivalent about the state of affairs. After all, if one had lived for seventy years in the outside world, one saw or at least knew of all kinds of people. . . . Insofar as one did not encounter, for the first time in his life, all kinds, Fun City was experienced by many residents as unnatural and a place that took some getting used to. In short, new residents in Fun City experienced a form of culture shock.[30]

Retirement communities are found predominantly in the Southern and Western states, such as Florida, Arizona, and California, but recently they have been developing at an increasing rate in other sections of the country. A study by Katherine Heintz of 1,033 New Jersey residents in five retirement communities found that they attracted mostly residents who had formerly lived in nearby cities in New York,

Pennsylvania, and New Jersey.[31] There appears to be a nationwide trend for the elderly to move short distances from their former urban homes and to relocate in the metropolitan fringe areas.

Most of the reasons given by the residents for their move to a New Jersey retirement community involved antipathy toward city life, reflected in such phrases as "sick of city life," "bad neighbors," "neighborhood deteriorating," "pollution," "too many kids," "tired of city's rat race," and "closed-in feeling."[32] Two important factors influencing the decision to move were the economic advantages and the proximity to their former residences. Although the people did not specify availability of planned leisure activities as a primary reason for moving to a retirement community, the appeal of such activities is shown by the fact that almost 75 percent of the residents participated in them.

The residents indicated that they were highly satisfied with their retirement community. Satisfaction was found to be positively correlated with the length of residence; that is, the longer people lived there, the more content they were. This high level of satisfaction was supported by the fact only about 7 percent said that they would like to move. Ninety percent said they would recommend such a community to their friends who were planning to move.

Most studies indicate high levels of social interaction among the residents of age-segregated communities. When work, family, and other roles are lost with age, retirement communities afford the elderly an opportunity to acquire new roles to take their place. On the other hand, retirement communities are definitely not for all older persons. Some cannot afford them, others do not wish to be isolated from younger age groups, or to be pressured into participating in social and recreational activities. But for those elderly who are leisure-oriented and who have the money and desire for this type of lifestyle, retirement communities represent a highly satisfactory living arrangement.

Summary

1. Sociologists define a group as two or more people who interact with one another in a standardized pattern and who share a sense of common identity. People who have some particular attribute in common are considered a category, not a group. But if members of a category begin to interact with one another and to share a sense of relatedness, they may become a group. Rose argues that older people in our society are in the process of being transformed from a category into a group. He also asserts that because of certain demographic and social trends that are occurring in our society, a subculture of aging is emerging. At the present time, there is not sufficient evidence to support his assumption.

2. Groups that we use to compare ourselves to and to measure our successes

and failures against are called reference groups. Reference groups provide us with a set of norms, attitudes, and values. At present, there is a lack of age-appropriate reference groups for the elderly, and for this reason, many older people continue to judge themselves by middle-age standards.

3. Groups may be analyzed by the type of relationship that exists among their members. Relationships that are intimate, personal, and sentimental characterize those found in primary groups. Primary groups help to support and sustain the individual, and they function as instruments of social control. By contrast, relationships in secondary groups are impersonal, superficial, and segmental.

4. Groups may also be analyzed by their degree of organization. An informal organization is a group that is loosely organized and occurs without deliberate planning or purpose; a formal organization is a highly organized group where policy, procedure, and objectives are formally stated. Voluntary associations are one type of formal organization in which membership is based on choice. The majority of studies of voluntary associations indicate that membership declines with age, that women remain active somewhat longer than men, and that older people who participated in voluntary associations when young tend to continue this pattern in later life.

5. One of the first associations of older people in this country was the Townsend Movement, which started in the early 1930s. The aim of the organization was to pass a law giving each retired person over age 60 a pension of $200 per month. Today, the largest group of older people is the AARP and its affiliates, the NRTA and AIM; these associations offer their members many services and programs. A somewhat different kind of association is the Gray Panthers, which is composed of both young and old people working together to fight problems of age discrimination. Still another kind of voluntary association for older people is the senior citizen center. Today, modern centers offer their members not only recreational opportunities but educational, cultural, health, and social services.

6. A community is a large inclusive territorial group. Communities may be classified by various criteria, including age. Retirement communities are composed of retired or semi-retired persons and are spatially isolated and relatively self-sufficient entities. Bultena and Wood compared the morale of older people living in retirement communities with the morale of those living in regular communities in Arizona. They found the morale higher for the residents of age-segregated communities. Most studies indicate that the residents of retirement communities manifest a high degree of social interaction and activity. Although retirement communities are not a universal solution to the problems of older people, for some they are proving to be a most satisfactory one.

Notes

1. *The Manchester Evening News*, December 10, 1973, and November 5, 1975.

2. Leonard Broom and Phillip Selznick, *Sociology* (5th ed.), Harper & Row, New York, 1973, p. 47.

3. Arnold M. Rose, "The Subculture of the Aging," *Older People and Their Social World*, eds. Arnold Rose and Warren Peterson, F. A. Davis, Philadelphia, 1965.

4. Ibid., p. 14.

5. Gordon L. Bultena, "Age-Grading in the Social Interaction of an Elderly Male Population," *Journal of Gerontology*, 23 (1968), 539–543.

6. Ibid., p. 543.

7. Rose, "The Subculture of the Aging," p. 7.

8. James D. Manney, Jr., *Aging in American Society*, The Institute of Gerontology, University of Michigan-Wayne State University, Ann Arbor, Mich., 1975, p. 19.

9. Gordon Bultena and Edward Powers, "Effects of Age-Grade Comparisons on Adjustment in Later Life," *Time, Roles, and Self in Old Age*, eds. Jaber F. Gubrium, Human Sciences Press, New York, 1976, pp. 165–177.

10. Ibid.

11. Vern L. Bengtson and Ron C. Manuel, "The Sociology of Aging," *Aging: Prospects and Issues*, ed. Richard H. Davis, Ethel Percy Andrus Gerontology Center, University of Southern California, 1976, p. 48.

12. Kingsley Davis, *Human Society*, Macmillan, New York, 1949, p. 294.

13. Zena Smith Blau, *Old Age in a Changing Society*, New Viewpoints, New York, 1973, p. 71.

14. F. J. Roethlisberger and W. J. Dickson, *Management and the Worker*, Harvard University Press, Cambridge, Mass., 1939.

15. Arlie R. Hochschild, *The Unexpected Community*, Prentice-Hall, Englewood Cliffs, N.J., 1973.

16. Ibid., p. 34.

17. Arlie Russell Hochschild, *The Unexpected Community*, © 1973, p. 75. Reprinted by permission of Prentice-Hall, Inc., Englewood Cliffs, New Jersey.

18. Arnold M. Rose, "The Impact of Aging on Voluntary Associations," *Handbook of Social Gerontology*, ed. Clark Tibbitts, The University of Chicago Press, Chicago, 1960, p. 666.

19. Robert J. Havighurst and Ruth Albrecht, *Older People*, Longmans Green, New York, 1953, p. 194.

20. Blau, *Old Age in a Changing Society*, p. 72.

21. Rose, "The Impact of Aging on Voluntary Associations," p. 678.

22. "Gray Panthers, Age and Youth in Action," Gray Panthers, Philadelphia, Pa., n.d., unpaged.

23. Gordon F. Streib, *Retirement Roles and Activities*, 1971 White House Conference on Aging, Background and Issues, U.S. Government Printing Office, Washington, D.C., February 1971, p. 25.

24. David Guttman and Phyllis R. Miller, "Perspective on the Provision of Social Services in Senior Citizen Centers," *The Gerontologist*, 12 (1974), 403–406.

25. Davis, *Human Society*, p. 313.

26. Ernest S. Burgess, ed., *Retirement Villages*, Division of Gerontology, University of Michigan, Ann Arbor, 1961, unpaged.

27. James A. Peterson and Aili Larson, "Social-Psychological Factors in Select-ing Retirement Housing," *Patterns of Living and Housing of Middle-Aged and Older People,* ed. Frances M. Carp, Public Health Service Publication No. 1496, Wash-ington, D.C., 1965.

28. Gordon L. Bultena and Vivian Wood, "The American Retirement Commu-nity: Bane or Blessing?" *Journal of Gerontology,* 24 no. 2 (1969), 209–217.

29. Ibid., p. 215.

30. Jerry Jacobs, *Older Persons and Retirement Communities,* Charles C Thomas, Springfield, Ill., 1975, pp. 70–71.

31. Katherine McMillan Heintz, *Retirement Communities,* The Center for Urban Policy Research, Rutgers-The State University of New Jersey, New Brunswick, N.J., 1976.

32. Ibid., p. 43.

For Further Study

Burgess, Ernest S., ed. *Retirement Villages.* Division of Gerontology, University of Michigan, Ann Arbor, 1961. Contains a collection of papers that were presented at a conference on the retirement villages.

Gubrium, Jaber F., ed. *Late Life: Communities and Environmental Policy.* Charles C Thomas, Springfield, Ill., 1974. This book contains papers dealing with the physical, formal, and cross-cultural environments of old age and some issues on environmental policy.

Heintz, Katherine M. *Retirement Communities.* The Center for Urban Policy Research, Rutgers-The State University of New Jersey, New Brunswick, N.J., 1976. This study deals with the characteristics of retirement communities, their occupants, and their impact upon the municipal environment.

Jacobs, Jerry. *Older Persons and Retirement Communities.* Charles C Thomas, Springfield, Ill., 1975. A case study of the residents of a high-rise retirement apartment building.

Mangum, Wiley P. "Retirement Villages." In *Foundations of Practical Gerontology,* edited by Rosamonde Boyd and Charles G. Oakes. University of South Carolina Press, Columbia, S.C., 1973. A good discussion of retirement villages.

Riley, Matilda White, and Anne Foner. *Aging and Society:* vol. I: *An Inventory of Research Findings.* Russell Sage Foundation, New York, 1968. Chapter 21 provides an excellent summary of research findings on voluntary associations.

Rose, Arnold M. "Impact of Aging on Voluntary Associations." In *Handbook of Social Gerontology,* edited by Clark Tibbitts. The University of Chicago Press, Chicago, 1960. Though somewhat outdated in places, it provides a penetrat-ing analysis of older people and voluntary associations.

————, "The Subculture of the Aging," and "Group Consciousness Among the Aging." In *Older People and Their Social World,* edited by Arnold Rose and Warren Peterson. F. A. Davis, Philadelphia, 1965. Each of these papers presents a theoretical framework for research in social gerontology.

9

Social Stratification and Aging

"All men are created equal but some are more equal than others" is a common saying. Inequality and social stratification are certainly inherent and pervasive in social life. Archaeological evidence reveals that social stratification was present among the ancient Greeks and Persians as well as among early preliterate societies. Yet people have always dreamed of a classless society in which inequality and distinctions of rank do not exist.

For thousands of years, social stratification has been a source of conflict and controversy and a subject of philosophical debate. Stratification not only dates back to antiquity, but is found in all known societies today. *Stratification* involves the ranking of individuals and families into higher and lower social positions according to their share of social rewards. Or it may simply be referred to as structured social inequality. The major dimensions of stratification involve the unequal distribution of such social rewards as wealth, power, and prestige.[1]

Dimensions of Stratification

Wealth

While Americans are among the world's wealthiest people, huge inequalities continue to exist in this country between the very rich and the very poor. At the present time, there are no indications of a trend toward equality. In fact, the pattern of the distribution of wealth (which includes property and other assets) seems to be fairly stable and highly concentrated.[2] Huge gaps also exist between the rich and the poor in the distribution of income (which includes salaries and wages). These disparities in income are more pronounced among certain categories of the population than others. For instance, poverty is more common among blacks, among those households with female heads, and among people who are age 65 or older, than it is among the general population.

The degree of inequality in the distribution of income among older persons is indicated by median incomes. In 1977 the median income of families with heads aged 65 and over was $9,110, while the median income of all families was $17,203. Income tends to fall sharply at retirement; overall, retired people live on about half their former incomes. Social security, pensions, and personal savings do not afford the majority of older people the same standard of living as they had before retirement. Elderly persons who have worked and saved for the future often find at retirement that their savings have been eroded away by inflation and taxes. But if they should choose to get a job to make ends meet, they are limited by an earnings ceiling ($5,000 in 1980).* If they earn more, they cannot collect full social security benefits. On the other hand, wealthier retired persons who may receive money from real estate, stocks, or bonds, but not from wages, are allowed to collect their full amount of social security.

In a study of employed as well as retired blue-collar workers, George Rosenberg noted an inverse relationship between age and income level.[3] He found that about 15 percent were poor among those persons between the ages of 45 and 54. The proportion of poverty rose to 25 percent in the 55 to 64 age group; in the 65 to 79 category, the proportion of poor reached 55 percent.

James Manney sums up the unequal distribution of income as follows:

> Younger people now enjoying higher living standards are building on an economy which was created by people now retired. Yet unless retirees own stock, variable annuities, or other securities, they have no way to share in the benefits of the increasing productivity which their work largely made possible. . . . Unless public income maintenance programs incorporate some mechanisms to distribute more wealth equitably among all groups in the population, a significant number of older people will always be poor or near-poor as measured by an ever-rising poverty line. In view of the trend toward ever-earlier retirement, the percentage of older people in this position may even increase. Economists call this phenomenon a trend toward relative economic deprivation. As economic growth and inflation wipe out the gains older people have made, their economic status will eventually deteriorate relative to the working population.[4]

Power

Another dimension of stratification closely related to the possession of money is power. Though there is not always a one-to-one correlation between them — not all powerful men are wealthy and not all wealthy men are powerful — in general, a strong relationship exists between

*This ceiling remains in force until age 72. Beginning in 1982 the age will be lowered to 70.

"MONEY MAY NOT BUY HAPPINESS — BUT
IT SURE CAN REMOVE YOU A
LONG WAY FROM MISERY."

money and power. David Popenoe divides power into two main types: personal and social.[5] He notes that people have *personal power* when they are able to choose the quality and type of life that they wish to lead and have access to the goods and services that they desire. This boils down to the individual having adequate financial resources. Many older people, because of their meager circumstances, are deprived of this type of power; they lack the freedom of choice and the power to control their own lives, and feel helpless and dependent.

Social power refers to the ability to control and influence the behavior of others. In most primitive societies, and in many traditional ones, because the elderly are valued for their wisdom and experience, much power is placed in their hands. They are looked to for leadership and guidance. In modern societies like our own, wealth and power tend to be concentrated largely among the middle-aged group. But because of seniority rules in bureaucracies, labor unions, and legislatures and because elective officials are not subject to mandatory retirement policies, older people exert disproportionate influence in this country.

Prestige

A third influence on social stratification is prestige. *Prestige* refers to the social recognition and respect that one receives from others. Usually a person's occupation is the major determinant of prestige. Prestige in American society comes from holding what is considered a high social position, such as being a professor, a lawyer, or a physician. Eugene Friedmann and Robert Havighurst interviewed physicians over 65 years of age in Cook County, Illinois, to explore what their work meant to them.[6] One meaning voiced by some physicians was that their profession was a source of prestige to them.

> Some doctors stated that to be a physician meant that one belonged to an elite class. It meant that one associated with important people and was in a position of leadership in the community. This feeling was expressed by Dr. I., who described his work as . . . "a nice clean profession. It has prestige and you can get into so many inaccessible places just by sending in your card." Dr. I. told of the time that he wanted to visit someone who was in jail. The attendant told him that he could not possibly get in. He just gave the attendant his card and the latter said with reverence, "Oh, come in, doctor."[7]

At retirement, individuals lose their occupational position, which often results in a decline in their prestige and social rewards. Professionals and other persons of high occupational status, however, frequently continue to identify with their occupations after retirement, and in this way they retain their titles and some of their former prestige. This practice is especially characteristic of doctors, professors, and judges, who continue to be called by their titles instead of "mister." Also persons of high military rank are often referred to as General or Colonel long after retirement.

Social Class

We have been discussing the reasons for social stratification in society — the unequal distribution of wealth, power, and prestige. Now let us examine the patterns that social stratification takes or the social class system in our society that results from these inequalities.

Social class may be defined as a category of individuals and families who share relatively equal amounts of social rewards. To determine class divisions, sociologists popularly use three criteria that are closely associated with one another — occupation, education, and income. In most cases, education is related to a good job, and a good job is usually related to a high income. Because of this correlation, it is not always necessary to know all three factors about a person to establish his or her social class membership. By knowing one factor — especially occupation, which is the main indicator of social class — we can make assumptions about the other two.

Class Divisions

Identifying distinct classes in the United States is difficult. The number of social classes is not fixed, and the boundaries between them are often blurred. While some sociologists identify only three classes — the upper class, middle class, and lower class — most sociologists generally prefer to use five or six basic categories. Lloyd Warner, in his study of a small New England town, "Yankee City," used six categories by dividing each of the major classes into an upper and lower level.[8] Later when he studied Jonesville in the Midwest, Warner used only five classes, combining the two upper classes.[9]

This same kind of class breakdown was followed by Havighurst and Albrecht when they described the social-class structure of Prairie City (Figure 9.1).[10] Though their work was done about three decades ago, it still contains more pertinent data on the lifestyles of the elderly at each class level than any other study. We will discuss the characteristics of each of the five basic social classes in Prairie City, and include a description of an elderly person or couple who represent each class. These class-related characteristics, of course, refer to a given people at a particular time and place.

THE UPPER CLASS   Although the upper class is the smallest group in Prairie City, its members are called the "top crowd," and the "Four Hundred." The members fall into two categories. One group, known as the "old families," has been in the community for four generations, and much of their wealth is largely in land. A second group consists of those who have only recently come to the community; they are the owners of the principal industries. The men in the upper class do not retire from their businesses or professions, but instead reduce their responsibilities to have the amount of leisure that they desire. While persons in this class are not visibly active in community affairs, they are always consulted on important issues, and they support the institutions in the community.

Havighurst and Albrecht give the following profile of an upper-class widow:

When Mrs. Mable Ross, 77, a white-haired, dignified little woman, walks down a Prairie City street she expects to be noticed by everyone who amounts to anything socially. She is not only the widow of Phillip Ross whose wide land holdings gave power and prestige to his voice in the

Figure 9.1   The distribution of social classes in Prairie City

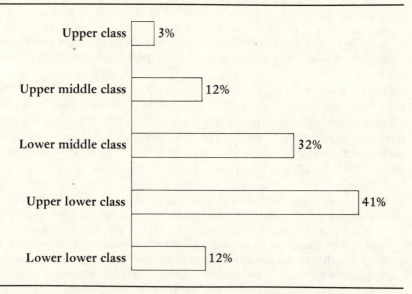

Upper class	3%
Upper middle class	12%
Lower middle class	32%
Upper lower class	41%
Lower lower class	12%

SOURCE: Adapted from Robert J. Havighurst and Ruth Albrecht, *Older People*, Longmans, Green, New York, 1953.

community, but, what is more, she is the granddaughter and heir of Lewis Collister, the early settler for whom parks and roadways have been named. . . . Visitors to Prairie City are routinely driven past the "Ross Corner" to view her fine old home. . . .

Since the death of her husband, fourteen years ago, she has assumed the management of the family properties. . . . Periods of ill health during the past several years have interrupted her travels and narrowed down her social and philanthropic activities. With considerable regularity however, she meets for luncheon at the Country Club with a small group of old friends, mostly widows close to her own age.[11]

THE UPPER-MIDDLE CLASS   The upper-middle class is composed of professionals, executives of industries, and owners of the larger retail businesses. They have above-average incomes, high educational levels, and live in nice homes. Members of this group are the political, social, and religious leaders of Prairie City. They have a general reputation for very high moral standards and are considered to be pillars of the community. Mr. and Mrs. Gray are an example of an upper-middle-class couple:

Mr. Gray, 68, a trim, broad-proportioned man always dressed in a neat gray suit, lives with his wife, 65, in a modern colonial home in the exclusive residential section of town. By the middle of most mornings he is in his busy retail store, looking over accounts in the back office or out in front greeting customers by their first names. Two of his sons are now in business with him and are taking over more and more responsibility. . . . He and his wife have both been prominent in club and civic affairs, holding offices and chairmanships in leading organizations. Today they participate less actively.[12]

THE LOWER-MIDDLE CLASS   Thirty-two percent of the residents of Prairie City fall into the lower-middle class. They provide the bulk of the membership in Prairie City's many organizations. "These are the people whose bridge parties, bunco clubs, and 'get-togethers' provide the most prominent news item in the society columns of the Prairie City Record."[13] Mr. Wayne is representative of this class:

Mr. Wayne, a retired railroad worker, is a slender, erect man of 70, with gray hair showing only at his temples. He is proud of the fact that most people who meet him underestimate his age. . . . His home, where he lives with his wife and unmarried son, is a neat, six-room bungalow on a street with rows of houses that are somewhat similar to his. When he retired five years ago he had been a foreman in the freight house for over ten years. . . .

During his working years, Mr. Wayne was active in union organizations and in his lodge. Today he attends meetings irregularly. . . . His retirement pension and a small annuity keep him from financial worry. . . . "I would say that my life has been very happy, and I am well satisfied with what I have accomplished. . . . I don't feel old, perhaps I feel middle-aged."[14]

THE UPPER-LOWER CLASS   The largest percentage of Prairie City's population (41 percent) are in the upper-lower class. The members of this class are too busy making a living to have much time to participate in voluntary organizations. These people are considered to be poor but respectable, and most are employed as semiskilled workers, laborers, and tenant farmers. The two revivalistic churches draw almost all their members from this group; they live in the poorer sections of the town and in some of the downtown buildings. Over half of the men over 65 in this class are still employed, while those who are not working or who are retired have to depend on help from their relatives or from old-age assistance. The Brandons are a typical upper-lower-class couple:

Mr. and Mrs. Brandon, both well along in their sixties, live out in a neighborhood between the canal bed and the river where the houses are small and scattered. . . . On Saturday and Sunday Mr. Brandon likes to fuss about the house and yard with his whittling or gardening. During the week when he returns from his day's stint as a janitor in a factory he has little energy for this kind of puttering. . . .

Mrs. Brandon . . . usually has one or two grandchildren under foot in the house. During the years her family was growing up she had little time for activities outside the home. Occasionally she attended a church social and helped in the serving. Mr. Brandon has paid union dues and membership in one lodge for many years. Today the Brandons' social activities consist of visiting with a few old friends and in the homes of their three children who live in Prairie City.[15]

THE LOWER-LOWER CLASS   While the upper-lower class are described as "poor but respectable," the lower-lower class is regarded as "poor but not respectable." Lower-lower class members are referred to as "the river rats" and "the damned Yellow Hammers," and are thought by the other residents to be dirty, lazy, dishonest, and of low moral standards. They have the least amount of education and the lowest income of any of the other classes. Approximately half of the lower-lower-class older people are receiving old-age assistance. A large segment of older men in this group have come in from nearby farms and towns when they could no longer work and have taken refuge in Prairie City. Mr. Benson is such a case:

> Oley Benson, 68, can be seen most any afternoon wending his way from the old brick rooming house near Main Street over to Harry's Tavern. For nearly forty years Prairie City has been Oley's headquarters, although for most of that time he has lived and worked on farms in the surrounding countryside. Most Saturday nights found him in town with some cronies prepared to celebrate the passing of another week. Three years ago, at 65, with all his worldly goods packed into a battered suitcase, he moved to Prairie City. Since then he has received an old-age pension check each month. . . .Occasionally, a big chunk of Oley's pension check gets lost in a crap game.[16]

Correlates of Class Membership

From Havighurst and Albrecht's description of Prairie City's five classes, it is evident that each social class has its own system of behavior, set of values, attitudes, and lifestyle. These class differences are perpetuated from one generation to the next. Prairie City's older people as well as the other age groups in the upper classes fare better than the elderly in the lower classes. As individuals move down the scale from the upper to the lower classes, life-opportunities and rewards become limited, and the probability that they will attain certain desirable goals and experiences decreases. Social class position has far-reaching consequences that penetrate every aspect of a person's daily life and social interaction. James Birren notes that "although each individual is unique, with particular genetic, psychological, and social characteristics, the accumulated effects of social class have an impact upon the way in which humans age."[17] Let us look at some of the factors associated with class membership and how they relate to aging and the aged.

LIFE EXPECTANCY How long a person may be expected to live is influenced by social class. Albert Mayer and Phillip Hauser found that the chances of longevity are definitely greater in the higher social classes. The differences in life span were 7.6 years between the upper-class and lower-class whites, and 6.0 years between the upper-class and lower-class blacks.[18]

ILLNESS.   Persons in the lower class are not only likely to die earlier than those in the upper class, but they also suffer more from physical and mental illness. A study by Robert Dovenmuehle and his associates — of 256 persons 60 years of age and older — found that persons of higher social levels had fewer limitations on physical functioning than those of lower levels.[19] In addition, persons in the lower levels have a higher incidence of impairment of vision, arteriosclerosis, cardiovascular disease, hypertension, pulmonary disease, and arthritis.

One of the most striking differences between the social classes is in the area of mental illness. Contrary to popular belief, for the population as a whole, there is a lower incidence of mental illness in the upper classes than in the lower classes; this tends to be the case for older people as well.

Margaret Clark and Barbara Anderson compared the social levels of persons 60 years of age and over who had undergone, or were in the process of undergoing treatment in a San Francisco hospital for mental disorders with the social levels of mentally healthy persons of similar ages who lived in the community.[20] The researchers found that the majority of hospital patients came from a considerably lower social level than the community residents did. Sixty-three percent of the community sample were from a high social level, compared to only 23 percent of the discharged hospital patients and to 14 percent of the hospital patients.

FRIENDSHIP PATTERNS Various studies reveal that the number of friends a person has in old age appears to be related to social class. Middle-class people have a larger number of friends than those in the working class.* Also, members of the working class are dependent on neighbors as a source of friends, while middle-class persons rely on other sources of friendship. As a corollary, Blau reports that widows in the working class are more isolated and have fewer social opportunities than widows in the middle class.[21]

---

*Working class is a broad term that refers to those who do manual work and usually includes blue-collar workers. It is often used synonymously for lower class.

AGE IDENTIFICATION   Feeling old tends to be related to social class. Rosow found in his Cleveland study that middle-class people aged 65 and over feel young or middle-aged as often as they feel old.[22] Among the working class sample, three out of every four persons thought of themselves as being older. While few persons look forward to the prospect of growing old, it seems that working-class people can more readily accept it. Rosow concludes:

> Those in the middle class are presumably more sensitive to the sheer implications of aging . . . and they are more demoralized by actual or impending age. Consequently, they deny their age. . . . For to identify oneself as old presumably represents a relatively greater loss of status and prestige to the middle class person than to the working class individual.[23]

RETIREMENT ADAPTATION   Retirement patterns vary with status level. In her study of 306 male retirees, Ida Simpson grouped workers into three general strata: upper white-collar workers, composed of professionals and executives; middle stratum, consisting of clerical workers, sales people, and skilled craftsmen and foremen; and lower blue-collar workers, composed of semiskilled service workers and laborers.[24] Of these three status levels, she found that though the upper white-collar workers received the greatest satisfaction from their work, they also made the most successful adaptation to retirement. Their adaptation was facilitated by their varied interests, their high level of community participation, and the freedom that their jobs afforded them to structure their own work routines. Although few of these men looked forward to retirement, when it came they adjusted well and were able to find meaningful substitutes for their work.

The middle level anticipated retirement the most. For them their work had little intrinsic meaning, and they looked forward to a life of leisure. In comparison to the upper white-collar workers, they had fewer interests and community roles, so they experienced more difficulty in finding substitutes for their work.

The blue-collar workers were not as enthusiastic about retirement as the middle level. They worried more about finances and felt a sense of helplessness toward life's events. In addition, their social relationships were limited to their family or neighbors, which gave them the fewest outlets in retirement. The blue-collar workers were the least successful in adapting to retirement.

FAMILY INTERACTION   Studies of the relationship between social class and visiting patterns have found that working-class persons visit older members of their family more often than middle-class persons do.

Figure 9.2 The life-styles of older people by social class.

	Vacation	Place for social life	Recreation	Rejuvenation aids
Upper class	 Mediterranean cruise	 Country club	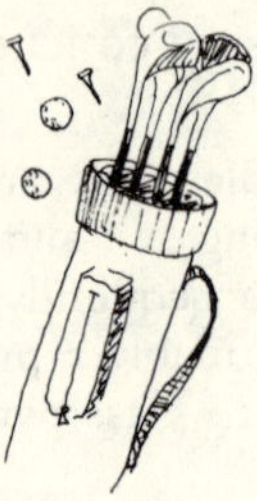 Golf	 Spas in Switzerland and Romania
Middle class	 Group bus tours	 Senior citizens center	 Shuffleboard	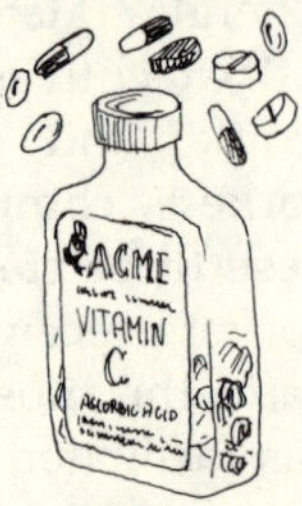 Vitamins
Lower class	 Visit sister Dora in Detroit	 Park bench	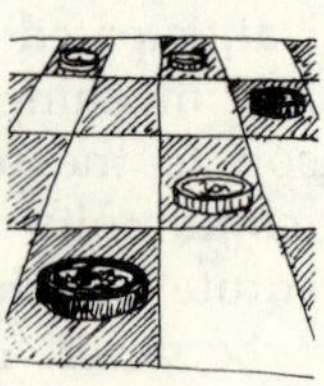 Checkers	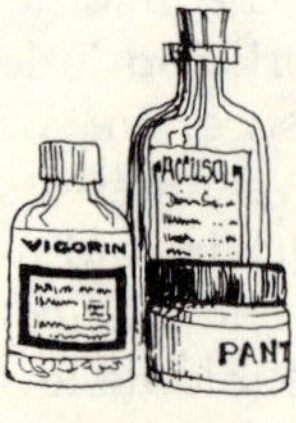 Patent medicines

Retirement rite	Retirement residence	Gifts to grandchildren under 18	Gifts to grandchildren over 18
Guest of honor at banquet	Condominiums or age-segregated apartment buildings	Money	Checking accounts and cars
Gold watch and group dinner	Retirement communities	Toys	Clothes
Handshake and a beer with the boys	Public housing or living with children	Cookies and pies	Cookies and pies

However, when geographic distance is controlled, middle-class persons visit their relatives as much as, if not more than, members of the working class. It appears, then, that social class affects visiting patterns because middle-class persons tend to move more and live farther from their relatives than those in the working class.[25]

Family-help patterns also vary by social class. Generally, parents in the middle class help their adult children by giving them financial assistance. Those in the lower classes supply less in the way of finances and rely more on the exchange of services.

In a study of grandparent roles, Albrecht found that males in the white-collar groups have more interaction with their grandchildren than those in the working class do. Overall, there was no significant difference in the grandmother role.[26] Other researchers have found that a stronger tie existed between grandparents and their grandchildren when they lived nearby, especially for those in the middle and upper classes.[27]

SOCIAL PARTICIPATION   Older persons in higher social levels participate more in community activities and tend to be more socially integrated into society than those in lower levels. In addition, the higher the level of income and education (often used as an index of social class), the greater the number of memberships in voluntary associations a person is likely to have. For older persons in the lower classes, social participation appears to revolve largely around their families and neighbors.

RESIDENTIAL MOBILITY   Change of residence takes place twice as often for older people in the lower classes, compared to those in the upper classes. Some research reveals that the poor elderly in urban areas continuously search for different housing. When older persons in the upper classes decide to relocate, they tend to move to age-segregated apartment complexes or to retirement communities.

LIFE SATISFACTION   A strong correlation exists between being satisfied with life and holding high social status. Older persons from the upper classes are more likely to evidence satisfaction with their lives than those in the lower classes. Family income appears to be one of the most important determinants of life satisfaction.

LEISURE TIME   How people use their leisure time varies with social class. Havighurst obtained information on leisure-time activities from a sample of 234 men and women in Kansas City between the ages of 40 and 70.[28] He found that the favorite activities of the upper-middle class were flower and landscape gardening and participation in sports and voluntary associations, while the lower-middle and lower-class people preferred television and manual-manipulative activities, such as home repairs and woodworking. Members of the lower-middle and upper-lower classes especially favored fishing. Visiting friends and relatives ranked highest among the lower-lower class as did vegetable gardening. All classes chose reading as a leisure-time activity about equally, with the exception of the lower class who showed the least interest in it.

Social Mobility

Social mobility refers to the vertical movement of persons or groups from one social class to another. Most people think of vertical social mobility as getting ahead and of moving up the social ladder as success. Getting a new or better job, marrying a person of higher status, and moving to a better neighborhood are all examples of upward social mobility. But vertical mobility can be downward as well. Instances of downward mobility would include loss or reduction of income, a job demotion, and in many cases, retirement and widowhood.

A common-place example of downward social mobility in old age is seen in the following instance:

> Mrs. Woods: an old lady with a lightly made, stately body, carried with pride and some pain. Her beautifully wrinkled skin was almost translucent, showing her high cheekbones.
>
> She would be pretty if not for the worried strain in her voice, face and hands, the shifting feet, distant eyes. A successful lawyer's wife, she had always been able to live in comfortable circumstances but was now under increasing financial pressure. She had outlived her savings.
>
> When her lawyer makes a visit she puts on the violet and blue print dress. She does not change her flat brown shoes. She pins her hair in a soft white knot in back. The lawyer was the family attorney for years. He comes to receive her endorsed checks and pay her bills. He makes out a check to the realty company for rent, and two other checks, one for the housekeeper who comes once a week, the other for food. He continues to help her now, when she is on public assistance of $92 per month.[29]

Rosow investigated downward social mobility among older people in the middle and working classes.[30] He used loss of income as an indicator of downward mobility because income is a major component of social class. Members in both social classes were equally matched in the proportion of retirees and widows who said they experienced a loss of income. As Table 9.1 shows, about one-fourth of the working class acknowledged that their class position declined, whereas only 14

Table 9.1   Social mobility of the retired and widowed by social class

	Mobility		
Social class	*Upward*	*Stable*	*Downward*
Working class	9%	65%	26%
Middle class	8	78	14

SOURCE: Irving Rosow, *Social Integration of the Aged*, Free Press, New York, 1967, p. 282.

percent of the middle class admitted a downward change. Rosow explains that growing old appears to be more threatening and demoralizing to people in higher-class positions because they have more to lose. Thus, members of the middle class are more likely than those of the lower class to deny or minimize any loss in status.

The amount of downward mobility in a society is an important indicator of whether or not it has an open- or closed-class system. Theoretically, an open-class system permits its members to move up and down the social hierarchy, depending on their own accomplishments or failings. In a closed-class system, on the other hand, mobility is severely restricted. A person is assigned a certain status, usually at birth, that cannot be changed. No class system is completely open or totally closed, but all systems can be placed on an open-to-closed continuum.

Industrial societies like our own have a fairly open-class system with considerable amounts of mobility. But how do those in the lower levels of our society view the class system and their chances for upward mobility? In a study of blue-collar workers in Philadelphia, Rosenberg analyzed the images that older workers had about the class system compared to those of younger workers.[31] When workers were asked whether or not they thought the class system was open or closed in terms of their own experience in getting ahead, a larger proportion of younger than of older workers indicated that it was a closed-class system. Those men currently in the labor force appeared to be more discontent and manifested more resentment than those who were retired. To explore beliefs about class system in the future, the men were asked what they thought would be the chance of working people getting ahead in the next ten years. Those still in the labor force tended to be more pessimistic about the future. A greater proportion of the younger men than of the older men believed that a closed-class system will prevent working-class advancement in the future. Rosenberg also examined the relationship between the economic context of the neighborhood where the workers lived and their image of the class system. He found that those older men who lived in the poorest neighborhoods were more likely to have a conception of a closed-class system.

Summary

1. Social stratification or structured social inequality is found in every known human society. Stratification refers to the ranking of individuals and families into higher and lower social positions according to their share of social rewards. These rewards involve wealth, power, and prestige.

2. Great inequalities exist in the distribution of income in the United States, especially among such categories in the population as the elderly. Power is also unequally distributed and may be divided into two types: personal and social. Personal power refers to the ability to control one's own life, while social power is the ability to control or influence the lives of others. Prestige, the social recognition that one receives from others, is largely determined by occupation. At retirement, a decline in prestige usually results.

3. Social classes are generally defined by occupation, education, and income. Though the number of social classes is not fixed and the divisions between the classes is often indistinct, most sociologists identify five or six classes. Havighurst and Albrecht found five classes in their study of older people in Prairie City. The smallest group of residents belonged to the upper class, which consisted of the older aristocratic families and the owners of Prairie City's principal industries. The upper-middle class members, made up of professionals, business executives, and owners of large retail businesses, were considered to be the community leaders. The lower-middle class provided the bulk of members in Prairie City's voluntary organizations. The largest class was the upper-lower category, which included those people who worked in semi-skilled manual jobs; they participated less than the higher classes in voluntary organizations. The lower-lower class included not only the most disadvantaged segment of the community, but also those persons thought to be dishonest, lazy, and of low moral standards.

4. Class membership relates to one's life chances and opportunities. Some of the varied aspects of life correlated with social class include: life expectancy, illness, friendship patterns, age identification, retirement adaptation, family interaction patterns, social participation, residential mobility, life satisfaction, and leisure time.

5. Social mobility refers to the vertical movement of persons or groups from one social class to another. Downward mobility is frequently found among those who are retired or widowed. Rosow observed that persons in the middle class found downward mobility harder to accept than those in the working class did. As a result those in the middle class deny or try to minimize any loss of status. Social mobility is an important indicator of whether or not a society has an open or closed class system. Rosenberg analyzed the images that older blue-collar workers and retirees held about the class system. On the whole, more older men than younger men tended to see the American class system as open and were more optimistic about the future and the chances for getting ahead.

Notes

1. Max Weber, *From Max Weber: Essays in Sociology*, trans. and ed. H. H. Gerth and C. Wright Mills, Oxford University Press, New York, 1946, pp. 180–195.

2. Daniel W. Rossides, *The American Class System*, Houghton Mifflin, Boston, 1976, pp. 126–128.

3. George S. Rosenberg, *The Worker Grows Old*, Jossey-Bass, San Francisco, 1970, pp. 9–10.

4. James D. Manney, Jr., *Aging in American Society*, Institute of Gerontology, University of Michigan-Wayne State University, Ann Arbor, 1975, pp. 126–127.

5. David Popenoe, *Sociology*, Appleton-Century-Crofts, New York, 1974, pp. 254–255.

6. Eugene A. Friedmann and Robert J. Havighurst, *The Meaning of Work and Retirement*, The University of Chicago Press, Chicago, 1954.

7. Ibid., p. 161.

8. W. Lloyd Warner and Paul S. Lunt, *The Social Life of a Modern Community*, vol. 1, *Yankee City Series*, Yale University Press, New Haven, 1941.

9. W. Lloyd Warner, ed., *Democracy in Jonesville*, Harper, New York, 1949.

10. Robert J. Havighurst and Ruth Albrecht, *Older People*, Longmans, Green, New York, 1953.

11. Ibid., p. 235.

12. Ibid., pp. 236–237.

13. Ibid., p. 241.

14. Ibid., pp. 239–241.

15. Ibid., pp. 241–242.

16. Ibid., pp. 243–244.

17. James E. Birren, *The Psychology of Aging*, Prentice-Hall, Englewood Cliffs, N.J., 1964, p. 25.

18. Albert J. Mayer and Phillip Hauser, "Class Differentials in Expectation of Life at Birth," *Class, Status and Power*, eds. Reinhard Bendix and Seymour M. Lipset, Free Press of Glencoe, Glencoe, Ill., 1953, pp. 281–284.

19. Robert H. Dovenmuehle, Ewald W. Busse, and Gustave Newman, "Physical Problems of Older People," *Normal Aging*, ed. Erdman Palmore, Duke University Press, Durham, N.C., 1970, pp. 29–39.

20. Margaret Clark and Barbara G. Anderson, *Culture and Aging*, Charles C Thomas, Springfield, Ill., 1967, pp. 442–443.

21. Zena Smith Blau, *Old Age in a Changing Society*, New Viewpoints, New York, 1973, p. 84.

22. Irving Rosow, *Social Integration of the Aged*, Free Press, New York, 1967, pp. 279–280.

23. Ibid., p. 280.

24. Ida Harper Simpson, "Problems of the Aging in Work and Retirement,

Foundations of Practical Gerontology, eds. Rosamonde R. Boyd and Charles G. Oakes, University of South Carolina Press, Columbia, S.C., 1973, pp. 167–170.

25. Vern L. Bengtson, Edward B. Olander, and Annus A. Haddad, "The Generation Gap and Aging Family Members," *Time, Roles and Self in Old Age*, eds. Jaber F. Gubrium, Human Sciences Press, New York, 1976, p. 251.

26. Ruth Albrecht, "The Family and Aging Seen Cross-Culturally," *Foundations of Practical Gerontology*, eds. Rosamonde R. Boyd and Charles G. Oakes, University of South Carolina Press, Columbia, S.C., 1973, p. 31.

27. Lillian E. Troll, Sheila J. Miller, and Robert C. Atchley, *Families in Later Life*, Wadsworth, Belmont, Calif., 1979, p. 113.

28. Robert J. Havighurst, "The Nature and Values of Meaningful Free-Time Activities," *Aging and Leisure*, ed. Robert W. Kleemeier, Oxford University Press, New York, 1961, p. 316.

29. Robert N. Butler, *Why Survive? Being Old in America*, Harper & Row, New York, 1975, p. 25.

30. Reprinted with permission of Macmillan Publishing Com., Inc. from *Social Integration of the Aged* by Irving Rosow. Copyright © 1967 by The Free Press, a Division of The Macmillan Company.

31. Rosenberg, *The Worker Grows Old*, pp. 169–184.

For Further Study

Coleman, Richard P., and Bernice L. Neugarten. *Social Status in the City*. Jossey-Bass, San Francisco, 1971. Deals with the social structure of Kansas City, Mo., in the 1950s.

Riley, Matilda W., Marilyn Johnson, and Anne Foner. *Aging and Society*: vol. 3, *A Sociology of Age Stratification*. Russell Sage Foundation, New York, 1972. Contains a theory of age stratification that parallels class stratification in some respects.

Rosenberg, George S. *The Worker Grows Old*. Jossey-Bass, San Francisco, 1970. Deals with the patterns of social participation among older men in the working class.

Rossides, Daniel W. *The American Class System*. Houghton Mifflin, Boston, 1976. An excellent text on social stratification in the United States.

Shanas, Ethel, Peter Townsend, Dorothy Wedderburn, Henning Friis, Poul Milhøj, and Jan Stehouwer. *Old People in Three Industrial Societies*. Atherton Press, New York, 1968. A cross-national study of the elderly in Denmark, Britain, and the United States, which offers valuable information on the relationship between the aged and social class in these three societies.

Streib, Gordon F. "Social Stratification and Aging." In *Handbook of Aging and the Social Sciences*, edited by Robert H. Binstock and Ethel Shanas. Van Nostrand Reinhold, New York, 1976. Provides a good systematic analysis of a neglected topic — the relationship between aging and social stratification.

10

The Elderly in Minority Groups

Not only do we use class membership as a basis for differentiating persons in American society (Chapter 9), but we also use membership in certain racial or ethnic groups.* The term *minority group* is often used to socially define a racial or ethnic segment of the population. Persons distinguished by such physical characteristics as skin color, hair texture, eyelid fold, or stature are identified as a *racial minority;* those distinguished by such cultural characteristics as language, religion, or national origin are identified as an *ethnic minority*.

Minority Status

Sociologists do not use the term *minority* in a numerical sense; they use it to denote some form of dominance. For instance, in the United States the blacks are a minority group and constitute about 11 percent of the population. But in the Union of South Africa where they make up 75 percent of the population, they are still considered a minority group because they are socially, politically, and economically dominated by the whites.

In the United States the dominant group has been and continues to be native-born, white, Anglo-Saxon Protestants (WASPS). Generally speaking, those in the population who do not share the characteristics of the dominant group are singled out for minority status. In essence then, a *minority group* is a category or group of people who in some ways differ from the dominant group in society and who because of this difference, are the objects of prejudice and discrimination, resulting in their being disadvantaged.

While prejudice and discrimination often occur together, they are not one and the same. It is possible to be prejudiced against a minority group without showing discrimination and vice versa. *Prejudice* refers to a state of mind and entails feelings and attitudes. *Discrimination* involves

*Though minorities have been traditionally designated as *groups* by sociologists, and we will follow this usage in the present chapter, they are not groups in the precise meaning of the term as defined in Chapter 8.

overt action in which members of a minority are treated unfavorably.[1] Robert Butler has coined the word *ageism* to describe prejudice against older people. He sees it as "a process of systematic stereotyping of and discrimination against people because they are old."[2]

Similar to social-class inequalities, minority group members have less access to the rewards of society — wealth, power, and prestige — than members of the dominant group do. Minority status limits opportunities and privileges, and as a result, minorities are often barred from full participation in society. Because of these conditions, some gerontologists argue that the elderly constitute a minority group.

The Elderly as a Minority Group

Leonard Breen points out that in many ways the elderly manifest characteristics of a minority group.[3] They have high visibility, they are subject to stereotyping, and they are the objects of prejudice and discrimination, especially in employment practices. Zena Blau also feels that the aged constitute a minority group "to the extent that they are barred from full and equal participation in the occupational structure, which in contemporary society is the principal determinant of status, wealth, and power."[4] A similar point of view is expressed by Ewald Busse and Eric Pfeiffer who believe that the aged hold the status of a deprived minority group.[5] They feel that older people, especially those who are retired, are often denied their share of opportunities and advantages available to the majority of our society.

In contrast to these views, Gordon Streib claims that they are not.[6] He lists six criteria associated with minority group status and argues that they do not apply to the condition of the elderly in our society.

1. Does the characteristic identify all who possess it throughout the life cycle?
2. Does the dominant group hold stereotypes and clichés about the aged regarding work performance and appropriate activities?
3. Do the aged view themselves as a separate and distinct group?
4. Is there a readiness to organize as an identifiable pressure group?
5. Do they have differential access to power, privileges, and rights?
6. Are the elderly deprived of economic and social security, as well as being subjected to residential and social isolation?

Streib claims that to view the elderly as a minority group only obscures their social role in society instead of clarifying it.

The aged do not share a distinct and separate culture; membership in the group defined as "aged" is not exclusive and permanent, but awaits all members of our society who live long enough. As a result, age is a less distinguishing group characteristic than others such as sex, occupation, social class, and the like. True, many aged persons possess distinctive physical characteristics. But even here there is a broad spectrum, and these "stigmata" do not normally justify differential and discriminatory treatment by others. The aged have little feeling of identification with their age group: they have a low degree of collective consciousness; hostility towards a depriving out-group is exceptional. The aged are not organized to advance their own interests and are not particularly attracted to such organizations. Nor are they systematically deprived of power and privileges. They are not herded in ghettos, deprived of civil rights, excluded from public facilities, or from jobs they are qualified to perform. That they are often underprivileged economi-cally and have more frequent health problems is more the result of handicaps that often accompany aging, than of social organization or group structure.[7]

Jerry Jacobs contends that much of Streib's refutation of the aged as a minority group applies to the elderly who are still working and part of the greater community and not to retired persons, especially those living in retirement communities.[8] Jacobs feels that many characteristics of minority status are seen among the residents of retirement communities like Fun City.

Figure 10.1   Five principal minorities of the population aged 65 and over in the United States, 1970

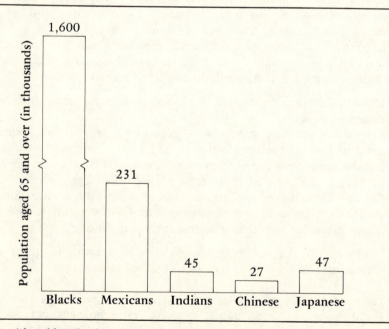

SOURCE: Adapted from data from the U.S. Bureau of the Census, 1970.

Fun City residents exhibit a "sense of consciousness of kind," are subject to "restrictions on political roles and activities," do not have "access to work," are "subject to residential segregation" (by way of subjecting others to it), do experience "social [and geographic] isolation," are as a group looked upon by the greater community as "less deserving of respect and consideration" (indeed, this is their self-perception of how others view them), and experience "less economic and social security" (real or perceived).[9]

As the elderly continue to develop more group identification and group consciousness, which are already becoming quite pronounced in many retirement communities, they will become increasingly more like a minority group. But whether or not the elderly constitute a "true" minority group is debatable. Undoubtedly, however, they possess many characteristics associated with minority group status.

America is a nation composed of hundreds of minority groups. These minority groups originated from three principal sources: the indigenous Indian population, the blacks brought from Africa as servants and slaves, and the immigrants who settled on our shores.

The five principal minority groups in the United States are the blacks, the Mexican-Americans, the Indians, the Chinese-Americans, and the Japanese-Americans (Figure 10.1). Brief sketches of the history and the experience of each group in this country follow, with a discussion of their present situation and problems of their elderly.

The Elderly in Minority Groups

The Black Americans

Americans of African ancestry are the largest minority group in the nation. They number nearly 25 million and comprise 11 percent of the population. Their history in this country includes over 100 years of exploitation and degradation.

The first blacks came to the new world as explorers and servants, not slaves. The precedent for slavery in America was established by the Spanish and Portuguese and later adopted by the English. The black population grew very slowly at first, even after slavery was legally established in the English Colonies. With the advent of the industrial revolution, which created a demand for raw materials, especially cotton, the demand for black slaves rapidly increased. By 1860 there were nearly 4 million blacks in slavery. Their price also increased; a healthy male between the ages of 16 and 24 was sold for $1,800 on the New Orleans market.

To protect the sizable investments of the slave owners, laws were enacted, known as the slave codes. These laws did not allow the slaves

When Dr. Ira Reid, a distinguished black sociologist, was asked what term would be most appropriate to describe Negroes, he replied that no appellation would please all. He felt that different age groups would, on the average, have different preferences. The very old would probably be preferred to be called "colored"; a slightly younger group would prefer "Afro-Asian"; a still younger group "Negro"; and the young would demand "black."

SOURCE: Donald P. Kent, "The Elderly in Minority Groups: Variant Patterns of Aging," *The Gerontologist*, 2, no. 1 (1971), Pt. II, 28.

to leave the premises without written permission of their owners. Slaves were not allowed to own property, to give evidence in court, or to make contracts. In addition, it was forbidden to teach them reading or writing.

In 1865 when the Thirteenth Amendment abolished slavery and involuntary servitude, discrimination and intimidation of the blacks still continued. The Jim Crow statutes of the 1890s served to make the blacks second-class citizens by excluding them from all private and public facilities used by whites. In 1896 the United States Supreme Court made "separate but equal" facilities the law of the land. This law stayed in effect until after World War II.

Since World War II, there has been an unprecedented migration of blacks from the South to northern cities. In 1940, 77 percent of the nation's blacks lived in the South, and by 1970 only slightly more than half remained. This migration can be attributed primarily to the better opportunities for employment in the North. Also, after the war mechanization of Southern farms increased greatly, and many rural blacks could no longer find work as field laborers or sharecroppers.

The Supreme Court declared segregation unconstitutional in 1954 and the Civil Rights Act was passed some ten years later. Since these events, black Americans have made great strides in the areas of employment, income, education, and housing. Yet, despite these gains, there is still a considerable gap between the races, which is even more pronounced among many elderly blacks who are said to experience the triple jeopardy of being black, old, and poor.

THE BLACK ELDERLY   In general, the nearly 2 million blacks age 65 and over have lower incomes, less education, poorer housing, and a lower quality of life than their white counterparts. The life expectancy of blacks at birth is far below that of whites. In 1976, life expectation for black men was 64.1 years, compared to 69.7 years for white men. For black women life expectancy was 72.6 years; for white women it was 77.3 years. Though fewer blacks survive to old age, the ones who do tend to live longer than the white elderly do. By the early seventies the life expectancy for blacks becomes greater than that for whites. This tendency may be due to the factor of natural selection, in which only the healthiest blacks who have been able to endure the hardships of younger years, survive to old age. By the same token, the hardships faced by blacks, including social and economic deprivations, are reflected in the fact that blacks perceive themselves as being old earlier and that they tend to age at a faster rate than whites.[10]

The income of families headed by blacks age 65 and over is much lower than for families headed by whites 65 and over. The median income of elderly husband-wife black families in 1976 was $6,457, whereas the median income of similar white families was $8,902.[11] Although the proportion of older Americans living below the poverty level has steadily fallen in the last decade and a half, 36 percent of the elderly blacks were still below the poverty level in 1974, compared to only 14 percent of the older whites. Older black females fare much worse than older black males. Sixty-nine percent of black women who live alone are poor, compared to 44 percent of the black males.

The level of educational attainment also differs between the races. In 1977, 38 percent of white males and 41 percent of white females age 65 and over had completed high school. In contrast, only 16 percent of black males and 14 percent of black females were high school graduates.

Another disparity between the races is in the area of nursing home and long-term care facilities. The percentage of blacks in these institutions is much lower than it is for whites. Some maintain this is due to the fact that blacks take care of their own.

It is a common assumption, perhaps with some basis in truth, that blacks and other minority-group members offer greater acceptance to their elderly and that both the older minority members and their families prefer that they remain within the home. This assumption has been attacked in recent years as an excuse on the part of the "white establishment" for not providing adequate long-term care facilities for nonwhites. The claim is made that nonwhites are underrepresented in these care facilities because of overt racial discrimination and because of serious economic limitations. The black elderly are found in these institutions at less than one-third the rate their population would indicate.[12]

To determine how the black aged differ from the many stereotypes held about them in our culture, Jacquelyne Jackson analyzed research findings in social gerontology and other related fields.[13] The aged black is often depicted as differing from the aged white in marital status, but Jackson found that no such difference existed. Neither did she find any evidence to substantiate the belief that blacks have a weaker family structure than whites. "For most aged Negroes with families, the family is the primary source of assistance (to the extent of its ability) and of primary group relationships.''[14] In addition, when socioeconomic status was held constant, Jackson found no significant differences between older blacks and whites regarding religious activity, health, and organizational participation. Contrary to earlier findings indicating that blacks had a low rate of organizational and political participation, some recent studies have shown that older blacks may even exhibit a slightly greater participation than whites.

The Mexican-Americans

The largest group of Spanish-speaking people in this country are the 6.6 million Americans of Mexican descent. Mexican-Americans, or Chicanos as they are commonly called, are concentrated in the five southwestern states of California, Arizona, New Mexico, Colorado, and Texas. As a whole, Mexican-Americans are poor and often jobless, have a high rate of illiteracy, and are plagued by discriminatory practices.

Some Mexican-Americans are descendants of the original settlers who occupied the southwestern part of the United States long before New England was colonized. At the end of the Mexican-American War in 1848, Mexico recognized the annexation of Texas by the United States and ceded the territory that now comprises the states of California, Nevada, and Utah, and parts of Arizona, New Mexico, Colorado, and Wyoming to the United States. The people living on these lands were given the option to move to Mexico or to become American citizens. Many of them remained, and today their descendants number about one million.

During the Mexican Revolution of 1911 to 1922, many well-to-do Mexicans began immigrating to the United States as political refugees. Others came because of the attraction of the agricultural labor market. It is estimated that between 1910 and 1930, about a million Mexicans entered this country. During the depression of the 1930s, immigration from Mexico was brought to a halt. Also many Mexican laborers, though United States citizens by birth, were deported by the truckloads back to Mexico in an effort to relieve the unemployment situation in this country.[15] Beginning about World War II, Mexican immigration resumed and has continued to the present time. Most of the recent immigrants have come in search of agricultural work. Thousands have entered this country illegally by wading or swimming across the Rio Grande (hence, some are referred to as "wetbacks").

Mexican-Americans have continued to preserve their language, along with many cultural traditions and values. Most live in distinct and relatively closed urban communities known as *barrios,* which serve to reinforce their cultural identity. Though the Mexican-Americans have not been socially excluded to the extent of the blacks, they have shared somewhat similar experiences in residential and school segregation. Both have suffered discrimination in employment and have been denied access to public accommodations. An 83-year-old Mexican-American woman whose ancestry in this country can be traced back for four centuries remarked, "You bend with the wind. And Anglo people are a strong wind. They want their own way; they can be like a tornado, out to pass over everyone as they go somewhere. . . . But we are outsiders in a land that is ours."[16]

THE MEXICAN-AMERICAN ELDERLY   The proportion of persons age 65 and over is unusually low among the Mexican-Americans. Only 4 percent of all Mexican-Americans are elderly, compared to 11 percent of all persons in this country. Several factors account for this. First, Mexican women have high fertility rates, which result in a disproportionate number of young persons in the population. Secondly, the most recent immigrants to the United States from Mexico are young. At the same time, Mexican-Americans leaving the United States are often older persons returning to Mexico to live out their remaining years. Finally, Mexican-Americans have a shorter life expectancy than the national average, so fewer persons survive to old age.

Most older Mexican-Americans have low incomes. In 1976, 35 percent of Mexican-American families with heads 65 years of age and over fell below the poverty level. Older Mexican-American females have much lower incomes than older males. The median income for elderly female Mexican-Americans was $1,927, compared to $3,112 for the males.

Because of their poverty and low educational attainment, and especially because of their language barrier, most older Mexican-Americans are separated from, and uninformed about the larger society. Diffusing information to them becomes a difficult problem. Frances Carp investigated the communication habits of older Mexican-Americans and the ways in which they obtain information.[17] She found that the difficulty in communication arises because the usual techniques for disseminating information are relatively ineffective. Though most listened regularly to the radio and watched television, two-thirds of the group said that they never read a newspaper. Sixty percent interviewed said they never read a magazine. "Much of the 'reading' consisted of looking at illustrations . . . for this generation of old people there is little hope of improving information dissemination through the printed word because their reading skills are very poor, both in English and in Spanish."[18]

The low level of literacy of older Mexican-Americans is borne out by the census data. In 1976, 70 percent of the Mexican-American women and 64 percent of the men 65 years of age and over had completed less than 5 years of school. About 4 percent of the women and 5 percent of the men had finished high school.

Many elderly Mexican-Americans have held strongly to their values and traditions. Like this man in New Mexico, they are a proud and independent people. (© 1973 by Alex Harris. Reprinted from *The Old Ones of New Mexico*, by Robert Coles [Albuquerque: University of New Mexico Press, 1973], by permission of the photographer and publisher.)

Perception of aging appears to vary among different groups in the population. In a West Texas study of 291 older Mexican-Americans, Ben Crouch found that nearly two-thirds of the sample considered old age to begin at 60 or below.[19] A similar finding was reported by Vern Bengtson and his associates in Southern California where they compared 1,269 Mexican-Americans, blacks, and Anglos.[20] The respondents were asked whether they thought of themselves as old, middle-aged, or young. Over 30 percent of the Mexican-Americans replied that they were old at age 60 (others felt old at younger ages), blacks replied at age 65, and Anglos did not feel old until they were about 70. These studies, as well as those cited earlier, indicate that perception of aging is related to socioeconomic status. Those of a lower socioeconomic status perceive the onset of old age as beginning much earlier than those of a higher socioeconomic status. Because blacks and Mexican-Americans are deprived minorities of essentially the same lower socioeconomic level, we would expect that they would perceive old age as starting sooner — and they do.

Bengtson reports that both Mexican-Americans and blacks view old age more negatively than Anglos do.[21] This negative view may in part reflect whether older people judge their own health to be good or bad. He found that in the 65–74 age group, 23 percent of Mexican-Americans considered their health to be poor, as did 27 percent of the blacks. In contrast, only 4 percent of the Anglos felt that they were in poor health.

The Native Americans

No other minority in the United States has suffered more injustice or abuse than the American Indian. Their deprivation is unequalled by any other group in our society. In 1977, there were 898,392 Indians, or Native Americans as they are often called. They live in every state of the union. Half the Indian population lives outside the boundaries of reservations in urban areas. About 30 percent live on reservations located in some 26 states.

At the time of Columbus, it is estimated that over a million Indians lived in the territory that now comprises the United States. They represented several hundred major tribes with countless subdivisions. Each of these tribal groups had their own distinctive culture and language. It has been said that the American Indians spoke more different languages than were used in the entire Old World.

At first the relationship between the early European settlers and their Indian neighbors was a peaceful one. In many cases, the Indians turned over large portions of land to them in return for goods, not understanding the European meaning of property rights. But later when the white settlers made additional demands for land, bitter disputes arose. If the Indians resisted, they were either driven away or annihilated.

As the invading whites moved westward, the policies of the federal government toward the Indians shifted between assimilation, leaving them alone, and extermination. In the first half of the nineteenth century an estimated 100,000 Indians were moved to the territories in the West. Many Indians died en route because of the harsh conditions under which they were forced to travel. Diseases introduced by Europeans also took a toll of Indian lives — more were lost than in military conflict.

The first of 267 reservations was established in the middle part of the nineteenth century. One purpose of the reservation was to help assimilate the Indians into the American way of life. In 1871 Congress declared that no Indian tribe could be recognized as an independent power, and the Indians were made wards of the federal government. In

Unemployment rates on Indian reservations are extremely high. These women on the Cherokee reservation in North Carolina are making items to sell to tourists. (Courtesy of Tennessee Valley Authority)

the years that followed, the government program to break up the tribal organizations and to force the Indians to "Americanize" met with utter failure. In 1933 the policy of the federal government toward the Indians was reversed. Instead of trying to assimilate the Indians, they were given freedom to preserve their identity and to retain the values and customs of their cultures. A year later the Indian Reorganization Act was passed, which allowed the Indians to form businesses and agricultural enterprises and to set up self-governing units. The first Americans were finally granted citizenship in 1924.

THE NATIVE AMERICAN ELDERLY   In 1977, there were 48,042 Indians aged 65 and over. Nearly half of them live on or near federal reservations. Even though the average life expectancy for the Indian has increased from 60.0 years in 1950 to 65.1 years in 1970, it is still below that of any group in the population.[22] Unemployment rates on reservations some-

The elderly Indian is considered the poorest of the poor. This 91-year-old Salish woman suffers from the effects of economic deprivation. (Courtesy of the Bureau of Indian Affairs)

times reach 50 percent and even higher. Few of the elderly have ever worked steadily, and because of this and the fact that many who were employed were not covered under social security, a large proportion of the Indian elderly are ineligible for social security benefits. In most cases, older Indians cannot look to their children for financial assistance because they also have an inadequate income. In 1970 the per capita income for all Indians in the United States was $1,573, and in 1975 it was $1,520 for Indians living on reservations.

Being the poorest of the poor, the elderly Indians suffer from hunger and malnutrition and have a high incidence of disease. Medical care, provided primarily by the Indian Health Service, is extremely inadequate. Also funds are lacking for hearing aids, eye glasses, and dentures.

A contributing factor to poor health and prevalence of disease among older Indians is substandard and overcrowded living conditions.* A study done in California revealed:

> Many older Native Americans live in crowded homes where there are from one to three families. Physical crowding promotes the spread of infectious diseases. Water, usually from wells, is often contaminated and the lack of refrigeration in many homes leads to contamination of foods. Open fires and stoves which are used for heating and cooking present burn hazards. Leaky roofs and damp houses contribute to colds, pneumonia, and lowered resistance to other diseases.[23]

The lack of nursing home and extended care facilities as well as their inaccessibility is still another problem confronting older Indians. Some states will not license nursing homes on Indian reservations. Often Indians are forced to go outside their communities to obtain this type of care.

> When a sick elderly Indian must be moved to a nursing home facility, it is usually not within his own community but several hundred miles away or even in another state. The normal trauma of being uprooted from home and familiar surroundings is intensified for the elderly Indian because he is surrounded by strangers who do not understand his language or cultural values and is too far from home for relatives or friends to visit. The attitude of many is typified by a remark one older Apache reportedly made to his relatives as he was being taken to a nursing home in Phoenix, Arizona. "Goodbye," he said. "The next time you see me I will be in a pine box."[24]

The plight of older Indians is further aggravated by their social and physical isolation. Most have little or no education. Many cannot speak English, and for those who do, it is a second language. A large percentage of elderly Indians live on or near reservations, generally in isolated rural areas and miles from a major urban center. Poor roads and lack of transportation make medical services and other facilities in these centers often inaccessible.

The Chinese-Americans

The Chinese and Japanese, though both Asian minorities in the United States, differ greatly in their history in this country. The first large influx

---

*In 1976, there were 86,500 Indian families living in substandard housing.

of Chinese to the United States began in the 1850s, precipitated by the famine in the Canton region of China and the need for contract laborers ("coolies") to help build U.S. railroads and work in the California gold mines. Many of those who had originally intended to return to China after improving their economic situation remained permanently. Later the Chinese began to shift to other occupations, including working on the farms and orchards of the West Coast. Because of the shortage of women in the Old West, many Chinese found it profitable to open small restaurants and hand laundries.

With the completion of the Central Pacific Railroad and the rise in unemployment, many whites began to fear competition from cheap Chinese labor. Anti-Chinese feelings intensified and open hostility ensued, many Chinese were beaten, harassed, and even lynched. In 1882, Congress passed the Chinese Exclusion Act making all Chinese immigration illegal. The Act was not repealed until 1943 when China became our military ally in World War II.

Much of the past prejudice and discrimination against Chinese-Americans has declined. During the last decade their number has increased by 84 percent, mostly due to immigration. Today there are 435,000 Chinese-Americans, and nearly all live in urban areas. Although there are many near-illiterate Chinese in the population, at the same time the proportion of Chinese-Americans who have completed college is more than double the national average and is the highest of any group in the United States.

THE CHINESE-AMERICAN ELDERLY   About 6 percent of the total Chinese-American population, or 27,000, are 65 and over. The Chinese population in the United States has been predominantly male since the beginning of this century. Though the differential between the sexes has been gradually decreasing, by 1970 elderly males still comprised 57 percent of their population and females 43 percent. This unusual sex ratio reflects the earlier immigration patterns.

The elderly Chinese have the highest rate of poverty of any of the other Asian-Americans. In 1970 nearly 30 percent were poor. Over half the Chinese elderly who are poor live alone, and most are males who never married because of the scarcity of Chinese women.

Traditionally, the Chinese have emphasized education for males, but not for females. This practice is reflected in the extremely high rate of illiteracy for elderly foreign-born females. (See Table 10.1) The elderly foreign-born males had 6.2 median years of school, compared to less than a year for females.

Elderly Chinese fall into two principal groups: those who came here as early immigrants to work as laborers, and recent immigrants who came as political refugees, when they were old, from the Communist

A major problem facing a significant number of Chinese elderly is their lack of fluency in English, which makes it difficult for them to obtain many needed services. (Jeroboam Inc. Ilka Hartmann—Photographer)

Table 10.1 Median years of school of Chinese and Japanese 65 years old and over by sex and nativity, 1970

	Chinese	*Japanese*
Males		
U.S. born	7.7 years	8.6 years
Foreign born	6.2	8.5
Females		
U.S. born	8.1	7.8
Foreign born	0.9	7.4

Source: Adapted from "A Study of Selected Socio-economic Characteristics of Ethnic Minorities Based on the 1970 Census," vol. II: *Asian Americans*, Department of Health, Education, and Welfare, Washington, D.C.

takeover. A major problem facing both groups is the language barrier, which separates them from the mainstream of American society as well as from other Chinese speaking another of the many different Chinese dialects.

In addition, not speaking English hampers their capacity to obtain many needed services, such as health care. In a study of health-care needs of 138 elderly persons in San Francisco's Chinatown, Frances Karp and Eunice Kataoka found that though serious health problems existed among the older residents, their resources for obtaining medical services on their own were extremely limited.[25] Besides the problem of communicating with the physician, they found that the majority of older Chinese-Americans live below the poverty level and cannot afford medical care. Eighty percent of the Chinese-American elderly who were interviewed in the study lived in a household with a yearly income of less than $4,000, nearly a third of them with a family income under $2,000. Most of the elderly respondents had no means of transportation and were restricted to those medical services within walking distance.

Many people believe that because of the Chinese concept of filial piety, respect, and devotion to parents, the aged Chinese have no problems and will be taken care of by their children. This practice is not generally followed today in America. As younger Chinese families have become Americanized, children have taken the highest position in the family and are considered more important than parents. Although many Chinese-Americans still give lip service to the concept of filial piety and believe it should be preserved, a discrepancy exists between the ideal and actual practice. In a study of Chinese aged in Los Angeles, Frances Wu notes that "financial support of parents was an ideal approved by both aged and middle-aged, but in practice, this support was rare."[26] Because of the popular belief that the Chinese elderly are cared for by

---

The following is an illustration of the concept of filial piety that has dominated the teachings of the Chinese for centuries: Kuo Chu was a poor man burdened with a wife, mother, and child. One day he said to his wife, "We are so poor that we cannot even support mother. Moreover, the little one shares mother's food. Why not bury this child? We may have another, but if mother should die, we could not get another one." The wife did not dare to contradict him. He began to dig the grave and suddenly discovered a vase full of gold, "A gift of heaven to the filial son."

SOURCE: Frances Y. T. Wu, "Mandarin-Speaking Aged Chinese in the Los Angeles Area," *The Gerontologist*, 15, no. 3 (1975), 274.

their families, they have often been overlooked in government appropriations for the needy elderly.

The Japanese-Americans

The Japanese immigrants began arriving in this country about 1880, 30 years after the Chinese. Like the Chinese, most were unskilled laborers who planned to return home after earning some money. Some worked on farms and in mines, while others went to the cities to become small merchants or to work as domestics or gardeners. Soon the prejudice against Chinese workers was also directed toward the Japanese. To decrease their immigration, President Theodore Roosevelt entered into a "Gentleman's Agreement" with the Japanese government in 1908. Under the agreement, Japan was not to permit laborers to emigrate to the United States. The Japanese government was, however, allowed to issue passports to the wives of Japanese men living in this country; many Japanese women were married by proxy, so that they could come to the United States as wives.

In 1942, following the attack on Pearl Harbor, 100,000 Japanese citizens and aliens were removed from the West Coast and interned in "security" camps in other parts of the country. The reason given for their evacuation was that all Americans of Japanese ancestry were considered to be potential traitors and saboteurs. Before leaving the West Coast, they were forced to sell their businesses and property within a few weeks, and because of this, they suffered great financial losses. After the war, many Japanese-Americans, depleted of their resources, found it difficult to start over again and to return to their former occupations.

Despite their financial losses during World War II and the retention by the general society of some prejudice against them, the Japanese have been remarkably successful in the last 30 years. Not only have they achieved the highest socioeconomic level of any racial minority in the United States, but they have surpassed the national average in income and educational attainment.

THE JAPANESE-AMERICAN ELDERLY In 1970 there were 591,000 Japanese-Americans in this country; about 47,000 were 65 and over. The Japanese population has shifted from being predominantly male to being predominantly female. Among the elderly, 43 percent of the population are males, and 57 percent are females. This increase is due not only to female longevity but to a higher percentage of female immigrants.

The elderly Japanese men have slightly higher educational attainment than the women. There is also only a small difference in schooling between Japanese who are foreign born and those born in the United States (See Table 10.1).

About one-fifth of all Japanese elderly are poor. The poverty rate is higher for those without their families in rural areas. Most of the elderly poor who live alone are women, usually widows. Like the older Chinese, the Japanese have problems in communicating, as many cannot speak English.

Minorities differ markedly from one another because each is a product of its distinctive cultural background and its own history in this country. But, because of their minority status and the prejudice and discrimination experienced, these groups share certain characteristics. The histories of black Americans, American Indians, and Mexican-Americans reflect a disproportionate amount of unemployment and poverty. Their wages are often low, their housing substandard, and their medical care inadequate.

The minority elderly not only endure the same deprived conditions that they did when younger, but their position has worsened. The elderly in each of the five minorities discussed above have the highest rate of poverty for their group. Because they trail far behind the younger members in education and language skills, they are often isolated, even within their own group. And to the existing discrimination pervading their lives, a new dimension is added — age discrimination.

Summary

1. Basically there are two types of minority groups: racial and ethnic. Persons belonging to a racial minority are distinguished from the dominant group by physical characteristics; those belonging to an ethnic group are distinguished by cultural characteristics. A minority group is a category or group of people who differ in some ways from the dominant group of society and, because of this, are the objects of prejudice and discrimination.

2. Prejudice is a state of mind, whereas discrimination involves overt action. Prejudice and discrimination directed against old people is called *ageism*. Because of ageism, some argue that the elderly constitute a minority group or have the characteristics of a minority group.

3. The five principal minority groups in our society are blacks, Mexican-Americans, American Indians, Chinese-Americans, and Japanese-Americans. The blacks are the largest minority group in the nation. Those 65 and over generally have lower incomes, less education, and poorer housing than do whites in the same age category. Contrary to stereotypes often held about older blacks, Jackson found that they are similar to their white counterparts in religious activity, health, and organizational participation.

4. The largest group of Spanish-speaking people in the nation are the Mexican-Americans. Mexican-Americans have an unusually low proportion of older

people in their population. Besides having low incomes and educational levels, Mexican-Americans are plagued by a language barrier, which limits their communication with the larger society. Research reveals that Mexican-Americans, as well as blacks, perceive old age as beginning sooner and view aging more negatively than whites do.

5. Of all the minority groups in our society, the most deprived are the American Indians, or Native Americans. In the middle of the nineteenth century, over 267 government reservations were established. Today about half of all older Indians live there. Their living conditions are characterized by extreme poverty, malnutrition, and a high incidence of disease; their houses are often substandard and overcrowded. Health services available to them are inadequate and often inaccessible.

6. In the 1850s, large numbers of young Chinese laborers immigrated to this country to work on the railroads and in the mines. Because of widespread feelings of prejudice and discrimination, laws were passed to halt their immigration. Today these early patterns of immigration are reflected in the unusual sex ratio of the elderly Chinese — more men than women. Although younger Chinese-Americans have the highest educational attainment of any group in the nation, many elderly Chinese have low levels of literacy. The elderly are not generally cared for by their families, as the tradition of filial piety appears to be gradually fading in this country.

7. Similar to the Chinese, the Japanese came here as laborers and soon became the object of prejudice and discrimination. Large numbers were unjustly interned during World War II in the interest of U.S. security. Though Japanese-Americans as a whole have above-average incomes, about one-fifth of the older Japanese are poor.

Notes

1. James W. Vander Zanden, *American Minority Relations* (3rd ed.), Ronald Press, New York, 1972, p. 26.

2. Robert N. Butler, *Why Survive? Being Old in America*, Harper & Row, New York, 1975, p. 12.

3. Leonard Z. Breen, "The Aging Individual," *Handbook of Social Gerontology*, ed. Clark Tibbitts, The University of Chicago Press, Chicago, p. 157.

4. Zena Smith Blau, *Old Age in a Changing Society*, New Viewpoints, New York, 1973, p. 97.

5. Ewald W. Busse and Eric Pfeiffer, "Introduction," *Behavior and Adaptation in Late Life*, eds. E. W. Busse and E. Pfeiffer, Little, Brown, Boston, 1977, p. 2.

6. Gordon F. Streib, "Are the Aged a Minority Group?" *Applied Sociology*, eds. Alvin W. Gouldner and S. M. Miller, Free Press, New York, 1965, pp. 311–328.

7. Reprinted with permission of Macmillan Publishing Co., Inc. from ibid., pp. 45–46. Copyright © 1967 by the Free Press, a division of The Macmillan Company.

8. Jerry Jacobs, *Fun City*, Holt, Rinehart & Winston, New York, 1974, p. 74.

9. Ibid.

10. Jacquelyne J. Jackson, "Aged Negroes: Their Cultural Departures from Statistical Stereotypes and Rural-Urban Differences," *The Gerontologist*, 10, no. 2 (1970), p. 141.

11. Robert Hill, "A Demographic Profile of the Black Elderly," *Aging*, September–October 1978, nos. 287–288, pp. 4–5.

12. Richard A. Kalish, *Late Adulthood: Perspectives on Human Development*, Brooks/Cole, Monterey, Calif., 1975, pp. 19–20.

13. Jackson, "Aged Negroes," pp. 140–145.

14. Ibid., p. 142.

15. Luis F. Hernandez, *"Mexican-Americans" in Minority Problems*, eds. Arnold M. Rose and Caroline B. Rose, Harper & Row, New York, 1965, pp. 60–69.

16. Robert Coles, *The Old Ones of New Mexico*, University of New Mexico Press, Albuquerque, 1974, p. 17.

17. Frances M. Carp, "Communicating with Elderly Mexican-Americans," *The Gerontologist*, 10, no. 2 (1970), 126–133.

18. Ibid., p. 131.

19. Ben M. Crouch, "Age and Institutional Support: Perceptions of Older Mexican-Americans," *The Journal of Gerontology*, 27 (1972), 525.

20. Vern L. Bengtson, et al., "The Impact of Social Structure on Aging Individuals," *Handbook of the Psychology of Aging*, eds. James E. Birren and K. Warner Schaie, Van Nostrand Reinhold, New York, 1977, pp. 340–341.

21. Bengtson et al., "The Impact of Social Structure on Aging Individuals," p. 340.

22. *American Indian Policy Review Commission, Final Report*, U.S. Government Printing Office, Washington, D.C., 1977, p. 91.

23. "Nutrition Program Aids California's Older Native Americans," *Aging*, September–October 1976, p. 11.

24. "Projects in Nevada Succeed in Helping Indians Help Themselves," *Aging*, September–October 1976, p. 18.

25. Frances M. Carp and Eunice Kataoka, "Health Care Problems of the Elderly of San Francisco's Chinatown," *The Gerontologist*, 16, no. 1 (1976), 30–38.

26. Frances Y. T. Wu, "Mandarin-Speaking Aged Chinese in the Los Angeles Area," *The Gerontologist*, 15 no. 3 (1975), 271–275; quote from p. 274.

For Further Study

Bell, Bill D., ed. *Contemporary Social Gerontology*. Charles C Thomas, Springfield, Ill., 1976. Section 8 consists of a series of papers on the minority elderly.

Coles, Robert. *The Old Ones of New Mexico*. University of New Mexico Press, Albuquerque, 1974. An insightful account of the elderly Mexican-American's view of life.

Hendricks, Jon, and C. Davis Hendricks. *Aging in Mass Society*. Winthrop, Cambridge, Mass. 1977. Chapter 13 contains a good discussion of the experiences of minority aging.

Rose, Peter. *They and We: Racial and Ethnic Relations in the United States*, 2nd ed. Random House, New York, 1974. A concise, clearly written introduction to minority group relations.

Vander Zanden, James W. *American Minority Relations*, 3rd ed. Ronald Press, New York, 1972. An excellent basic text for the study of minority relations.

Youmans, E. Grant, ed. *Older Rural Americans*. University of Kentucky Press, Lexington, 1967. A sociological perspective on the elderly who live in rural environments. Chapters include the older American Indians, the older Spanish-speaking people, and the older rural blacks.

IV

Social Institutions
and the Elderly

11

The Family

A wit once remarked that "marriage is a great institution, but who wants to live in an institution?" This statement combines both the popular usage and the sociological meaning of *institution*. Most people think of an institution as a place of complete or partial confinement where a specific group of individuals lives — for example, prisons, hospitals, orphanages, schools, and nursing homes. In sociology, the term *institution* is used as an abstraction and refers to normative patterns and established procedures, not to a particular place or a concrete entity. In the sociological sense, you cannot see, belong to, or live in an institution.

Institutions

An institution may be thought of as a regulatory agency that channels human action much in the way that instincts channel animal behavior.[1] Peter Berger notes that "institutions provide procedures through which human conduct is patterned, compelled to go, in grooves deemed desirable to society."[2] An *institution*, then, may be defined as an organized cluster of norms — folkways, mores, and laws — that surround an important social need or activity of a society. In other words, an institution is a conventional way of pursuing an activity important to society.

Every known society has these five basic social institutions in one form or another: the family, the economy, the political system, religion, and education. So necessary are institutions that no society could survive without them. Each institution fulfills at least one major function (see Table 11.1).

In Part Four we will examine these five social institutions, emphasizing the roles of the elderly in them and how roles in each of these institutions change with age. Now let us discuss the first institution to which all human beings are introduced — the family.

Table 11.1   The five basic social institutions and their functions

Institution	Function
Family	Procreation and child-rearing
Economy	The production and distribution of goods and services
Political system	Maintenance of societal order
Religion	Preservation and reaffirmation of sacred traditions and shared values
Education	The transmission of cultural values, knowledge, and skills

Patterns of Family Organization

A Cross-cultural Perspective

Anthropologists and sociologists have recorded an amazing variety of family patterns that exist or have existed in different societies of the world. Many patterns differ greatly from our own and seem strange to us. By the same token, American family patterns appear strange to people of other cultures, who are equally ethnocentric.

Societies vary greatly in their processes for selecting mates. In many places, marriage arrangements are made by the heads of families. Their authority in these matters is often reinforced by the requirement that a bride price be paid to the girl's family by the boy's parents. In ancient Greece and in China until recently, brides and grooms did not see each other until just before the wedding ceremony. In some societies, girls and boys are married when only two or three years of age. Up to about a generation ago, an Arab's choice of a wife was often restricted to marrying his cousin on his father's side. In many societies it is a common custom for young girls to marry elderly men; as a result, the young men experience difficulty obtaining wives and often have to marry old women or widows.

Societies also differ in the degree of interaction between family members. Mother-in-law avoidance is a common custom among many peoples; the Aranda of Australia, for instance, do not allow the men to look at, or even speak to their mothers-in-law. The Semang believe in a certain amount of avoidance between mother and son and between father and daughter, while the Baganda often send their first child to live with the father's brother.[3] In an Israeli kibbutz, children live apart from their parents and visit them only at certain times each day. This last style of living is designed to weaken ties between parents and children and to eliminate family-centeredness. The kibbutz provides us with an example of family life very different from our own.[4]

The Israeli *kibbutzim* (plural of *kibbutz*) are agricultural settlements organized around the principle of communal living. All able-bodied adults work at whatever task is assigned to them for the welfare of the collective. The task of child-rearing is taken over by communal institutions. Children are trained and educated by special nurses and teachers. The parents' role is limited to a warm, affectional, indulgent relationship without involving discipline or other means of socializing the child. This pattern is more like the interaction between grandparents and grandchildren in American society.

The kibbutz has solved many problems associated with aging. A fixed retirement age does not exist; instead a person gradually withdraws from the occupational sphere beginning at age 55. Older persons work shorter hours and are given lighter, less strenuous tasks. The elderly who can no longer work are secure — all their basic needs including food, housing, and health care are provided. According to Yonina Talmon, however, the emphasis on work and productivity, characteristic of all kibbutzim, produces feelings of guilt among nonproductive older members.

Older people tend to compensate for the loss of their work role by shifting their focus to the family. The parent-child relationship assumes greater importance for them, and grandchildren become a major preoccupation. Even though communal institutions take over most child care, grandparents assist parents. For example, when children visit their parents at the end of the work day, sometimes grandparents help out by entertaining the children. Or, when the parents go on vacations or leave the kibbutz, grandparents take their place. In most families, emotional ties between grandparents and their grandchildren are strong. Though the bulk of older persons' needs are provided by the kibbutz, children perform important domestic and personal chores for them when they become sick or incapacitated.

> In the support and care of aged relatives the children only supplement collective institutions. Their limited liabilities and duties do not, in most cases, interfere with their normal life routines. The curtailment and limitation of obligations seem to reinforce rather than weaken family relationships. As a rule, it does not undermine the sense of responsibility toward old parents; quite the contrary; the children are able to help spontaneously and generously. The relationship is free of the feeling of resentment and of the sense of guilt engendered by too heavy responsibilities.[5]

Older people with no children, or whose children have left the collective, tend to compensate for this lack by increased participation in communal affairs. Friends and neighbors usually take over some functions that children normally perform and serve as foster families. Some older people who are childless attach themselves to the family of a friend or neighbor and act as additional grandparents.

Nuclear and Extended Families

The *nuclear family*, the most basic of all family types, is composed of a husband, a wife, and their children. When several nuclear families are joined together by an extension of parent-child relationships, this is called an *extended*, or three-generation, *family* — typically a married couple, their unmarried children, their married children and spouses, and their grandchildren, all living together.

The general thesis throughout much sociological literature is that the extended family, the norm in early agrarian America, has greatly declined, and that today the nuclear family is the dominant form. Many sociologists argue that this change in family organization is responsible for many problems that confront the elderly.

The major cause of this shift from the extended to the nuclear family is considered to be industrialization. Proponents of this view argue that with industrialization, workers are required to move to where job opportunities are available. This geographical mobility tends to undermine the kinship bonds in the extended family by decreasing the frequency and intimacy of contact between its members. David Popenoe observes that industrialization has made it possible for women to work outside the home, a practice that diminishes the importance of some basic functions of the extended family.[6] At the same time, the nuclear family, with its more limited set of responsibilities, has been strengthened. Finally, and probably the most important reason given for the change in family organization, is the loss of the family as a productive unit:

> In an agrarian society, each member of the family does economically productive work. Children, the elderly, and the handicapped do less than able-bodied adults, but they each make a contribution to the economic welfare of the family unit. The extended family thus offers an economic advantage. In an industrial society, however, the young, the elderly, and the physically handicapped are unemployable. They produce little for the family unit, yet they consume at the same rate as a producer. The extended family unit, with aged parents or other dependent relatives, becomes a burden rather than an advantage.[7]

In the transformation of the extended family into the nuclear family, it was believed that not only did older people lose their economic role in the household, along with other functions, but they also became

isolated from their children and relatives. Recent studies have contra-
dicted these notions. First, it has been found that extended families
were no more prevalent in the past than they are now. So the family did
not evolve from an extended into a nuclear family form, but has
remained much the same. Clark Tibbitts points out that "it is now clear
that the nuclear parent-child family has always been the modal family
type in the United States and that three-generation families have always
been relatively rare."[8]

Since few people lived to old age in the past, it would have been
impossible for the extended family to be the predominant family type.
Much of the nostalgia for the farm family of the past, where older people
enjoyed the economic security and emotional satisfaction of being part
of a large household of kinfolk, is based on fiction and not fact. William
Goode asserts that idealization of the classical American family of the
past only obscures much of its real character.

> When we penetrate the confusing mists of recent history, we find few
> examples of this "classical" family. Grandma's farm was not economically
> self-sufficient. Few families stayed together as large aggregations of kinfolk.
> Most houses were small, not large. We now *see* more large old houses than
> small ones; they survived longer because they were likely to have been better
> constructed. The one-room cabins rotted away. . . . Indeed, we find, as in so
> many other pictures of the glowing past, that in each past generation people
> write of a period *still* more remote, *their* grandparents' generation, when
> things really were much better.[9]

Another misconception that has been examined is that old people
who live alone or apart from their children are isolated from them. This
myth of alienation is based on two sources: professional workers and the
elderly themselves. Professional workers often develop a distorted view
because they deal with older clients alienated from their families or with
some family problems that more than likely began before they became
old. About one-fifth of all elderly people in the United States are
childless, and they are the most likely of all to believe that aged parents
are neglected by their children.[10]

Intergenerational Relationships

Parent-Child Relationships

Nearly all studies find that older people prefer to live near, but not with,
their children. Most elderly desire to remain in their own homes to
retain their independence and to avoid impinging on their children's
freedom. However, separate homes are not always possible in situations
where older people are in poor health or lack adequate finances to live

alone. Despite this preference for living apart, about one-third of the persons 65 and over who have children live with them.

INTERACTION WITH CHILDREN   The majority of older people who live alone enjoy a high degree of interaction with one or more of their adult children. In their study of the elderly in Denmark, Great Britain, and the United States, Ethel Shanas and her associates found that while most older parents live apart from their children, they maintain regular contact with at least one child.[11] Nearly two-thirds of the older people surveyed said that they had seen at least one child during the 24-hour period preceding the interview. In all three countries the majority of older people had at least one child who lived within a 30-minutes' distance from them. Other studies reveal that even when geographic distances are great, regular contact is maintained between parents and their children by letters, telephone, and extended visits. "Feelings of affection toward kin, especially aging parents, seem to override spatial distances."[12]

The old maxim that "a son's a son till he gets a wife and a daughter's a daughter all her life" appears to have some validity. Married daughters seem to have closer ties and contact with their parents than married sons do.[13] Some investigators have found that females keep in closer touch with relatives on both sides of the family than do males, and that a middle-aged couple tends to be closer to the wife's family than to the husband's family.[14]

Some gerontologists maintain that as parents age, the parent-child relationship reverses itself: the parent assumes the former dependency role of the child, while the child takes on the supportive role of the parent. Margaret Blenkner disagrees, arguing that *role-reversal* is not a normal, but a pathological condition of neurotic or emotionally immature or disturbed older persons.[15] She believes that instead of the adult child assuming the parental role, he or she takes on a more mature filial role. This role is seen as a natural outgrowth of the increasing maturity of the adult child as he or she reaches middle age. The role "involves being depended on and therefore being dependable insofar as the parent is concerned."[16] Blenkner refers to this stage as *filial maturity*. She sees it as a part of the developmental process in which children begin to recognize parents as individuals with their own needs, rights, limitations, and distinctive life histories.

PATTERNS OF MUTUAL ASSISTANCE   Many studies of intergenerational family relationships have concentrated on the mutual-aid patterns that exist between parents and their adult children. Mutual aid flows in two directions: from adult children to their parents, and from the parents to their children. When aged parents are infirm or financially deprived, children inevitably give more help than they receive.

Jan Stehouwer has distinguished two forms of help.[17] The first type is composed of nonessential, informal services that people perform for each other when they live nearby; these services require little effort, such as a son carrying packages for his elderly mother. The second type is deliberately organized and constitutes essential help, for example, when an older couple takes over their daughter's household responsibilities in an emergency.

Marvin Sussman and Lee Burchinal have pinpointed a number of help patterns that seem to be more prevalent among middle-class and working-class families: the exchange of gifts, advice, economic assistance, and various services.[18] Certain services that adult children are expected to perform on a regular basis for their aged parents are considered acts of filial responsibility and are done voluntarily. These services include "physical care, the providing of shelter, escorting, shopping, performing household tasks, sharing of leisure time, etc."[19] Other forms of help may be given periodically for such ceremonial occasions as funerals or in time of crisis or illness.

The type of mutual aid tends to vary by the sexes of the parents and the children. Older men typically assist their children in household repairs, while elderly women often help out with baby-sitting and cooking. Sons and daughters do not generally receive the same kind of assistance; adult male children are likely to receive financial aid, and daughters to receive a greater share of services from their parents.

Economic aid between parents and their adult children also varies with social class. As a rule, the lower classes supply less in the way of finances and rely more on the exchange of services and shared living arrangements. The middle classes are more likely to provide financial help. Regardless of class, the direction of financial assistance most frequently flows from parents to children. Sussman and Burchinal describe the pattern of aid among the middle class at different stages of the life cycle:

> During the early years of the child's marriage the flow of aid is from parents to children. As children become middle-aged the stream may be reversed, children now help their aged parents. Middle-class, middle-aged children may be giving subsidies to young married children and aged parents at the same time. A frequent pattern of aid is to turn to the needs of aging and often ailing parents after children have been aided in beginning their marriage and careers.[20]

In recent years there has been a trend toward a decrease in the financial reliance of older people on their children. Tibbitts indicates that less than 5 percent of the elderly's income comes from a direct transfer of money from children to their parents.[21] The elderly today look to governmental agencies and private pension arrangements for the bulk of their economic maintenance. In other words, responsibility for the support of parents has shifted from an individual to a collective responsibility.

This trend is reflected in the marked increase in the number of financial-assistance programs administered by large-scale governmental organizations or bureaucracies. In addition to social security, older people are guaranteed a minimum income through Supplemental Security Income (SSI) and are given medical coverage through Medicare and Medicaid. Other governmental aids include subsidized housing, meal programs, and income-tax exemptions. Older people often rely on their children and other relatives for information about these programs and for assistance in dealing with them. Sussman notes that many relationships of older people with their children today center around coping with bureaucratic organizations.[22] Children often act as mediators and buffers between the organizations and their aged parents.

Grandparent-Grandchild Relationships

Over the past decades, the family cycle has speeded up. As people married at younger ages, they became parents and also grandparents at earlier ages than in previous generations. Grandparenthood has become a middle-age event, and great-grandparenthood is an old-age phenomenon. Today with increased longevity, children have more living grandparents than ever before (see Table 11.2).

PERCEPTIONS OF GRANDPARENTS In a study of 70 middle-class older couples, Bernice Neugarten and Karol Weinstein found that not everyone enjoys being a grandparent.[23] A third of the respondents experienced difficulty in performing the grandparent role satisfactorily and felt that the role was uncomfortable, unrewarding, and disappointing. The study also revealed that the grandparent role holds different

Table 11.2 Percentage of 10-year-olds having living grandparents

Year	Number of living grandparents		
	1	2	4
1920	80	40	11
1970	95	75	71

SOURCE: Adapted from *Aging,* February–March 1973, p. 12.

meanings for different people. For some, it gives a feeling of biological renewal and continuity; they derive a sense of immortality through their grandchildren. Others feel that the grandparent role provides them with emotional self-fulfillment and the satisfaction of being a teacher and a resource person. A few saw grandparenthood as a chance for vicarious achievement, that is, they felt that grandchildren might accomplish what they and their children had not.

The grandparent role tends to be so varied that Neugarten and Weinstein were able to distinguish five types of grandparents:

1. The *formal* grandparent enjoys giving presents and indulging grandchildren, but is careful not to encroach on the parents' responsibility and authority.

2. The *fun seeker* has an informal, playful relationship with grandchildren and often sees them as a source of leisure activity. The grandparents in this group, instead of indulging their grandchildren, tend to emphasize mutual satisfaction.

3. The *surrogate parent* role pertains to grandmothers whose daughters work and who are responsible for the care of grandchildren during the day.

4. The *reservoir of family wisdom* type refers mostly to grandfathers who maintain an authoritarian position in the family and dispense knowledge and special skills.

5. The *distant figure* grandparent has only brief contacts with grandchildren on holidays and special occasions, seeing them infrequently otherwise.

The style of grandparenting also relates to age. The fun seekers and distant figure types are found more frequently among younger grandparents, whereas the formal grandparents are more typical of older grandparents. Grandparents tend to enjoy their grandchildren more as young children than when they reach adolescence and beyond.[24] According to one grandparent, "As you get older, you like small children more, because the older children don't like to be bothered with older people."[25] Margaret Clark and Barbara Anderson explain that "as these children advance in years, the earlier aura they might have perceived to surround the awesome personages of their grandparents begins to dim. The grandfolks do not seem to be as competent as they were."[26]

PERCEPTIONS OF GRANDCHILDREN The type of grandparent that one prefers tends to be related to the age of the grandchild. Kahana and Kahana found that preschool age children valued indulgent grandparents who gave them food and presents, whereas slightly older ones wanted grandparents to be active and "fun-sharing."[27] Joan Robertson reports that young adults between the ages of 18 and 26 described the ideal grandparent as "one who loves and enjoys grandchildren," "who visits them," "shows interest," and "is helpful when needed."[28]

In a survey of 500 junior high and high school students, the authors found that most of the respondents had a positive attitude toward their grandparents.[29] When asked what they liked most about their grandparents, the most frequent response was "they are nice," followed by "they are easier to talk to than my parents," and "they listen to me and understand my problems." The most often repeated criticism of grandparents was they were "old-fashioned." Some students felt that grandparents complained too much, while others found them boring and too talkative. When the students were asked in what ways they could help their grandparents, they replied: "visiting them or writing them more often," "doing work around their house," and "loving them."

The attitudes of children toward the elderly are often influenced by their own experience within the family. L. de Moyne Bekker and Charles Taylor found that young people who had grandparents and great-grandparents had fewer prejudices against older persons than those who did not.[30] Rosalie Gilford and Dean Black explored how grandchildren develop positive sentiments for their grandparents.[31] Their findings suggest that attitudes and feelings toward grandparents are largely transmitted from parent to child and tend to persist into adulthood. There has been some speculation that children observe how their parents relate to their grandparents and often treat their parents similarly when they get old. The following version of a common European folk tale illustrates this point:

> A family would not let the grandfather eat at the table with the rest of them. Instead, they placed his food in a little wooden trough some distance from the others, and there, out of sight and hearing, the old man ate his meals. One day the middle-aged father came across his young son hammering some nails into a couple of boards. "What are you doing?" the father asked. Glancing up from his work, the son replied, "It's for you when you get old." Shocked by that glimpse of his own future, the father hastily invited the old man to rejoin the family at the table.[32]

The Foster Grandparent Program, even though outside the family situation, demonstrates the value of the grandchild-grandparent relationship. This program provides an opportunity for older persons to work on a one-to-one basis with special needs children in a variety of residential and community settings.

Opposite page: The Foster Grandparent Program provides older persons with an opportunity to work with children in day-care centers, hospitals, schools, and private homes. (ACTION)

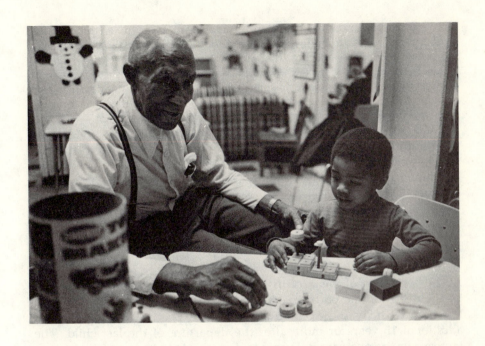

The unusual aspect of the Foster Grandparent Program is that it is of enormous benefit to both the doer and the recipient. For the children, the kindness, patience, and love that they receive improve their lives. In many cases, the children served show improvement in their physical, social, and psychological development. In some cases, the individual attention that each older volunteer gives each child results in early release of the child from the institution or the early termination of costly special treatment.[33]

In addition, this program gives older persons a chance to make a valuable contribution to their communities and, in so doing, feel useful and needed. Many foster grandparents attest to the fact that the satisfaction and increased sense of self-esteem derived from working with children contributes to their physical and mental well-being.

Older Husband and Wife Relationships

At the beginning of this century, over half of all marriages were broken by the death of one partner, usually the husband, before the last child left home. Today the average couple can expect to live together an additional 15 years or more after the departure of the last child. The increase in the postparental years is due mainly to longer life expectancies and smaller, more closely spaced families. Researchers have found that couples often enjoy greater satisfaction with their marriages after the children have left home. Some sociologists feel that this upswing continues into the later years, while others find that it is limited to the immediate "post-launching" period.

Wayne Thompson and Gordon Streib have divided the postparental period into these stages: (1) the family of late maturity, in which the husband and wife are between the ages of 45 and 54; (2) the family of preretirement, in the 55 to 64 age range; (3) the family of early retirement, between ages 65 to 74; and (4) the family of later retirement, for those still together at age 75 and over.[34] Our interest lies in the last two postparental stages and their consequences for the marital relationship.

The high male mortality rate characterizes the family of early retirement. In 1977, 80 percent of the males and only 49 percent of the females in the 65–74-year-old age group were married. Studies of the effects of retirement on the marital relationship focus mainly on the changes in role differentiation and the sharing of household chores.[35] After retirement, husbands usually become more involved with homemaking and domestic activities. The sharing of household tasks is associated with a growth in companionship and common interests. Alan Kerchoff found that in households where husbands participated in domestic chores, the morale of both the husband and wife was higher than in households where husbands did not participate.[36] On the other

For the happily married older couple, marriage can be a source of great satisfaction and comfort, especially during the retirement years. (Jeroboam Inc. Mitchell Payne)

hand, some husbands may consider housework degrading, and some wives may resent their husbands' interference in the domestic domain.

Several studies suggest that a significant proportion of wives do not look forward to their husband's retirement. Many wives feel that "there will be more housework to do, that their daily routine will be disrupted, that they do not want their husbands home all day, and that they will have to live on a lower income."[37] Heyman and Jeffers found a positive correlation between the length of a husband's retirement and the proportion of wives stating that they regretted that their spouses had stopped working.[38]

A husband's retirement is likely to bring a couple together in a way that they have not experienced since the first years of their marriage. Before retiring, their interests centered around child-rearing and earning a living; now their interests are directed toward one another. For some couples the intense interaction of the retirement years may increase their appreciation of each other and bring them closer together. For others the intimacy of the relationship may put a strain on the marriage: "daily absence from home except over the weekends may have enabled many husbands to adjust to the marital relationship which under conditions of closer contact they might have found explosive or intolerable."[39]

As couples reach the later retirement stage, age 75 and over, Clark and Anderson have observed that successful marriages are based on a mutual interdependency that has a symbiotic quality. This is especially

"Tell me, Edgar, did you, at any of those times you went out for a loaf of bread, ever toy with the idea of never coming back?" (Drawing by Frascino; © 1974. The New Yorker Magazine, Inc.)

true in situations where the husband or wife or both are ill and need the care and support of the other.[40] In addition, they report that happy older marriages are based on a greater social equality in the relationship. "Rather than the feminine subordination to a husband, . . . husband and wife appear more as social equals, dividing up the labor of the household, blending the masculine and feminine into one tight little social unit."[41]

Widowhood

One of the greatest fears of happily married husbands and wives is the fear of widowhood. The woman is more likely to be widowed than the man. In 1978, more than half (52 percent) of all women over age 65 were widowed, while most older men (78 percent) were married. Or, put another way, widows outnumber widowers by about five to one, due to

Widowhood Among the Witotos of Amazonia

When a man dies, his widow, after her period of mourning is over, has the choice of remaining in the house under the protection of his brother or the chief, returning to her own clan, marrying again, or becoming an informal village prostitute.

SOURCE: George P. Murdock, *Our Primitive Contemporaries*, Macmillan, New York, 1934, p. 467.

women's longer life expectancies and their tendency to marry older men.

Some sociologists have suggested that the problems of widowhood are more serious for women than for men. Widows tend to fare worse in terms of remarriage and finances. Because of the greater availability of women over 65, the widower has a wide choice. In addition, unlike the older woman, the widower is not limited to his own age group but can, and often does select a marital partner much younger than himself. In 1976, the remarriage rate for older men was 8.8 times that for older women. Though social relationships with the opposite sex are limited for older women and their chances for remarriage small, they find some compensation in the likelihood of having a large group of other widows from which to select friends.

Widows constitute the poorest segment of the older population. About one-fourth have incomes below the poverty level. Some reasons for their financially disadvantaged position include: (1) social security benefits drop by one-third following the death of the husband; (2) when women are primary beneficiaries, they usually have lower earnings than men on which to base social security benefits; and (3) only about 2 percent of elderly widows receive benefits from private pension plans after the death of their husbands.[42]

On the other hand, other sociologists argue that the problems a surviving husband faces are more difficult than those of a surviving wife. The widower is often confronted with the management of household affairs for which he may be totally unprepared. For some men, domestic tasks and responsibilities appear overwhelming. Furthermore, the widower experiences more difficulty in finding an adequate substitute for the intimacy of the primary relationship that was once provided by the wife.[43]

Perhaps because widowhood is more often encountered by older wives than older husbands, studies find that more women than men are likely to report that they had thought about the possibility of losing their mates. Thus, many women go through a "rehearsal for widowhood," in which they begin to prepare themselves psychologically for some of the

Though the opportunities for remarriage for older widows are limited due to the fewer available men, they have a large group of other widows from which to select friends. (Black Star. Jean Shapiro—Photographer)

problems and adjustments they are likely to encounter when their husbands die.[44]

Alternative Forms of Family

After the death of a spouse, many older people are unwilling or unable to live alone. The traditional alternatives previously open to them were either to move in with their children or to live in a nursing home or some other institution for the aged. Today a growing proportion of older people are rejecting these choices and, like some in the younger generation, are experimenting with new, alternative forms of family life.

Senior Citizens' Communes

Communal living is not new, but the fact that such an arrangement might meet the needs of the elderly is new. According to Gordon Streib and Ruth Streib, two social trends in our society have led to the idea of communal living for the older population.[45] First, because of the increased number and proportion of people 65 and over, more attention is being given to their needs and problems, including their living environment. Secondly, the emergence of a communal movement among young people has given rise to the idea that communal arrangements might provide a solution to some problems of older people. Streib and Streib suggest that "since old age and retirement for many are marked by a shift in roles and activities which deemphasize work, individualism, competition, and the accumulation of wealth, it is argued that the elderly might benefit from an environment involving cooperation, sharing of expenses, and the provision of emotional supports."[46]

One noteworthy example of a modified form of communal living is the Share-A-Home Association, which consists of a network of private residences located primarily in Florida. Started in 1960 as a nonprofit organization, these homes allow older persons to live together as a family by sharing expenses and functioning as a single household unit. In this environment the members not only fulfill their basic needs, but also provide one another with companionship and emotional support. The power and decision-making in the household rests solely in the hands of the residents. Their authority ranges from hiring and firing the staff and voting on new members, to decisions regarding menus and entertainment.

A case involving a Share-A-Home group in Winter Park, Florida, gave a new legal definition to what constitutes a family.[47] In 1971 the Orange County Board of Commissioners filed a suit against a Share-A-Home

---

When Older Couples Remarry the Success Rate Is High

Couples who remarry late in life have an excellent chance of making a success of their unions. According to Walter C. McKain, professor of sociology at the University of Connecticut who studied the lives of 100 aging couples five years after they were married, only six out of the 100 appeared to be failures.

Some were married for the third or fourth time. All the men were at least 65, the women at least 60, when they wed.

Companionship was listed as the major reason for remarrying by almost 75 percent of the men and 66 percent of the women. Others listed the need to stretch retirement incomes.

A number of the men said they were looking for a live-in cook, housekeeper or nurse. Some of the women claimed they craved a home of their own with a man around it.

SOURCE: Modern Maturity, February–March 1973, p. 57. © American Association of Retired Persons.

Association, claiming that it was a boarding house, and as such was in violation of the single-family zoning ordinance in that neighborhood. The Share-A-Home group in question consisted of 12 older people, aged 61 to 94, who had formed a communal-type family and were living in an old 27-room house. The Orange County code defines a family as "one or more persons occupying a dwelling and living as a single housekeeping unit."[48] Because these persons were living in the same household, sharing the same kitchen, splitting living costs, and giving each other support and understanding, they were found to be a bona fide family. (The main argument for not recognizing them as family was that they were not related.) The presiding judge ruled that the group met the legal definition of a family and that "any group that pools its resources with the intention of sharing the joys and sorrows of family life is a family."[49]

The Share-A-Home Association is set up so that the home is truly a home and not an institution. By pooling their financial resources, persons can enjoy a higher standard of living than they could afford alone. For those elderly who have limited incomes, are lonely, and are no longer totally independent, the Share-A-Home Association appears to offer them a viable solution.

Polygyny

Several gerontologists have suggested that polygynous marriages for older people (when a husband has two or more wives at the same time) would compensate for the excess of women in that age category. A leading exponent of this marriage alternative is Victor Kessel.[50] Instead of facing 15 to 20 years of widowhood, a woman over 60 would have a chance to remarry if men over 60 married two to five wives. This marital arrangement would not only afford older people the opportunity to establish a new family group consisting of wives and their spouse, but according to Kessel, such an arrangement would include at least seven advantages.

First, he notes that married couples have a more balanced diet than widows or widowers, who often have little or no incentive to cook for themselves and do not enjoy eating alone. By living as a family, members would find the mealtime atmosphere greatly improved. Secondly, by family members pooling their resources, they could live more adequately and graciously.

A third advantage of polygyny, according to Kessel, is that in the event of illness, the husband and wives could share the burden of nursing. Also many elderly are hospitalized because they live alone and have no one to take care of them; in this situation, infirm persons could remain at home with people to look after them.

Sometimes older people do not have the stamina or strength to do all the work necessary to maintain a household. Thus, a fourth advantage would be that several women working together and dividing the domestic tasks could lighten the load considerably. Many older widows who grew up in a society that considered sex outside marriage a serious transgression cannot accept such relationships; their sexual activity ceased with the death of their husbands. The fifth advantage of a polygynous marriage would be for an older woman to have a legally sanctioned sexual partner.

A sixth benefit of a polygynous family arrangement is that it would help combat depression resulting from feelings of loneliness and uselessness. "It is knowing that one is a member of a distinct group that produces a feeling of belonging, with a consequent reason to live."[51] Lastly, because of the rivalry that exists in a polygynous family, Kessel believes that it can increase pride in appearance and emphasize good grooming. Although he acknowledges that jealousy and rivalry may often lead to family disruption, he feels that all the other advantages of plural marriage far outweigh this disadvantage.

George Rosenberg raises objections to a polygynous family structure for the elderly.[52] In particular, he feels that monogamous values are so firmly implanted in our society that there is no reason to believe an older woman can or would want to discard these values. Furthermore, he notes that a polygynous remarriage would have economic consequences on kinship ties, especially where inheritance is involved. Polygyny would lead to a dispersal of inheritance outside the original family lineage and, in turn, would be disruptive to the present kinship system.

Cohabitation

Another variant family form is cohabitation, commonly referred to as "living together." In recent years this lifestyle has been adopted by varied segments of the population from young adults to the elderly. In the 1970 census, 18,000 couples age 65 and over listed themselves as living together, and that figure almost certainly underestimates the real total.

Living together has proven to be a very satisfactory solution for some older people. A significant proportion of the elderly who cohabitate do so because they fear being penalized financially. In the past, many older men and women avoided remarriage in order to draw maximum social security benefits, but recently social security regulations have changed, so older couples will no longer lose any part of their benefits if they marry. In some cases women do not remarry in order to retain their widow's benefits from the union or private pension plans. Also, the problems that each older person faces with his or her children over inheritance are minimized in this type of living arrangement.

Although cohabitation affords older people the advantage of companionship, emotional support, and sexual expression, at the same time many suffer from deep feelings of guilt and anxiety about deviating from societal norms. Plagued by religious convictions, some consider themselves "living in sin." In an effort to resolve their conflicts, they may seek the help of trained professionals and ministers. Dr. Benton Gaskell, a minister in Pomona, California, relates how he dealt with an elderly couple who came to him for help.

> "They were in their 70s . . . and living together clandestinely because they couldn't afford to marry since they would lose pension income. They said they felt "faithless" to their late spouses, never knew what to tell their children or friends, and were in spiritual distress over their predicament. They asked me to ease their guilt by solemnizing their union in the sight of God."
>
> For Dr. Gaskell, the plea presented a quandary. A minister may not conduct a marriage ceremony if there is no marriage license. Nor could he compromise the church. Yet he could not turn away the couple's plea. After consultation with his staff, Dr. Gaskell fashioned a ritual which enabled him formally to bless the couple's "union." With this emotional support, the couple were able to live together openly. "I don't know what they told their friends or family," says Dr. Gaskell, "and I don't care. I know what they told me. 'We feel better about ourselves now,' they said. 'It makes us feel our relationship is all right.' "[53]

A variety of alternatives to conventional marriage, in addition to the ones above, may offer solutions to the needs of some elderly. Today, the changing demographic structure of our population — the growth in the percentage of older people in the population and the large number of women who survive their husbands — requires that we explore new types of relationships between the sexes. Many older people may choose to have either conventional relationships or none at all. But for those who wish to try alternatives, the option should be open to them.

Summary

1. An institution is a cluster of norms surrounding an important social need of a society. Every known society has five basic social institutions: the family, the economy, the political system, religion, and education.

2. Family patterns vary widely in different societies. Many patterns in other cultures seem strange to Americans, and our ways seem equally strange to them. The Israeli kibbutz is an example of a twentieth-century society that has tried to minimize the family and its functions.

3. The most basic of all family types is the nuclear family. When several nuclear families are combined generationally they form an extended family. Contrary to what many believe, the extended family was no more prevalent in the past than

it is today. The nuclear family has always represented the modal pattern for the elderly in American society.

4. Though most older people live apart from their children, they are not isolated from them. They maintain contact with at least one child on a regular basis. Mutual-aid patterns between parents and their adult children flow in both directions, and tend to vary by age, sex, and social class. Blenkner asserts that role-reversal is not a natural outcome of the relationship between aging parents and their children. She suggests that a better term for the stage when adult children can be depended on when needed by parents is *filial maturity*.

5. Grandparenthood now occurs at earlier ages, and children have more living grandparents today than ever before. Neugarten distinguishes five types of grandparents: the formal grandparent, the fun seeker, the surrogate parent, the reservoir of family wisdom, and the distant figure grandparent. The grandparent-grandchild relationship, as well as the type of grandparents that grandchildren prefer, appears to be influenced by the children's age, and their experiences within the family.

6. The postparental period in a marriage has been greatly extended in recent years. Thompson and Streib have divided this period into four stages, the last two stages being the family of early retirement and the family of later retirement. The family of early retirement centers around the changes in role differentiation and the sharing of household tasks. In the family of later retirement, an increased mutual interdependence often develops between husband and wife.

7. Widowhood is a greater problem for elderly women than men. Over half of all women over age 65 are widows, who constitute one of the lowest economic segments in our population.

8. Today many older people, like the young adults, are looking for experimental alternatives to traditional marriage. An example of a modified form of communal living is the Share-A-Home Association, in which older people live together as a family unit, pooling living expenses and providing support to one another. Kessel has proposed polygynous marriages for people aged 60 and over to reduce the number of women in that age group who are unmarried. Living together is another lifestyle that has been adopted by some older people. These and other alternatives to traditional marriage may prove to be ways of solving some marital and family problems of the elderly.

Notes

1. Peter L. Berger, citing Arnold Gehlen, *Invitation to Sociology*, Anchor Books, Doubleday, Garden City, N.Y., 1963, p. 87.

2. Ibid.

3. For some good sources of cultural variations in the family see Stuart A. Queen and Robert W. Habenstein, *The Family in Various Cultures*, J. B. Lippincott, Philadelphia, 1974; and George P. Murdock, *Our Primitive Contemporaries*, Macmillan, New York, 1934.

4. This summary is taken largely from Yonina Talmon, "Aging in Israel, a Planned Society," *American Journal of Sociology*, 67 (1971), 284–295.

5. Talmon, "Aging in Israel, a Planned Society," p. 289.

6. David Popenoe, *Sociology* (3rd ed.), Prentice-Hall, Englewood Cliffs, N.J., 1977, pp. 191–192.

7. Ibid., p. 192.

8. Clark Tibbitts, "Some Social Aspects of Gerontology," *The Gerontologist*, 8, no. 2 (1968), 132.

9. William J. Goode, *World Revolution and Family Patterns*, Free Press of Glencoe, New York, 1963, p. 7.

10. Margaret Blenkner, "Social Work and Family Relationships in Later Life," in *Social Structure and the Family*, eds. Ethel Shanas and Gordon F. Streib, Prentice-Hall, Englewood Cliffs, N.J., 1965, pp. 48–50.

11. Ethel Shanas, et al., *Old People in Three Industrial Societies*, Atherton Press, New York, 1968, pp. 192–196.

12. Vern L. Bengtson, Edward B. Olander, and Anees A. Haddad, "The Generation Gap and Aging Family Members," in *Time, Roles, and Self in Old Age,* ed. Jaber F. Gubrium, Human Sciences Press, New York, 1976, p. 253.

13. Marvin B. Sussman, "Relationships of Adult Children with Their Parents," in *Social Structure and the Family*, eds. Ethel Shanas and Gordon F. Streib, Prentice-Hall, Englewood Cliffs, N.J., 1965, p. 81.

14. Richard A. Kalish, *Late Adulthood: Perspectives on Human Development*, Brooks/Cole, Monterey, Calif., 1975, p. 80.

15. Blenker, "Social Work and Family Relationships in Late Life," pp. 57–58.

16. Ibid., p. 57.

17. Shanas, et al., *Old People in Three Industrial Societies*, pp. 203–204.

18. Sussman, "Relationships of Adult Children with Their Parents," pp. 68–71.

19. Ibid., p. 70.

20. Marvin B. Sussman and Lee Burchinal, "Parental Aid to Married Children: Implications for Family Functioning," *Marriage and Family Living*, 24 (November 1962), 320–332.

21. Clark Tibbitts, "Older Americans in the Family Context," *Aging*, April–May 1977, p. 9.

22. Marvin B. Sussman, "Family Life of Old People," in *Handbook of Aging and the Social Sciences*, eds. Robert H. Binstock and Ethel Shanas, Van Nostrand Reinhold, New York, 1976, p. 221.

23. Bernice L. Neugarten and Karol K. Weinstein, "The Changing American Grandparent," in *Middle Age and Aging*, ed. Bernice L. Neugarten, The University of Chicago Press, Chicago, 1968, pp. 280–285.

24. Boaz Kahana and Eva Kahana, "Grandparenthood from the Perspective of the Developing Grandchild," *Developmental Psychology*, 3, no. 1 (1970), 98–105.

25. Margaret Clark and Barbara Anderson, *Culture and Aging*, Charles C Thomas, Springfield, Ill., p. 292.

26. Ibid.

27. Kahana and Kahana, "Grandparenthood from the Perspective of the Developing Grandchild," p. 102.

28. Joan Robertson, "Significance of Grandparents' Perception of Young Adult Grandchildren," *The Gerontologist*, 16, no. 2 (1976), 137–140.

29. William E. Cole and Diana K. Harris, *The Elderly in America*, Allyn & Bacon, Boston, 1977, pp. 44–45.

30. L. de Moyne Bekker and Charles Taylor, "Attitudes Toward the Aged in a Multigenerational Sample," *Journal of Gerontology*, 21, no. 1 (1966), 115–118.

31. Vivian Wood and Joan Robertson citing Rosalie Gilford and Dean Black, "The Significance of Grandparenthood," in *Time, Roles, and Self in Old Age*, ed. Jaber F. Gubrium, Human Sciences Press, New York, 1976, pp. 287–288.

32. Rochelle Jones, *The Other Generation: The New Power of Older People*, © 1977, pp. 77–78. Reprinted by permission of Prentice-Hall, Inc., Englewood Cliffs, New Jersey.

33. Lorin A. Baumhover and Joan D. Jones, eds., *Handbook of American Aging Programs*, Greenwood Press, Westport, Conn., 1977, p. 79.

34. Wayne E. Thompson and Gordon F. Streib, "Meaningful Activity in a Family Context," in *Aging and Leisure*, ed. Robert W. Kleemeier, Oxford University Press, New York, 1961, pp. 177–211.

35. Lillian Troll, "The Family of Later Life: A Decade Review," *Journal of Marriage and the Family*, 33 (1971), 274.

36. Alan C. Kerchoff, "Family Patterns and Morale in Retirement," in *Social Aspects of Aging*, eds. Ida Simpson and John McKinney, Duke University Press, Durham, N.C., 1966, p. 191.

37. Wilma Donahue, Harold Orbach, and Otto Pollak, "Retirement: The Emerging Social Pattern," in *Handbook of Social Gerontology*, ed. Clark Tibbitts, The University of Chicago Press, Chicago, 1960, p. 371.

38. Dorothy Heyman and Frances C. Jeffers, "Wives and Retirement: A Pilot Study," *Journal of Gerontology*, 23 (1968), 488–496.

39. Donahue, et al., "Retirement: The Emerging Social Pattern," p. 371.

40. Clark and Anderson, *Culture and Aging*, p. 238.

41. Ibid., p. 241.

42. James H. Schulz, *The Economics of Aging*, Wadsworth, Belmont, Calif., 1976, pp. 159–160.

43. Felix M. Berardo, "Survivorship and Isolation: The Case of the Aged Widower," *The Family Coordinator*, 19 (January 1970), 22.

44. Kalish, *Late Adulthood: Perspectives on Human Development*, p. 84.

45. Gordon F. Streib and Ruth B. Streib, "Communes and the Aging," *American Behavioral Scientist*, 19 (November–December 1975), 176–189.

46. Ibid., p. 177.

47. Sussman, "Family Life of Old People," pp. 231–232.

48. Ibid., p. 231.

49. Jones, *The Other Generation*, p. 58.

50. Victor Kessel, "Polygyny After Sixty," in *The Family in Search of a Future*, ed. Herbert A. Otto, Appleton-Century-Crofts, New York, 1970, pp. 137–143.

51. Ibid., p. 141.

52. George S. Rosenberg, "Implications of New Models of the Family for the Aging Population," in *The Family in Search of a Future*, ed. Herbert A. Otto, Appleton-Century-Crofts, New York, 1970, pp. 171–181.

53. Norman M. Lobsenz, "Sex and the Senior Citizen," *New York Times Magazine*, January 20, 1974. © 1974 by The New York Times Company. Reprinted by permission.

For Further Study

Kephart, William M. *The Family, Society, and the Individual* (3rd ed.. Houghton Mifflin, Boston, 1972. A good basic text for the study of the family.

Lopata, Helena Z. *Widowhood in an American City*. Schenkman, Cambridge, Mass., 1973. Contains the result of an extensive study of widows from varying social classes and backgrounds.

Shanas, Ethel, and Gordon F. Streib, eds. *Social Structure and the Family: Generational Relations*. Prentice-Hall, Englewood Cliffs, N.J., 1965. Using an interdisciplinary approach, this volume contains an excellent collection of papers on intergenerational relationships and the social structure of the family in later life.

————, and Marvin B. Sussman, eds. *Family, Bureaucracy and the Elderly*. Duke University Press, Durham, N.C., 1977. The papers in this book explore the ways in which older people and their families deal with the various bureaucracies in our society and the effect of these bureaucracies on family relationships.

Skolnick, Arlene S., and Jerome H. Skolnick, eds. *The Family in Transition*. Little, Brown, Boston, 1971. A book of readings that challenges both the popular and professional views of marriage, sexuality, child rearing, and family organization.

Sussman, Marvin B. "Family Life of Old People." In *Handbook of Aging and the Social Sciences*, edited by Robert H. Binstock and Ethel Shanas. Van Nostrand Reinhold, New York, 1976. A good analysis of the changes taking place in the structure of the family and the behavior of its members.

Troll, Lillian E., Sheila J. Miller, and Robert C. Atchley. *Families in Later Life*. Wadsworth, Belmont, Calif., 1979. Provides a concise coverage of the literature of the familial lives of older people in the United States.

12

The Economy: Work
and Retirement

Unlike the solitary wasp, virtually no human being can subsist by his or her own efforts alone. In human society, cultural adaptation implies an interdependent relationship among its members to produce the necessities for existence. This interdependence entails a division of labor and a specialization that evoke the need for some system of exchange. A society, then, must not only provide for the production of goods and services essential for the survival and welfare of its members, but it must also devise some orderly and efficient means of allocation, due to the inevitable scarcity of these items.

The norms and ideas controlling the production and distribution of scarce goods and services in a society constitute its *economic institutions*.[1] These institutions frame the world of work. This chapter focuses primarily on work and the departure from it — retirement — in relation to the older person.

The Meaning and Function of Work

Historically, *work* has carried different meanings at various times and places. Among the ancient Greeks the word for *work, ponos,* was derived from the word for *sorrow.* Work was regarded as fit only for slaves, because affluent Greeks felt it degraded the mind and corrupted the soul. The Latin word for *labor* means both work and toil in the sense of suffering. The Hebrews looked on work as Adam's punishment, the necessity of having to toil for a living: "In the sweat of thy face shalt thou eat bread."[2] The first Christians did work as a penance.

With the advent of the Protestant Reformation, the Christian concept of work took on a totally new meaning. Work began to be characterized as a religious devotion. The Calvinist doctrine of predestination held that only through hard work could individuals get evidence that they had God's favor and were chosen for salvation. Work was equated with prayer and was considered a personal calling or mission.

Though most people in our society today do not look on work as a

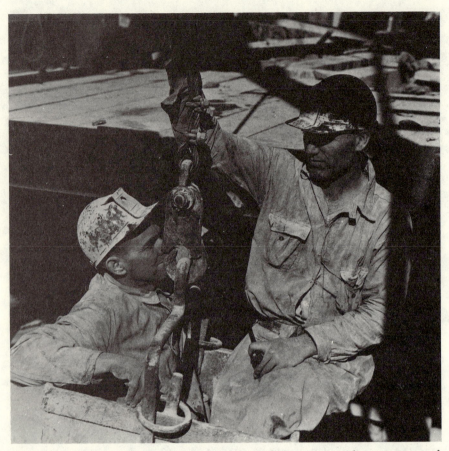

The lives of most people center around work, as it provides a source of identification and fulfillment and fixes one's position in society. (Courtesy of Tennessee Valley Authority)

sign of salvation, they are still guided by a strong work ethic. Eugene Friedmann and Robert Havighurst identify five general functions that work performs in the lives of individuals.[3] The first and most obvious function is that the job gives persons income or some financial return by which to maintain themselves. In exchange, workers are expected to produce something or to make some economic contribution. A second function of work is that of regulating life-activity. Work usually requires the individual to be at a certain place during certain days and hours. In this way, the job determines to a great extent where, when, and how people are to spend a large portion of their time. This demand gives order and routine to their lives.

Retirement Means Losing the Important
Part of One's Name

I have yet to see anyone mention one problem that bothers most men when they retire. This problem is the sudden loss of personal identification except for a name. This is what I mean. Let's take a fellow named John Jones. He has worked for a firm named General Endeavor (or General Motors or General Electric) for 30 or 40 years. He has long been accustomed to thinking of himself in relation to his firm. When introducing himself to a stranger, he has said, "I'm Jones of General Endeavor." He knew he had a fixed place in the business world and he was identified with his organization. He was accustomed to thinking of himself as part of his firm.

Then John Jones retired and one day he walked into a room filled with strangers and he heard his own voice saying, "I'm John Jones." It shook him to realize that he no longer was John Jones of General Endeavor. He was just John Jones period. He was on his own. The experience left him feeling curiously adrift without the old anchor of identification he had always thrown out when meeting someone. He felt as though he were floating about in space without identity, even though he had a name and was a member of the human race. "I'm John Jones and I belong to the human race" was hardly adequate. . . .

SOURCE: Don Whitehead, *Knoxville News-Sentinel*, October 4, 1977, p. 24.

A third function of work is that it gives persons a sense of identity. The job helps them describe themselves. As Everett Hughes has noted, "a man's job is his price tag and calling card."[4] Most people describe themselves by the company or organization for which they work. The importance of this job-related identification becomes most pronounced at retirement, when individuals feel a sudden loss of identity. Along with the identity, persons carry the position or status that society has attached to their particular job. Although each person occupies many different statuses, usually the job provides the key status and bears heavily on social standing in the community.

A fourth function of work is that a job serves as a base for social relationships. It is a principal source of social contact and of a major reference group. Finally, a fifth function of work is that it affords the worker a cluster of meaningful life experiences. "It is a source of contacts with persons, objects, and ideas. It is a market place where the worker's store of life-experience is enriched through interaction with the world about him and where he receives new ideas, expresses his own ideas, and modifies his conception of the world and of himself in relation to it."[5]

The Older Worker

Labor Force Participation

In 1900, 68.3 percent of the males age 65 and over were in the labor force. Since that time, except for the period during World War II when an acute labor shortage drew many older persons back into the labor force, the participation rate of older men in the labor force has progressively declined. By 1960 the number of older men in the labor force had dropped to about one-third, and today only about one-fifth of those aged 65 and over work (Table 12.1). This decline reflects the increase in early retirement programs, the enforcement of mandatory retirement policies, and the decrease in self-employment.[6]

The proportion of women aged 65 and over in the labor force has changed little in the past 25 years, except for a slight decline in the last decade. The employment rates of older women have fluctuated between 8 and 11 percent. Presently, about 8 percent of older women continue to work.

As shown in Table 12.1, the employment patterns for older black males is similar to that of whites. Historically, older black women have had much higher employment rates than their white counterparts. But the worker proportions have been converging, so the differences between the two are now minimal.

Projections by the Bureau of Labor Statistics indicate that the downward trends in employment of the elderly are expected to continue into the future for both sexes.[7] By 1990, it is estimated that only about

Table 12.1 Labor force participation for the population 65 and over, by race and sex, 1950–1990

Race and sex	1950	1955	1960	1965	1970	1975	1980	1990
All classes								
Male	45.8	39.6	33.1	27.9	26.8	21.7	20.1	16.8
Female	9.7	10.6	10.8	10.0	9.7	8.3	8.0	7.5
Blacks and other races								
Male	45.5	40.0	31.2	27.9	27.4	20.9	a	a
Female	16.5	12.1	12.8	12.9	12.2	10.5	a	a

[a]Data not available.

SOURCE: Adapted from U.S. Bureau of the Census, *Current Population Reports*, Special Studies Series P-23, No. 59, U.S. Government Printing Office, Washington, D.C., 1976, p. 51.

16.8 percent of the male population aged 65 and over will be in the labor force. For women, the drop will decrease only to 7.5 percent.

Characteristics of Older Workers

When compared to the younger adult population, older workers have a disadvantaged position in the labor force. This situation is due to erroneous beliefs about older workers. The U.S. Department of Labor has listed five of the more common myths about older workers and the facts concerning them.

1. *Older workers are too slow — they can't meet the production requirements.* Studies show no significant drop in performance and productivity in older workers. Many older workers exceed the average output of younger employees.

2. *Older workers can't meet the physical demands of our jobs.* Job analysis indicates that less than 14 percent of jobs today require great strength and heavy lifting. Labor-saving machinery makes it possible for older workers to handle most jobs without difficulty.

3. *You can't depend on older workers — they're absent from work too often.* According to surveys, workers 65 and over have a good record of attendance in comparison with other age groups.

4. *Older workers are not adaptable — they're hard to train because they can't accept change.* Evaluations of older jobseekers show that a high proportion are flexible in accepting change in their occupation and earnings. Adaptability depends on the individual: many young people are set in their ways, and many older workers adjust to change readily.

5. *Hiring older workers increases our pension and insurance costs. . . .* Costs of group life, accident, and health insurance and workmen's compensation are not materially increased by hiring older workers. Most pension plans provide for benefits related to length of service or earnings, or both.[8]

Other reasons that account for the disadvantaged position of older workers include their lower educational attainment, their obsolescent skills, and management's preference for younger workers in a competitive economy. As a consequence, older people are overrepresented in some occupational groups.

The older worker's best chance for being employed is in farming and in the proprietary occupations, where he is self-employed, and in low-paid service jobs such as janitorial work. His chances are about equal to those of the younger worker in sales, semi-skilled work, and skilled craft work, and considerably less in professional, technical, clerical and laboring occupations.[9]

Older people are often found in the self-employed category because it affords them the advantages of setting their own hours and work pace, as well as making their own decisions about retirement. The proportion of men employed in service occupations increases steadily with age. Such jobs as janitor, desk clerk in a hotel or motel, night watchman, or guard are more apt to be filled by older men. Older women are frequently employed to do baby-sitting or light housework.[10]

Older workers are less occupationally mobile than their younger counterparts. By the age of 50, few workers are apt to change jobs voluntarily, for several reasons. In middle age, workers are more likely to be settled down in jobs that they consider to be permanent. Workers, as a rule, do not want to give up their seniority or their fringe benefits.[11] But probably the most significant reason why older workers refrain from leaving their job is the fear of not being able to find another. This fear is not without justification. After age 45, finding a job becomes more difficult, which is reflected in the fact that duration of unemployment tends to increase with age. In 1975 the average period of unemployment for males between the ages of 45 and 54 was about 19 weeks, and for females about 16 weeks. The average time of unemployment for both men and women aged 65 is six months.[12]

Despite the fact that older workers encounter great problems in finding another job once they are unemployed, the unemployment rates for older workers are low. Though at first this seems paradoxical, the situation is explained by what is called "hidden unemployment." The unemployment rate reflects only those *actively* seeking work, and omits those older workers who become discouraged and drop out of the labor force after finding their search for employment futile. These people are then no longer classified as unemployed.

> Unemployment is often a demoralizing experience: many men find it difficult to maintain self-respect when they are out of work. The line of least resistance for the man aged 65 or over is to declare himself retired or, at least, to deny that he is seeking work. According to the definitions used by the Bureau of Census, a man who is not employed must be seeking work to be considered unemployed. If he is not seeking work, he is classified as being out of the labor force. Being out of the labor force is more respectable than being unemployed.[13]

Age Discrimination in Employment

Age discrimination in employment begins earlier than most people realize. For example, a 48-year-old woman in Atlanta was dismissed from her job when her company decided to eliminate older employees and retain younger workers. One man was turned down when he applied for the position of an FBI agent on the grounds that he was too old. He was 35.

A report in 1965 by William Wirtz, then Secretary of Labor, revealed that the most obvious form of age discrimination in employment was the employers' policies not to hire people over a given age.[14] At that time, one-fourth of job openings were closed to applicants over 45 years of age, and one-half were closed to applicants over age 55. Wirtz concluded:

> Approximately one million productive man-years are not utilized each year because workers over 45 are unemployed; many more productive years are lost because of forced, compulsory, or automatic retirement. Though the social cost, e.g., in the form of lost inventions, ideas, leadership, etc., cannot be estimated, approximately one billion dollars of unemployment insurance payments annually can be attributed to unemployment due to age. The potential loss of production might result in two or three times the unemployment insurance payments attributable to discrimination.[15]

Since 1967, when the Age Discrimination in Employment Act was passed, age discrimination in hiring, promoting, and dismissing employees has been against the law. This Act, designed to protect workers between the ages of 40 and 65, makes it unlawful for an employment agency to refuse to refer a client to a prospective employer for a job because of age. Also it is unlawful for prospective employers to state age preferences in help-wanted advertisements. Since the law has been in effect, nearly 11,000 persons have been awarded more than $48 million in damages and back pay. During 1975 alone, the Department of Labor found 6,000 companies had violated the law and thereby had deprived workers of over 6.5 million dollars due them. Many workers have been successful in recovering lost pay, damages, reinstatement privileges, and other benefits. One of the largest age discrimination settlements to date involved the employees of the Standard Oil Company of California. The company was forced to reinstate 120 employees who were terminated on the basis of age, and to give 2 million dollars in back pay to 160 others.

In 1978 the Age Discrimination in Employment Act was amended to include persons up to 70 years of age, instead of 65. These changes officially outlawed 65 as the age of mandatory retirement in the United States for most workers and abolished it altogether for federal employees. Although many proponents of flexible retirement policies look on this legislation as a significant step in the right direction, they feel that the law did not go far enough. They argue that the upper limit of age 70 should be removed because it constitutes age discrimination, and that mandatory retirement should be considered unlawful at any age.

If age is to be used as a basis for distributing jobs to workers, then I would establish a lottery and draw numbers. This year, if 38 is the age drawn, everyone aged 38 will be thrown out of work. Next year perhaps it will be 29 or 52. Such a lottery would be precisely as equitable as firing people who are, say, 65 or refusing to hire them at, say, 55.

SOURCE: Harriet Miller, quoted by Cyril Brickfield in "Why We Oppose Mandatory Retirement," *Modern Maturity*, August–September 1977, p. 40.

The Age of Retirement

Flexible Versus Mandatory Retirement

The debate on flexible retirement based on ability versus mandatory retirement based on a certain age has been a perennial issue in gerontology for several decades. As early as 1948, Otto Pollack in his pioneering work, *Social Adjustment in Old Age*, called for the need for research on the attitudes toward flexible and mandatory retirement practices.[16] In 1960, Wilma Donahue and her associates wrote: "The single most important issue in retirement policy today is the question of compulsory retirement at a fixed age. . . . Probably no other topic has occasioned more discussion and controversy in recent years or received as much attention."[17]

Actually, the issue goes back to 1777 when the first American mandatory retirement laws were enacted in New York. At that time a provision was introduced into the New York state constitution to require judges to leave the bench at a certain age. By 1820, six other states had passed similar laws. These mandatory ages for retirement of judges usually ranged between 60 and 70. One of the earliest opponents of mandatory retirement was former President John Adams who, at age 89, said that he could never forgive those states "for turning out venerable men."[18]

Despite the raising of the retirement age to 70, the debate on flexible versus mandatory retirement continues. Some arguments for flexible retirement are summarized by Erdman Palmore:

1. Mandatory retirement is discriminatory and contrary to the principal of equal employment opportunities.
2. Age is not an accurate indicator of the abilities of older people.
3. Flexible retirement would more fully utilize the experiences, skills, and potentials of older people.
4. Flexible retirement would increase the income of the elderly and reduce transfer payments necessary for income maintenance.

5. Flexible retirement would lessen the resentment caused by mandatory retirement.[19]

The major arguments in support of mandatory retirement are summarized below, and after each argument the opposing point of view is given.

One argument for mandatory retirement is that it assures everyone equal treatment. An employer does not have to discriminate between employees by telling some workers they may continue to work and others that they must go. One automobile executive points out that the practice of having everyone retire at the same time helps individuals maintain their dignity.

> It's customary when people retire at General Motors to have a retirement party. There's reason for celebration. The man or woman has earned retirement, and they have a big fun party. . . . You're not saying poor old Joe no longer has the mental or physical power so he's got to go. Everybody knows that (at GM) at age 68, people are going to be retired. There is no stigma attached to that.[20]

On the other hand, though proponents of flexible retirement recognize that there is a face-saving benefit to mandatory retirement, they argue that it penalizes the competent older workers. In other words, it is unfair to force all workers to retire in order to protect a small group of workers from being stigmatized.

Many corporate executives maintain that a fixed retirement age is needed to open up job opportunities for young people. Without such an age, many feel that the size of the work force will increase, as will unemployment. This argument is based on the premise that society can provide only a limited number of jobs. Most economists today feel that this argument is no longer acceptable. Even if it were, Representative Claude Pepper raises the question: Why should a young person have more right to a job than an older person? "To take jobs away from the old to give to the young apparently assumes that given a choice between young and old, the elderly should suffer."[21] It is more a question of rights and equity than one of economics.[22]

Another closely related argument holds that mandatory retirement provides promotional opportunities and strengthens incentives for younger people. Without fixed retirement, seniority and tenure practices would result in a slowdown or blockage of the upward mobility of younger employees. Palmore suggests that a solution to this problem would be "to eliminate seniority and tenure provisions at a fixed age and require the older workers to compete periodically for their jobs on the basis of ability rather than seniority."[23]

That older workers are not as productive as younger workers is one of the most popular arguments used by those in favor of mandatory

Through mandatory retirement policies, the skills and experiences of many older persons are being wasted, and they feel useless and without purpose. (Allen Green/Visual Departures)

retirement. As we mentioned previously, this argument has no factual basis. Research reveals that, with the exception of physically demanding labor and time-paced tasks, older workers perform as well as, if not better than, younger workers. In addition, they are more likely to have fewer absences and accidents, and to be far more dependable than their younger counterparts.

A key argument is that without mandatory retirement, health and pension plans would be more difficult to administer. Some corporate executives feel that the stability and solvency of pension plans require a fixed age. A counter argument is that by allowing those older workers who desire to continue working to do so, some strain on the social security system could be eased. Instead of taking from the system, these workers would continue to contribute to it. Likewise, fewer demands would be made upon private pension funds. Health-insurance costs of companies would not be greatly affected because at age 65, Medicare assumes most of the cost of health-care payments that the employer once financed.

Still others argue that mandatory retirement allows a company and its employees to plan better for the future by having a fixed date in which retirement must take place. But workers change jobs, become ill, or take early retirement at various times before the mandatory age, and companies are able to adjust to these circumstances, apparently with little difficulty. Without mandatory retirement, workers could choose their particular time to retire and could give the company advance notice.

Early Retirement

If the present trend continues, mandatory retirement may be purely an academic question within the next two decades. Each year, more and more people are choosing *early retirement* (retiring before age 65). In the decade from 1964 to 1974, the number of workers retiring early under social security tripled. In 1964, 2.6 million workers had retired on social security before age 65, equalling 25 percent of all retired workers collecting social security benefits. By 1974, the figure had increased to 8 million workers, or 52.6 percent of all retired workers receiving benefits.[24] Today about 60 percent of all retired workers have started to draw benefits before age 65. Bernice Neugarten predicts that by the year 2000, the retirement age will be around 55, and most people will have twice as many retirement years as the people today have.[25]

In a survey of company policies on early retirement, Mark Greene and Charles Pyron found in 1969 that 93 percent had provisions for early retirement in their private pension plans. Minimum age requirements for eligibility varied from age 50 to 62, with the most common requirement being a minimum age of 55. Most plans contained minimum service requirements varying between 10 and 20 years.[26]

The trend toward early retirement gained momentum in the early 1960s as more and more industrial workers were given options to retire early, along with increased retirement benefits. Early retirement has become increasingly prevalent in recent years as unions have bargained successfully for earlier retirement provisions. This has been especially true in the case of automobile workers. Harold Orbach reported that as early as 1962, 35 percent of the automobile workers had chosen early retirement.[27] In 1973 the United Automobile Workers union adopted the "30 and out plan." Under this plan, regardless of age, an automobile worker is eligible to collect a pension after 30 years of service. At the present time it is about $800 per month. Many persons as young as age 48 or 49 are able to qualify for full pension benefits.

A. William Pollman studied 442 members of the United Automobile Workers between the ages of 60 to 65 to determine their reasons for choosing early retirement.[28] His analysis indicated that an adequate retirement income was the main reason they gave. Poor health ranked second, followed by a desire for more free time. Job and work dissatisfaction were not listed among the most important reasons by the respondents.

Most studies reveal that workers who choose to retire early report high degrees of satisfaction with their retirement experience. E. F. Messer found in a study of federal civil service workers, who had retired as early as 55 and 60 years of age, that 68 percent said they would certainly retire again under the same conditions. Twenty-four percent said they probably would.[29]

A wide range of businesses and industries have been making early retirement attractive to their employees by offering lump-sum payments, pension supplements, and larger pension benefits. Early retirement has caught on with blue-collar and professional workers alike. The lowering of the age of eligibility for social security benefits to age 62, along with rising social security benefits, has given further impetus to this trend.

Another factor expected to have an impact on mandatory retirement policies in the United States is a predicted labor shortage. Loether points out that when labor shortages occur, there is pressure not only to hold on to older workers, but to bring retired workers back into the labor force.

> During World War II there was a temporary reversal of the long-term trend toward decreasing labor force participation of older men; in 1940, the participation rate for men 65 and over was 42.2. The rate began to climb with the outbreak of the war, reaching . . . 50.8 per cent in 1945. Thereafter, the rate returned to its long-term pattern of decreasing participation.[30]

Countries experiencing chronic labor shortages look on older workers as a valuable resource. Japan is an example of an industrial nation in which older workers are encouraged to remain in the labor force and where efforts are being made to raise the retirement age. In the United States, the decline in the birth rate during the last 15 years is expected to create a shortage of people in the labor force under the age of 65 by the year 2000. As a result, there will be societal pressure to retain older workers. It is highly likely that with such a shortage, the mandatory age for retirement will be raised from its present 70 to, say, 75 — or it may be abolished altogether.

The Meaning of Retirement

In many places of the world, retirement as we know it is a rarity. Cessation of work in most preliterate societies occurs only when the individual is too feeble to perform any type of productive activity. The aged are expected to continue to engage in whatever economic function that they are capable of doing, shifting from heavy labor to lighter, less strenuous tasks. In this way, they retain a sense of usefulness and a place in the productive activities of the group.

> Retirement is a word unknown to the peasants of the Andes. Healthy people continue to labor, although in reduced form, just as long as they are physically able to do so. Appropriate to the older members of the household are such tasks as weeding the fields near the house, scaring the birds away from the fields when the crops are maturing, minding the house when the younger members of the household are away tending distant fields or herding animals or going away on a trading expedition. Elders also play an important role in the care and supervision of children.[31]

Retirement is a relatively recent development in modern industrialized societies. It is the creation of "an economically non-productive role for large numbers of people whose labor is not considered essential to or necessary for the functioning of the economic order."[32] Retirement entails the transition from an economically productive role, which is clear-cut and well defined, to an economically nonproductive role, which is somewhat vague and ambiguous. This lack of clarity in the retirement role is due to its new and unique social position, for which there is no precedence. People used to work throughout their adult lives out of necessity. Today a new period has been added to the life cycle, in which people live out their last 10 to 15 years without having to work. They constitute a new social category known as retirees.

Retirement, like work, does not have the same meaning for all individuals. For some, retirement is the realization of a lifelong goal and represents the happiest time of their life; for others, it is a time of bitterness and frustration. Still others view it with shock and disbelief — something they never thought would happen to them.

> Mr. Hartsell was called to my office once a month for a year before he was 65 and told of company policy. He only laughed. When the day came that he had been warned about, he couldn't believe it and went home and went to bed although in perfect health. Three months later his wife was desperate. She said he wouldn't get out of bed, refused to read or look at TV, and would talk of nothing but the job he had lost. . . .[33]

Frances Carp observes that retirement has many meanings.

> The end of individual worth and social contact, a haven of rest, relief from an unpleasant, overtaxing, or health-draining job, or completion of commitment to society and initiation of self-realization. It may be a ceremony between one career and another; it may represent the opportunity to start one's "real"

lifework or to draw two paychecks. Second and even third careers are becoming more common among men and among women whose first career is motherhood.[34]

Satisfaction with Retirement

Overall satisfaction with life and higher morale are greater among older people who are still working than among those who have retired. This difference is partly due to the fact that those in the labor force usually have a higher socioeconomic status and are in better health than retirees. According to a 1965 Harris Poll, 61 percent of the retirees report that retirement has fulfilled their expectation for a good life, while 33 percent have found retirement less satisfying than they expected it to be.[35] Those persons who were dissatisfied gave such reasons as financial problems, poor health, and the fact that they missed working. Among the reasons given by those who reported satisfaction with retirement were the enjoyment of leisure and hobbies and the freedom to do as they pleased.

In a comprehensive study of retirement among both men and women, Gordon Streib and Clement Schneider report that about a third (31 percent) of their retired respondents are satisfied with retirement and feel that it turned out better than expected.[36] Nearly two-thirds (65 percent) said that it has turned out about the way they expected, while 4 percent feel it is worse. Interviews with some of these people reveal a wide range of responses to retirement. Some people were extremely satisfied; one man said, "Retirement means everything to me. I'm so happy about the whole set-up. When I was 68 I was retired, I was pleased. I'm having a good time." Others had mixed feelings about retirement. "I don't like it. I like to work. But then, some days I get up and maybe I don't feel so well, and the weather is bad outside, and then I think it might not be so bad after all to stay in bed. The main problem is finding something to do." Finally, some were bitter about their retirement situation. One man said, "I dislike retirement. Personally, I think it is better to keep busy. When you are not occupied and not useful, you feel like a back number. The world gets along without you."[37]

Satisfaction in retirement is related to factors that precede the retirement event. Wayne Thompson states that for the achievement of satisfaction in retirement, "the two most important factors are an accurate preconception of retirement and a favorable pre-retirement attitude toward retirement."[38] In line with this view, numerous preretirement preparation programs have been developed in the last two decades by business, industry, labor unions, and educational institutions (see Chapter 6). In addition to giving workers some idea of what

"They didn't give me a gold watch. They gave me a corduroy leisure suit."
(Drawing by Weber; © 1974. The New Yorker Magazine, Inc.)

retirement will be like, and trying to create a more positive attitude toward it, most programs attempt to encourage participants to plan constructively for retirement and to act on these plans before they retire. How effective these preretirement programs have been is difficult to ascertain.

Another significant factor in achieving satisfaction in retirement and influencing attitude toward retirement is the expected retirement income. In general, persons who have a favorable view toward retirement are also more likely to be confident about the adequacy of their retirement finances.

The specific occupational group to which one belongs also affects satisfaction in retirement. Streib and Schneider report that professionals include a higher proportion of satisfied retirees than any other group in their sample.[39] Simpson found that although professionals and executives make the most satisfactory adjustment to retirement of any category of workers, they are also the least likely to want to retire because of the intrinsic rewards that work affords them.[40] Yet, despite their reluctance to retire, they have the best retirement experience because of their ample financial circumstances and their personal and social resources, which enable them to seek out meaningful substitute roles. She notes that the middle stratum, composed of such occupations as clerical workers, salespersons, and craftsmen, has a less satisfying experience with retirement than professionals, while the lower stratum of blue-collar workers has the least satisfying experience of all.

The Effects of Retirement

In addition to research on the changes after retirement in personal and social circumstances and their effect on the retiree, factors influenced by retirement have also been investigated.

Health

One of the most popular beliefs about retirement is that it has a deleterious effect on health and in some instances can lead to a premature death. It is generally assumed that the abrupt cessation of a pattern of high activity and the shift to a slower pace at retirement contribute to physical decline. Stories about people who worked "day and night" and then, several months after retirement, died suddenly are common.

Research findings do not support this premise. Instead, most studies reveal that retirement does not adversely effect health; in fact, in some cases, health actually improves after retirement. Although the retirement population does contain a disproportionate number of people in poor health, retirement did not cause their health to decline; they retired because they were in poor health. Poor health is the main reason people give for taking early or voluntary retirement. Streib and Schneider, using data obtained from a longitudinal analysis, report the same pattern of changes in health in those retired and those still working. They found that among unskilled workers there was a slight improvement in health after retirement.[41]

Mental Health

Because of the belief that work has a therapeutic value, it is popularly assumed that without work, mental ailments ensue. Little evidence supports this view.

Lifelong patterns of illness, both mental and physical, have often been overlooked as the basic causes of mental illness after retirement; and the interrelationship between lifelong patterns of health, economic circumstances, and the generic problems of advanced age, when carefully examined, lend little credence to retirement itself as a cause of mental illness.[42]

Income

At retirement most people experience a sharp reduction in income, usually about half their preretirement earnings. Finances play a significant part in the decision to retire. Once individuals feel they have enough financial resources, then other factors such as health and the desire for more free time influence the time of retirement. J. N. Edwards and D. L. Klemmack report that the family income was the single most important determinant of life satisfaction and morale in retirement.[43]

Social Relationships

Another popular belief is that retirement marks a decline in social relationships. Research reveals that in most cases withdrawal from the labor force does not automatically result in a reduction of social contact with family, friends, or neighbors. Retirees are no more likely than workers to change their patterns of seeing their children, visiting with family and friends, and participating in community and associational activities.[44] Simpson and her associates found that the factor having the most influence on social participation in retirement is the status of the retiree's occupation.[45] Retired professionals have the highest degree of involvement, followed by middle status workers, with the semi-skilled having the least involvement. The researchers also discovered that if social involvements are not established before retirement, it is highly unlikely that they will be initiated after retirement.

The Marital Relationship

Retirement affects the marital relationship of couples in many ways. When the husband retires, the wife who has been a lifelong homemaker must adjust her daily routines to his presence. Some consensus is usually reached regarding the division of household tasks. While some wives complain of "half as much income and twice as much husband," they also report that their husband's retirement affords greater companionship. Generally, if a husband and wife enjoy a good relationship prior to retirement, retirement will increase, rather than decrease, marital satisfaction. But spouses who were able to adjust to each other only because they were apart each day may find that retirement creates a strain on their relationship (see Chapter 11).

Age Identification

In a study in Elmira, New York, Zena Blau found that retired older people are more likely to feel old than those still working.[46] Eighteen percent of the employed people in their sixties thought of themselves as old, compared to 37 percent of retirees the same age. Conflicting findings are reported by Streib and Schneider, who note that there is a pattern of increasing older-age identification, regardless of whether a person continues to work.[47]

Women and Retirement

People generally believe that retirement is not as traumatic for women as it is for men. Some writers point out that a woman worker has the roles of homemaker and career person; she retains the former, which alleviates the impact of retirement.[48] Others suggest that retirement is easier for a woman because she has "effectively retired once before from her primary family role as mother and thus by age 65 has already negotiated one more or less successful transition."[49]

Recent research has questioned these assumptions and suggests that retirement may be as difficult, if not more difficult, for women than for men. Streib and Schneider report that women are more unwilling to retire than men are. Among the women retirees in their sample, 57 percent were reluctant to retire, compared to 49 percent of the men. These researchers point out that women who are still working at 65 are those who have consciously selected the work role in preference to the homemaker role and, consequently, are more committed to it. Also their study reveals that women who retire report a sharper increase in feelings of uselessness than male retirees.[50] In comparing men and women retirees, Robert Atchley found that women frequently had more difficulty in getting used to retirement and were less likely to find it satisfactory. Also, older women tended to be more lonely and depressed than their male counterparts.[51]

Evidence shows that the marital status of women is related to their time of retirement. Women who are divorced or widowed are more likely to retire later than those who are married. This decision may be due to economic reasons as well as to the fact that married women often choose to retire when their husbands do, even though in most cases the wives are younger than their husbands.[52]

It is generally assumed that women who have worked have a more restricted social network after retirement because they have not had time to make friends outside of the work situation. To investigate this assumption, Judith Fox studied the effect of retirement on the social life of 212 middle-class women.[53] She found that women who have worked much of their lives have the same, if not more, social involvement than lifelong homemakers do. Retirees perceive that they have fewer social contacts than those women still working; however, retirees' interaction with friends and neighbors tends to increase. Fox hypothesizes that retired women are more dependent on social contacts outside the family than are women who have been housewives and never worked. The data suggest that upon retirement, women accelerate their informal friendships and neighborhood roles to compensate for the loss of work-related friendships.

Work After Retirement

About 20 percent of American males and 8 percent of the females continue to work after the traditional retirement age of 65 (Table 12.1) and are sometimes referred to as the "working retired." Gerda Fillenbaum in a study of working-retired men tried to determine which variables are most closely associated with work after retirement.[54] Her findings reveal that the working retired differ mainly from the nonworking retired in that they have more education, have intended to continue working when retired, and are less likely to report a decline in health. In addition, the working retired have less financial need to work and belonged to a larger number of voluntary associations. She indicates that the major reasons inducing certain persons to continue working after officially retiring are their greater involvement in work as well as occupational success and recognition.

Individuals who work beyond the traditional retirement tend to fall into these categories: (1) those who retire and take a part-time job; (2) those who embark on a second career; (3) and those who continue working at the same job. The largest proportion of workers aged 65 and over who continue to work do so on a part-time basis. This situation is due mainly to their preference for part-time work and to the earnings' limitation ceiling of the social security system, which discourages full-time employment. Part-time jobs and the type of work available usually carry low wages. Many part-time workers are exempt from the minimum wage laws.

Another group of people are successful in launching new careers after retirement. Some persons go into a new career because they are bored and disappointed with retirement, others because of financial reasons, and some because they want to fulfill a lifelong dream.[55] While second careers are not the modal pattern in American society, they are

Retirement for some persons means the beginning of a successful second career. After this woman retired from the classroom, she began a new job as a communications consultant for an engineering firm. (NRTA)

Generally, persons who work after retirement are strongly committed to their jobs. This 71-year-old man continues to put in a 40-hour-week as an executive of a large bank. (Photograph by Hal Morris. Reprinted from *Dynamic Years.*)

George Washington retired three times; each time he became depressed and introspective. The first time at the age of 26 while in command of the Virginia Militia in 1758, he decided to retire because of poor health. In a letter to a friend he wrote, "I have not too much reason to apprehend an approaching decay." With the outbreak of the Revolutionary War, he was recalled from retirement and, against his wish, was placed in command of the Continental Army. In 1783, he retired again; his words, "The scene is at length closed. I will move gently down the stream of life until I sleep with my fathers." But again, at 51, he was recalled to serve as the first President of the Constitutional Convention.

SOURCE: Edward L. Bortz, "Beyond Retirement," in *Retirement*, ed. Frances M. Carp, Behavioral Publications, New York, 1972, pp. 352–353.

becoming a more frequent phenomenon, especially with the trend toward earlier retirement in government units, business, and industry. Second careers have long been a pattern for the military because of the 20-year-minimum requirement for retirement, which means that many military personnel can retire in their early forties. General Dwight D. Eisenhower after his retirement from the army began his second career as a college president at the age of 58, and started a third career at 62 as President of the United States.

The third category, those who continue to work at their occupations, often are self-employed. Richard Barfield and James Morgan found that self-employment is the most important factor in determining a late retirement, that is, retirement at age 70 and older. Other significant factors include an expected low retirement income and a current low income. Job satisfaction is also important; people who enjoy their work tend to postpone retirement.[56]

Summary

1. Through the ages, work has had a variety of meanings and has fulfilled numerous functions. Today, work performs five general functions for most individuals: (1) it provides income; (2) it regulates life-activity; (3) it gives a person a sense of identity; (4) it is the source of social relationships; and (5) it offers a set of meaningful life-experiences.

2. The proportion of older males, both white and black, in the labor force has steadily declined during this century. The number of older women in the labor force, except for a slight decline in the last decade, has changed only slightly. Black females continue to have somewhat higher employment rates than white females, but the differences between the rates are disappearing.

3. There are many misconceptions about older workers' productivity, absentee-ism rates, and adaptability. Older workers are handicapped in the labor market by their low educational levels, their obsolescent skills, and the preference of employers for younger workers. As a result, they are overrepresented in farming, service work, and proprietary occupations in which they are self-employed. Older workers are less mobile occupationally than younger workers are; after age 50, few change jobs voluntarily because it is difficult for them to get a new job. Many times when older people cannot find work, they drop out of the labor force and declare themselves retired.

4. The Age Discrimination in Employment Act (1967) protects workers between the ages of 40 and 65 from discriminatory practices in employment. In 1978 the Act was amended to include workers up to the age of 70. The debate on flexible versus mandatory retirement has been one of the most hotly contested issues in gerontology. Proponents of flexible retirement policies argue that they allow for a fuller utilization of the skills and experiences of older people, increase their income, and lessen the resentment caused by mandatory retirement. The major arguments for mandatory retirement include: (1) it spares the worker the stigma of being dismissed; (2) it opens up jobs and promotional opportunities for younger workers; (3) older workers are less productive than younger workers; and (4) it allows the company and the individual to plan better for the future.

5. Early retirement is becoming increasingly popular since the early 1960s. Originally promoted by labor unions for industrial workers, the trend toward early retirement has spread to many businesses and industries and has become popular with both blue-collar and professional workers.

6. Retirement is a modern phenomenon and is becoming a new stage in the life cycle. Like work, retirement has different meanings for different people. Reasons given by those satisfied with retirement are that it gives them more time to enjoy leisure activities and freedom to do as they please. Those dissatisfied with retirement gave financial problems and poor health as reasons. Satisfaction in retirement is related to a person's preretirement attitude, retirement income, and specific occupational category. Professionals and executives show the most satisfactory adjustment to retirement.

7. Studies show that if retirement has any effect on health at all, it is a beneficial one. Studies also reveal that the level of social involvement changes little or not at all in retirement.

8. Recent research suggests that retirement can be as traumatic for women as it is for men. In fact, women are more reluctant to retire than men are. Women who retire also have greater feelings of uselessness and are more depressed and lonelier than men.

9. Persons who are deeply involved in their work, who are successful, and who have received status and recognition on the job are the most likely to continue working past retirement age. Individuals who continue to work after the customary retirement age can be divided into three groups: those who work part-time, those who pursue a second career, and those who continue working at the same job. The largest proportion of older workers are engaged in part-time employment. Second careers are becoming increasingly more common, as many workers opt for early retirement.

Notes

1. Kingsley Davis, *Human Society*, Macmillan, New York, 1949, pp. 451–452.

2. Genesis 3:19.

3. Eugene A. Friedmann and Robert J. Havighurst, *The Meaning of Work and Retirement*, The University of Chicago Press, Chicago, 1954, pp. 3–5.

4. Everett Hughes quoted by George Maddox in "Adaptation to Retirement," *The Gerontologist*, 10, no. 1 (1970), Pt. II, 15.

5. Friedmann and Havighurst, *The Meaning of Work and Retirement*, pp. 4–5.

6. U.S. Bureau of the Census, *Current Population Reports*, Special Studies Series P-23, No. 59, U.S. Government Printing Office, Washington, D.C., 1976, pp. 49–50.

7. Robert Clark and Joseph Spengler, "Population Aging in the Twenty-first Century," *Aging*, January–February 1978, p. 11.

8. U.S. Department of Labor, The Manpower Administration, *Back to Work After Retirement*, U.S. Government Printing Office, Washington, D.C., 1971, p. 5.

9. Ida H. Simpson, "Problems of the Aging in Work and Retirement," in *Foundations of Practical Gerontology*, eds. Rosamonde Boyd and Charles Oakes, University of South Carolina Press, Columbia, 1973, p. 161.

10. Herman J. Loether, *Problems of Aging*, Dickenson, Belmont, Calif., 1975, pp. 64–65.

11. Ibid., p. 65.

12. *Fact Book on Aging: A Profile of America's Older Population*, The National Council on the Aging, Washington, D.C., 1978, p. 82.

13. Loether, *Problems of Aging*, pp. 65–66.

14. James H. Schulz, *Retirement*, 1971 White House Conference on Aging, Background and Issues, U.S. Government Printing Office, Washington, D.C., 1971, p. 27.

15. Ibid.

16. Otto Pollack, *Social Adjustment in Old Age*, Social Science Research Council, New York, 1948, p. 116.

17. Wilma Donahue, Harold Orbach, and Otto Pollack, "Retirement: The Emerging Social Pattern," in *Handbook of Social Gerontology*, ed. Clark Tibbitts, The University of Chicago Press, Chicago, 1960, p. 355.

18. David H. Fischer, *Growing Old in America*, Oxford University Press, New York, 1978, p. 80.

19. Erdman Palmore, "Compulsory Versus Flexible Retirement: Issues and Facts," *The Gerontologist*, 12, no. 4 (1972), 344–345. Also, see R. K. Burns, quoted by Wilma Donahue, et al., "Retirement: The Emerging Social Pattern," in *Handbook of Social Gerontology*, ed. Clark Tibbitts, The University of Chicago Press, Chicago, 1960, pp. 355–356.

20. *U.S. News and World Report*, October 3, 1977, p. 31.

21. Representative Claude Pepper, "We Shouldn't Have to Retire at 65," *Parade*, September 4, 1977, p. 15.

22. "Now, the Revolt of the Old," *Time*, October 10, 1977, pp. 18–19.

23. Palmore, "Compulsory Versus Flexible Retirement," p. 26.

24. *U.S. News and World Report*, May 13, 1974, p. 59.

25. Bernice L. Neugarten, "The Future and Young-Old," *The Gerontologist*, 15, no. 1 (1975), 7.

26. Schultz, *Retirement*, 1971 White House Conference on Aging, p. 25.

27. Harold L. Orbach, "Social and Institutional Aspects of Industrial Workers' Retirement Patterns," in *Trends in Early Retirement*, Occasional Papers in Gerontology, no. 4, Institute of Gerontology, University of Michigan-Wayne State University, Ann Arbor, 1969, pp. 1–26.

28. A. William Pollman, "Early Retirement: A Comparison of Poor Health to Other Retirement Factors," *Journal of Gerontology*, 26, no. 1 (1971), 41–45.

29. E. F. Messer, "Thirty-Eight Years Is a Plenty," in *Trends in Early Retirement*, Occasional Papers in Gerontology, no. 4, Institute of Gerontology, University of Michigan-Wayne State University, Ann Arbor, 1969, pp. 50–66.

30. Loether, *Problems of Aging*, p. 71.

31. Allan R. Holmberg, "Age in the Andes," in *Aging and Leisure*, ed. Robert W. Kleemeier, Oxford University Press, New York, 1961, p. 89.

32. Harold L. Orbach, "Societal Values and the Institutionalization of Retirement," in *Processes of Aging*, vol. 2, eds. Richard Williams, Clark Tibbitts, and Wilma Donahue, Atherton Press, New York, 1963, p. 389.

33. William E. Cole and Diana K. Harris, *The Elderly in America*, Allyn & Bacon, Boston, 1977, p. 58.

34. Frances M. Carp, "Background and Statement of Purpose," in *The Retirement Process*, ed. Frances M. Carp. U.S. Government Printing Office, Washington, D.C., 1966, p. 8.

35. Louis Harris, "Pleasant Retirement Expected," *The Washington Post*, November 28, 1965.

36. Gordon F. Streib and Clement J. Schneider, *Retirement in American Society: Impact and Process*, Cornell University Press, Ithaca, N.Y., 1971, p. 139.

37. Ibid., pp. 139–142.

38. Wayne E. Thompson, "Pre-Retirement Anticipation and Adjustment in Retirement," *Journal of Social Issues*, 14, no. 2 (1958), 43.

39. Streib and Schneider, *Retirement in American Society*, p. 131.

40. Simpson, "Problems of the Aging in Work and Retirement," pp. 168–170.

41. Streib and Schneider, *Retirement in American Society*, pp. 62–79.

42. Eugene A. Friedmann and Harold L. Orbach, "Adjustment to Retirement," in *American Handbook of Psychiatry*, vol. 1, ed. Silvano Arieti, Basic Books, New York, 1974, pp. 625–626.

43. J. N. Edwards and D. L. Klemmack, "Correlates of Life Satisfaction: A Re-Examination," *Journal of Gerontology*, 28, no. 4 (1973), 497–502.

44. Gordon F. Streib, "A Longitudinal Study of Retirement," in *Final Report to the Social Security Administration*, U.S. Government Printing Office, Washington, D.C., 1965, p. 3.

45. Ida H. Simpson, Kurt W. Bach, and John D. McKinney, "Work and Retirement," in *Social Aspects of Aging*, eds. Ida H. Simpson and John C. McKinney, Duke University Press, Durham, N.C., 1966, pp. 68–74.

46. Zena S. Blau, *Old Age in a Changing Society*, New Viewpoints, New York, 1973, pp. 104–105.

47. Streib and Schneider, *Retirement in American Society*, pp. 160–161.

48. Robert N. Butler and Myrna I. Lewis, *Aging and Mental Health*, C. V. Mosby, St. Louis, 1977, p. 37.

49. Vern L. Bengtson, Patricia L. Kasschau and Pauline K. Ragan, "The Impact of Social Structure on Aging Individuals," in *Handbook of the Psychology of Aging*, eds. James E. Birren and K. Warner Schaie, Van Nostrand Rheinhold, New York, 1977, p. 334.

50. Streib and Schneider, *Retirement in American Society*, pp. 50–51, 161.

51. Robert C. Atchley, "Selected Social and Psychological Differences Between Men and Women in Later Life," *Journal of Gerontology*, 31, no. 2 (1976), 204–211.

52. Alan Sheldon, Peter J. McEwan, and Carol P. Ryser, *Retirement Patterns and Predictions*, U.S. Government Printing Office, Washington, D.C., 1975, p. 144.

53. Judith H. Fox, "Effects of Retirement and Former Work Life on Women's Adaptation in Old Age," *Journal of Gerontology*, 32, no. 2 (1977), 196–202.

54. Gerda G. Fillenbaum, "The Working Retired," *Journal of Gerontology*, 26, no. 1 (1971), 82–89.

55. Gordon F. Streib, *Retirement Roles and Activities*, 1971 White House Conference on Aging, Background and Issues, U.S. Government Printing Office, Washington, D.C., 1971, p. 15.

56. Richard E. Barfield and James N. Morgan, *Early Retirement: The Decision and the Experience*, Institute for Social Research, University of Michigan, Ann Arbor, 1969.

For Further Study

Atchley, Robert C. *The Sociology of Retirement*. Schenkman, Cambridge, Mass., 1976. A concise book covering the various aspects of retirement.

Carp, Frances M., ed. *Retirement*. Behavioral Publications, New York, 1972. A collection of academic and popular papers that view retirement from a variety of perspectives.

Friedmann, Eugene A., and Harold L. Orbach. "Adjustment to Retirement." In *American Handbook of Psychiatry*, edited by Silvano Arieti. Basic Books, New York, 1974. A summary article on retirement written from a sociological perspective.

Sheppard, Harold L. "Work and Retirement." In *Handbook of Aging and the Social Sciences*, edited by Robert Binstock and Ethel Shanas. Van Nostrand Reinhold,

New York, 1976. An article that covers the participation of older people in the labor force and some issues involved in retirement.

————, and Sara E. Rix. *The Graying of Working America*. Free Press, New York, 1977. A penetrating analysis of retirement-age policy.

Smelser, Neil J. *The Sociology of Economic Life* (2nd ed.). Prentice-Hall, Englewood Cliffs, N.J., 1976. A short book that focuses on the relationship between society and the economy.

Streib, Gordon F. and Clement J. Schneider. *Retirement in American Society*. Cornell University Press, Ithaca, N.Y., 1971. Contains the research findings from the Cornell Study of Occupational Retirement.

13

The Political System
and Aging

Man is not only a social animal, but according to Aristotle he is also a political animal. Some form of political system or government is found even in the simplest societies. The *political institution* serves to maintain social order, to protect against outside enemies, and to plan and coordinate for the general welfare. In addition to these functions, the political institution also provides for the distribution of power.

The process by which people acquire and exercise power over others is known as *politics*. Politics has been referred to as the science of "who gets what, when, and how."[1] In other words, it determines who shall be given what power in government, and when and how it shall be given. In this chapter we shall examine the attitudes and participation of older people in politics. What is the impact of senior citizen organizations on the political system? What is the government's involvement in programs for the elderly? Lastly, what is the future of the aged in politics?

Political Attitudes and Behavior

Attitudes and Issues

It is popularly assumed that with age people become more politically conservative. Cross-sectional studies, which account for the bulk of the research in this area, show that in comparison with younger adults, older people do tend to be more conservative. But cross-sectional studies do not tell us whether or not there is a change in political attitudes with age.

To understand the political attitudes and behavior of older people fully, three distinct, but interrelated factors must be taken into account: the *age cohort* to which older people belong, that is, individuals born during approximately the same time period; the aging process throughout the life cycle; and the period or historical effects on all age groups in the population.[2] First, the cohort effect must be considered, because the time in which people grew up and received their early socialization plays an important part in interpreting their political attitudes and behavior.

> Data on persons who are old at the time of measurement may reveal more about the shared experiences and perceptions of that particular older generation — exposure at approximately the same age and time to common patterns of schooling, family life, economic cycles, wars and political events — than about anything intrinsic to the processes of aging.[3]

Second, political attitudes and behavior may be influenced by the aging process or by the maturational changes that occur at different stages in the life cycle. For instance, the elderly's support of government programs for medical aid may increase; also, physical decline may curtail political participation. Third, period or historical effects must be considered, as social and political events greatly alter the patterns of party identification and change the degree of popularity of the two major American parties.

By a technique called *cohort analysis*, which examines cross-sectional and longitudinal data at the same time, these three factors may be more readily observed and identified. Briefly, cohort analysis when used to study political attitudes does so through a sequence of cross-sectional attitudes surveys. Each survey is arranged in such a way that persons of similar ages may be followed over a period of time. For example, suppose we had data from three attitude surveys taken ten years apart, from 1950 to 1970, in which the respondents had been placed into age groups of five-year intervals. Those respondents who had been 30 to 35 years old in 1950 would be 40 to 45 in 1960, and 50 to 55 in 1970. In this way it is possible to trace different generations or age cohorts over time through a series of surveys.

Through this method of analysis, Norval Glenn found two important facts about the relationship between age and political attitudes. First, "people have typically become less, rather than more conservative as they have grown older, in conformity with general societal trends."[4] Second, persons in their fifties and sixties generally are more liberal than when they were in their thirties and forties. Though older people have tended to change in the same direction as the total adult population, the liberalization has been slower. Thus, compared to others in the population, the elderly appear to have become more conservative, but compared with their own younger attitudes, they actually have become more liberal.

There is no clear-cut relationship between age and political issues. The response of people to political issues tends to be governed more by their early socialization or by their present social and economic circumstances than by age.[5] People who grew up in the 1920s naturally have a different orientation on such issues as abortion, legalization of marijuana, interracial marriage, and school integration than younger adults do.

The relationship of age to political issues may also reflect changes that occur through the life cycle and the individual's present circumstances. For example, parents who have young children in school are more likely to be receptive to increasing school taxes than older persons whose children are grown and who live on a fixed income. In the same way, we would expect older people to support tax proposals to better their own financial situations. But we also find that such proposals are equally supported by younger age groups. For instance, in 1975 a Harris Poll revealed that a comparable number of older and younger people believe that social security payments to the elderly should automatically increase with rises in the cost of living.[6] The poll also found that those under 65 agreed even more strongly than those over 65 with the statement that the "government should help support older people with the taxes collected from all Americans." The same percentage of people over 65 as under 65 felt that "nobody should be forced to retire because of age, if he wants to continue working and is still able to do a good job."

Party Identification

As people age, do they tend to affiliate with the Republican party? In 1962, John Crittenden, using data from national surveys that spanned a 12-year period from 1946 to 1958, found that as persons grew older, they tended to become Republicans.[7] In re-analyzing Crittenden's data longitudinally across generations, instead of making cross-sectional comparisons, Neal Cutler reported that the increase in Republicanism was for all age groups, in conformity with a national trend.[8] He found no consistent relationship between aging and identification with the Republican party.

In a later study, Norval Glenn and Ted Hefner doubled the time span (1945–1969) and increased the sample size that Crittenden had used.[9] In addition, their data came from the entire nation, whereas Crittenden's were only for the nonsouthern population. Their findings also indicate no increase in Republicanism as a result of the aging process. They maintain that data from cross-sectional studies showing a positive relationship between Republicanism and aging reflect generational differences rather than the effects of aging. Glenn and Hefner conclude "This study should rather conclusively lay to rest the once prevalent belief that the aging process has been an important influence for Republicanism in the United States."[10]

Though age is not associated with the party a person chooses, it is related to whether or not a person identifies with a political party. Party identification does not decline in the later years but becomes stronger the longer that it lasts. In a study of the American voter, Norman Nie and his associates report that "the data are consistent with the view that the strength of party affiliation grows with age. In each year one finds a . . . smaller percentage of the older age groups with no party attachment."[11] This stronger sense of party identification among older people is related to the greater length of time that they have had to become attached to a party and to develop loyalty to it. Because of this strong identification, they become less and less susceptible to shifting their allegiance to another party.

> The longer a person associates himself with a group the stronger his attachment to it becomes and the more difficult it is to induce him to defect from the group or show disloyalty to its standards. In the political sphere this means that older people having had more time to develop a strong partisan self-image, are notably more stable in their voting than younger people and less likely to be moved by the political winds of the time. It is particularly interesting that in the election of 1968 George Wallace drew a larger proportion of votes from the under-35 generation than he did from any of the older cohorts. Although one might have expected Mr. Wallace's emphasis on "law and order" and containment of the racial protest to appeal to older people, survey evidence demonstrates that it was the people over 65 who were least responsive to his appeal.[12]

Voting and Political Interest

Considerable evidence exists to show high voting rates among older people. Voting participation is lowest among those persons under 25; it rapidly increases during the upper middle-age groups (55–64) before gradually dropping off. Figure 13.1 shows the variation in voting by sex, a difference that becomes more pronounced in the later years. In the 65 to 74 age group, 70.9 percent of the men voted, compared to 63.0 percent of the women. By age 75 and over, 62.9 percent of the men voted, while only 50.1 percent of the women voted. Though women tend to vote less frequently than men, voting participation for both sexes declines in the later stages of the life cycle. This drop is usually due to factors other than age. The older population has a preponderance of females, and since women usually vote less frequently than men, this partly accounts for the decline in voting. Also, because educational attainment is positively associated with voting participation and older people tend to have lower educational levels than younger persons have, voting by the elderly is less.[13]

When controls are introduced for both sex and education, the drop in voting among males 65 and over almost disappears (see Table 13.1). The table also shows that differences in the percentage voting are greater among those persons with elementary school education than among

Figure 13.1   Recent voting by age and sex, November 1976

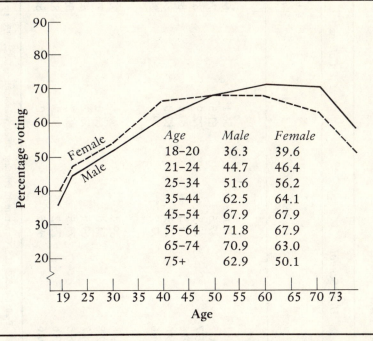

Age	Male	Female
18–20	36.3	39.6
21–24	44.7	46.4
25–34	51.6	56.2
35–44	62.5	64.1
45–54	67.9	67.9
55–64	71.8	67.9
65–74	70.9	63.0
75+	62.9	50.1

SOURCE: Adapted from Herman B. Brotman, "Voter Participation in November 1976," *The Gerontologist*, 17, No. 2 (1977), 157–159.

those with college education. On the whole, larger differences in voting rates appear within age groups than between them.

In comparing the voting frequency of older and younger persons in presidential and congressional elections, Rochelle Jones notes:

> In the 1972 presidential election, 87 per cent of the registered voters over 65 went to the polls. Only 55 per cent of the people under 65 voted. In previous presidential elections, people in their seventies and eighties, despite the frequent handicaps of age, physical infirmities, and ill health, have turned out with greater frequency than people in their early twenties. About 75 per cent of people in their seventies and 66 per cent of people in their eighties have voted in presidential elections. In nonpresidential election years when the voting turnout usually drops dramatically, older adults continue to go to the polls in large numbers. About 80 per cent of the over-65 registered voters turned out in 1974.[14]

Older people not only vote more frequently than younger persons do, but they manifest higher levels of political interest. Norval Glenn and Michael Grimes found that the highest percentage reporting a great

Table 13.1 Voting by sex, age, and education, November 1976

Sex and age	Elementary		High School		College	
	0–7 years	8 years	1–3 years	4 years	1–3 years	4 years or more
Male						
18-24	6.5%	13.1%	20.1%	36.6%	56.1%	69.8%
25-34	11.5	30.4	30.7	47.6	61.5	74.6
35-44	30.2	41.7	45.7	62.1	72.9	81.4
45-54	36.7	55.5	58.8	71.5	80.6	84.6
55-64	49.4	63.5	69.6	77.1	82.0	86.1
65+	52.4	65.7	74.6	77.7	79.9	84.3
Female						
18-24	8.2	12.2	19.6	39.4	59.6	75.0
25-34	13.4	20.0	32.8	54.0	66.0	79.0
35-44	23.0	38.9	44.7	69.5	77.2	83.5
45-54	33.7	46.9	58.5	73.5	80.2	85.0
55-64	42.8	55.5	63.6	75.2	80.0	82.6
65+	36.1	52.4	60.6	69.5	77.0	80.4

SOURCE: Adapted from U.S. Bureau of the Census, *Current Population Reports*, 1978, P-20, No. 322, U.S. Government Printing Office, Washington, D.C., 1976, pp. 57-59.

deal of interest in politics to be people aged 60 and older.[15] They explain that older people do not have the distractions that they had at earlier stages of the life cycle. When they were young, their immediate problems of families and careers made demands on their time and energy, continuing in a modified form in the middle years. By retirement age, fewer distractions allow more time for political matters, which also compensate for the lack of other activities and interests. Glenn and Grimes note also that with age, political activity may become a source of satisfaction and an end itself, rather than a means toward achieving an ideal or pursuing self-interests.

Age and Leadership

Older people also appear to occupy a disproportionate number of leadership positions. Such positions of high rank as Supreme Court Justice or President of the United States are often dominated by persons in their middle and later years. Harvey Lehman's study, *Age and Achievement*, reveals that the largest number of Supreme Court Justices began their appointment between the ages of 55 to 59.[16] Although some served in their thirties and others in their nineties, the majority served between the ages of 65 to 69. Lehman notes that 80 percent of Supreme Court service has been rendered by men over 65 (Figure 13.2).

Albert Johns and his co-authors point out that federal judges are not

Figure 13.2   Ages of 70 Justices of the U.S. Supreme Court

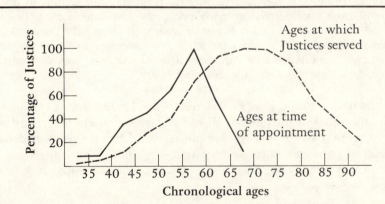

SOURCE: Harvey C. Lehman, *Age and Achievement*, Princeton University Press, Princeton, N.J., 1953, p. 171.

William O. Douglas served over 36 years as a U.S. Supreme Court Justice, longer than any other Justice in history, and was 77 when he resigned. (UPI)

subject to mandatory retirement and are virtually appointed for a lifetime:

> Some critics of the federal judiciary suggest that judges should, like members of other professions, be forced to retire at a reasonable age. It is believed that old judges are very likely to become physically or mentally infirm and that such disabilities could affect the quality of their decisions. . . . On the other hand, it is desirable to have experienced and competent people on the federal bench. Infirmity became an issue in 1974 and 1975 when Justice William O. Douglas suffered a stroke. His physical condition forced him to absent himself from proceedings on many occasions, thus late in 1975, Douglas ended the speculation and criticism by resigning. During the presidency of Franklin Roosevelt, Congress passed a law that was designed to make retirement a more desirable option for federal judges. It was decided that after age seventy they could retire at full salary.[17]

Lehman also found that Presidents of the United States were most frequently between the ages of 55 and 59 when first elected.[18] Furthermore, the two major parties are most likely to choose presidential candidates, both successful and unsuccessful, in this age range.

As life expectancy has increased, so has the average age of political leaders:

> In the early Republic the median age of Cabinet officers was forty-seven. In the mid-twentieth century it was sixty. At the same time the median age of

The U.S. Constitution, written in 1787, was not unmindful of the value of age; it set 30 as the minimum age for Senators. At the time, the life expectancy was about 30, so only half the Americans born were expected to reach that age. A higher age limit might not have left enough living Americans from which to make a good choice.

SOURCE: Isaac Asimov, "The Pursuit of Youth," *Ladies Home Journal,* June 1974, p. 154.

United States Senators advanced from forty-five in 1799 to fifty-seven in 1925. . . . Leaders in twentieth-century America are not merely older on the average, they also tend to vary less in their ages. From 1900 to 1940, no Speaker of the United States House of Representatives was elected under the age of sixty except Nicholas Longworth, who in 1925 was chosen at the age of fifty-six.[19]

Joseph Schlesinger reports an age timetable for political leaders that corresponds to the hierarchy of offices. For instance, United States representatives usually enter the House between the ages of 35 and 40, governors are elected between 45 and 50, and senators are elected for the first time between 50 and 55. He concludes that the older a politician is, the higher the office that he or she is likely to hold.[20]

Senior Citizen Organizations

In recent years, older people have become increasingly mobilized politically through their membership and participation in age-based organizations. Public officials have begun to recognize the credentials of these groups, and more and more they are being included in the national policy processes and decisions that concern the elderly. Binstock points out that these organizations have basically three types of power available to them.[21] First, their ready access to public officials gives the elderly a chance to present their proposals and work to block others they oppose. Second, this access to public officials affords them an opportunity to frame many issues of policy pertinent to aging and also to initiate issues for public debate. A third type of power is the "electoral bluff." Although the large membership of many age-based organizations represents an electoral force that most politicians do not wish to offend, the potential power of these organizations is a bluff because it is doubtful that older people will vote as a cohesive bloc. Binstock observes, "Within moderate limits, public officials are responsive to the interpretations of the interest groups; and the interest groups keep their interpretations within these moderate limits, never putting forth radical proposals that might force politicians to call the bluff of the aging vote."[22]

At present, about ten groups are involved in national politics, more or less exclusively on behalf of the elderly. These organizations include: the National Council on the Aging (NCOA), a loose confederation of social welfare agencies; the American Gerontological Society, a multidisciplinary professional organization; and the National Caucus on the Black Aged, a coalition of professionals focusing on the problems of older blacks. Four groups are trade associations: the American Association of Homes for the Aging, the American Nursing Home Association, the National Council of Health Care Services, and the National Association of State Units on Aging. In addition, there are three mass-membership organizations: the National Association of Retired Federal Employees (NARFE); the National Council of Senior Citizens (NCSC); and the National Retired Teachers Association and the American Association of Retired Persons, which function politically as one organization (NRTA-AARP).[23]

The NRTA-AARP, the largest association of older people began with the political matter of state pensions and federal tax benefits for retired teachers, and its goals have always included a political dimension, though this has played a subordinate role in the organization. Primary emphasis has been directed toward benefits for the association's membership. The AARP has gained a reputation since the early 1970s as being nonpartisan, but the second largest association, the NCSC, is closely identified with the Democratic party and is more politically active. The NCSC had its origins in political involvement with the Senior Citizens for Kennedy Movement in 1960 and then directed its efforts toward the fight for the congressional enactment of Medicare. Since the passage of the bill, the NCSC has expanded its political goals to include a broad range of other political issues.

The NCSC and the AARP also differ in their stands on various issues, particularly on the earnings limitation ceiling of the social security system and on national health insurance. For instance, the AARP has long pursued the goal of abolishing the ceiling on the amount of earnings a person may receive and still collect social security benefits. The Association maintains that the earnings ceiling not only stifles initiative, but penalizes those who need to work to make ends meet. On the other hand, the NCSC argues that the ceiling must be retained in order to conserve funds to pay social security benefits to those who are unable to work. Furthermore, the NCSC feels that removing the ceiling would result in a "gratuitous benefit given retired doctors, lawyers, and others who can continue to make money, although formally retired."[24] The respective positions of the two groups on the earnings limit reflect the basic composition of their membership. AARP consists mainly of middle-class members, many of whom are professionals and can continue to work beyond retirement age if they so desire. The NCSC is composed primarily of working-class members who have no employment options after retirement age.[25]

Though both AARP and NCSC favor the establishment of a national health care plan for all citizens, they differ in how it should be implemented. The difference of opinion between the two organizations is, in part, related to the fact that the leadership of the NCSC is strongly labor-oriented while the NRTA-AARP is closely tied to the insurance industry. AARP has urged the prompt enactment of the Comprehensive Medicare Reform Act; the NCSC supports the labor-endorsed National Health Security bill. The NCSC has charged that the Medicare reforms advocated by AARP fail to protect the working population, undermine Medicare, and benefit the insurance industry.[26] AARP spokesmen maintain that millions of older Americans need adequate medical care now and can no longer wait for the improvement of existing programs.[27]

Government Involvement

In 1935 when the Social Security Act was signed into law, President Franklin D. Roosevelt remarked: "We can never insure one hundred per cent of the population against one hundred per cent of the hazards and vicissitudes of life, but we have tried to frame a law which will give some measure of protection . . . against poverty-ridden old age."[28] This act marked the beginning of the government's involvement in the problems of the elderly.

Exactly thirty years elapsed before the enactment of two other important pieces of legislation that have greatly affected the lives of older people. In 1965 Congress passed the Medicare Bill and the Older Americans Act. Under the Medicare program, millions of older people receive federal assistance in paying their hospital and doctor bills. The Older Americans Act established the Administration on Aging (AoA), which is under the jurisdiction of the Secretary of Health, Education, and Welfare. Through the AoA, financial grants are authorized to states to develop and improve a variety of programs and services for older people. The Older Americans Act spelled out specific government responsibilities and objectives for the elderly; these objectives are contained in Title I of the Act.

1. An adequate income in retirement in accordance with the American standard of living.
2. The best possible physical and mental health which science can make available and without regard to economic status.
3. Suitable housing, independently selected, designed and located with reference to special needs and available at costs which older citizens can afford.

4. Full restorative services for those who require institutional care.
5. Opportunity for employment with no discriminatory personnel practices because of age.
6. Retirement in health, honor, dignity — after years of contribution to the economy.
7. Pursuit of meaningful activity within the widest range of civic, cultural, and recreational opportunities.
8. Efficient community services, including access to low-cost transportation, which provide social assistance in a coordinated manner and which are readily available when needed.
9. Immediate benefit from proven research knowledge which can sustain and improve health and happiness.
10. Freedom, independence, and the free exercise of individual initiative in planning and managing their own lives.[29]

The 1960s are often thought of as the turning point in the government's responsiveness to the needs of the elderly. Prior to that time, older Americans not only suffered from the lack of concern for their problems, but with the exception of social security, the federal government almost totally failed to recognize that the elderly had any problems at all.

The government's awareness of its responsibilities for older people was evidenced in 1960 when Congress authorized a White House Conference on Aging to be held in 1961. Each state assessed the needs of its older people through a series of studies and inventories and reported their findings to the conference. From these proceedings emerged a comprehensive set of recommendations for action on a nationwide basis to meet the needs of the elderly. It is generally recognized that this conference made a major contribution to the enactment of Medicare, as well as laying the groundwork for the Older Americans Act.

The second White House Conference convened a decade later, in the fall of 1971. Some observers have felt that this conference fell short of its intended goals and had no significant results. But Pratt argues to the contrary:

> There is strong presumptive evidence that the 1971 White House Conference on aging has had a major effect on the trend of events during the subsequent two and one-half years. The impact is measurable partly in the significant legislative developments of the period and, not less importantly, in developments internal to the larger senior-citizen organizations.[30]

Byron Gold classifies the government's programs and services designed to improve the circumstances of the elderly into six categories.[31] First, cash transfer programs help assure older people a more adequate income, such as social security and Supplemental Security Income (SSI). SSI, which replaced the Old Age Assistance Program, establishes an income floor for the elderly. The second category includes noncash benefits and services that have a measurable economic value, exemplified by Medicare, Medicaid, housing subsidies, and food stamps. The third area is the protection of the rights of older people through legislation, such as the Age Discrimination in Employment Act, raising the mandatory retirement age to 70, and pension-reform legislation. The Employee Retirement Income Security Act expanded previous legislation regulating private pension plans and, for the first time, set certain minimum pension standards.

The support of biomedical, social, and behavioral research related to the aging process is a fourth area. The Research on Aging Act of 1974 authorized the establishment of the National Institute on Aging to conduct research and to study the diseases and special problems of the elderly. A fifth role of the government is the delivery of services to the elderly through grants to private and public organizations at the state and local level under Titles III and VII of the Older Americans Act. For example, Title VII provides for meals to be served under the nutrition program; older people are served meals at centralized locations, or for those unable to go to these sites, meals are delivered at their homes. Lastly, a sixth role is the coordination at state and local levels of the resources, services, and programs made available in the five preceding categories.

The government's concern for the elderly may be limited in the long run by the expansion of their needs. With the increasing numbers of persons who are chronologically aged and of those who are retiring from the labor force at earlier ages, the government may find it more difficult in the future to meet their needs and fulfill the responsibilities that it has already undertaken.[32] Rochelle Jones suggests that some sort of backlash against older people is inevitable as the economic burden on the taxpayer increases.

> The backlash will grow as the government assumes a larger share of society's support for older adults and as workers feel the tax bite of supporting the aging, nonproductive sector of the population. In an age-segregated society, the burden of support for older adults is steadily shifted from the family to the government. The young will no longer contribute directly to the support of their parents. Instead, they will give their tax dollars to an impersonal government to be revolved through a variety of assistance programs for the support of unknown masses of older adults. The resentment will intensify as the level of support increases.[33]

The Aged in Future Politics

Though much has been written about senior power, there is no evidence at this time that older people are likely to exercise this power and vote as a bloc. Binstock points out that even if the proportion of older voters during the next few decades were to double, it is unlikely that it would result in a cohesive aging vote that could determine the outcome of elections.[34] The generational cohorts who will be 65 years of age between now and 2020 have already demonstrated their political diversity.

> And because each age cohort includes people who differ profoundly in many important conditions of life, it is not likely that any age group will be very homogenous in its attitudes. The evidence which national surveys provide us does in fact demonstrate that attitudinal differences between age groups are far less impressive than those within age groups. . . . Age groups will continue to remain as heterogeneous in economic, social, and geographical characteristics as they are now, and this heterogeneity will frustrate attempts to make common cause among people who resemble each other only in their age.[35]

While Neal Cutler and John Schmidhauser agree that the elderly are not likely to vote as a cohesive bloc, they do suggest that age is going to play an increasingly important role in politics in the future.[36] They cite several factors to support this conclusion, including changes in the demographic and educational composition of the population. The size and proportion of the older population is steadily increasing and will continue to do so for some time. By the year 2020, it is estimated that there will be about 45 million persons aged 65 and over, representing over 15 percent of the population. As the size of the older population increases, more retirees will be economically dependent on a relatively decreasing number of workers. Currently, there are 30 social security beneficiaries for every 100 workers; early in the next century there will be 52 recipients for every 100 workers. In addition, the fact that the average age of retirement is becoming lower will further increase the economic burden on the working population. Because social security and other pension systems ultimately pose a political question, age will be an important issue in politics in the future.

A second factor to consider is whether the aged themselves will substantially be involved in politics in the future. Because of changes in educational opportunities, the electorate has become better educated. In 2020, those persons aged 65 and over will be represented by a cohort that already has high levels of educational attainment. Since education is a major predictor of political participation, it may be assumed that tomorrow's elderly will be even more involved in political affairs than older people today.

Summary

1. To gain a clearer understanding of the political attitudes and behavior of older people, the generational cohort, the aging, and the period effects must be taken

into account. Through the technique of cohort analysis, which examines cross-sectional and longitudinal data at the same time, these effects are more readily observed.

2. Instead of people becoming more conservative with age, Glenn reports that they have actually become more liberal, in conformity with the general trends of society. Though older persons tend to be more conservative than younger persons, in comparison to their younger selves they have become more liberal.

3. The relationship between age and political issues is not clear-cut. The way people respond to political issues tends to be governed more by their early socialization and present circumstances than by age. Although there is no increase in Republicanism as a result of aging, aging does tend to be associated with party identification because party identification increases with age. Party ties are strongest among older people and they are the least susceptible to shifting their allegiance to another party.

4. Older people have a higher voting turnout than do younger persons. Voting is lowest among persons under 25 and increases up to the middle sixties before gradually declining. But when education and sex are held constant, the drop in voting among males 65 and over almost disappears. Political interest is also higher among the older rather than the younger segments of the population. Glenn and Grimes found that the highest percentage of people reporting a great deal of interest in politics was among people aged 60 and over.

5. Positions of leadership are occupied by a disproportionate number of older people. The majority of Supreme Court Justices have served between the ages of 65 to 69, and Presidents of the United States are most often between 55 and 59 years of age when they take office.

6. The elderly have become increasingly mobilized politically through their membership in senior citizen organizations. Two of the largest organizations of older people are the NRTA-AARP and the NCSC. The NRTA-AARP is nonpartisan and is composed largely of middle-class persons. The NCSC, which consists mainly of working-class members, is closely identified with the Democratic party. Two major points of divergence between the two groups concern national health insurance and the earnings ceiling of the social security system.

7. The government's involvement with the problems of the elderly began with the passage of the Social Security Act in 1935. Since that time, two of the most significant pieces of legislation for the elderly have been the Medicare Bill and the Older Americans Act. The federal government performs many services for older people. These include cash transfer programs, noncash benefits and services, the protection of the rights of older people, the support of research on aging, and the delivery and coordination of services to the elderly.

8. Most authorities agree that there is little evidence at this time that older people will vote as a cohesive bloc. However, it is likely that age will play an important part in future politics for two reasons: social security and other pension systems are ultimately a political question, and a more highly educated older population will become even more involved in politics in the future.

Notes

1. Harold D. Laswell, *Politics: Who Gets What, When, How?* McGraw-Hill, New York, 1936.

2. Robert B. Hudson and Robert H. Binstock, "Political Systems and Aging" in *Handbook of Aging and the Social Sciences*, eds. Robert H. Binstock and Ethel Shanas, Van Nostrand Reinhold, New York, 1976, pp. 369–370.

3. Ibid., p. 370.

4. Norval D. Glenn, "Aging and Conservatism," *The Annals of the American Academy of Political and Social Science*, 415 (September 1974), 185.

5. Angus Campbell, "Politics Through the Life Cycle," *The Gerontologist*, 2, no. 2 (1971), Pt. I, 112–117.

6. Louis Harris and Associates, *The Myth and Reality of Aging in America*, The National Council on the Aging, Washington, D.C., 1975, pp. 210–226.

7. John Crittenden, "Aging and Party Affiliation," *Public Opinion Quarterly*, 26, (1962), 648–657. Also see Angus Campbell, et al., *The American Voter*, Wiley, New York, 1960, pp. 165–167.

8. Neal E. Cutler, "Generation, Maturation, and Party Affiliation: A Cohort Analysis," *Public Opinion Quarterly*, 33 (1969–70), 583–588.

9. Norval Glenn and Ted Hefner, "Further Evidence on Aging and Party Identification," *Public Opinion Quarterly*, 36 (1972), 31–47.

10. Ibid., p. 47.

11. Norman Nie, Sidney Verba, and John Petrocik, *The Changing American Voter*, Harvard University Press, Cambridge, Mass., 1976, p. 60.

12. Campbell, "Politics Through the Life Cycle," p. 113.

13. Hudson and Binstock, "Political Systems and Aging," pp. 375–376.

14. Rochelle Jones, *The Other Generation: The New Power of Older People*, © 1977, pp. 237–238. Reprinted by permission of Prentice-Hall, Inc., Englewood Cliffs, New Jersey.

15. Norval Glenn and Michael Grimes, "Aging, Voting, and Political Interest," *American Sociological Review*, 33 (August 1968), 572.

16. Harvey C. Lehman, *Age and Achievement*, Princeton University Press, Princeton, N.J., 1953, pp. 170–171.

17. Albert Johns, Andrew Tuttle, and Robert Bigler, *American Politics in Transition*, Kendall/Hunt Publishing Company, Dubuque, Iowa, 1977, p. 92.

18. Ibid., p. 164.

19. David H. Fischer, *Growing Old in America*, Oxford University Press, 1978, New York, pp. 136–137.

20. Joseph A. Schlesinger, *Ambition and Politics: Political Careers in the United States*, Rand McNally, Chicago, 1966, pp. 175–192.

21. Robert H. Binstock, "Aging and the Future of American Politics," *The Annals of the American Academy of Political and Social Science*, 415, September 1974, p. 206.

22. Ibid.

23. Henry J. Pratt, *The Gray Lobby*, The University of Chicago Press, Chicago, 1976, p. 87.

24. *AARP News Bulletin*, December 1977, p. 6.

25. Pratt, *The Gray Lobby*, p. 101.

26. Ibid., p. 102.

27. Lorin A. Baumhover and Joan D. Jones, *Handbook of American Aging Programs*, Greenwood Press, Westport, Conn., 1977, p. 172.

28. Samuel I. Rosenman, *The Public Papers and Addresses of Franklin D. Roosevelt*, Random House, New York, 1938, p. 324.

29. U.S. Department of Health, Education and Welfare, *Older Americans Act of 1965, as Amended, and Related Acts*, U.S. Government Printing Office, Washington, D.C., December 1974, pp. 2–3.

30. Pratt, *The Gray Lobby*, p. 152.

31. Byron D. Gold, "The Role of the Federal Government in the Provision of Social Services to Older Persons," *The Annals of the American Academy of Political and Social Science*, 415 (September 1974), 56.

32. Hudson and Binstock, "Political Systems and Aging," p. 397.

33. Rochelle Jones, *The Other Generation: The New Power of Older People*, © 1977, p. 229. Reprinted by permission of Prentice-Hall, Inc., Englewood Cliffs, New Jersey.

34. Binstock, "Aging and the Future of American Politics," p. 203.

35. Campbell, "Politics Through the Life Cycle," p. 117.

36. Neal E. Cutler and John R. Schmidhauser, "Age and Political Behavior," in *Aging: Scientific Perspectives and Social Issues*, eds. Diana S. Woodruff and James E. Birren, D. Van Nostrand, New York, 1975, pp. 397–403.

For Further Study

Baumhover, Lorin A., and Joan D. Jones. *Handbook of American Aging Programs.* Greenwood Press, Westport, Conn., 1977. Examines a number of programs that are having a significant impact on the lives of older people.

Binstock, Robert H. "Aging and American Politics." In *The Later Years: Social Applications of Gerontology*, edited by Richard A. Kalish. Brooks/Cole, Monterey, Calif., 1977. This article deals with interest group politics and the activities of aged-based organizations.

Campbell, Angus, Phillip Converse, Warren Miller, and Donald Stokes. *The American Voter.* Wiley, New York, 1960. Provides an extensive examination of voting and the political system. It focuses on party identification, the impact of government policies on political preferences, and the effect of electoral behavior on politics.

Cutler, Neal E., and John R. Schmidhauser. "Age and Political Behavior." In *Aging: Scientific Perspectives and Social Issues*, edited by Diana S. Woodruff and

James E. Birren. D. Van Nostrand, New York, 1975. Emphasizes the importance of the increasingly large number of older people on the political scene and their potential as a source of intervention to improve the conditions of the elderly.

Donahue, Wilma, and Clark Tibbitts. *Politics of Age*. Division of Gerontology, University of Michigan, Ann Arbor, 1962. A pioneering study of age and politics.

Foner, Ann. "The Polity." In *Aging and Society*, vol. 3: *A Sociology of Age Stratification*, edited by Matilda White Riley, Marilyn Johnson, and Ann Foner. Russell Sage Foundation, New York, 1972. This essay deals with how the political system can be organized within a theory of age stratification.

Pratt, Henry J. *The Gray Lobby*. The University of Chicago Press, Chicago, 1976. An excellent book which for the first time deals with the origin of collective concern for the aging.

14

Religion and Aging

When King Tutankhamun's tomb was discovered in the 1920s, the world was awed by the magnificent 3,300-year-old treasures that it contained. Among the gilt and gold objects were amulets to protect the king in his travels through the underworld, as well as tools to do any labor that the gods might assign to him. The Neanderthal burial sites dating back over 100,000 years reveal that the departed were also supplied with tools for the afterlife. Though made of stone and certainly not as elaborate as those of King Tut, they attest to the presence of religion even then.[1]

Religion is such a pervasive and universal phenomenon that every society from earliest known times has had some system of religious beliefs and practices. The variations are endless. Some people believe in many gods. For instance, the Ifugoas of the Philippines have some 1,500 distinct gods. A few religious groups believe in one god, while still others do not believe in any gods. Instead of gods, some religions focus on souls or spirits. In different times and places, a large variety of things have been deified, ranging from oceans, mountains, and trees to ducks, rabbits, cows, lizards, frogs, and worms. In Africa, the Dahomey believe that all people have at least three souls and that adult males have four. Some groups think that after death the soul journeys to a spirit world in the West or to an underworld beneath the sea.

Old Age and Religion

Old age has characteristically been associated with religion in many primitive societies. The elderly are peculiarly qualified to perform a dominant role in the religious life of preliterate people for several reasons. First, due to the fact that they have lived so long, older persons have had the opportunity to accumulate a vast knowledge of religious affairs and practices. Secondly, it has been generally accepted that since they would soon be spirits themselves, they were the logical intermediaries between this world and the next, and between the living and their ancestors.[2] Finally, "survival to a great age was sufficiently uncommon to seem unnatural or even supernatural. One way of making sense of

Pope John XXIII became head of the Roman Catholic Church in 1958 at the age of 77. (UPI)

such a world was to believe that age was itself endowed with super-natural properties."[3]

Thus, it is not surprising that the highest religious offices of the Aztecs, Incas, and Todas were held by old men. In some societies old women also performed religious duties. The aged patriarchs were the family priests among the Samoans and the Ainu of Japan. Leo Simmons observes that the attributes of old age were assigned to the various gods in primitive societies: "they were almost always described as worldly wise and very powerful — and, although aged, never stupid or senile. . . . It would almost appear that the aged have created gods in their own image."[4]

The tendency to visualize deities or religious figures as old persons occurs throughout history. In seventeenth-century America, Puritan writers often described God as an old man with a white beard, an image that has persisted. But the Puritan concept of an angel was quite different from the one most people hold today. They pictured an angel as a man in his seventies. In early America, according to David Fischer, "When a white-haired septuagenarian suddenly appeared in the New England town of Hadley, some of the inhabitants mistook him for a heavenly messenger."[5]

The close tie between old age and religion is also reflected in word usage. For example, *priest* is derived from the Greek work *presbyteros* meaning elder. The word *venerable* is used as a title for an Anglican archdeacon. In the Roman Catholic Church, veneration is used for those who have obtained the first of the three degrees of sanctity. In addition, the popes of the Catholic Church have usually been older men; from 1800 to the present, the average age of a pope at the time of his election has been 65.

Harvey Lehman plotted the ages at which 51 men served as popes of the Roman Catholic Church, the ages at which 101 persons served as presidents of religious organizations, and the ages at which 54 persons founded religious sects and societies (Figure 14.1).[6] His data reveal that more than 97 percent of the popes were past age 50 and over 65 percent were 65 years of age and over. Ninety-three percent of the presidents of non-Catholic religious organizations served when they were past 50, and 56 percent when they were past 65. In addition, he found that out of 148 Protestant bishops, most served as bishops between the ages of 70 to 74. His study further suggests that though new religious movements are most likely to be started by individuals in their 30s, their leadership is likely to come from older persons after they become well established. Writing in 1923, G. Stanley Hall observed:

> Thus it came that, while men in their prime conceived the great religions, the old made them prevail. Thus, too, instituted and dogmatic religion owes its existence chiefly to men past the meridian of life. The old did not invent belief

Figure 14.1 Ages of religious leaders versus ages of founders of religions, religious sects, and societies

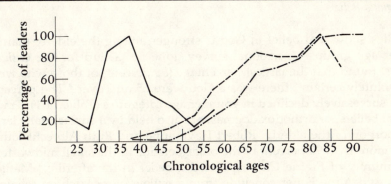

——— 54 founders of religions, religious sects, and societies

—·— 51 popes of the Roman Catholic Church who served for a total of 495 years

——— 101 presidents of other religious organizations who served for a total of 770 years

SOURCE: Harvey C. Lehman, *Age and Achievement*, Princeton University Press, Princeton, N.J., 1953, p. 173.

in supernatural powers or persons but needed and used it to sustain their position when physical inferiority would have otherwise compelled them to step aside and so they made themselves mediators between gods and men. They directed and presided over rites and ceremonies and took possession of the keys of the next world, enforced orthodoxies for the sake of the order, and established and equipped the young to aid them in their work. They were behind the scenes and held the secrets, realizing the utility to society and also to themselves."[7]

Some Dimensions of Religiosity

A popularly held view in our society is that people become increasingly more religious as they age and that there is an inevitable turning toward religion in later life. Presumably, the religious fervor of the elderly is related to the problem of their approaching demise, as well as to their concern with the hereafter. In addition, since the elderly have so much time for contemplation, it is only natural that they think more about religion.

The above common-sense view about age and religion has little or no basis in fact. Yet, this folklore is not only widely accepted by the general public, but by some social scientists as well, contrary to research findings about religious attitudes and activities of the aged.

Religious Beliefs

Studies show that belief in God is stronger among the elderly than in other age groups. A national survey done by Gallup for the *Catholic Digest* found that the largest percentage (86 percent) of those who were "absolutely certain" there was a God were 65 and over.[8] The percentages successively declined in younger age categories (Table 14.1). Traditional beliefs, or orthodox dogmas, are also held by a substantially large proportion of the elderly. Robert Havighurst and Ruth Albrecht found that more than 90 percent of the older persons in the small midwestern community of Prairie City expressed a belief in the afterlife.[9] Matilda Riley and Anne Foner conclude from a review of research on religion: "belief in God and immortality is firmly ingrained in most older people, as well as in the public at large."[10]

Importance of Religion

Most of the available evidence indicates that religion appears to be more important to older people than to younger people. In a series of

Table 14.1   Belief in God

			Age			
Belief	18–24	25–34	35–44	45–54	55–64	65+
Absolutely certain	71%	80%	81%	83%	85%	86%
Fairly sure	17	14	12	11	8	9
Quite sure	4	3	3	2	4	2
Not at all sure	3	a	1	2	1	2
Do not believe	4	2	1	2	2	1
Do not know	1	1	2	a	a	a

aLess than 1 percent.
SOURCE: Adapted from George Gallup Opinion Surveys, *Catholic Digest*, 30 (June 1966), 19. Copyright 1966 by The College of St. Thomas, and reprinted with permission of the *Catholic Digest*.

interviews of centenarians by the Social Security Administration, many attributed their long lives to religious reasons.[11] For example, "the Lord is keeping me here to carry on His work," "God has been good to me," and "I'm still here because the Lord wants me to live." According to a 1975 Harris Poll, 71 percent of those aged 65 and over felt that religion was "very important in their lives," compared to 49 percent of those under 65.[12] Only 7 percent of the elderly felt that religion was "hardly important at all" (Table 14.2). An earlier study done by Gallup obtained similar results.[13] In both studies the percentage of those who regarded religion as being very important was greatest in the older age group.

Because older people attach more importance to religion than younger adults do, and belief in God is stronger among the elderly than in other age groups, many researchers have concluded that religious feelings increase with advancing age. Studies of this relationship have typically been based on cross-sectional data, which compare older and younger people at the same point in time. Cross-sectional research makes the assumption that the attitudes and activities of the younger generation accurately represent those of older persons when they were young. But, like political attitudes and behavior discussed in Chapter 13, in order to understand the differences in religious beliefs between generations, we must take into account the age cohort to which older people belong, as well as the effects of the aging process. In addition, the effects of historical periods must also be considered because of the changing place of religion in our society. As David Moberg observes:

Whether the differences in religious beliefs between the generations are a result of the aging process or of divergent experiences during the formative

Table 14.2   Importance of religion

	Age	
Belief	*18–64*	*65+*
Very important	49%	71%
Somewhat important	33	21
Hardly important at all	17	7
Not sure	1	1

SOURCE: Reprinted from *The Myth and Reality of Aging in America*, a study prepared by Louis Harris and Associates, Inc. for The National Council on the Aging, Inc., Washington, D.C. © 1975, p. 181.

years of childhood and youth, which are linked with different social and historical circumstances, is unknown. Longitudinal research might reveal considerably different conclusions from the cross-sectional studies which provide the foundation for current generalizations about age variations in the ideological dimension of religion.[14]

One such longitudinal study is reported by Dan Blazer and Erdman Palmore from an analysis of religious activities and attitudes of 272 community residents over an 18-year period.[15] Subjects were interviewed at two- to three-year intervals beginning in 1957. Measures of religious activities included church attendance, listening to church services on radio and television, and reading the Bible. Religious attitudes were determined by agreement or disagreement with such statements as "religion is a great comfort" and "religion is the most important thing to me." Their findings reveal that positive religious attitudes remain fairly stable over time with no significant increase or decrease. If individuals were religious or nonreligious when young, chances are they will continue to have the same basic religious orientation when old. This contradicts the common view that people become increasingly religious as they age. While Blazer and Palmore found no change in religious attitudes, their findings do show a gradual decline in religious activities in the later years (Figure 14.2).

Church Attendance

A major form of religious activity is church attendance. A substantial amount of research has been done on the relationship between aging and church attendance. Howard Bahr has classified the findings of these

Figure 14.2 Religious attitudes and activities over time

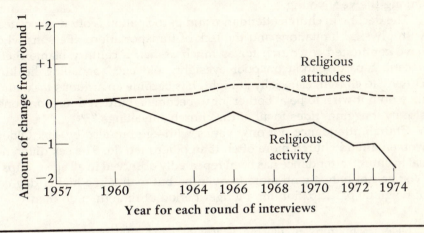

Year for each round of interviews

SOURCE: Dan Blazer and Erdman Palmore, "Religion and Aging in a Longitudinal Panel," *The Gerontologist*, 16, No. 1 (1976), Pt. 1, 84.

studies into four major models: the "traditional" model, the "stability" model, the "family cycle" model, and the "disengagement" model.[16] The traditional model reveals a steady drop in church attendance from the ages of 18 to 35, the lowest point being between 30 to 35, after which church activity increases until old age. The stability model asserts that there is no relationship between aging and church attendance and that the pattern of church attendance remains stable throughout one's lifetime. The family cycle model relates church attendance to stages of the family cycle. The peak in church attendance for this model is when children reach Sunday school age. As children grow up and leave home, the frequency of church attendance begins to drop. Lastly, the disengagement model, like the disengagement theory of aging, assumes that as one ages there is a mutual withdrawal that takes place between the individual and society, with a steady decline after middle age in church attendance.

The majority of studies contradict the stability model and indicate that church attendance varies with age. Of the other three models, most of the available evidence supports the disengagement model. Riley and Foner in their inventory of research on religion concluded that church attendance tends to decrease rather than increase in old age.[17] Moberg also observes that most research findings indicate that church attendance tends to decline in the later years.[18] At what age the decline in church attendance occurs is not clear. Some studies report that the drop begins in the late sixties or early seventies, while others find that it occurs much later. The Harris Poll reports that church attendance tends to decline among those 80 and over.[19] Their 1975 survey reveals that church attendance is highest between the ages of 55 and 79 and lowest among the very young.

The decline in church attendance and participation is often associated with physical limitations and the lack of transportation. "Persons who have commuted to church for as much as half a century blame their declining participation on poor eyesight, 'old age,' or failing health. Driving to church, especially at night, has become an arduous task, and they do not wish to be a 'bother' or to become a burden upon someone else by 'begging' rides to all of the church's meetings."[20]

Church attendance not only varies with age but also by sex. Older women attend church more often than older men do. The sex differential in church attendance has been repeatedly observed in all age groups. Women not only attend more frequently, but maintain a higher degree of religious participation for a longer period of time than do men.

> Older men drop out of church activity more rapidly than women do, probably because their activities are more involved with administrative and teaching positions, in which there is considerable turnover, with new officers being elected annually. Women, on the other hand, have the women's organizations to keep them occupied, and, even though they may drop out of leadership roles, they have many meetings to attend during the week.
>
> Furthermore, older women often find themselves in demand for service at church dinners, as well as for sewing, quilting, and other church projects. Older women are generally of more use in a church than older men, and, for this reason, they get more out of church life.[21]

Religious preference is also associated with church attendance. Among the elderly, as well as other age categories, Catholics attend church more frequently than do Protestants, while Jews attend least of all. Bernard Lazerwitz found that among persons age 65 and over, 66 percent of the Catholics attended church regularly, compared to 40 percent of the Protestants, and 25 percent of the Jews.[22]

Adjustment and Religion

Most studies concur that church attendance and participation, both past and present, are related to a satisfactory adjustment in later life. Other indicators of religiosity found to be positively associated with being well adjusted are Bible reading, listening to church sermons on the radio and television, and a belief in immortality. The relationship between religious involvement and personal adjustment is unclear. As Moberg puts it: "either those who are well-adjusted engage in many religious activities or else engaging in many religious activities contributes to a good adjustment in old age."[23]

One investigation found that happiness is associated with frequency of church attendance. The "very happy" attended church most often, while the "less happy" attended the least of all.[24] Another study reported that life satisfaction is positively correlated with church-related activities.[25] Blazer and Palmore suggest that religion becomes increasingly important for the personal adjustment of many elderly.[26] They found that happiness, a sense of usefulness, and personal adjustment are significantly related to religious activity and attitude.[27] In a study of 5,000 persons aged 60 and over in four midwestern states, Moberg and Taves investigated the relationship between church participation and adjustment in old age.[28] They found that church members had higher personal adjustment scores than nonmembers, and that church leaders (officers and committee persons) had higher scores than other church members. The researchers concluded that the evidence overwhelmingly supports the hypothesis that church participation is related to a good personal adjustment in the later years.

On the other hand, Margaret Clark and Barbara Anderson in a study of two groups of older persons — mentally healthy community residents and mentally ill hospital patients — found frequent church attendance to be more characteristic of the mentally ill subjects.[29] This can be partly attributed to the fact that many of the mentally ill aged are unhappy and fearful, and as a result, they turn to religion for consolation and emotional support. A hospital subject reports: "I am a great religious person. It helps me as much as medicine does. Religion is food for our well-being, makes us more hopeful. I need consolation all the time."[30]

Clark and Anderson observed that the community subjects were less concerned than the hospital subjects with the emotional support that religious beliefs provide and saw more value in the social aspects of church attendance. For example, Mrs. Burbank noted that the social aspect of religion meant the most to her, adding that religion is "a good discipline and a source for an older person for acquaintances and friendships."[31] Another difference between the two groups was on the subject of immortality. The mentally ill aged had less tolerance of uncertainty about death and more fear of death, than did the mentally healthy subjects. A typical attitude of the community subjects was accepting death as an inevitable fact of life.

Moberg reports that among geriatric patients in a state hospital, the preferred topic for discussion at therapy sessions was religion.

> Religious beliefs and faith in God helped disorganized members to overcome their grief when unhappy, lonesome, and despondent. They were eager to discuss a better life after death; other members sensed the support religion

gave them because they themselves also received greater "ego strength" from religion.[32]

Functions and Dysfunctions of Religion

Religion functions primarily at two levels: the psychological (or individual) level and the social (or group) level. For the individual who in faith accepts the basic teachings of a religion, religion may perform certain psychological functions during the later years. Milton Barron cites four such functions: (1) to help face impending death; (2) to help find and maintain a sense of meaningfulness and significance in life; (3) to help accept the inevitable losses of old age; and (4) to help discover and utilize the compensatory values that are potential in old age.[33]

At the social level, the church brings together people of all ages and helps reduce isolation of the elderly by affording them the opportunity for social interaction. Esther Twente observes that for many elderly people, religious pursuits, especially in small communities, help activate and nurture social relationships.[34] "Opportunities to meet friends and exchange news about one another and about mutual acquaintances are important. Sympathy, support, pleasantries, encouragement, and jokes find expression and the older person experiences warmth and reassurance as he feels himself one of the group."[35]

Even when a person can no longer participate in church activities, the importance of continued interaction with church representatives is illustrated by the following example:

> An eighty-one-year-old woman, Mrs. Lang was suffering from a crippling form of arthritis which made her homebound. She had always been a warm, vital, outgoing person who, until three years earlier, was active in her church and contributed her handiwork to the Ladies' Circle. Now, she says, she understands what it means to "cast one's bread upon the waters." She does not know what she would have done were it not for the visits from her minister, who is a source of spiritual comfort, and from the members of the Ladies' Circle. Through these visits she is kept informed as to what is happening in her church, and they make her feel that she still "belongs," that it does not matter that she can no longer help her church — now it is their turn to help her.[36]

Visits from a clergyman or the lack of them may also create problems. Many older people who are homebound, hospitalized, or in nursing homes expect to be visited regularly by their clergyman or church representatives. When these expectations are not met, they may feel neglected or offended. Surveying 606 elderly persons in Long Beach, Charles McCann asked for additional ways in which the church could serve them.[37] They placed home visits at the top of the list. Moberg states that clergy visits to older people when they are ill may have a negative, instead of a positive, effect.[38] In some cases when a clergyman calls, ill persons may become afraid that they are about to die.

Many elderly people whose finances are limited feel guilty about attending church because they can only afford a meager contribution or in some instances cannot make one. Sometimes older persons may feel that they are being shunned by the church because of this lack of financial support. A case in point is Mrs. Brown: "I was always active in my church and, like my father before me, I always contributed when I was able. Now that I am poor, and cannot make donations, my church seems to have no use for me."[39]

Another problem that many older persons face is the feeling that they no longer have a place in the life of their church. After years of faithful service, many complain that their leadership roles and responsibilities are being taken over by younger persons. In addition, some argue that their advice is no longer sought and their opinions are ignored.

Church Associations and Programs

Church-related or religious associations rank second only to lodges and fraternal organizations in terms of membership among older people. Those active in church-related groups also tend to participate in other voluntary organizations. As Moberg explains: "It is not unreasonable to think that associating with people in church-related activities and organizations contributes to knowledge of other voluntary organizations; friendships in the church with persons who are members of other groups may lead to social participation in them."[41]

Besides meeting the spiritual needs of the elderly, churches and religious organizations offer older members a wide range of services and programs. These fall into three main categories: housing and institutional care, service programs, and volunteer projects. Religious organizations have helped to establish and maintain retirement homes and communities and convalescent and long-term-care facilities for the elderly. A number of religious homes for the aged have an outstanding reputation for excellence. One such example is the Jewish Home for the Aged in New York, one of the largest nonprofit institutions for the care of older people. In 1970 there were 1,500 nonprofit homes for the aged in the United States under the auspices of various religious organizations (Table 14.3).

Some congregations offer older persons continuing education programs, social clubs, and counseling and referral services. Churches not only provide services for older people, but also give them the opportunity to serve others through such programs as telephone reassurance, in which older people who live alone are called each day. Many churches

Table 14.3 Types of nonprofit homes for the aging

Type of home	Number of homes	Average number of beds	Total number of patients
Religious	1,500	84	117,180
Government (municipal)	670	105	63,000
Others (benevolent, fraternal, trust)	1,225	60	66,150
Summary	3,395		246,330

SOURCE: From Butler, Robert N., and Lewis, Myrna I: *Aging and mental health,* ed. 2, St. Louis, 1977, The C. V. Mosby Co.; based on data from Frank Zelenka, American Association of Homes for the Aging; from Selected institutional characteristics of long-term care facilities, Department of Health Care Administration, George Washington University Long-term Care Monograph No. 4, Jan., 1970.

also provide transportation, mobile meals, and tape-recorded church services for their elderly members.

Summary

1. The close tie between religion and old age is characteristic of not only primitive but modern societies. Though religious movements are often started by younger persons, religious leadership is most likely to be concentrated among the elderly.

2. Older persons tend to have a stronger belief in God and to consider religion more important in their lives than younger persons do. The dissimilarity in the religious orientation between younger and older people appears to be the result of generational differences, not the aging process. No evidence indicates that there is a turning toward religion in old age. Religious attitudes appear to be fairly stable and show no dramatic change in later life.

3. While religious attitudes appear to remain constant, religious activities tend to decline in later life, especially church attendance. Bahr has classified the relationship between church and the aging into four groups: the traditional model, the stability model, the family cycle model, and the disengagement model. Most studies tend to support the disengagement model. Church attendance varies with sex and religious preference. More older women attend church than older men do, and continue to do so until later ages. Among those persons 65 and over, as with other age categories, Roman Catholics attend church more regularly than do Protestants, with Jews having the lowest attendance.

4. Many researchers state that church attendance and participation are related to a good adjustment in old age. On the other hand, frequent church attendance is also characteristic of the mentally ill. Mentally ill persons look to religion for

consolation and emotional support, while mentally healthy persons are more often concerned with the social aspects.

5. Religion performs many psychological and social functions for the older person. Its psychological functions include helping one to face death and to discover and maintain a feeling of the meaningfulness in life. At the social level, religion helps reduce social isolation and fosters group interaction. Religion can also be dysfunctional in that older people who are ill or homebound often feel neglected and upset when not visited regularly by a clergyman. On the other hand, in some instances ill persons may jump to the conclusion that they are about to die when they receive a visit from their minister, rabbi, or priest. Other problems faced by some older persons include feeling they are being pushed out of their roles in church affairs by younger persons and that their opinions and ideas are no longer needed.

6. Churches offer older people a variety of services and programs. These include institutional care, continuing education, social clubs, and counseling and referral services.

Notes

1. William Howells, *Mankind So Far*, Doubleday, Garden City, N.Y., 1948, p. 164.

2. Jack Goody, "Aging in Nonindustrial Societies," in *Handbook of Aging and the Social Sciences*, eds., Robert H. Binstock and Ethel Shanas, Van Nostrand Reinhold, New York, 1976, pp. 127–128.

3. David H. Fischer, *Growing Old in America*, Oxford University Press, New York, 1978, p. 34.

4. Leo W. Simmons, *The Role of the Aged in Primitive Society*, Yale University Press, New Haven, 1945, p. 74.

5. Fischer, *Growing Old in America*, pp. 34–35.

6. Harvey C. Lehman, *Age and Achievement*, Princeton University Press, Princeton, N.J., 1953, pp. 173–174.

7. G. Stanley Hall quoted in ibid., p. 174.

8. George Gallup Opinion Surveys, *Catholic Digest*, 30 (June 1966), 19.

9. Robert J. Havighurst and Ruth Albrecht, *Older People*, Longmans, Green, New York, 1953, p. 202.

10. Matilda Riley and Anne Foner, *Aging and Society*, vol. 1: *An Inventory of Research Findings*, Russell Sage Foundation, New York, 1958, p. 493.

11. *America's Centenarians*, U.S. Department of Health, Education, and Welfare, Social Security Administration, Washington, D.C., 1972, vols. 1 and 5, unpaged.

12. Louis Harris and Associates, *The Myth and Reality of Aging in America*, The National Council on the Aging, Washington, D.C., 1975, pp. 180–181.

13. George Gallup Public Opinion Surveys, *Catholic Digest*, 30 (October 1966), 122–127.

14. David O. Moberg, "Religiosity in Old Age," *The Gerontologist*, 5, no. 2 (1965), 80.

15. Dan Blazer and Erdman Palmore, "Religion and Aging in a Longitudinal Panel," *The Gerontologist*, 16, no. 1 (February 1976), Pt. 1, 82–85.

16. Howard M. Bahr, "Aging and Religious Disaffiliation," *Social Forces*, 49 (September 1970), 59–71.

17. Riley and Foner, *Aging and Society*, 1: 489.

18. Moberg, "Religiosity in Old Age," p. 82.

19. Harris and Associates, *The Myth and Reality of Aging in America*, p. 180.

20. David O. Moberg, "The Integration of Older Members in the Church Congregation," in *Older People and Their Social World*, eds. Arnold M. Rose and Warren A. Peterson, F. A. Davis, Philadelphia, 1965, p. 136.

21. Havighurst and Albrecht, *Older People*, p. 203.

22. Bernard Lazerwitz, "Some Factors Associated with Variations in Church Attendance," *Social Forces*, 39, (May 1961), 301–309.

23. Moberg, "Religiosity in Old Age," p. 85.

24. C. T. O'Reilly and M. M. Pembroke quoted in ibid., p. 84.

25. John N. Edwards and David L. Klemmack, "Correlates of Life Satisfaction: A Re-examination," *The Journal of Gerontology*, 28, no. 4 (October 1973), 497–502.

26. Blazer and Palmore, "Religion and Aging in a Longitudinal Panel," p. 85.

27. Ibid.

28. David O. Moberg and Marvin J. Taves, "Church Participation and Adjustment in Old Age," in *Older People and Their Social World*, eds. Arnold M. Rose and Warren A. Peterson, F. A. Davis, Philadelphia, 1965, pp. 113–124.

29. Margaret Clark and Barbara Anderson, *Culture and Aging*, Charles C Thomas, Springfield, Ill., 1967.

30. Ibid., pp. 335–336.

31. Ibid., p. 336.

32. Moberg, "Religiosity in Old Age," p. 84.

33. Milton L. Barron, *The Aging American: An Introduction to Social Gerontology and Geriatrics*, Thomas Y. Crowell, New York, 1961, p. 166.

34. Esther E. Twente, *Never Too Old*, Jossey-Bass, San Francisco, 1970.

35. Ibid., p. 65.

36. Minna Field, *Aging with Honor and Dignity*, Charles C Thomas, Springfield, Ill., 1968, p. 141.

37. Charles W. McCann quoted in Phillip E. Hammond, "Aging and the Minister," in *Aging and Society*, vol 2, eds. Matilda Riley, John Riley, and Marilyn Johnson, Russell Sage Foundation, New York, 1969, p. 304.

38. David O. Moberg, "Spiritual Well-Being in Late Life," in *Late Life* ed. Jaber F. Gubrium, Charles C Thomas, Springfield, Ill., 1974.

39. Twente, *Never Too Old*, p. 65.

40. Moberg, "Religiosity in Old Age," p. 83.

For Further Study

Barron, Milton L. *The Aging American: An Introduction to Social Gerontology and Geriatrics*. Thomas Y. Crowell, New York, 1961. See Chapter 11 which explores the relationship between religion and aging.

Maves, Paul B. "Aging, Religion, and the Church." In *Handbook of Social Gerontology*, edited by Clark Tibbitts. The University of Chicago Press, Chicago, 1960. A good discussion about the religious activities and interests of older people and about what churches are doing to meet the needs of the elderly.

Moberg, David O. "Religion in the Later Years." In *The Daily Needs and Interests of Older Persons*, edited by Adeline M. Hoffman. Charles C Thomas, Springfield, Ill., 1970. A brief overview of the role of religion in the lives of the elderly.

———. "Spiritual Well-Being in Late Life." In *Late Life*, edited by Jaber F. Gubrium. Charles C Thomas, Springfield, Ill., 1974. Deals with older people's spiritual worlds and the satisfaction of their spiritual needs.

O'Dea, Thomas. *The Sociology of Religion*. Prentice-Hall, Englewood Cliffs, N.J., 1966. A concise, clear introduction to the sociology of religion.

Riley, Matilda, and Anne Foner. *Aging and Society*, vol 1: *An Inventory of Research Findings*. Russell Sage Foundation, New York, 1968. Chapter 20 summarizes the available knowledge in the area of religion and aging.

15

Education and Aging

Over two hundred years ago the philosopher Immanuel Kant wrote: "Man becomes man through education; he is what education makes him." In this statement Kant emphasizes the primary function of the educational process — socialization. Through socialization people acquire the skills, values, and roles that make it possible for them to become members of society (see Chapter 6). The school is the agency in our society that has the responsibility of socializing the young in certain skills and values. It gives them much of the knowledge they will need as adults and trains them to do necessary work.

Education is a major social institution in all industrialized societies. The growth of mass education in the United States began about a hundred years ago and coincided with the shift from an agricultural to an industrial economy. Industrialization requires not only that workers be able to read and write, but also that they learn new skills and techniques in order to perform specialized roles within the division of labor. Schools were developed to provide such training.

At many university campuses today, one gets the distinct impression of being in a large industrial center, rather than at a center for learning. In fact, when we consider the number of our population involved in formal education in elementary schools, high schools, and colleges either as students, teachers, or suppliers of school goods and services, education is the largest single industry in the United States and the major employer in our society.

The number of Americans attending school has steadily increased. Currently, around 60 million Americans are enrolled in schools. The number of years spent in school has also increased, as schooling is beginning earlier in the life cycle. In 1977, about 4.6 million children (nearly 50 percent) from three to five years old were enrolled in nursery and kindergarten programs.[1] At the other end of the continuum, in 1974, 400,000 persons age 65 and over were enrolled in educational institutions or taking courses.[2]

Barriers to Learning

Kingsley Davis observes that every society sets up certain barriers to learning through defective instructional techniques and lack of proper motives and incentives.[3] "All told, societies vary enormously in their waste of human learning ability, but they all waste it. Since modern scientists have such difficulty in perfecting teaching techniques, in measuring capacities and talents, and in motivating people to learn, there is little wonder that societies have also bungled the job."[4]

Older people in our society face a formidable barrier to learning because of the many myths that prevail regarding their inability to learn. Despite evidence that "you are never too old to learn," some educators hold steadfastly to the belief that the elderly cannot benefit from educational activities. Over two decades ago, Clark Tibbitts and Merrill Rogers, in noting the lack of interest in adult education for older people, remarked: "Skepticism on the part of adult educators, as well as many aging people themselves, regarding the learning capacity of older men and women seems to be an important factor in retarding a faster growth."[5] As a result, the role of education in old age has been largely neglected in the past.

The myths about the elderly's learning ability not only have affected the attitudes of the general public and the professionals who work with older people, but have served to undermine the confidence of older people in themselves, acting as a self-fulfilling prophecy. Howard McClusky makes the following observation about the elderly's low participation rates in learning activities:

> It is also possible that older people, especially in later years, have gnawing, unacknowledged doubts about their continuing ability to learn. This loss of "educational nerve" may have become so regressive that the elderly are extremely reluctant to expose themselves to the embarrassment, and in their eyes even ridicule, that participation might possibly entail.[6]

Educational Levels

Older people were born and educated in an era when the opportunity for free mass public education was more limited. As a result, the educational level of older people, as we have previously noted, is far below that of the overall adult population. In 1978, about 2.2 million persons (10 percent) 65 and over had either no schooling or less than five years and were therefore classified as "functionally illiterate."[7] In 1975, the median years of school completed for persons 65 and over was 9.0, compared to 12.3 years for the entire adult population. In that same

An increasing number of older persons are enrolling in college after retirement, audit college classes, or take noncredit courses. Some people earn a degree like Mary Brasch, who received her bachelor's degree at age 87. (NRTA-AARP)

year, a little over a third of the elderly were high school graduates, while almost two-thirds of the adults in general had received a high school education (Table 15.1).

The educational attainment of the older population has been steadily increasing, just as it has for the entire population 25 years and older. In 1975, the percentage of high school graduates among persons 65 and over nearly doubled the figure for 1952. By the year 2000, the educational gap between younger and older populations is expected to narrow considerably. One reason is that the elderly in the future will have much more formal education than they do today. The number of median years of school completed by them will rise to over twelve years, or a little better than a high school education, by 2000 (Table 15.2). At the same time, the pattern of an increasing educational attainment for younger people may be over. The long-term trend of a continuous rise in school enrollment rates began to reverse itself in the 1970s. Richard Freeman predicts that though there will be an increase during the 1980s, the 1990s will fall below the level of the late 1960s.[8]

In addition, the low levels of educational attainment of the elderly are also related to the immigration patterns of the past. Prior to World War I, a great influx of young immigrants came to this country. These persons now make up a significant proportion of the older population. In 1970, 15 percent of those 65 and over were foreign born. In comparison with the general population, they have lower levels of

Table 15.1 Educational attainment of the population 65 years and over and 25 years and over, by sex, 1965–1980

Sex and year	Median school years completed		Percentage of high school graduates	
	65 years old and over	25 years old and over	65 years old and over	25 years old and over
Both sexes				
1965	8.5	11.8	23.5%	49.0%
1970	8.7	12.2	28.3	55.2
1975	9.0	12.3	35.2	62.6
1980	9.7	12.4	37.9	65.4
Males				
1965	8.3	11.7	21.8	48.0
1970	8.6	12.2	25.9	55.0
1975	8.9	12.4	33.4	63.1
1980	9.4	12.5	36.3	66.5
Females				
1965	8.6	12.0	24.7	49.9
1970	8.8	12.1	30.1	55.4
1975	9.4	12.3	36.5	62.1
1980	9.9	12.4	38.9	64.4

SOURCE: Adapted from U.S. Bureau of the Census, *Current Population Reports,* Special Studies Series P-23, No. 59, U.S. Government Printing Office, Washington, D.C., 1976, p. 50.

Table 15.2 Educational status of the elderly

Age	1970	2000[a]
Median years of schooling completed		
55–64	10.6	12.5
65–74	8.8	12.3
75+	8.5	12.1[b]
Percentage of cohort that are high school graduates		
55–64	40.4%	71.5%
65–74	29.2	61.7
75+	24.1	54.2[b]

[a]The projections for the year 2000 assume that no additional education is completed after 1970 and that differential mortality rates do not influence the measures of educational attainment for the cohort. Thus, the estimates may somewhat underestimate the educational attainment of these cohorts in 2000.
[b]Only population aged 75–84 is represented in these figures.
SOURCE: Robert Clark and Joseph Spengler, "Population Aging in the Twenty-first Century," *Aging,* January–February 1978, p. 11.

education and higher rates of illiteracy. Language difficulties encountered by this group are underscored in a survey conducted in 1975 by the Bureau of the Census.[9] The survey indicates that 1 million persons (5 percent) 65 and over usually speak a language other than English. The proportion of foreign-born elderly has been declining as the older immigrants die and, under the present system, there are fewer recent immigrants. This decline is expected to accelerate in the coming years.

Adult Education

Background and Scope

The history of adult education in the United States from colonial times to the present has been a repetitious one, in which specific needs arose and programs were developed to try to meet them. As each need was met or it declined in importance, the focus of adult education shifted to another concern.

In its earliest beginnings, adult education was mainly associated with the task of teaching adults to read so they could attain salvation through studying the Holy Scriptures. Later, during the Revolutionary and Civil war periods, adult education became closely identified with the need for an enlightened citizenry, a view that was the outgrowth of the ideal that people must be educated to fulfill their responsibilities as citizens of a democracy.[10]

Between the Civil War and World War I, adult education shifted its focus to more specific programs, such as vocational education and public affairs. But the main concern of this period centered around the Americanization of the large number of immigrants. In order for them to become assimilated, it was necessary that they learn the common language, attitudes, and values of American society. In 1926 the American Association for Adult Education was founded, launching adult education as a distinct field of social practice. Since 1930, adult education has rapidly expanded.[11]

At present, a wide range of activities comprise the field of adult education, including credit and noncredit courses, lectures, discussion groups, correspondence courses, education by television, and on-the-job training. In addition, these activities are conducted by a myriad of institutions and agencies — colleges and universities, public schools, libraries, labor unions, business and industry, churches, and community centers.

Up to the mid-1950s, adult educators largely confined their efforts to teaching persons from their early twenties to middle age. In 1955 with the publication of Wilma Donahue's pioneer book, *Education for Later Maturity*, the field of adult education was expanded to include the later stages of the life cycle.[12] The name given this new area of adult education is *educational gerontology*. Educational gerontology is the place where adult education and social gerontology meet. David Peterson defines educational gerontology as "the study and practice of instructional endeavors for and about aged and aging individuals."[13] He views it as including educational programs designed for older people, instructional endeavors for the general public about aging, and programs for those who are working or intend to work with the elderly in a professional capacity.

Participation in Adult Education

Most studies show that as people advance in age, their level of participation in adult education tends to drop. John Johnstone and Ramon Rivera studied the participation rates of people by age categories in lecture series, study groups, and discussion groups sponsored by various organizations and institutions.[14] The researchers found that the highest participation rate, 22 percent, occurs in the 40 to 49 age group, followed by 13 percent of those between the ages of 50 to 59. Only 6 percent participated in the 60 to 69 group, and 2 percent in the over 70 group.

Several reasons account for the lower participation of older people. Many elderly are inhibited from taking part in educational activities because of their fear of failure. Some think that education is for the young and that they would feel childish in such a setting. Another reason is that older people are difficult to reach and recruit for educational programs, as they often are outside the mainstream of the regular channels of communication and community services. Finally, some persons are unable to participate because of their lack of physical mobility or transportation. Transportation becomes even more of a problem for those wishing to attend evening classes because many elderly people find night driving difficult and public transportation generally inadequate.

The lower participation rates of older people in adult education programs are also related to their lower levels of educational attainment. It is generally assumed that education begets education. The more formal education persons have, the more likely they are to participate in educational programs. For example, among those 65 and over, 7 percent of the college graduates were enrolled in educational institutions or were taking courses, compared to 1 percent of those with some high school education or less (Table 15.3).

When persons 65 years of age and older were asked why they took courses, the 1975 Harris Poll found that the majority, 76 percent, said it was to expand their general knowledge about some field or hobby.

Table 15.3 Percentage of persons enrolled in educational institutions or taking courses, by previous level of education, 1974

Age	Some high school or less	High school graduate/ some college	College graduate
18–54	5%	18%	25%
55–64	2	8	11
65 and over	1	3	7
Total	3	16	23

SOURCE: Reprinted from *The Myth and Reality of Aging in America*, a study prepared by Louis Harris and Associates, Inc. for The National Council on the Aging, Inc., Washington, D.C. © 1975, p. 107.

Thirty-nine percent reported it was to make good use of their time, while 28 percent said it was to be with other people.[15]

Some argue that older people have not taken advantage of the educational opportunities available to them. Yet, educational programs for older people have received the lowest priority in adult education, and educators have shown only limited interest in this area and have failed, for the most part, to develop programs designed to meet the specific needs and goals of older people. Of the programs geared toward older people, many are of inferior quality and are poorly planned. Often such programs underrate the intellectual and creative abilities of older persons. Some offer only a brief recreational diversion with little or no challenge.

> While society expresses concern about improving their physical and material condition, the aged are seldom provided with the resources they need for relevance and a sense of worth. We tend to place them in "playpens" by providing recreation and similar endeavors while doing almost nothing to furnish them with the means to keep mentally alert. We strip them of most of their meaningful roles on the assumption they are incapable of carrying them out effectively, with the rationalization that they deserve the right to rest and take it easy. Recreational activities are not sufficient to maintain mental abilities, contact with society, identity and sense of significance as a person.[16]

Some Functions of Education

Fulfillment of Needs

Education fulfills many important needs in the lives of older people. It serves to maintain contact with others, expands horizons, and helps to create and develop meaningful activities. But most important of all, education helps older people maintain their physical and mental well-being.

> There is empirical evidence that mental deterioration . . . occurs primarily among low-skilled, less-educated people whose work does not require the exercise of higher mental faculties or the acquisition of new knowledge. A recent study of retirants of better-than-average education found an overall excellence of health and mental ability, with only minor differences in either respect, between that group and a group of men in their early twenties. In fact, the retirants, on the average, had higher intelligence ratings than the young men in the comparison group.[17]

The rationale for educational programming for older people is that adults, regardless of age, have needs that can best be satisfied by an increase in knowledge and skills.[18] Howard McClusky divides the educational needs of older people into these four categories: coping needs, expressive needs, contributive needs, and influence needs.[19]

Coping needs refer to the basic requirements that must be met before other needs can be realized, and are essential to daily living and survival. These educational needs include programs for adult basic education (the three Rs), health education, income maintenance, legal advice, housing selection, family adjustments, and the most beneficial use of leisure time.

The next category, expressive needs, refers to those areas in which people participate for the sake of the activities themselves and not as a means of achieving some goal. Such activities give a person pleasure and enjoyment in their own right. Education may provide such an outlet through the learning of certain skills or hobbies. Also many older adults enjoy taking credit and noncredit courses at colleges or universities.

The third category, contributive needs, are those that fulfill the desire to be useful — to find a meaningful role, to be of service to others, and to develop new competencies. These needs can be realized through participation in various types of community activities and programs. One such program is Foster Grandparents, which provides low-income elderly with the opportunity to make a useful contribution to their community through giving personalized care to children with special needs in both institutional and noninstitutional settings (see Chapter 11). Before starting this service, Foster Grandparents receive 40 hours of orientation; once in the program, they take part in regularly scheduled in-service training sessions.

The last category is called influence needs. Through leadership training and instruction by adult education agencies, older people can be assisted in gaining the attention of public officials to obtain needed services and programs for themselves. In this way, not only will they have more power in directing and controlling their own lives, but they can help bring about change in society. The Gray Panthers movement is an example of the influence that older people can have when they become committed to changing social policies and national priorities.

Lifelong Learning

Education is being viewed increasingly as a continuous process of lifelong learning, rather than as learning restricted to the early stages of life. Educational opportunities over the life span, especially in the later years, are expected to be in great demand in the future. This demand will be due mainly to the lengthening of life expectancy, the rise in the educational levels of the elderly accompanied by their subsequent interest in education, and the acceleration of change in society.

In describing the role of education throughout adulthood, Cyril Houle divides the adult life span into four periods: young independent adulthood, early middle age, early old age, and later old age.[20] Of particular interest are the last two stages: early old age, beginning at 55 and extending to 75; and later old age, from 75 and over.

Education performs several important functions in early old age. First, education can help the individual to plan a strategy to bring about a successful adjustment in the later years. Next, besides diminishing disengagement, it can also assist in re-engagement, by giving persons the ability to take part in new interests and activities. In addition, education can be one of those activities that helps to fill the time for older people.

Learning in later old age is usually related to a sense of personal need, which includes spending time in a satisfying manner and continuing to contribute to society. For many elderly persons, education affords them the opportunity to interact with persons of all age groups and to remain involved in community affairs and activities. Lastly, learning in old age, as well as throughout other stages of the life cycle, contributes to a vitality of both mind and body.

In the past, persons experienced a much slower rate of change in their lifetimes than people do today. This fact was especially true of those living in farming communities, where the environment remained much the same from one generation to the next. All the necessary skills and knowledge needed for a lifetime were learned in the early years of one's education.

But in today's rapidly changing technological society, education has no cut-off point. The challenges of a changing society demand that education be continuous not only to prevent intellectual obsolescence, but to counterbalance skill obsolescence in the job market. New skills must be learned in order to hold a job or to qualify for re-employment.

For many years it was an accepted fact that skill obsolescence was an inevitable occurrence in older workers and that not much could be done about it. In recent years a positive solution to the problem has been found through retraining programs designed to improve the older workers' skills and to make them more employable.

In the early 1960s, manpower training programs were instituted by the federal government for this purpose; to date, only a small proportion of workers have participated in them. The Senate Special Committee on Aging reported that in 1975, older workers accounted for only 8.8 percent of all participants in the manpower programs, although 31 percent of all long-term unemployed persons were in this age group.[21] The reasons for the low participation rates of older workers stem in part from their reluctance to enter training programs, as well as from the fear that they will be unable to be placed once they are trained.

For those older workers who do become participants in manpower training programs, their completion rates tend to be higher than younger enrollees'. The type of jobs for which older workers are trained differ from those of younger workers; most older workers receive training related to agricultural employment and service-type occupations. One year after completion of training, the proportion of employment for older workers is almost the same as that for the younger trainees.[22]

Life-Cycle Education

Life-cycle education differs from lifelong learning. Robert Butler refers to this type of education as that in "which different psychological, personal, familial, occupational and other tasks related to specific processes and stages of life are taught."[23] He emphasizes the need to understand and prepare for the transitions that take place throughout the life cycle, such as marriage, parenthood, and retirement.

In recent years, one of the most promising areas for life-cycle education has been preretirement education, or preparation for retirement. Currently preretirement planning programs are being offered by business and industry, universities, labor unions, and other organizations, usually some three to five years before retirement. In this way, employees anticipate many decisions involved in making the transition from worker to retiree.

For retirement education to be most beneficial, it should begin much earlier than it is usually offered. Some gerontologists argue that preretirement preparation should begin as early as high school or college. Early education for retirement gives a person the opportunity to plan for an adequate retirement income, to take preventive measures in health maintenance, and to develop hobbies and interests for the retirement years. Not only retirement preparation, but other life-cycle transitions may be taught successfully long before they are experienced.

The Role of Colleges and Universities

The number of colleges and universities offering courses, workshops, conferences, and educational television programming in the area of aging has increased rapidly in recent years. In 1976, a survey done by the Association for Gerontology in Higher Education reported 1,275 institutions involved in aging-related educational activities. Universities comprised 27 percent of this activity, four-year colleges 29 percent, and junior and community colleges 33 percent.[24] Higher education in the field of aging involves two separate but interrelated aspects: education *about* older people, and education *for* older people. From these two perspectives, let us discuss some services that colleges and universities perform relating to gerontology.

Education About Older People

Gerontology education, which refers to the study of aging, involves course work usually at a college or university. Students enroll in these courses usually for two reasons: to understand the aging process and the problems of the elderly in our society, without regard for applying this knowledge in a professional role; and to prepare for a career in the field, which may entail work in research, teaching, administration, or delivery of services to the elderly. Many universities and colleges provide programs of continuing education for professionals to upgrade their service potential. Some schools also offer correspondence courses for this purpose.[25]

Most retirement courses are very superficial. All you're offering is telling us what our incomes will be when we retire, how we should live and what hobbies we might look for. You ought to be thinking about how we might want more education for one thing. Middle-aged and older people almost never get into graduate school, you know, but the community colleges are begging for us to come in and take a little basketry.

SOURCE: Maggie Kuhn, as quoted in Ira F. Ehrlich and Phyllis D. Ehrlich, "A Four-part Framework to Meet the Responsibilities of Higher Education to Gerontology," *Educational Gerontology*, 1, no. 3 (1976), 258–259.

Besides instruction, the university has the responsibility of developing new knowledge through research activities, thus making knowledge available for use in present and future aging programs. University personnel often assist those who work with older people by serving on boards of community organizations, sponsoring seminars and workshops, and speaking to community service groups. Another major service that universities and colleges perform is the dissemination of information about aging through pamphlets, books, and articles. Educational television and radio programs under the auspices of universities have also been especially useful.[26]

Education for Older People

The educational programs offered by colleges and universities that attract older people are generally noncredit courses of two basic types. One type is composed of programs designed to help older people develop coping skills and competencies for facing the problems of old age. The other type consists of general courses for self-enrichment and intellectual growth.

Some institutions have focused their educational activities for older people in short-term programs, such as the Elderhostel. The name *Elderhostel* refers to a network of colleges and universities that offer one week mini-courses during the summer months to men and women aged 60 and over at a very low cost.[27] Presently, this ranges from $75 to $115 per week. The participants live on campus and take college-level courses taught by regular faculty members. This program started in 1975 as a summer experiment at the University of New Hampshire and four other New Hampshire colleges and has spread rapidly. By the summer of 1979, Elderhostel programs were being offered by 235 colleges and universities in 38 states, with an enrollment of between 13,000 to 14,000.

Community colleges have been most active in developing innovative noncredit programs for the elderly. Much of their success has been due to their congenial social atmosphere, flexibility in program content, and styles of teaching. In addition, community colleges have employed active recruitment and outreach efforts. Lillian Glickman and her associates point out: "Elders are looking for meaningful use of their time, while community colleges with their motivation, initiative, and resources, are looking — for both financial and philosophical reasons — to serve new groups. An alliance between the two seems natural and mutually advantageous."[28]

North Hennepin Community College in Brooklyn, Minnesota, is an example of successful program development on behalf of the elderly.[29] This college has an enrollment of over 2,000 area residents who are 55 years of age and older. It offers 35 specially designed noncredit courses,

The Elderhostel program is a unique educational experience for older persons offered by over 200 colleges and universities. (Courtesy of Elderhostel)

Minnesota's North Hennepin Community College has welcomed hundreds of elderly students, and an excellent relationship has developed between them and the young persons enrolled there. Rap sessions between the two groups and an annual spring dance that pairs off the old with the young offer opportunities for old–young interaction. (Courtesy of North Hennepin Community College)

which fall into these categories: enrichment, advocacy, retirement planning, and retraining for second careers. Older students are also encouraged to take regular courses for credit or noncredit. The elderly are fully integrated into campus life, and they take an active role in all phases of program planning and development.

Summary

1. Education is a major social institution in industrialized societies. The most common function of the institution is cultural transmission. The growth of mass education in the United States which began a century ago was made necessary by industrialization.

2. Myths regarding the older person's inability to learn have been too readily accepted by the general public and by adult educators. These myths have served to retard the growth of adult education and to undermine older persons' confidence in their ability to learn.

3. Currently, the level of educational attainment of older people is far below that

of the total population. This is due to the fact that older people were born and educated in a period when the opportunity for mass education was much more limited. The educational attainment of the older population as well as that for the entire population has been steadily rising.

4. The field of adult education encompasses a wide range of activities that take place in a variety of settings. In the 1950s, adult education was expanded to include the later stages of the life cycle. The name given this new area is educational gerontology, which is characterized as "the study and practice of instructional endeavors for and about aging individuals."

5. Lower levels of participation in adult education are associated with advancing age and with lower educational attainments. Educational programs for older people have received the lowest priority in the adult education field. Most programs fail to meet the needs of the elderly. On the whole, they underestimate the intelligence and creative ability of the elderly.

6. Many important needs of older people can be fulfilled through education. McClusky classifies the educational needs of older people into four types: coping, expressive, contributive, and influence. Education is being viewed increasingly as a continuous process that covers the entire life span. In a rapidly changing society, lifelong education is essential to prevent intellectual and skill obsolescence. On the other hand, life-cycle education is an important factor in preparing for, and adjusting to the transitions an individual must make throughout life.

7. In recent years, colleges and universities have become increasingly involved in age-related activities. Gerontology education has two separate but interrelated aspects: education about older people and education for older people. Education about older people either involves instruction about the aging process for personal understanding or provides professional training for a career in the field of aging. Education for older people focuses on instruction in coping skills for the elderly or for continuing enrichment and intellectual growth. Community colleges have been most active and successful in providing both types of programs for older people.

Notes

1. U.S. Bureau of the Census, *Statistical Abstract of the United States: 1978*, U.S. Government Printing Office, Washington, D.C., 1978, p. 142.

2. Louis Harris and Associates, *The Myth and Reality of Aging in America*, The National Council on the Aging, Washington, D.C., 1975, p. 106.

3. Kingsley Davis, *Human Society*, Macmillan, New York, 1949, pp. 203–204.

4. Ibid., p. 204.

5. Clark Tibbitts and Merrill Rogers, "Aging in the Contemporary Scene," in *Education for Later Maturity*, ed. Wilma Donahue, Whiteside and William Morrow, New York, 1955, pp. 32–33.

6. Howard Y. McClusky, *Education*, 1971 White House Conference on Aging, Background and Issues, U.S. Government Printing Office, Washington, D.C., 1971, p. 20.

7. U.S. Senate, *Developments in Aging: 1978*, A Report of the Special Committee on Aging, U.S. Government Printing Office, Washington, D.C., 1979, p. xxii.

8. Richard Freeman, quoted in Robert Clark and Joseph Spengler, "Population Aging in the Twenty-first Century," *Aging*, January–February 1978, p. 10.

9. Donald G. Fowles, "Some Prospects for the Future Elderly Population," *Statistical Reports on Older Americans*, National Clearinghouse on Aging, Administration on Aging, January 1978, p. 11.

10. Wayne L. Schroeder, "Adult Education Defined and Described," in *Handbook of Adult Education*, eds. Robert Smith, George Aker, and J. R. Kidd, Macmillan, New York, 1970, pp. 26–27.

11. Ibid.

12. Wilma Donahue, *Education for Later Maturity*, Whiteside and William Morrow, New York, 1955.

13. David A. Peterson, "Educational Gerontology: The State of the Art," *Educational Gerontology*, 1, no. 1 (1976), 62.

14. John W. Johnstone and Ramon Rivera, *Volunteers for Learning*, Aldine, Chicago, 1965, p. 73.

15. Harris, *The Myth and Reality of Aging in America*, p. 108.

16. Jack London, "The Social Setting for Adult Education," in *Handbook of Adult Education*, ed. Robert Smith, George Aker, and J. R. Kidd, Macmillan, New York, 1970, pp. 15–16.

17. Zena S. Blau, *Old Age in a Changing Society*, New Viewpoints, New York, 1973, p. 141.

18. Peterson, "Educational Gerontology," p. 64.

19. McClusky, *Education*, pp. 2–5.

20. Cyril O. Houle, "The Changing Goals of Education in the Perspective of Lifelong Learning," *International Review of Education*, 20, no. 4 (1974), 430–446.

21. U.S. Senate, *Developments in Aging: 1976*, A Report of the Special Committee on Aging, U.S. Government Printing Office, Washington, D.C., 1976, p. 147.

22. Harold L. Sheppard, "Aging and Manpower Development," in *Aging and Society*, vol. 2, eds. Matilda Riley, John Riley, Jr., and Marilyn Johnson, Russell Sage Foundation, New York, 1969, pp. 175–177.

23. Robert N. Butler, *Why Survive? Being Old in America*, Harper & Row, New York, 1975, p. 389.

24. David Peterson, "An Overview of Gerontology Education," in *Gerontology in Higher Education: Perspective and Issues*, eds. Mildred Seltzer, Harvey Sterns, and Tom Hickey, Wadsworth, Belmont, Calif., 1978, p. 16.

25. Ibid., p. 17.

26. Bonny Russell, "Special Service Aspects of College and University Programs," in *Gerontology in Higher Education: Perspectives and Issues*, eds. Mildred Seltzer, Harvey Stearns, and Tom Hickey, Wadsworth, Belmont, Calif., 1978, pp. 176–185.

27. Martin P. Knowlton, "Liberal Arts: The Elderhostel Plan for Survival," *Educational Gerontology*, 2, no. 1 (1977), 87–93.

28. Lillian L. Glickman, Benjamin S. Hersey, and I. Ira Goldberg, *Community Colleges Respond to Elders*, National Institute of Education, U.S. Government Printing Office, Washington, D.C., 1975, p. 4.

29. Ibid., pp. 11–13.

For Further Study

Birren, James E., and Diana S. Woodruff. "Human Development over the Life Span Through Education." In *Life-Span Developmental Psychology*, edited by Paul B. Baltes and K. Warner Schaie. Academic Press, New York, 1973, pp. 305–337. This paper discusses the strategies, means, and prospects for life-span education.

Brookover, Wilber B., and Edsel L. Erickson. *Sociology of Education*. Dorsey, Homewood, Ill., 1975. A good textbook in the sociology of education. It examines the reciprocal influence of education and other social institutions.

Donahue, Wilma. *Education for Later Maturity*. Whiteside and William Morrow, New York, 1955. A pioneering effort on both the theoretical and practical aspects of education for the elderly.

Eklund, Lowell, "Aging and the Field of Education." In *Aging and Society*, vol. 2, edited by Matilda Riley, John Riley, Jr., and Marilyn Johnson. Russell Sage Foundation, New York, 1969, pp. 324–351. This chapter focuses on the biological, physiological, and psychological factors relevant to education for older people.

McClusky, Howard Y. *Education*. 1971 White House Conference on Aging, Background and Issues. U.S. Government Printing Office, Washington, D.C., 1971. This paper covers the need for education in the later years and the present situation, goals, and issues of educational programs for the elderly.

Peterson, David A. "The Role of Gerontology in Adult Education." In *The Later Years: Social Applications of Gerontology*, edited by Richard A. Kalish. Brooks/ Cole, Monterey, Calif., 1977, pp. 233–243. An article that emphasizes the various educational needs of older adults and what can be done to meet them.

Seltzer, Mildred, Harvey Sterns, and Tom Hickey. *Gerontology in Higher Education: Perspectives and Issues*. Wadsworth, Belmont, Calif., 1978. A collection of papers from the 1977 meeting of the Association for Gerontology in Higher Education.

V

Social Problems
of the Elderly

16

The Economic Status of the Elderly

All of us are familiar with the plight of elderly people who are struggling to live on a limited income. Should we look on this as a personal or a social problem? What is the distinction between the two? A personal problem is a condition that is linked to individual suffering and does not affect a large number of people; its causes and solutions lie within individuals and their immediate environment. On the other hand, a social problem is a condition that adversely affects a large number of people, and its causes and solutions lie outside individuals and their immediate environment.[1] For example, if only one or two elderly persons were living in poverty, we might determine that the source of their problem was poor planning, not saving for retirement, or laziness. This would constitute a personal problem. But when large numbers of older people are living in poverty, the situation becomes a social problem, and as such requires that we look beyond individuals and their immediate environment to the economic and political institutions in society for causes and solutions.

Sociologists are primarily interested in social problems, not in personal ones. A *social problem* may be defined as a condition that a significant number of people believe to be undesirable and feel that something should be done to correct it. By this definition, the increasing number of older people in our population does not in itself constitute a social problem. Longevity is not considered an undesirable condition, but rather an achievement that has been highly valued and sought after in most societies from the beginning of recorded time (Chapter 2). As for doing something to correct the situation, not many people would advocate employing measures to reduce longevity or the size of the older population. The social problem concerning the elderly lies in the fact that the major social institutions have not kept pace with the rapid increase in the number of older people nor made the necessary adaptations to their needs.[2] In addition, our society's changing values are beginning to define many conditions that have existed among older people as no longer tolerable. Instead of accepting these conditions as

Older females living alone have a higher incidence of poverty than do males in similar circumstances. This 91-year-old woman was arrested and jailed for shoplifting $15.00 worth of food so that she would not starve. (UPI)

inevitable or taking them for granted as we have done in the past, we are now seeing these conditions as social problems that can be changed through social action.

Throughout this book we have been discussing the problems that the elderly face. Some problems have resulted from physiological changes; others have been associated with societal values and beliefs, role loss, a decline in status, and age discrimination. In this part, we will examine the elderly's problems regarding economic status, health care, transportation, housing, and crime. Finally, we will discuss death and dying in a social context.

Most people think that the elderly, having met their major economic obligations, need less income than younger persons. In general, older people do spend less money, but often it is because they have less money to spend. In addition, among the very old, expenses for illness and institutionalization tend to increase dramatically. For some, poverty is a lifelong condition only worsened in old age. For others, poverty is a new condition, occurring after retirement when income is often cut by one-half or two-thirds. Some retirees are forced to give up many things because they lack money.

> I don't is a most accurate description of the older adult living in retirement. I don't entertain. I don't go out with friends. I don't eat in restaurants. I don't go to movies. I don't buy new clothes. I don't ride subways and buses. I don't buy cake. I don't eat a lot. I don't take care of my health like I should. I don't, I don't, I don't.[3]

Income and Poverty

Median Income

One way of showing the disadvantaged economic position of the elderly is by comparing their median incomes with those of the younger population.* Since 1960, the income levels of older families have been about one half of those families under age 65. In 1977 the median annual income of families with heads 65 and over was $9,110, compared to $17,203 for families with younger heads (Table 16.1). *Unrelated individuals*, that is, those persons who live alone or with nonrelatives, have substantially lower incomes than those who live in family settings. The median income for unrelated individuals 65 and over in 1977 was $3,829, or about two-fifths of the median income of older families. These data reflect the economic hardships of the elderly who live alone.

Though the income of older people is still far below that of the younger segment of the population, it has steadily been increasing. Between 1970 and 1976, the median income of older families rose by 18 percent; the income of individuals 65 years of age and over grew by 22 percent.[4] Some factors contributing to the improvement of the economic situation of the elderly have been the increasing coverage of older

---

*Median income is the point at which families or individuals can be divided into two equal income groups, with half of them receiving an income below the median and with half of them above it.

Table 16.1   Trends in median money income of families and
unrelated individuals by age, 1960–1977

Year	Median income of families		Median income of unrelated individuals	
	Heads under 65	Heads over 65	Under 65	Over 65
1960	$ 5,905	$2,897	$2,571	$1,053
1961	6,099	3,026	2,589	1,106
1962	6,336	3,204	2,644	1,248
1963	6,644	3,352	2,881	1,277
1964	6,981	3,376	3,094	1,297
1965	7,413	3,514	3,344	1,378
1966	7,922	3,645	3,443	1,443
1967	8,504	3,928	3,655	1,480
1968	9,198	4,592	4,073	1,734
1969	10,085	4,803	4,314	1,855
1970	10,541	5,053	4,616	1,951
1971	10,976	5,453	4,783	2,199
1972	11,870	5,968	5,018	2,397
1973	12,935	6,426	5,547	2,725
1974	13,823	7,505	6,080	2,984
1975	14,698	8,057	6,460	3,311
1976	15,912	8,721	7,030	3,495
1977	17,203	9,110	7,674	3,829

SOURCE: Adapted from Herman B. Brotman, "Income and Poverty in the Older Population in 1975,"
The Gerontologist, 17, no. 1 (1977), 23. The 1976 figures are from U.S. Senate, *Developments in Aging: 1977*,
A Report of the Special Committee on Aging, U.S. Government Printing Office, Washington, D.C.,
1978, p. xvi. The 1977 figures are from U.S. Senate, *Developments in Aging: 1978*, A Report of the Special
Committee on Aging, U.S. Government Printing Office, Washington, D.C., 1979, p. xvi.

people by private and public pension plans, the implementation of the
Supplemental Security Income Program (SSI), social security increases,
and improvements in other income maintenance programs.

Income Distribution

Figure 16.1 presents the income distribution of older couples and
unrelated individuals. Nearly 32 percent of couples with husbands 65
and over had incomes of less than $6,000 in 1976. At the other end of the

Figure 16.1 Distribution by income of older couples and unrelated individuals, 1976

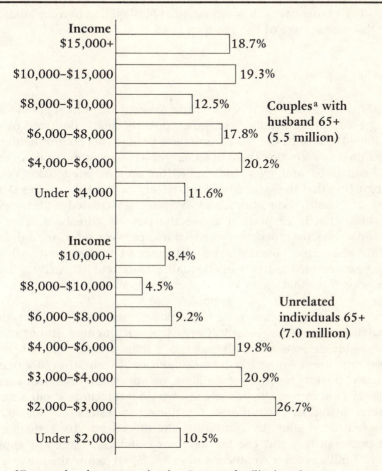

ᵃFor couples, data are restricted to 2-person families in order
to exclude income received by other family members in larger families.

SOURCE: National Clearing House on Aging, *Facts About Older Americans, 1978*, U.S. Goverment Printing Office, Washington, D.C., 1979.

income scale, 18.7 percent of older couples received incomes of $15,000 or more. The income of unrelated individuals 65 and over was skewed much more toward the lower end of the scale. Nearly 78 percent had incomes of less than $6,000, and about 37 percent received incomes under $3,000.

Though the aged are disproportionately represented in the poorer segments of the population, they are also disproportionately represented in the very rich segment. The average age of millionaires in the United States for both sexes is about 60. A list compiled by *Fortune* of 66 individuals whose wealth is estimated at $150 million or more, indicated that the median age of the group was 65.[5]

Poverty Level

In 1977, 14.1 percent of persons 65 and over, or 3.2 million people, were living below the officially determined poverty line — deprived of what are considered to be the basic necessities of life. This determination was based on a poverty threshold of $3,637 for a two-person family in which the head is 65 and over and $2,895 for an unrelated older person. Recognizing that these threshold figures are extremely low, the Department of Health, Education, and Welfare has created a "near-poor" threshold that is 25 percent above the poverty threshold. This new threshold was designed to include those persons who, though living slightly above the poverty level, still cannot be considered as having enough money to maintain an adequate standard of living. By using the near-poor threshold as an index of poverty, about another 2.3 million older persons are seen as marginally poor.[6]

In addition to these recognized poor, there is a "hidden-poor" population among the elderly. Census poverty figures do not include those older persons who, though poor themselves, live with others (mostly relatives) whose incomes are sufficient to raise the older persons out of the poverty level. Over a million are not classified as poor because of this. Furthermore, the poverty figures do not include about a million persons living in institutions. Of these, an estimated 500,000 are projected to be poor. By combining the official poverty statistics, the near-poor figures, and the hidden-poor estimates, there are approximately 7 million older Americans who live either below the poverty line or very near to it. Yet the United States is one of the wealthiest nations in the world with a gross national product of over $1.8 trillion.

Poverty is not evenly distributed throughout the older population, but varies by race and sex. In 1977, the percentage of elderly blacks living below the poverty level was 36.3, or about three times that of the whites.[7] Older females living alone or with nonrelatives reflect a higher incidence of poverty than their male counterparts. Black females living alone have the highest percentage of poverty of all categories.

The proportion of all older persons living below the poverty level has been dropping steadily for a number of years. According to the census poverty figures in 1959, 35.2 percent of all the elderly were poor, compared to 14.1 percent in 1977. The greatest decline in poverty among the older population during the 1970s occurred among older males

A large number of older persons live below the poverty level or very close to it.
(Karen R. Preuss © 1977)

living in family settings. Little or no decline took place among older females and elderly minority group members. Largely due to their lower earnings and intermittent work histories, these two groups have limited financial resources to rely on after retirement.[8]

Public Sources of Income

To gain a clearer picture of the financial situation of older people, it is necessary to look at the major sources of their income, both public and private, and to understand some of the programs from which this income is derived.

Social Security

As Table 16.2 shows, the most common source of the elderly's income is social security. It accounts for over half the income for 70 percent of older individuals and for 50 percent of the income of older couples.[9] Though social security has long been considered the financial bedrock

Table 16.2 Income sources for families and unrelated individuals 65 years and over, 1975

Income source	Percentage with income from designated source	
	Family	*Unrelated individual*
Social security and railroad retirement	90.9%	90.1%
Personal assets (interest, dividends, rent)	64.4	53.8
Wages or salary	41.7	13.5
Private, military and federal employee pensions	35.7	22.9
Veterans, unemployment, and workmen's compensation	12.3	8.6
Supplementary security income	8.4	13.9

SOURCE: Adapted from *Fact Book on Aging: A Profile of America's Older Population,* The National Council on the Aging, Inc., Washington, D.C. © 1978, p. 56.

Ida M. Fuller in January 1940, at age 76, was the first social security beneficiary, with benefits of $22.54 per month. (Social Security Administration)

for millions of older Americans, it was originally designed and conceived as a supplement to the income of older people.

When the Social Security Act was signed into law in 1935, it made provisions for two federal-state programs: (1) unemployment insurance, and (2) assistance to three groups of low-income persons (the aged, the blind, and dependent children). In addition, it established a federal old-age insurance system designed to provide basic retirement income after the age of 65 for workers insured under the system. This old-age insurance became popularly known as "social security."

Since the passage of the Social Security Act, many changes have been made to improve the protection it gives to wage-earners and to extend this protection to their families. Originally, the Act covered only workers when they retired, but in 1939 it was amended to provide benefits to the workers' dependents at retirement, as well as to the workers' survivors at their death. With the addition of these benefits, the program was then called old-age and survivors' insurance (OASI). In the beginning, the social security program covered only those who worked in industry or commerce, but by the 1950s coverage was extended to include household and farm workers, self-employed persons, state and local employees, members of the armed forces, and clergymen. To protect workers against the loss of earnings due to total disability, disability insurance was later added to the system. In 1965, the social security program was expanded once more with the passage of national health insurance, or Medicare, for those 65 and over. The program is now formally referred to as old-age, survivors, disability, and health insurance (OASDHI).[10]

For our present discussion, we will consider only the old age and survivors' insurance portion of OASDHI. This aspect of the program may be divided into these categories: basic benefits, minimum benefits, dependent benefits, early retirement benefits, delayed retirement benefits, the retirement test, and survivors' benefits.[11]

BASIC BENEFITS   Basic benefits are paid at age 65 and are based upon the workers' average yearly earnings under social security over a period of years. But, regardless of how much a worker has earned, there is a limit set on the amount of the benefit. The maximum monthly benefit for a worker retiring at age 65 in 1979 was $553.30, and the maximum benefit paid to a couple was $829.95. As a result of legislation passed in 1972, social security benefits are adjusted annually for cost-of-living increases. The maximum benefits that social security recipients may receive have increased dramatically over the years. The average monthly payment to a retired worker in 1979 was $283, and to a couple, $482.

MINIMUM BENEFITS   Workers who would receive only very low basic benefits because of low lifetime earnings are given a special minimum benefit, which is larger than the amount that they would normally have been entitled to under their basic benefit. Like maximum benefits, minimum benefits have also steadily increased. In 1979, the minimum benefit for a 65-year-old single worker was $121.80 and for a couple it was $182.70 prior to the 1979 cost-of-living increase.

DEPENDENT BENEFITS   Dependent benefits are equal to half of the workers' basic benefits and may be paid to their spouse and children under age 18 (18–22 if full-time students). In cases where a wife has worked and is qualified to receive social security, she has the option to draw a pension based either on her work record or on her husband's (reduced by half), depending on which is higher.

This situation raises the question of whether or not the working wife is being treated fairly. During their working years, a husband and wife are considered as separate tax units, and together they pay more into the system than a family where only the husband works and earns the same amount. Yet, at retirement, the husband and wife are treated as one unit and are thus entitled to only one benefit. Often a working wife may receive no more or even less in retirement benefits than a nonworking wife. The working wife, however, does receive disability protection and has the option to retire at 62 even if her husband continues to work. As the participation rates of women in the labor force continue to increase, the issue of their retirement benefits is expected to become highly controversial.

EARLY RETIREMENT BENEFITS   Early retirement benefits may be paid to beneficiaries as early as age 62, but the amount is permanently reduced to take into account the longer period over which they must be paid. Before 1962, workers could not receive any benefits until they reached the age of 65. The law was changed in 1956 to permit women to receive reduced benefits at 62, and in 1961 the same option was given to men. At the present time, almost 60 percent of all retired workers are receiving reduced benefits because they retired before age 65. The proportion of workers taking early retirement is expected to increase in the future.

DELAYED RETIREMENT BENEFITS   In the past, workers who delayed retirement received an increase in retirement benefits of 1 percent for each year that they worked beyond age 65 without drawing social security benefits. Beginning in 1982, the delayed retirement credit will be increased to 3 percent for each year from age 65 to 72 that a worker is eligible to receive benefits but does not take them.

THE RETIREMENT TEST   The retirement test refers to the fact that persons from 65 to 72 years of age are allowed to earn only a certain amount of money to still be eligible to receive their full social security benefits. When this limitation is reached ($5,000 in 1980), benefits are reduced one dollar for every two dollars earned. This earnings ceiling will increase by $500 each year through 1982. Also, beginning in 1982 the age at which beneficiaries may receive full benefits, regardless of their earnings, will be lowered from age 72 to 70.

The retirement test has probably been the target for more criticism than any other aspect of the social security program. Many persons argue that it destroys a person's incentive to work and penalizes those with low pensions who need to work. Others maintain that it is discriminatory because it takes into account only earned income and not income received from nonwork sources, such as stocks and bonds, dividends, rents, interest, or insurance annuities. Many opponents of the retirement test feel that it should be eliminated completely. If this were done, the estimated cost to the government would be about $4 billion per year, whereas the present strategy of liberalizing the retirement test costs less than $1 billion.

SURVIVORS' BENEFITS Survivors' benefits are payable to the widow or dependent widower beginning at age 60. In the past, benefits were reduced in most cases by 50 percent if the widow or widower remarried. This reduction resulted in many elderly couples living together, rather than marrying, to avoid a cut in benefits. Since January 1979, widows and widowers who remarry at age 60 and later no longer have their benefits reduced. Unmarried children of a deceased worker can receive benefits until they are 18, or until 22 if full-time students.

The social security program is essentially a transfer of money from the young working population to the elderly retired population. This money is derived from payroll taxes — the employee pays a certain amount that is matched by the employer. To support the system, the payroll tax rate and the amount of income taxed have risen over the years. Between 1937 and 1949, the basic social security payroll tax rate was 1 percent each from the employee and the employer on the first $3,000 of earned income. By 1979, the tax rate was 6.13 percent on the first $22,900 of earned income.

Much criticism of social security stems from the larger bite taken out of the worker's paycheck as well as from the regressive character of the payroll tax. Unlike the federal income tax, which is progressive — the more you make, the more you pay — the social security tax is based on the premise that the more you make, the less you pay. For example, persons earning $22,900 or less in 1979 were taxed at the rate of 6.13 percent on their entire income, while those who earned more were not taxed on earnings after the $22,900 mark was reached. Thus, higher salaried workers pay a lower proportion of their income in social security taxes than lower salaried workers. Put in dollars, a worker earning $50,000 pays the same amount ($1,403) into the system as one earning $22,900, but the amount represents only 2.8 percent of the higher income.

Also, social security does not allow for exemptions and does not apply to nonearned income, only to wages. This situation further increases the disparity between the higher and lower income groups. Many persons who earn too little to pay income taxes still must pay social security taxes. More than half of all American taxpayers pay more to the Social Security Administration than they pay in income taxes.

Another major criticism of the social security program is that the benefits are inadequate. Yet, from 1967 to 1974, aggregate benefits increased by 90.5 percent as a result of five across-the-board raises during this period. In addition, social security benefits automatically increase with the cost-of-living index. But social security increases have managed only to keep up with the rising price levels, with much of the rise offset by inflation. In 1975, the average social security payment for a retired couple was only $72 above the poverty level. For the single retiree, the average benefit was below the poverty level.[12]

With workers retiring earlier and living longer, the ratio between those who pay into the social security system and those who collect from it has changed markedly. This situation, along with continual increases in social security benefits, has caused much concern about the depletion of the social security trust fund, which acts as a cushion against deficits. In the past few years, payments have been exceeding revenues; for example, in 1976 social security benefits exceeded revenues by $4.3 billion, and the trust fund was dipped into to make up the difference. The 1977 amendments to the Social Security Act considerably strengthened the financing of the trust fund. The trust fund balance is expected to increase from $32.3 billion in 1977 to $115.9 billion by 1987, and is projected to provide a surplus for the next 25 years and a manageable deficit for the next 75 years.[13]

To finance the social security program, the obvious solution is to continue to raise social security taxes. The 1977 legislation calls for raises in payroll taxes so that by 1987 the tax rate will have increased to 7.15 percent on earnings up to an estimated $42,000. An alternative would be to finance social security out of the general revenue. Some people argue that the solution lies in changing the payroll tax either by making the tax progressive and allowing for exemptions or by combining the social security tax with the income tax. No matter what changes occur in the financing of social security, one thing is certain: to provide adequately for the retirement period in the future, there will be an increasing financial burden on the working population.

> Social security has enjoyed long-standing public acceptance and support. It is a vital arm of our national policy of income security and dignity for the retired. . . . Unfortunately, we jeopardize the future acceptance and viability of this great social experiment by enacting too high a cost for its financing. Already the working public is increasingly alarmed by present social security tax rates. This displeasure will build tremendously in the decade ahead when the social security tax, even now the largest tax for over 50 per cent of America's households, increases dramatically.[14]

Basically, the issue is whether or not we want to live better in our retirement years at the expense of a lower standard of living during our working years.[15]

Supplemental Security Income

In addition to social security, the Social Security Administration administers the Supplemental Security Income Program, which went into operation in 1974. SSI replaced the federal-state assistance program for the low-income aged, blind, and disabled that was originally established under the Social Security Act of 1935. SSI is the first federal program to provide a guaranteed minimum income for any segment of the population. Unlike social security, it is financed from general revenues. Because it is a federal program, the requirements for eligibility as well as minimum standards are uniform throughout the nation. Nearly all the states are now currently adding money to the program to raise the level of payments.

Approximately 2 million persons aged 65 years and over received SSI benefits in 1978; 70 percent of them also received social security payments.[16] Persons with no income receive the full amount of SSI. Those who have other sources of income, but still fall below the minimum income level, receive SSI money to bring them up to this level. In 1979 this minimum was $208.20 per month for individuals and $312.30 for couples. As social security benefits increase each year, the number of SSI recipients is gradually declining.

Private Sources of Income

Private Pension Plans

In recent years the growth of private pensions has been widespread. Over 35 million workers now have private pension coverage. Private pension plans may be classified into two types: contributory and noncontributory plans. A contributory plan requires that an employee pay part of the cost, whereas noncontributory plans, which are the most common, are financed totally by the employer. Retirement benefits are determined in a variety of ways. Some companies provide the same retirement benefits to all eligible employees. Others base their benefits on the number of years of service, or on the employee's earnings, or a combination of both.[17]

Two key characteristics of pension plans are vesting and portability. *Vesting* refers to the right of employees to receive the pension benefits they have accumulated if they leave the plan before retirement. *Portability* refers to the transfer of pension rights from one plan to another when the worker changes jobs. Social security provides a good example of portability in the public sector; credits toward benefits accumulate under the social security system for workers no matter how often they change jobs. In the private sector, Teacher's Insurance and Annuity Association (TIAA) offers portability; university and college professors can transfer their pension benefits from one institution to another as their affiliations change.[18]

Nearly all pension plans contain early retirement options so that workers can receive their benefits before the customary retirement age. Usually such options require that the worker meet a minimum age requirement, or minimum years-of-service requirement, or both. The "30 and out" plan of the United Automobile Workers, mentioned in Chapter 12, uses only years of service as qualification for full pension benefits. American Telephone and Telegraph Company combines age with years of service. Employees are given the option to retire at age 55 after 20 years of service on full pension, or they may retire at age 50 after 25 years of service but with reduced benefits.[19]

The flagrant abuse and mismanagement of private pension plans prompted the passage of the Employment Retirement Income Security Act in 1974. Prior to this legislation, some companies required 30 years or more of continuous service for an employee to become vested. Many employees often lost their pension rights when they changed jobs, were laid off, or were terminated. When companies went out of business or were purchased by other companies, workers were often unable to collect their pensions, or at best, only small portions of them. The Studebaker plant closing provides an illustration of this situation.

> In 1963 . . . some four thousand employees of Studebaker Corporation's South Bend, Indiana, plant found that their pensions amounted to little after the factory closed down. There was not enough money in the fund to pay benefits, although Studebaker had honored all its contract obligations. Men who had worked for the company for thirty and forty years got 15 per cent of their promised pensions; many others received nothing.[20]

The Employment Retirement Income Security Act has greatly improved the prospects that pension promises will be fulfilled. This legislation regulates and supervises private pension plans and provides basic protection against the loss of retirement benefits. To insure that there will be enough money to pay the benefits promised, the pension law sets minimum standards for building up the funds that finance pensions. This law regulates both the timing and amount of vesting so that employees may receive a larger part or all of their pension benefits in fewer years. In this way, those who switch jobs will have a better chance to collect a pension when they retire. Also the law provides for a government corporation that will pay pensions up to a certain amount if the company goes out of business or cannot meet its obligations. Finally, the law establishes strict rules to prevent the misuse of pension funds.[21]

Personal Assets

Table 16.2 shows that nearly two-thirds of the older families and over one-half of the unrelated individuals received income from personal assets in 1975. Yet, the proportion of their income from such sources is relatively small. A 1972 social security survey found that over one-half of the elderly persons with income from assets received less than one-fifth of their total income from this source. Only 15 percent received half or more of their income from personal assets.[22]

An earlier social security survey in 1968 revealed that the majority of elderly couples and unrelated individuals had less than $5,000 in liquid assets, such as savings, stocks, and bonds. Indeed, 43 percent of these couples and 61 percent of the unrelated individuals had assets of under $1,000. The survey also found that the most common, nonliquid asset of older people is equity in a home. About 80 percent of older couples own their homes; of these, about four-fifths have fully paid their mortgages.[23]

Income Adequacy

Measuring Adequacy

Measuring the level of financial adequacy for older people or setting standards to determine it is a difficult process. One of the most common approaches uses budgets prepared by the Bureau of Labor Statistics. These budgets are designed for couples in urban areas, with the husband aged 65 or over and both partners retired. It is assumed that the couples are self-supporting and in relatively good health, live in their own homes, and are able to take care of themselves. The budget lists the costs of major items required to meet the normal needs of retired couples at three different standards of living: lower, intermediate, and higher. The budgets are adjusted annually for changes in the Consumer Price Index.

In 1977 the Bureau of Labor Statistics set the budget for retired couples at $5,031 for the lower level, $7,198 for the intermediate level, and $10,711 for the higher level. As Table 16.3 shows, from 1971 through 1977, the percentages of elderly couples with incomes below the three budget levels have steadily declined. In 1977, 39.4 percent of the elderly couples had incomes below the intermediate budget level, and 17.7 percent had incomes below the lower level.

As an alternative to using budgets as an indicator of whether or not income is adequate, David Peterson suggests a perceptual approach for measuring financial adequacy.[24] Through this method, valuable insight into the way older people view their financial situation may be gained.

This method rests on the assumption that an individual can determine the adequacy of his own finances; in fact, he is probably the only person who is in a position to do so since only he can incorporate consideration of his past level of living, his changing needs, his housing situation, the number of

"Why, you've been absolutely right all along, Theodore! The best *was* yet to be!"
(Drawing by Robert Day; © 1971. The New Yorker Magazine, Inc.)

persons he must provide for, his assets, medical expenses, debts, etc. The perceptual method is employed by asking older people how adequate they think their financial situation is and accepting their judgment as the measure of financial adequacy.[25]

Peterson surveyed 462 older persons in Southeastern Michigan to determine how they perceived their financial situation. His findings reveal that 57 percent of the respondents felt their present finances to be inadequate, 35 percent viewed their incomes as adequate, and another 8 percent saw them as partially adequate. He found that females, blacks, and those living alone — the same segments of the population heavily represented among the elderly poor — were more likely to report their finances as inadequate.

Peterson's data also showed that persons in the lower income levels tended to have lower financial expectations than those in the higher levels. Individuals in the lower categories felt that only a small increase was needed in their income to raise them to what they considered to be

Table 16.3   Elderly couples with income below the three budget levels of the Bureau of Labor Statistics, 1971–1977

	Budgets for a retired couple			Percentage of elderly couples with income below the budget levels		
Year	Lower	Inter-mediate	Higher	Lower	Inter-mediate	Higher
1971	$3,319	$4,771	$ 7,158	26.4%	47.8%	71.3%
1972	3,442	4,959	7,426	22.0	44.3	68.4
1973	3,791	5,442	8,072	22.2	44.4	67.9
1974	4,228	6,041	8,969	22.0	43.8	68.0
1975	4,501	6,465	9,598	20.1	41.4	65.1
1976	4,695	6,738	10,048	17.8	39.0	62.2
1977	5,031	7,198	10,711	17.7	39.4	63.6

SOURCE: Adapted from National Clearing House on Aging, *Statistical Notes*, Administration on Aging, Washington, D.C., January 1979, p. 3.

an adequate level. He concludes that financial adequacy is best seen in relative terms, instead of specific amounts of money: "The average older person regardless of present level of income stated that to reach adequacy, his family income would need to be increased by 33%."[26]

Inflation

What was considered to be an adequate income at the time of retirement may become inadequate during postretirement years. The relative economic position of an individual or a family tends to decline with advancing age, mainly due to inflation. Most people believe that among the elderly population, inflation affects those persons in the lower income levels more than those in the upper income levels. Just the opposite is true. Lower income elderly who depend mainly on social security have been protected to some extent from inflation since 1975 with benefit increases each June when the Consumer Price Index rises 3 percent or more. Also, SSI and the food stamp program both automatically adjust their benefits for inflation within a relatively short lag period. Thus, inflation is more of a serious problem among the higher income elderly, who suffer a greater loss from inflation in proportion to their incomes because many of their assets come from sources which

Old people should share in any rise in the economy and in its expansion — not just its inflation which erodes purchasing power. Old people should reap late life dividends for lifelong investments in America. Other Western nations have their pensioners share in the general productivity and give higher percentages of their gross national product to the aged. We provide neither the public services nor the money required.

SOURCE: Robert N. Butler, *The International Journal of Aging and Human Development*, Baywood, Farmingdale, N.Y., 1973, pp. 277–279.

have fixed dollar amounts, such as bonds, private pensions, and personal savings.[27]

Older persons spend a greater proportion of their income for housing, food, transportation, and health care than do younger persons. On the average, these four items account for more than $4 out of every $5 in an elderly family's budget.[28] The largest portion of the elderly's budget, 28.9 percent, is spent for housing, followed by 21.4 percent for food, 12.8 percent for transportation, and 8.3 percent for health care.[29] Since 1973 the spiraling costs of utilities and fuel have been especially hard on older people living on limited incomes. A 97-year-old man reports that the cost of fuel and electricity has gotten so high that only by cutting back on food and other necessities is he able to keep his home warm and lighted. "You know that it ain't right. But I just go ahead and try to starve it out."[30]

Summary

1. Social problems differ from personal problems in that they affect a large number of people and their causes lie outside the individual. A social problem is a condition that a significant number of people believe to be undesirable and feel that something should be done to correct it. By this definition, the growing size of the older population does not itself constitute a social problem. But the fact that needed changes in the major social institutions have not kept pace with the increases in the elderly population has led to social problems.

2. The median income of the elderly is about half that of the younger population. Older persons who live in family settings have higher incomes than those individuals who live alone or with nonrelatives. In 1977, 14.1 percent of the persons aged 65 and over were below the poverty level. Poverty is highest among older blacks and females living alone. The proportion of older persons living below the poverty level has been steadily declining in recent years.

3. Some sources from which the elderly derive their income include social security, SSI, private pensions, and personal assets. Of these, social security provides the major source of income. Over the years, social security benefits

have been changed to give added protection to workers and their families. The aspect of the social security program that provides for old age and survivors' insurance may be divided into these categories: basic benefits, minimum benefits, dependent benefits, early retirement benefits, delayed retirement benefits, the retirement test, and survivors' benefits. The social security system has been greatly criticized in recent years. Some criticize the retirement test, which puts an earnings ceiling on money a worker may earn and still draw full social security benefits. Another criticism is of the regressive nature of the payroll tax. Lower income workers carry the heaviest tax burden, and many who do not earn enough to pay income taxes still must pay social security taxes. The large numbers of older people drawing social security benefits, together with the trend toward earlier retirement, have put an increased strain on the social security trust fund.

4. SSI, which replaced the federal-state assistance program in 1974, is the first federal program to provide a guaranteed minimum income for a considerable segment of the population. Those elderly who have other sources of income but fall below the minimum income level receive additional money to bring them up to the minimum level. Others with no income receive the full amount of SSI.

5. Private pension plans have become widespread in recent years. Most plans are financed by the employer and provide for early retirement benefits. A key characteristic of a pension plan is vesting, which makes it possible to retain the pension benefits that workers have accumulated if they are discharged or change jobs. Another characteristic is portability, which allows employees to transfer their pension rights to another plan. In 1974, the Employment Retirement Income Security Act was passed to help protect workers against the loss of retirement benefits and to regulate and supervise private pension plans.

6. Though nearly two-thirds of the older families and one-half of the unrelated individuals receive income from personal assets, the proportion of their income derived from such sources is relatively small. The most common asset older people possess is equity in their home.

7. To determine income adequacy, a widely used measure is the budgets for retired couples prepared by the Bureau of Labor Statistics. These budgets are designed for three standards of living: lower, intermediate, and higher. Peterson has suggested that another way of determining income adequacy is to use a perceptual method. Older people are asked how adequate they think their financial situation is, and their judgments are used as measures of income adequacy.

8. Inflation is an increasing problem for many older people who live primarily on a fixed income. The elderly in the lower income levels tend to be protected somewhat from inflation by the automatic adjustments in cost-of-living increases for social security and SSI. Persons in the higher income levels suffer a greater loss from inflation in proportion to their incomes because much of their income is derived from sources that have fixed dollar amounts. The greatest percentage of the income of the elderly is spent for housing, followed by food, transportation, and health care.

Notes

1. Robert H. Lauer, *Social Problems and the Quality of Life*, Wm. C. Brown, Dubuque, Iowa, 1978, p. 3

2. Bernice L. Neugarten, "The Aged in American Society," in *Social Problems: A Modern Approach*, ed. Howard S. Becker, Wiley, New York, 1966, pp. 167–196.

3. U.S. Senate, Special Committee on Aging, quoted by Blanche Fitzpatrick, "Economics of Aging," in *Understanding Aging: A Multidisciplinary Approach*, eds. Marian Spencer and Caroline Dorr, Appleton-Century-Crofts, New York, 1975, p. 131.

4. Donald G. Fowles, "Some Prospects for the Future Elderly Population," *Statistical Reports on Older Americans*, National Clearing House on Aging, Administration on Aging, January 1978, p. 11.

5. Gordon F. Streib, "Social Stratification and Aging," in *Handbook of Aging and the Social Sciences*, eds. Robert H. Binstock and Ethel Shanas, Van Nostrand Reinhold, New York, 1976, p. 171.

6. National Clearing House on Aging, *Statistical Notes*, Administration on Aging, Washington, D.C., January 1979, p. 6.

7. U.S. Senate, *Developments in Aging: 1978*, A Report of the Special Committee on Aging, U.S. Government Printing Office, Washington, D.C., 1979, p. 39.

8. Fowles, "Some Prospects for the Future Elderly Population," p. 14.

9. U.S. Senate, *Developments in Aging: 1978*, p. viii.

10. U.S. Department of Health, Education, and Welfare, *Your Social Security*, U.S. Government Printing Office, Washington, D.C., 1974, pp. 5–6.

11. Much of the following discussion is drawn from James H. Schulz, *The Economics of Aging*, Wadsworth, Belmont, Calif., 1976, pp. 92–99.

12. *Fact Book on Aging: A Profile of America's Older Population*, The National Council on the Aging, Washington, D.C., 1978, p. 57.

13. U.S. Senate, *Developments in Aging: 1978*, pp. 2–10.

14. Ibid., p. 15.

15. Schulz, *The Economics of Aging*, p. 171.

16. U.S. Senate, *Developments in Aging: 1978*, p. 11.

17. Schulz, *The Economics of Aging*, p. 116.

18. Yung-Ping Chen, *Income*, 1971 White House Conference on Aging, Background and Issues, U.S. Government Printing Office, Washington, D.C., 1971, pp. 37–38.

19. *U.S. News and World Report*, May 13, 1974.

20. Robert N. Butler, *Why Survive? Being Old in America*, Harper & Row, New York, 1975, p. 49.

21. "The New Pension Law Could Be Good News for You," *Changing Times*, December 1974, pp. 7–10.

22. *Fact Book on Aging*, p. 60.

23. James H. Schulz, "Income Distribution and the Aging," in *Handbook of Aging and the Social Sciences*, eds. Robert H. Binstock and Ethel Shanas, Van Nostrand Reinhold, New York, 1976, pp. 571–572.

24. David A. Peterson, "Financial Adequacy in Retirement: Perceptions of Older Americans," *The Gerontologist*, 12, no. 4 (1972), 379–383.

25. Ibid., p. 380.

26. Ibid., p. 383.

27. Juanita M. Kreps, "The Economy and the Aged," in *Handbook of Aging and the Social Sciences*, eds. Robert H. Binstock and Ethel Shanas, Van Nostrand Reinhold, New York, 1976, p. 278. Also see Schulz, *The Economics of Aging*, pp. 31–32.

28. U.S. Senate, *Developments on Aging: 1978*, p. 33.

29. Ibid., p. xviii.

30. *Newsweek*, March 29, 1975, p. 75.

For Further Study

Chen, Yung-Ping Chen. *Income*. The 1971 White House Conference on Aging, Background and Issues. U.S. Government Printing Office, Washington, D.C., 1971. This paper concerns the income needs and the present income status of the elderly.

Fitzpatrick, Blanche. "Economics of Aging." In *Understanding Aging: A Multidisciplinary Approach*, edited by Marian G. Spencer and Caroline J. Dorr. Appleton-Century-Crofts, New York, 1975. A discussion of the causes of poverty among the aged in the 1970s.

Kreps, Juanita M. "The Economy and the Aged." In *Handbook of Aging and the Social Sciences*, edited by Robert H. Binstock and Ethel Shanas, Van Nostrand Reinhold, New York, 1976. A good article concerning economic growth and fluctuations as they affect the economic position of the elderly and the impact of the aged on the economy.

Neugarten, Bernice L., and Robert L. Havighurst, eds. *Social Policy, Social Ethics, and the Aging Society*. U.S. Government Printing Office, Washington, D.C., 1976. Includes a collection of papers on the income and economic welfare of the elderly.

Schulz, James H. *The Economics of Aging*. Wadsworth, Belmont, Calif., 1976. A short, clearly written account of the economic status of the aged with emphasis on private and public pension programs.

Seltzer, Mildred M., Sherry L. Corbett, and Robert C. Atchley. *Social Problems of the Aging: Readings*. Wadsworth, Belmont, Calif., 1978. A good overview of some of the problems relating to aging.

Walther, Robin Jane. "Economics and the Older Population." In *Aging, Scientific Perspectives and Social Issues*, eds. Diana S. Woodruff and James E. Birren. D. Van Nostrand, New York, 1975. This chapter suggests ways in which economists are contributing to the efforts to improve the elderly's economic position.

17

Health and Illness

Today we regard epilepsy as an illness, but in some societies in the past the epileptic was glorified. A man subject to such attacks was often the hero of an old Arab epic. He was more likely to receive admiration rather than treatment. Among the Abkhasians, overweight persons are looked on as ill. Though some forms of obesity may require medical attention in American society, nevertheless, we do not believe that all overweight persons are sick.

Health and illness, then, are not only viewed as physical problems, but have social aspects as well. What constitutes illness is subject to social definition, a definition in our society which differs greatly from what it was in the past. With advances in modern medicine, the definition has been greatly expanded and standards of wellness have changed. For example, malaria with its accompanying chills and fever calls for prompt medical attention today. But this was not the case in the mid-1800s when malaria, common among persons in the Mississippi Valley, was referred to as *ague* and accepted as a normal physical condition. People would often remark, "He's not sick, he's just got the ague."[1] By the same token, it is not uncommon today for physicians and patients alike to define many illnesses as "natural" and dismiss them under the guise of "it's just old age."

Illness affects society in many ways. Persons who are ill are not able to perform the necessary tasks of daily living and their social roles. In turn, they are expected to play a role that Talcott Parsons calls "the sick role."[2] One of the main characteristics of this role is the shift from independence to dependence. This role is particularly disturbing to most adults in our society because of the high value that we place on independence. Complementary to the sick role are the roles that family, friends, and medical personnel perform to help restore the sick person to a normal functioning state.

Illness exacts a high economic cost from our society in lost man hours, decreased productivity, and health care services. In 1977, total personal health care expenditures exceeded $142 billion. Though persons age 65 and over represent almost 11 percent of the total population, they accounted for almost 30 percent of the personal health care expenditures, or about $41 billion. The per capita health costs for persons over 65 are nearly three and a half times greater than for those under 65.[3]

Health looms large as a problem for the elderly. In most opinion polls, older people rank health and health care costs near the top of their list of concerns. In the 1975 Harris Poll, the elderly considered poor health to be the major drawback of old age.[4] When the elderly were asked what they personally experienced as "very serious" or "somewhat serious" problems, 50 percent ranked poor health first.

In order to understand the health care problems and needs of the elderly, let us begin by discussing their health status. Though health is difficult to measure, a number of indicators are used, including mortality, morbidity and disability rates, and self-health assessments.

Health Status of the Elderly

Mortality

Mortality rates are the oldest and a widely accepted indicator of health status. The majority of deaths in the United States are deaths of older persons. In 1975 the elderly accounted for over 64 percent of the deaths. In the decade between 1965 and 1975, the annual death rates for the elderly dropped about 11 percent, the greatest decline occurring among the 85 and over age group.[5]

Death rates have been consistently higher among older males than females, and the gap between them has widened considerably in recent years. In 1900 the death rate for males aged 65 and over was 6 percent higher than that for females. By mid-century it was 27 percent higher. In 1975 the death rate for older males was 47 percent higher than for older females.[6]

Death rates and life expectancy are closely related. As death rates decline, life expectancy increases. In 1976, average life expectancy at birth was 72.8 years. The gap in life expectancies between the sexes has become increasingly wider: for males, 69.0 years, but for females, 76.7 years. Since 1900, average life expectancy at birth has increased by 25 years, due mainly to the reduction in infant and childhood mortality rates.

At the other end of the life cycle, only a small improvement has been made in ameliorating the chronic conditions and diseases that are the major killers of older persons. Though more people are reaching 65 today than ever before, the number of years that they are living after that has only increased by about four years since the turn of the century.

Heart disease, stroke, and cancer, in that order, are the leading causes of deaths among the older population in the United States (Table

Table 17.1 Ten leading causes of death for persons age 65 and over in the United States, 1975

Rank[a]	Cause of death	Both sexes	Male	Female
		Deaths per 100,000 population		
1	Diseases of heart	2,403.9	2,933.0	2,036.7
2	Cancer (malignant neoplasms)	961.1	1,301.1	725.2
3	Stroke (cerebrovascular)	729.7	740.5	722.1
4	Influenza and pneumonia	187.1	239.2	150.9
5	Arteriosclerosis	123.0	119.8	125.2
6	Diabetes	112.9	102.8	119.9
7	Accidents	109.6	140.6	88.1
	Motor vehicle	25.3	38.7	16.0
	All others	84.3	101.9	72.1
8	Bronchitis, emphysema, and asthma	80.5	152.5	30.5
9	Cirrhosis of the liver	36.6	58.1	21.6
10	Infections of the kidney	23.2	—	—
	All causes	5,432.4	6,702.7	4,550.9

[a]Rank order for both sexes.
SOURCE: Adapted from U.S. Department of Health, Education, and Welfare, National Center for Health Statistics, *Health, United States, 1976–1977*, U.S. Government Printing Office, Washington, D.C., 1977, p. 7.

17.1). Declines in heart disease and stroke are responsible for much of the decrease in the mortality rates among the older population. Between 1965 and 1976, the death rate of older persons from heart disease dropped 14 percent and that for strokes, 22 percent. But the rate for deaths from cancer increased by 11 percent. These three diseases accounted for three-fourths of all the deaths of older people.[7]

Morbidity and Disability

The older population has a lower incidence of acute illnesses than younger persons have. The most common acute conditions affecting the elderly are certain infective diseases and respiratory conditions. Like younger persons, the elderly have flu, colds, and other illnesses of short duration. They also suffer a high rate of accidental injuries, which cause short-term restrictions and can result in permanent limitation of mobility.

Acute illnesses generally involve disability of a short-term nature, usually lasting less than three months. The effects of acute conditions are commonly measured by time lost from work, the number of days of restricted activity, and days spent in bed. As we noted previously, the older employee loses fewer days per year from work than the younger worker. In 1965 an older employee lost on the average of 8 days per year from work, and in 1975 about 4 days per year. This decline may be due to the fact that because of improved early retirement benefits, workers in poor health are leaving the labor force much earlier.[8]

While the number of days lost from work for the elderly has decreased over a 10-year period, the average number of disability days has remained much the same. Days of restricted activity and bed-disability increase with age, and tend to be higher for women than for men and highest among those in the low-income levels.[9] Older persons were restricted in their activity on an average of 38.4 days per year in 1975. In comparison, the younger population had only 17.9 days of restricted activity. In 1975 the average number of bed-disability days per year for the general population was 6.6 days, while that for persons 65 and over was twice that amount, or 12.9 days. Though older persons suffer from fewer acute diseases than younger persons do, their higher number of disability days is due to the fact that when older persons do become ill, they require a longer recovery period. Still, the average number of days spent in bed by an older person is much lower than most people expect — the myth persists that older people are always ill and spend much of their time in bed.[10]

In contrast to acute illnesses, chronic illnesses, which constitute the bulk of health care problems of the elderly, have no medical cure. They have been called the "companions of the aged."[11] They range from minor aches and pains to long-term disability. Some common chronic conditions among the elderly include high blood pressure, arthritis, heart disease, diabetes, and vision and hearing impairments. Chronic conditions tend to vary by sex. For example, older women have higher rates than men for arthritis, diabetes, high blood pressure and vision impairments. Older men have higher rates of asthma, chronic bronchitis, hernias, ulcers, and hearing impairments.[12]. Over 80 percent of older persons have at least one chronic condition, but for over half of these persons, these conditions do not interfere with, or restrict their activities. On the other hand, for some older persons such conditions may lead to long-term disability.

Long-term disability refers to a reduction in a person's normal activities as a result of a chronic condition. In 1975 about 47 percent of the noninstitutionalized elderly said that they were limited in activity.

Six percent reported a limitation, but it was not in their major activity, such as work or keeping house; 23 percent were limited in the amount or kind of major activity; and 17 percent suffered severe limitations and were unable to carry on their major activity.[13] The major causes of activity limitation are two chronic conditions, heart disease and arthritis or rheumatism. Together, these two conditions account for nearly half the restrictions imposed on older people.

Activity limitations tend to be related to various demographic characteristics. For instance, those with the fewest restrictions tend to be between the ages of 65 and 74, are women, and are white. In addition, higher income and educational levels are also associated with less limitation on activity.[14]

Disability can also be measured in terms of the ability that a person has to move about freely. A 1972 survey of the noninstitutionalized population 65 or over found that most older persons (82 percent) had no serious restrictions on their mobility. Among the 18 percent of elderly who did, 6 percent could move around alone but with some trouble, 7 percent needed help to get around, and 5 percent were homebound.[15]

Self-health Assessment

A third measure of health status is the perception that the individual has of his or her physical condition. The majority of older persons view themselves as being in good health. In a 1975 survey the National Center for Health Statistics reported that 68.9 percent of the elderly they interviewed considered their health to be good or excellent, whereas only 8.6 percent rated themselves as being in poor health (Table 17.2). These figures may be a surprise because of the high incidence of chronic illnesses and impairments that afflict the elderly. But George Maddox and Elizabeth Douglass observe that good health to most people does not generally mean the complete absence of any morbid condition, but only that the illness present does not significantly interfere with physical and social functioning. They also found that older persons tend to display a realistic orientation toward evaluating their health status, and that their evaluation coincides with their physician's health assessment, in two out of three cases.[16]

Table 17.2 shows that more than twice as many persons in the low-income level (12.2 percent) rated themselves in poor health as those in the higher income levels (5.8 percent) did. In addition, 16.3 percent of the minority elderly considered their health poor, compared to 7.8 percent of the whites in the survey. The fact that minority group members tend to view their health as poorer than that of elderly whites is noted in other studies.[17]

Table 17.2   Self-assessment of health status for persons 65 years and over, by selected demographic characteristics, 1975

Demographic characteristic	Health status			
	Excellent	Good	Fair	Poor
Sex and age				
Male	28.1%	40.0%	21.4%	9.4%
65–74 years	28.5	39.8	21.5	9.3
75 years and over	27.5	40.3	21.3	9.8
Female	28.9	40.6	21.6	8.0
65–74 years	29.2	41.4	21.5	7.2
75 years and over	28.6	39.3	21.8	9.4
Race				
White	29.4	40.8	21.0	7.8
All other	20.6	35.5	26.7	16.3
Family income				
Less than $5,000	23.3	38.7	24.9	12.2
$5,000–$9,999	29.8	41.3	21.4	6.8
$10,000–$14,999	31.6	42.7	19.9	5.1
$15,000 or more	38.7	40.3	13.9	5.8
Total	28.6	40.3	21.5	8.6

SOURCE: Adapted from U.S. Department of Health, Education, and Welfare, National Center for Health Statistics, *Health, United States, 1976–1977*, U.S. Government Printing Office, Washington, D.C., 1977, p. 12.

Major Types of Health Care

Ambulatory Care

Despite the greater incidence of chronic conditions and impairments among persons 65 and over, they visit a physician only one-third more times than persons under 65. Older persons had on the average of 6.9 visits per year in 1976, compared to 4.7 visits for those younger.[18] Overall, the average number of physician contacts per year have remained much the same for the elderly since the advent of Medicare. But Medicare has been responsible for some shifts within the elderly population: the number of physician contacts per person has decreased for the elderly nonpoor and increased for the poor. As a result, the gap between the two groups' rates of physician utilization is narrowing.[19]

The majority of older persons view themselves as being in good health in comparison with other persons their age, and function well despite one or more chronic conditions. (Courtesy of Tennessee Commission on Aging)

Between 1950 and 1974 the number of physicians in the United States increased by nearly 70 percent, and the ratio of physicians to population increased by 22 percent.[20] While the physician-population ratio has been improving steadily, the uneven geographical distribution of physician manpower continues to be a growing problem, especially for older people. Younger physicians are less likely to set up their practice in older central city neighborhoods, smaller communities, and rural areas, the very places with high proportions of elderly persons. The problem is further aggravated by the lack of mobility of many older people.

Oldest Physician

The oldest doctor to continue practice is Frederick Walter Whitney Dawson. He received his license in London, England, on January 1, 1901. He was still practicing in New Zealand in April, 1975, in his 99th year.

SOURCE: *Guinness Book of World Records*, Sterling, New York, 1978, p. 379.

Physicians tend to give low priority to the needs of older people for two reasons. The first reason is the misconception that being sick is a necessary part of being old. But some elderly also believe that symptoms of illness are normal and inevitable results of aging and do not seek help. A study done by the University of Illinois of 900 elderly persons who were homebound revealed that many of them were too ill even to walk to the door.[21] They had gone for months without seeking medical aid, and thought that because they were old, they were supposed to be sick. Because older people are expected to be ill, physicians tend to write off symptoms as "normal" in an elderly person. Patients may complain of feeling ill and of being confused and disoriented, and physicians often assure them that such behavior is to be expected with advanced years, instead of probing deeper for causes of symptoms. Thus, routinely treatable illnesses, such as heart attacks, viral infections, and even appendicitis, may go undiagnosed. Older patients are continually told, "What do you expect for a person of your age?" A story is told of an elderly woman who went to her physician complaining of not feeling well. The doctor said, "You must remember that you're not getting any younger." "I know that, doctor," she replied, "I just want to keep getting older."

The second reason why physicians give low priority to the needs of the elderly relates to their medical training, which focuses primarily on acute illnesses. Physicians often see positive, sometimes dramatic results in the treatment of younger patients with acute illnesses, and derive reward and satisfaction in curing them. By contrast, older people suffer from chronic illnesses with no known medical cure, a situation particularly frustrating and depressing to many physicians. Unable to heal the older patients, the physician can only help them adapt to their situation.

Geriatric medicine has received little or no attention in American medical schools, creating great gaps in physicians' knowledge about treating older people. In a 1976 survey conducted by a congressional committee, questionnaires were sent to all 104 of the country's medical

"Honest, Doc – if I'd known I was gonna live
this long, I'd have taken better care of myself..."

schools. Only 10 schools indicated that they had or were planning to include geriatrics as a specialty area.[22]

Hospital Care

Older persons have about twice as many hospital stays as younger persons and their stays last almost twice as long. In 1974, persons aged 65 to 74 spent, on the average, 3.3 days per year in a short-stay hospital; for those aged 75 and over, the average was 5.6 days.[23] Among those hospitalized during 1976, the average length of stay for older persons was 11.6 days, compared to 6.9 days for those under 65.[24]

Men are more likely to be hospitalized than women, starting at the age of 55 and continuing through the older years. There seems to be no apparent explanation for this trend. Higher death rates are not a reason, as death rates are higher for men at every age. Nor does it seem to be related to delaying hospital care until after retirement, because the hospital rate for men continues high even ten years after the usual retirement age.[25]

Since the implementation of Medicare, the proportion of older persons admitted to hospitals has steadily increased. Though elderly persons are more likely to be hospitalized today than a decade ago, once in the hospital they do not stay as long. The greatest increase in short-stay hospital care has been among the elderly poor, who because of Medicare are now able to afford in-patient hospital care.

Many older people who do not have a regular doctor and whose income is limited rely on the emergency rooms of voluntary, nonprofit, and public hospitals when they become ill. Some strategies used by these hospitals to deal with the elderly include:

1. *The emergency-room hustle.* This is primarily a technique to avoid dealing with the problems of the older person. The doctor gives the patient a cursory examination, decides nothing is wrong and the patient is told to go home and to return at another time.

2. *The transfer.* Voluntary hospitals may refuse care to elderly people. They often transfer them to overloaded and under-financed public hospitals.

3. *The shuttle.* This is a variation of the transfer tactic. Patients are moved from one place to another until a hospital breaks down and admits them. Sometimes patients die in the ambulance.[26]

Nursing Home Care

Another widely held misconception about older people is that a large percentage of them require institutional care. But only 4 to 5 percent of persons 65 and over (about 1 million) are in nursing homes. A much larger proportion (26 percent), however, will enter such an institution at sometime during their lives. The average patient in a nursing home is 82, female, white, and alone (Table 17.3). Of the 23,000 nursing homes in the United States, three-fourths are comparatively small, with fewer than 100 beds.

The greatest impetus to the creation of nursing homes in the United States was the passage of the Social Security Act in 1935. Prior to that time, the number of facilities for the aged were few in number. The majority of the aged who could not provide for themselves and had no family who could help them generally lived in county almshouses, popularly referred to as the "poor farm" or "poor house."

After the enactment of social security, the number of facilities run for profit to serve the newly monied aged population grew rapidly. Most of these early accommodations were organized as small, private boarding homes. At that time, recipients of the federal-state program of Old Age Assistance (OAA) were considered ineligible to collect monthly benefits

Table 17.3 A profile of America's one million nursing home patients

They are old:	Average age 82; 70% are over 70.
Most are female:	Women outnumber men 3 to 1.
Most are widowed:	Only 10% have a living spouse. Widowed, 63%; never married, 22%; divorced, 5%.
They are alone:	More than 50% have no close relatives.
They are white:	Whites, 96%; blacks, 2%; others, 2%.
They come from home:	Some 31% came from hospitals; 13% from other nursing homes; the remainder from their own homes.
Length of stay:	An average of 2.4 years.
Few can walk:	Less than 50% are ambulatory.
They are disabled:	At least 55% are mentally impaired; 33% are incontinent.
They take many drugs:	Average 4.2 drugs each day.
Few have visitors:	More than 60% have no visitors at all.
Few will leave:	Only 20% will return home. Some will be transferred to hospitals, but the vast majority will die in the nursing home.

SOURCE: Frank E. Moss and Val J. Halamandaris, *Too Old, Too Sick, Too Bad*, Aspen Systems Corporation, Germantown, Md., 1977, p. 8.

if they lived in a public institution.* Thousands of these residents moved into private boarding homes. With the passage of time, these homes began to hire nurses and to call themselves "nursing homes." Most states began licensing these facilities by the mid-1950s.

The passage of the Medicare Bill in 1965 gave nursing homes their biggest boost. The bill provided for federal reimbursement of all reasonable costs incurred by patients who qualified for rehabilitation or skilled nursing home services; it also provided, through Medicaid, for nursing home care for those with limited assets. This modification in the health care financing system, together with the increasing demand for beds as the aging population increased, accounts for most of the current boom in nursing homes. Since 1960, nursing homes have grown from a $500 million industry to one of about $15 billion in 1979 (Figure 17.1).

*The law was changed in 1950 to allow persons in public institutions to collect OAA benefits.

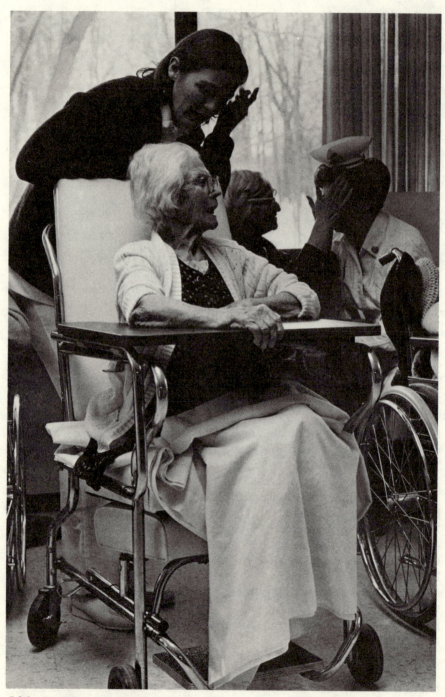

Of the 23,000 nursing homes in the United States, many are poorly staffed and do not meet adequate standards, but a number of homes like this one are well run and provide excellent care for their patients. (*Leslie Starobin*)

Figure 17.1 Estimated gains in number of U.S. nursing homes, beds, employees, and expenditures for care, contrasted with the increase in the number of older Americans, by percent, 1960–1976

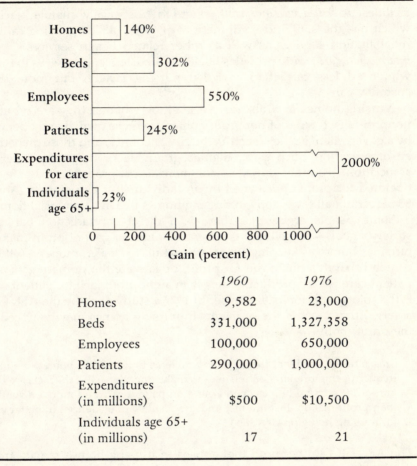

	1960	*1976*
Homes	9,582	23,000
Beds	331,000	1,327,358
Employees	100,000	650,000
Patients	290,000	1,000,000
Expenditures (in millions)	$500	$10,500
Individuals age 65+ (in millions)	17	21

Source: Frank E. Moss and Val J. Halamandaris, *Too Old, Too Sick, Too Bad*, Aspen Systems Corporation, Germantown, Md., 1977, p. 7.

TYPES OF FACILITIES   Homes for the aged should be distinguished from nursing homes. Homes for the aged are nonprofit institutions, usually sponsored by churches or fraternal organizations, and are designed for people who are physically well, but socially dependent. In the event of serious illness, persons are often transferred to nursing homes. In recent years, some homes for the aged have added medical facilities for their residents.

The term *nursing home* refers to many different kinds of facilities with a wide range of functions. Generally, a *nursing home* is any facility that gives some level of nursing care.[27] When classified by levels of care designated by the Medicare and Medicaid programs, nursing homes fall into two categories: skilled nursing facilities and intermediate care facilities. A *skilled nursing facility* refers to "a specially qualified facility which has the staff and equipment to provide skilled nursing care or rehabilitation services as well as other related health services."[28] An *intermediate care facility* provides health-related care and services to those who need less care than a skilled nursing facility, but more than custodial care.*

Nursing homes may also be classified by whether they are profit or nonprofit. Two types of nonprofit homes are those owned and operated by a government agency, such as the city or county, and those owned by an organization, such as a religious group, labor union, or fraternal association. Another type, a commercial or proprietary home, is operated for profit and owned by an individual or corporation. About 80 percent of all the elderly in nursing homes live in commercial homes.

Some people argue that there is a direct contradiction between society's goal — rehabilitating patients — and the goal of profit-making nursing homes — keeping their beds full to make money. Others contend that in a home run for profit, dollars are the primary goal and patient care is a by-product, whereas in a nonprofit facility, patient care is the sole reason for its existence. In 1977 a study done by the AFL-CIO asserted that most of the problems in nursing homes may be traced to the profit motive.

> This is not to state that there are no problems in non-profit homes, the most frequent being pressure on relatives to make donations. But the facts are that non-profit nursing homes spend more on patient care and more on staffing than profit-making institutions, and the results are evidenced in better care for nursing home residents.[29]

The AFL-CIO study found that abuses in nursing homes ranged from deaths due to injury or neglect to profiteering, bribes, poor food, unsanitary conditions, and violations of the fire safety codes.

PROBLEMS OF POOR CARE AND ABUSE   In recent years, one account after another has continued to reveal negligence and mistreatment of nursing home patients. For example, in Houston an elderly woman was so neglected that her death was not discovered until rigor mortis had set in. Another woman had to be hospitalized because of rat bites.[30] A witness

---

*Prior to the 1972 Social Security Amendments, the term *extended care facility* was used to denote a rehabilitative institution that helped the patient bridge the gap from hospital to home. Since then, this type of care is now included in a skilled nursing facility.

in Iowa testified: "I know that these people go hungry. I know that they lie there day after day in their own filth. I know that they have their mouths taped shut with adhesive tape — because they dared to ask for a bedpan at 2 o'clock in the afternoon, while the aides played cards."[31]

Such exposés of neglect and abuse have resulted in some major improvements in nursing homes in the last few years. It should also be noted that though many nursing homes fall far below the standards necessary to assure the physical and social well-being of their patients, some homes do their best to provide high quality care.

Much criticism of nursing homes concerns their inadequate medical care. Butler points out:

> Many states do not even require a principal physician, let alone a medical director, for a nursing home, and when they do there is no assurance that the physician regards himself as responsible for the patients. Doctors seldom conduct rounds. . . . Family doctors tend not to visit patients in nursing homes if they are too far away. Other doctors do "gang visits," seeing a number of patients quickly.[32]

Despite their name, nurses are scarce in nursing homes. Currently, approximately 65,000 registered nurses, divided into three shifts a day, care for about a million patients. The poor image that nursing homes have do not attract registered nurses. Those employed in these facilities are often overburdened with administrative duties and awesome responsibilities. Working conditions are often poor and wages are low. A similar situation applies to the 45,000 licensed practical nurses who work in these institutions. Because of this, 80 to 90 percent of the care in nursing homes is left in the hands of untrained aides and orderlies, who are paid minimum wages. Their turnover rate is exceedingly high, reaching about 75 percent a year. Most problems of poor care and abuse in nursing homes stem from their almost total dependence on untrained personnel.[33]

Drug abuse is another problem in nursing homes. Frank Moss and Val Halamandaris report the following situation:

> It has been charged that as much as 40 to 50 per cent of nursing home drugs may be administered in error. . . . Moreover, there is . . . abundant evidence of adverse reactions and death resulting from carelessly administered drugs. . . . The flow of drugs through America's 23,000 nursing homes is almost totally without controls. It is haphazard. It is inefficient. . . . In short, the use of drugs in a nursing home has become a kind of pharmaceutical Russian roulette.[34]

Tranquilizers account for one-fifth of all the drugs supplied to nursing homes. Many nursing homes give their patients tranquilizers to make them more manageable and to minimize work for the staff.

Health Care Costs

Health costs in this country are a major problem for all age groups. The elderly have been most severely affected because of their higher risks of illness and disability, as well as the special services and facilities that they require. Per capita health care expenditures for persons under age 65 in 1977 rose to $514, while for persons age 65 and over, the rate was three and a half times that amount, or $1,745. Hospital care accounts for the largest proportion of health care costs for the elderly (44 percent), followed by 26 percent for nursing home care, and 17 percent for physicians' services.[35]

Medicare payments are handled by private insurance organizations under contract with the government. Under Medicare, older persons pay a certain amount or a share of their medical costs. Medicare has two parts: Part A, hospital insurance, and Part B, medical insurance. Medicare's hospital insurance helps pay for hospital care, for care in a skilled nursing facility after a hospital stay, and for home health care. The second part of Medicare, medical insurance, helps pay for doctors' services, outpatient hospital care, and a number of other items not covered under Part A. Among the services and supplies that Medicare does not pay for are prescription drugs, dental services, eye glasses, hearing aids, and long-term care in a nursing home.[36]

Medicaid, a federal-state program, is administered by the Department of Health, Education, and Welfare. The government pays between 50 to 78 percent of the costs incurred by the states. Those persons who cannot pay their part of the costs of services covered under Medicare or for other health care expenses are eligible for help from the Medicaid program. Presently, the largest share of Medicaid funds (39 percent) pays for nursing home care.

In 1977, $18.3 billion was spent for Medicare. Even with this huge expenditure, it still failed to provide adequate medical coverage and protection for older people. Fifty-six percent of the health care needs of older people were paid out of their own pockets or through private insurance, Medicare covering only 44 percent. When Medicare's premiums and cost-sharing amounts are deducted, Medicare actually only paid for 41 percent of the health care expenditures of older people in 1977.[37]

In addition, Medicare does not protect the incomes of older people. Most elderly are plagued by the fear that they will lose their life savings if they are confined in a nursing home. Today the average cost of staying in a nursing home is $800 per month, a tremendous financial burden for most persons. Only after persons have depleted all their financial assets will Medicaid assume the cost of nursing home care. Medicare is geared toward short-term acute illnesses and makes no provision for diseases and disabilities that require long-term care, completely ignoring the greatest medical problem of the elderly.

Both Medicare and Medicaid programs have been partly responsible for the rampant inflation in health care costs, especially in hospital costs and nursing home care. Hospital rooms that cost $15 a day 25 years ago are now over $176. Since 1960, expenditures for hospital care have risen by almost 552 percent, while expenditures for nursing home care have increased by 2,108 percent.[38] These inflated rates have imposed a heavy burden on the very population that the programs were originally intended to help. Premiums and cost-sharing amounts under Medicare have continued to increase. The gaps have widened between items and services covered by Medicare and those to be paid out-of-pocket. Robert Butler and Myrna Lewis note: "Ironically, the out-of-pocket cost of medical care has actually risen for older people since the introduction of Medicare because of increases in physicians' fees, hospital costs, and the general inflationary spiral."[39] In 1966, the direct out-of-pocket health costs on a per capita basis were $237 for those 65 and over, and by 1977, they had reached $463 (Table 17.4).

Finally, fraud and abuse have been prevalent in both the Medicare and Medicaid programs. The submission of false claims and the acceptance of kickbacks are two of the more common schemes. In 1977 the Medicare-Medicaid Anti-Fraud and Abuse Amendments were signed into law; they were designed to strengthen penalties for persons convicted of program-related violations and to identify and prosecute

Table 17.4 Per capita expenditures for personal health care, by source of payment and age, 1966 and 1977

Age and year	Total cost[a]	Direct out-of-pocket cost	Total paid by other sources	Govern-ment	Private health insurance	Philan-thropy & industry
Under 65						
1966	$ 155	$ 79	$ 76	$ 30	$ 42	$ 3
1977	514	164	350	150	187	13
65 and over						
1966	445	237	209	133	71	5
1977	1,745	463	1,282	1,169	101	13

[a]Costs may not add to total shown because of rounding.
SOURCE: U.S. Senate, *Developments in Aging: 1978*, A Report of the Special Committee on Aging, U.S. Government Printing Office, Washington, D.C., 1979, p. xx.

cases involving fraudulent and abusive practices. The legislation made the defrauding of Medicare and Medicaid a felony instead of a misdemeanor.[40]

Summary

1. Illness is a social as well as a physical phenomenon. The social definition of illness has varied in different places and at different times. Illness exacts a high price from society in terms of lost productivity and the cost of maintaining health care services.

2. Death rates for the elderly have been steadily declining. Females have had a consistently lower death rate and a higher life expectancy than males. The gap between the two sexes in death rates and life expectancy have considerably widened in recent years in favor of females. The leading causes of death among the older population in the United States are heart disease, stroke, and cancer. The rates for heart disease and stroke have declined in the last decade, while they have increased for cancer.

3. Older people have fewer acute illnesses than younger people do. Acute illnesses generally involve disability of a short-term nature and are measured by time lost from work and disability days. Older workers lose less time from their jobs because of illness than younger workers do, whereas days of restricted activity and days spent in bed are twice as high for the elderly as for their younger counterparts.

4. Chronic illnesses are the major health problem of older people. Unlike acute illnesses, they have no known medical cures. Over 80 percent of the elderly have one or more chronic conditions, but about half of these persons suffer no limitation of activity. The two major causes of activity limitation among older people are heart disease and arthritis or rheumatism.

5. In a 1975 survey, nearly 70 percent of persons 65 and over reported that their health was good or excellent. More than twice as many persons in the low income group as those in the upper income levels considered their health to be poor. Minority group elderly view their health as being poorer than elderly whites do. Most older persons are able to realistically evaluate their own health status, and their assessments tend to coincide with those of their physicians.

6. Older people see their physicians about one-third more often than do younger persons. Between 1950 and 1974 the physician-population ratio improved, but the uneven geographical distribution of physician manpower is still a problem. The needs of the elderly are given low priority by physicians for two major reasons: (1) many physicians write off symptoms of illness in older persons as untreatable, and (2) physicians find it more rewarding to treat acute illnesses that can be cured than to treat the chronic illnesses that afflict older people.

7. The number of days spent in a hospital increases with age. In 1976, the average length of a hospital stay was nearly 5 days longer for older persons than for younger persons. Older men are more likely to be hospitalized than older

women. Although more elderly are hospitalized today than a decade ago, the length of stay in the hospital has shortened.

8. About a million older persons are in the nation's 23,000 nursing homes. The development of nursing homes in this country can be traced back to the Social Security Act of 1935. The passage of the Medicare Bill in 1965 along with the growth of the older population are mainly responsible for the current nursing home boom. Nursing homes may be classified into two broad categories: the skilled nursing home with high level care and rehabilitation services, and the intermediate nursing facility, which lies between a skilled nursing home and a custodial care facility. Eighty percent of all nursing homes in this country are profit-making enterprises. Some argue that the profit motive directly contradicts the best interests of the nursing home patient. Accounts in recent years have revealed neglect and abuse of nursing home patients. Many problems stem from the lack of doctors and nurses on nursing home staffs. Most patient care is left to untrained orderlies and aides.

9. Health care costs are three and a half times higher for persons 65 and over than they are for younger persons. Under Medicare, older persons pay a certain amount of their medical expenses. Those who cannot pay this amount are eligible for Medicaid, a federal-state program. In 1977, Medicare covered only 44 percent of the health care costs of the elderly. Since the initiation of Medicare and Medicaid, the elderly now spend more in out-of-pocket payments for health care than they did before.

Notes

1. William Caudill, "Applied Anthropology in Medicine," in *Anthropology Today*, ed. A. L. Kroeber, The University of Chicago, Chicago, 1953, p. 780.

2. Talcott Parsons, *The Social System*, Free Press, Glencoe, Ill., 1951, p. 436.

3. U.S. Senate, *Developments in Aging: 1978*, A Report of the Special Committee on Aging, U.S. Government Printing Office, Washington, D.C., 1979, p. xix.

4. Louis Harris and Associates, *The Myth and Reality of Aging in America*, The National Council on the Aging, Washington, D.C., 1975, p. 19.

5. U.S. Senate, *Developments in Aging: 1978*, p. xxi.

6. U.S. Department of Health, Education, and Welfare, National Center for Health Statistics, *Health, United States, 1976–1977*, U.S. Government Printing Office, Washington, D.C., 1977, p. 5.

7. U.S. Senate, *Developments in Aging: 1978*, p. xxi.

8. U.S. Department of Health, Education, and Welfare, *Health, United States, 1976–1977*, pp. 7–8.

9. Ethel Shanas and George Maddox, "Aging, Health, and Health Resources," in *Handbook of Aging and the Social Sciences*, eds. Robert H. Binstock and Ethel Shanas, Van Nostrand Reinhold, New York, 1976, p. 604.

10. *Fact Book on Aging: A Profile of America's Older Population*, The National Council on the Aging, Washington, D.C., 1978, p. 119.

11. National Center for Health Statistics, *Health in the Later Years of Life: Data from the National Center for Health Statistics*, U.S. Government Printing Office, Washington, D.C., 1971, p. 17.

12. U.S. Department of Health, Education, and Welfare, *Health, United States, 1976–1977*, p. 10.

13. Ibid., p. 11.

14. Ibid.

15. Ibid.

16. George Maddox and Elizabeth Douglass, "Self-Assessment of Health: A Longitudinal Study of Elderly Subjects," *Journal of Health and Social Behavior*, 14, no. 1 (1973), 87–93.

17. For example, see Vern L. Bengtson, Patricia Kasschan, and Pauline Ragan, "The Impact of Social Structure on Aging Individuals," in *Handbook of the Psychology of Aging*, eds. James H. Birren and K. Warner Schaie, Van Nostrand Reinhold, New York, 1977, p. 340.

18. U.S. Department of Health, Education, and Welfare, *Facts About Older Americans, 1978*, U.S. Government Printing Office, Washington, D.C., 1979, unpaged.

19. U.S. Department of Health, Education, and Welfare, *Health, United States, 1976–1977*, p. 14.

20. Ibid., p. 301.

21. *Time*, August 3, 1970, p. 51.

22. Frank E. Moss and Val J. Halamandaris, *Too Old, Too Sick, Too Bad*, Aspen Systems Corporation, Germantown, Md., 1977, p. 174.

23. U.S. Senate, *Developments in Aging: 1978*, p. xxi.

24. U.S. Department of Health, Education, and Welfare, *Facts About Older Americans*, 1978.

25. U.S. Department of Health, Education, and Welfare, *Health, United States, 1976–1977*, p. 17.

26. Robert N. Butler, *Why Survive? Being Old in America*, Harper & Row, New York, 1975, pp. 188–189.

27. U.S. Department of Health, Education, and Welfare, *Health, United States, 1976–1977*, p. 292.

28. U.S. Department of Health, Education, and Welfare, *Your Medicare Handbook*, U.S. Government Printing Office, Washington, D.C., 1979, p. 17.

29. U.S. Senate, *Developments in Aging: 1977*, A Report of the Special Committee on Aging, U.S. Government Printing Office, Washington, D.C., 1978, p. 87.

30. *U.S. News and World Report*, April 24, 1978, p. 56.

31. Moss and Halamandaris, *Too Old, Too Sick, Too Bad*, pp. 25–26.

32. Butler, *Why Survive? Being Old in America*, p. 264.

33. Moss and Halamandaris, *Too Old, Too Sick, Too Bad*, pp. 185–191.

34. Ibid., p. 39.

35. U.S. Senate, *Developments in Aging: 1978*, p. xix.

36. U.S. Department of Health, Education, and Welfare, *Your Medicare Handbook*, U.S. Government Printing Office, Washington, D.C., 1979, pp. 5, 42–43.

37. U.S. Senate, *Developments in Aging: 1978*, p. 42.

38. Ibid., pp. 53–54.

39. Robert N. Butler and Myrna I. Lewis, *Aging and Mental Health*, C. V. Mosby, St. Louis, 1977, p. 144.

40. U.S. Senate, *Developments in Aging: 1977*, pp. 80–82.

For Further Study

Butler, Robert N. *Why Survive? Being Old in America*. Harper & Row, New York, 1975. Chapters 7 and 9 give a highly readable account of the problems encountered by the elderly in securing medical services and long-term nursing care.

Chinn, Austin, Edwin Colby, and Edith G. Robins. *Physical and Mental Health*. 1971 White House Conference on Aging, Background and Issues. U.S. Government Printing Office, Washington, D.C., 1971. Part One of this paper deals with health needs of the elderly and the current programs designed to meet them.

Gubrium, Jaber F. *Living and Dying at Murray Manor*. St. Martin's Press, New York, 1975. A participant observation study of a nonprofit church-related nursing home.

Kalish, Richard A. *The Later Years, Social Applications of Gerontology*. Brooks/Cole, Monterey, Calif., 1977. Chapters 5 and 7 contain materials from a variety of sources that focus on health, illness, and health services.

Kart, Cary S., Eileen S. Metress, and James F. Metress. *Aging and Health*. Addison-Wesley, Menlo Park, Calif., 1978. An introductory text on the basic health concerns of older people with an emphasis on the biological aspects of aging.

Mendelson, Mary Adelaide. *Tender Loving Greed*. Alfred A. Knopf, New York, 1974. An exposé of the conditions that exist in the American nursing home industry.

Shanas, Ethel, and George L. Maddox. "Aging, Health, and Organization of Health Resources." In *Handbook of Aging and the Social Sciences*, edited by Robert H. Binstock and Ethel Shanas, Van Nostrand Reinhold, New York, 1976, pp. 592–618. A comprehensive article on some important social concerns regarding health care for the elderly.

18

Housing and Transportation for the Elderly

Because the elderly spend an increasingly larger proportion of their time at home, housing plays an important role in their lives. Their living environment includes not only the housing unit in which they live, but other aspects, such as shopping facilities, medical services, and transportation. In fact, a very important element in the living environment of an older person is the availability of adequate transportation. The value of good transportation may even outweigh the quality of the living unit itself. For an elderly person who does not drive, a home or an apartment may become a virtual prison if transportation is inaccessible.

Both housing and transportation then can have a decided impact on the quality of life and the lifestyles of elderly persons. Although there is a growing commitment to provide adequate housing and transportation for the elderly, these items remain major problems for them. In this chapter, after reviewing types of housing in which older people live, we will look at the major federal programs that assist the elderly in their housing needs. Then we will examine the sources of the transportation problem and the government's response to the problem.

Types of Housing

Almost a third of the elderly live in substandard, deteriorating, and dilapidated housing.[1] Many elderly not only cannot afford better housing, but find that there is insufficient housing available to them. Much that is available is not adequate for their needs.

> The housing situation — which was acute at the time of the White House Conference on aging in 1971 — has now become critical. Three years of a housing moratorium — coupled with rampant inflation — have made decent, safe, sanitary housing at manageable rental costs unavailable to a growing number of elderly persons in this country.[2]

As it is for other age groups in the population, the housing accommodations of the elderly cover a wide spectrum. We have previously discussed the retirement community as an option for older people.

Other options and types of housing include home ownership, living in an apartment or mobile home, and single-room occupancy.

Home Ownership

About 7 of every 10 elderly persons who are heads of households own their homes.[3] For most elderly people, their home is their major asset. The median value of homes owned by older people was $25,300 in 1976, compared to $34,000 for homes owned by younger persons.[4] Because homes owned by older people were usually purchased when they were younger, the dwellings are generally older, in older neighborhoods, and more likely to be substandard than the homes owned by younger adults. Nearly 5 million older people own houses that are more than 37 years old.[5] Some older people are "overhoused" in terms of room and square footage since their children have left home. They often prefer to remain in their own homes amid familiar surroundings, despite the fact that large, older homes are often expensive and difficult to maintain.

In the period between 1970 to 1976, property taxes rose by 47 percent. Property taxes are called regressive taxes because they are based not on ability to pay but rather on the property's value. As a result, older persons must pay a disproportionately large percentage of their often low income for taxes. For example, the typical urban home owner spends about 3.4 percent of his or her income on property taxes, whereas the elderly home owner pays an average of 8.1 percent. It has been estimated that older persons with incomes under $2,000 spend on an average of 15.8 percent of their incomes on property taxes. In one known case, an elderly widow with a yearly income of $1,176 paid $796, or 70 percent of her income, for property taxes.[6]

Nearly all states now have some type of property tax relief programs for older people, usually in the form of circuit-breaker programs or homestead exemptions. Circuit-breaker programs provide tax cuts or refunds when property taxes go above specified percentages of income; homestead exemptions remove a portion of property value from taxation. Despite such legislation, many older people still pay more taxes than they can afford. The financial plight of the elderly home owner has been further intensified in recent years by the rising costs of fuel. In 1976, many low-income elderly spent one-fourth of their incomes on home heating bills, and frequently costs ran even higher.[7]

Apartments

An alternative to owning a home is renting. About 30 percent of the housing units occupied by older people are rental properties.[8] Older people who rent are often unable to compete with younger persons for

Elderly renters tend to live in older, run-down apartment buildings where conveniences are few, and security is poor. (National Council on the Aging)

adequate housing. As a result, many elderly renters live in older apartment buildings located in areas of the city where rents are low and living conditions are the least desirable. Rents continue to rise as landlords shift the burden of increased taxes and maintenance onto their tenants. This inflation is especially hard on the elderly, who are already paying on the average of 35 percent of their incomes for rent, and those 75 and over, who pay as much as 48 percent.[9]

Mobile Homes

An increasingly popular housing alternative for older people, especially among working-class retirees, is mobile-home living. Mobile-home living is most frequently found in states with mild climates like Florida, Arizona, and California. The homogeneity of a mobile home park community often provides the elderly with security and companionship in addition to low-cost housing. Many parks have a restriction on the age of a mobile home (usually 5 years), to be admitted into the park. As a result, owners who want to move to another park with their over-age models often have difficulty finding one that will take them. As Sheila Johnson points out, this problem faces many older people who buy a mobile home when they retire and later on do not have enough money to replace it.

Some of these people may spend their 60s in a mobile-home park in a semi-rural, recreation area but find that in their 70s or 80s they want to move back to an urban area in order to be closer to their children or to hospital and shopping facilities. One elderly couple . . . had spent ten years in a mobile-home park near the ocean before they discovered that their mobile home was rusting due to the salt air — a problem they hadn't foreseen and which contributed to their decision to move back to the Bay Area. They spent six months looking for a park that would be willing to take them.[10]

In mobile home parks where spaces are rented, the residents are subject to rent increases by park owners. Many older people have no choice but to pay more rent because of the problems involved in moving to another park. Even if they were to find a park that would accept their older mobile home, they often can ill afford the expense of moving. Johnson observes that some older mobile home parks do cater to the elderly who cannot afford or qualify for the newer mobile home parks, but "they are often rather run-down in appearance . . . they are inhabited by retired, working-class individuals, some of them living in ancient and minuscule trailers, who are trying to remain independent on small pension or social security payments."[11]

Single-Room Occupancy

Many elderly persons live in inner-city hotels and rooming houses in which they have single-room occupancy (SROs), usually with shared or community bath and no kitchen unit. Research indicates that the elderly are present in high proportions where SROs are found. The elderly population in the center of the city may be as high as 49 percent.[12] SROs are not only limited to large cities, but are found in smaller communities as well.

The SRO population has been described as the "least visible of an invisible population."[13] The urban renewal efforts of the 1960s first brought the existence of the SRO population to the attention of the public. The demolition of many old hotels sent thousands of older residents into the streets to search for other low-rent accommodations.[14] The commercial areas and centers of the city in which SROs are found have been hardest hit by both public and private development. Phyllis Ehrlich notes that about 30 hotels in St. Louis that provided residences for the elderly have been razed since 1960:

Furthermore, the majority of the hotels in which the aged population now reside were constructed before 1910 and are approaching the point of terminal decay. The elderly manage to stay just one step ahead of the "headache ball" by going from one hotel to another as the structures become dilapidated and slated for redevelopment. . . . The downtown elderly, most with limited incomes, find themselves with fewer and fewer housing and service options.[15]

A situation that aroused much public indignation occurred in San Francisco in 1977. Forty elderly Chinese and Filipino residents were evicted from a hotel located at the edge of Chinatown because it was being torn down for commercial development. Over 330 law-enforcement officers were on the scene as 2,000 persons demonstrated against the evictions.[16]

It has been generally accepted that SROs constitute undesirable housing because many units were built for transients and are not suitable for permanent residence. Also, most of these structures are old and deteriorating. Recently, the view has been advanced that SROs help preserve and maintain a lifestyle that some older persons prefer and find advantageous. Personal security may be enhanced because people are always on the premises, sometimes including a desk clerk or custodian. Also many older persons value the security, cleanliness, and heat that a hotel or rooming house provides more than they do a private bath or kitchen unit.[17] In addition, the downtown location of the SROs allows older people to be within walking distance of nearby stores, restaurants, and cafeterias.

Federally Supported Housing Programs

A number of housing programs since the 1950s have been designed specifically for the elderly, or serve low-income families in which the elderly are well represented. Although such programs have done much to provide housing for older people, much more needs to be done.

Public Housing

Public housing began with the passage of the Housing Act of 1937, which was designed to assist low-income families. Not until 1956 was the act amended to provide public housing specifically for the elderly. Despite this act, low-cost public housing for all age groups including the elderly is in short supply. Since the beginning of the government-supported public housing program, the total number of public units constructed had only risen slightly above a million by 1976. Of these, 450,000 (44 percent) were occupied by the elderly.[18]

Public housing units for older people are a low priority item for federal spending. Rochelle Jones indicates that the elderly remain on waiting lists for public housing projects often as long as three to four years.

> In New York City, when 96 apartments were opened up, 5,000 older adults applied. In Los Angeles, applicants at federal housing projects for older adults have been told that there are waiting lists of 3,000 to 6,000 applicants. In New Jersey, state officials estimated a need for 70,000 additional apartments in low and moderate income housing projects to accommodate the number of eligible older adults by 1980. At the same time, they had no hope of meeting this goal. During the administration of Richard Nixon, funds for such projects were frozen, guaranteeing a three-to-four year backlog in housing even if the original had been adequate, which it was not.[19]

The Direct Loan Program: Section 202

Probably one of the most popular federal housing programs for the elderly has been Section 202. Authorized in 1959, it originally provided long-term loans directly from the federal government to nonprofit groups or sponsors to build housing for the elderly and handicapped. Under this program, the government made direct 3 percent loans for 50-year terms to meet total construction costs. The low interest rate was designed to make possible low and reasonable rents for the moderate- to low-income elderly. In a ten-year period, the program built 45,000 units in 330 projects.[20]

The 202 program was criticized mainly because the loans had to be appropriated by Congress and thus had a considerable impact on the national budget. The defenders of Section 202 maintained that it was still the most economical way to obtain good housing. The program was suspended in 1969 due to much opposition, only to be revived in 1974 largely due to the efforts of various groups and individuals representing the interests of the elderly. Significant changes were made in the 202 program in 1974 in order to strengthen and revitalize it: (1) providing more housing assistance to elderly persons with lower incomes than had been possible before; (2) making loans from the U.S. Treasury at the prevailing government interest rate, instead of from the national budget; and (3) raising the level of funding for the program.

The Rent Subsidy Program: Section 8

This program, which began in 1974, is currently the major federal means of housing assistance. It was developed to replace two programs, public housing and Section 236, the Interest Subsidy Program. Briefly, Section 236 encouraged private sponsors to build rental housing within the means of lower income families including the elderly. To reduce the monthly rent, the Department of Housing and Urban Development (HUD) paid all the sponsor's interest above 1 percent for the life of the mortgage. This program was not only extremely expensive for the federal government to operate, but it did not sufficiently meet the housing needs of low-income families, especially the elderly. Section 236 was suspended in 1973.

Section 8, which replaced Section 236, provides rent supplements to persons with low incomes and guarantees that assisted households will pay no more than 25 percent of their income for rent and no less than 15 percent. HUD contracts with private owners for the leasing of units to individuals and families who meet the eligibility requirements for public housing. HUD pays the difference between the fair market rent and the amount the tenant is required to pay. Under this program, eligible persons are permitted to choose their own dwellings instead of leaving the selection up to HUD or the local housing authority. They may choose from new construction or rehabilitated and existing housing of various types including apartment hotels, single-family dwellings, or multifamily structures. Section 8 housing assistance payments are also provided for eligible lower income families who live in projects financed under Section 202. The elderly have benefited more than any other age group from the Section 8 program. About 44 percent of the participants in the program are older persons.

The Transportation Problem

Being without transportation has been compared to having a modern kitchen with all the latest appliances and yet having no electricity.[21] This lack restricts one's life-space, limits contacts and activities with others, and makes goods and services difficult, if not impossible, to obtain. Lack of transportation plagues a large percentage of older people.

The transportation problems of the elderly originate mainly from these interrelated factors: (1) many older people have low incomes and cannot afford the cost of transportation; (2) the transportation system in our society is dominated by privately owned and operated automobiles; (3) physical limitations and design barriers inhibit many elderly from driving and using public transportation; and (4) many older people live in areas, both urban and rural, where transportation systems are inadequate or nonexistent.[22]

Low Income

Transportation costs are sufficiently high to represent the third largest item in the elderly family's budget after housing and food. Because of

The two most frequent forms of transportation for the elderly are public transportation and walking. (Tennessee Commission on Aging)

their low incomes and the fact that about 14 percent of the elderly live below the poverty level, the cost of public transportation is one barrier to its utilization. Public transportation fares have steadily increased in recent years; two or three separate fares are often needed for multizone trips. To ease the cost of public transportation for older people, some 145 transit systems now offer reduced fares.[23] Usually this reduction, which runs between 25 and 50 percent of the regular fare, applies to those persons 65 or over. In most cases it is offered only at nonpeak hours when optimum service has substantially tapered off. Even with reduced fares, many older persons still find transportation an expensive item on their limited budgets.

Robert Butler feels that reduced fares tend to place older persons in the position of second class citizens.[24] An example of what can happen follows: "Someone observed a bus driver say to an older woman, 'It's five of ten and you know damned well that your half fare is no good until ten o'clock so get off the bus.' The old woman shrunk a bit more and stumbled off the bus."[25] Though reduced fares are a way of compensating for the low income of the elderly, there is a question about whether financial assistance should be provided in this way. Some people argue that by guaranteeing older people a more sufficient income, they could then afford transportation at regular market prices and that reduced fares would not be necessary.

Though income is related to automobile ownership at all ages, the relationship is especially pronounced in the case of the elderly with their higher proportion of low incomes. As the costs of buying, operating, and maintaining an automobile have skyrocketed in recent years, more and more older people cannot afford a car, and many elderly have been forced to sell their cars.

Many older people who need to work to supplement their incomes cannot because of inadequate transportation. Others do so with great difficulty: "Mr. W., age 67, is trying to support himself and his wife. The only job he can get is during a split shift. The bus schedule is inadequate; he must wait an hour for a bus twice a day, making his work day intolerably long."[26]

Private Automobile Dominance

A major source of the transportation problem for older people is the dominance of the private automobile in American society. Its widespread use has resulted in extending the area of urban residence beyond the fixed routes of public transportation. Many homes and destinations today are only accessible by automobile. Furthermore, the bulk of our transportation resources are allocated to highways and to road construction, with only a small portion being earmarked for public transit systems and facilities.

The percentage of older households that own automobiles is much less than that of their younger counterparts. A 1974 Census Bureau Survey found that nearly 40 percent of older households did not own a car, compared to only 15 percent of younger households.[27] Table 18.1 shows that the percentage not owning cars remains fairly stable up until age 54, and then increases. Beginning with age 65, there is a marked drop in ownership.

Among the elderly who own cars, the amount of driving declines with age, and problems often arise with licensing and insurance. It is estimated that about 42 percent of those 65 or over have a driver's license.[28] Many states require a re-examination for licenses at specified age levels with varying renewal periods and restrictions. Automobile insurance companies discriminate against older drivers by frequently denying them coverage, cancelling their policies, or raising their insurance rates to intolerable levels.

Being without a car or access to one, a significant number of older people are limited to public transportation and walking. As the automobile has become the primary source of transportation in our society, public transportation systems have rapidly declined in numbers and scope. With fewer people riding buses, bus fares have gone up, routes have been cut back and cancelled, and hours of service have been

Table 18.1   Households not owning automobiles, by age of head, 1974

Age of household head	Percentage
Under 25 years	19.0%
25–29 years	14.1
30–34 years	12.8
35–44 years	12.4
45–54 years	13.7
55–64 years	18.0
65 years and over	39.0

SOURCE: Reprinted from *Fact Book on Aging: A Profile of America's Older Population*, The National Council on the Aging, Inc., Washington, D.C. © 1978, p. 216.

reduced. These changes, in turn, result in an even greater decline in riders. As a consequence, many public transit systems have experienced financial difficulties or have been forced to discontinue service altogether.

Walking becomes a problem in an automobile-oriented society. The smooth and rapid flow of automobile traffic takes precedence over pedestrian movements. Light signals, traffic and street signs, and the like are geared to the driver, not the pedestrian. Sidewalks, crosswalks, pedestrian routes, and pedestrian control signals are often absent. Many times traffic lights change too rapidly to allow one to walk safely across the street. All these factors contribute to a disproportionately high pedestrian accident rate among persons 65 and over. As Lewis Mumford notes: "To bring the pedestrian back into the picture, one must treat him with the respect and honor we now accord only to the automobile."[29]

In a study of the mobility patterns of 709 retired persons in San Antonio, Texas, Frances Carp found that walking was not looked on favorably as a means of transportation.[30] Only 3 percent of the respondents said walking was a satisfactory means of getting places; 53 percent said that it met their needs very poorly, while none felt it met their needs well. Carp reports that the more the retirees walked, the more negative was their evaluation. The major reasons given for the unsatisfactory evaluation of walking included: (1) most destinations were beyond walking distance, especially if packages or bundles were to be carried on the return trip; (2) fear that walking might result in an injury, such as being hit by a car, falling, or being attacked; and (3) fatigue and chronic health problems.

Transportation Barriers

The mobility problems of the elderly are further compounded by changes that generally occur with the aging process, such as a decline in sensory acuity, a loss of agility, and a slower response rate. These changes not only make driving more hazardous for the older person, but are magnified by the growing complexities of traffic conditions. Fast speeds on expressways and interstates, increased traffic and congestion, and directional signs that must be read and interpreted rapidly combine to make driving more difficult for the older person, and also force some to give up driving entirely.

> Although he may possess considerable driving experience, if declines occur in his sensory and perceptual processes and motor skills, his reaction times may be slowed, increasing the probability of an accident in demanding urban driving situations. As a result of a decline in visual acuity and peripheral vision, the elderly driver has more difficulty interpreting traffic lights and signs and in seeing cars approaching from the side. Consequently, he may have to restrict his driving to daytime hours or to less demanding traffic situations.[31]

Carp's study in San Antonio found that among the retirees surveyed, their access to automobiles was limited.[32] Only one-third of the respondents were drivers. Of these, less than half felt free to drive "anywhere." The majority had restrictions imposed either by themselves or by licensing authorities. Many had decided that they should no longer drive at night because of poor vision, others had been issued licenses for daytime driving only. A significant proportion would not drive even during daylight hours on expressways, downtown, or in new parts of town. Some only drove within their immediate neighborhoods.

Some of the factors that reduce driving ability also reduce the older person's capacity for using public transportation. High bus steps, rapidly closing doors, stiff exit doors, and poorly placed handrails constitute formidable structural barriers for the elderly. Equally difficult to cope with are long flights of stairs, turnstiles, and fast-moving escalators in subway stations (Table 18.2).

Many older persons also face psychological barriers to the use of public transit systems, such as uncertainty and the fear of getting lost. Bus and train schedules are difficult to read and interpret, signs may be confusing and illegible, and the information conveyed over a loudspeaker or by a bus driver is often inaudible even to those without hearing difficulties. Another obstacle to the elderly's use of public transportation is that many are afraid to walk between their homes and bus stops or subway stations for fear of street crime. In recent years,

Table 18.2   Travel barriers confronting the elderly and disabled

Physical barriers	*Operational barriers*

Vehicles
High step required to enter
Difficult to get into or out
  of seats
Seats not available/forced
  to stand
Difficult to reach handholds
Cannot see out for landmarks
No place to put packages
Cannot see or hear location
  information
Nonvisible signs
	Vehicles
	Frequency of service
	Driver assistance/attitude
	Acceleration/deceleration
	Information presentation
	Schedules maintenance
	Inadequate or inappropriate
	  routes
	Too many transfers

Terminals
Long stairs
Long walks
Poor fare collection facilities
Poor posting of information
Poor crowd flow design
Insufficient seating
Little interface with other
  modes
	Terminals
	Employee assistance/attitude poor
	Information clarity and
	  dissemination inadequate
	Length of stops too short
	Crowd flow nondirected
	Little or no interface with other
	  modes

Transit stops
Insufficient shelter
Platform incompatible with vehicle
Inadequate posting of information
	Transit stops
	Poor location:
	  for safety
	  for convenience
	Not enough stops
	Information displayed
	  insufficient or confusing

SOURCE: Richard K. Brail, James W. Hughes, and Carol A. Arthur, *Transportation Services for the Disabled and Elderly,* Center for Urban Policy Research, Rutgers University, New Brunswick, N.J., 1976, p. 26.

older people standing at bus stops have been prime targets for purse snatchers and robbers.

Place of Residence

Mobility is a particularly acute problem among those elderly who live in suburban and rural areas where transportation is either inadequate,

Public transportation poses many problems for older persons who have difficulty with steps or with hearing or reading location information. (Jeroboam Inc. Karen R. Preuss)

inaccessible, or unavailable. The problem is especially critical among the nation's nearly 6 million rural elderly. Older rural residents who cannot drive or can no longer afford an automobile are in a much worse transportation situation than their urban counterparts. Their isolation is greater, and their incomes generally less. As a result, necessary medical and social services are frequently inaccessible to them. In many rural areas, public transportation has completely disappeared as the bus has been replaced by the automobile. In the last 15 years, 146 bus systems have been discontinued, most of them in places of less than 25,000 population.[33] The needs of the rural elderly have received increased attention in the past few years through a series of hearings conducted by the Senate Special Committee on Aging and from practitioners in the field of aging.

Government Response to Transportation Needs

The issue of transportation for older people was not given major policy attention by the federal government until the passage of the Urban Mass Transportation Act in 1964. The act provided for long-term federal commitment to the development of new and improved transit facilities; a 1970 amendment authorized that a proportion of its funding (1.5 percent) be directed toward the special transportation needs of the elderly and handicapped. This amendment recognized for the first time that the mobility problems of the elderly and handicapped differ from those of other transit users.

> The elderly and handicapped persons have the same right as other persons to utilize mass transportation facilities and services; that special efforts shall be made in the planning and design of mass transportation facilities and services so that the availability to elderly and handicapped persons of mass transportation which they can effectively utilize will be assured; and that all Federal programs offering assistance in the field of mass transportation . . . should contain provisions implementing this policy.[34]

In an effort to aid the financial plight of the mass transit systems, the Federal-Aid Highway Act of 1973 permitted states under certain conditions to transfer funds from unwanted interstate highway systems to public transit funds. Urbanized areas also were permitted under certain conditions to use revenues from the Highway Trust Fund for mass transit improvements. Amendments to this act provided for grants and loans to private nonprofit corporations and associations to assist in providing transportation to meet the special needs of the elderly and handicapped.[35]

The National Mass Transit Act in 1974 provided for reduced transit fares for the elderly. This act stipulated that fares paid by the elderly and handicapped during off-peak hours in all projects funded by the Department of Transportation (DOT) were not to be more than one-half of those paid by general users during peak hours.

Since 1979, all new public transit buses purchased with federal assistance have been required to have barrier-free design features that will make them more accessible to elderly and handicapped persons. These new full-sized buses must have a floor height not to exceed 22 inches and must be equipped with either a ramp or a hydraulic lift for boarding.

Summary

1. Housing and transportation are major problems of the older population. Nearly a third of the elderly live in deteriorated or substandard housing, not only because they cannot afford better housing, but because there is a shortage of suitable housing to accommodate the needs of older people.

2. The majority of households headed by older persons are owner-occupied. Many of their homes are old, need extensive repair, and are increasingly expensive to maintain. Property taxes often present a financial burden to an older home owner despite tax relief programs that exist in most states. Rapidly rising fuel and energy bills in recent years have compounded the elderly home owner's plight. Many elderly renters, having lower incomes, are unable to compete with younger persons for housing; as a result, they live in deteriorating, older apartment buildings in less desirable parts of the community. Yet, older persons spend a third or more of their income for rent.

3. Mobile home living is common among working-class retirees. Mobile home communities provide their residents with safety, companionship, and inexpensive housing. When mobile homes are past five years old, however, many of the newer parks will not accept them, which makes moving difficult for many elderly mobile home owners. For some elderly, single-room occupancy in a downtown hotel or rooming house is the preferred lifestyle. This type of housing offers the advantage of having people on the premises at all times and the convenience of being within walking distance of stores and restaurants. In recent years, both public and private developers have forced the demolition of many old hotels in the center of cities, displacing large numbers of SRO residents.

4. Currently, the major federal programs for the elderly renter are public housing, the Direct Loan Program (Section 202), and Rent Subsidy program (Section 8). Public housing for the elderly is in short supply and remains a low priority item in the federal budget. Section 202, one of the most responsive government programs to the elderly's needs, was designed to make long-term, low-interest loans to nonprofit sponsors to build housing for older people. Though the program was suspended in 1969, it was reinstated in 1974. Section 8 at the present time is the major federal means of housing assistance. It provides rent supplements to low-income families and individuals. Persons eligible for this program may choose their own kind of housing and pay no more than 25 percent of their income for rent. Over 40 percent of the participants in the program are elderly persons.

5. Like housing, transportation is a critical problem for a significant percentage of older people. The transportation problems of the elderly stem from low incomes, the dominance of the private automobile, transportation barriers, and residences with no access to public transportation facilities.

6. The low income of the elderly is a major obstacle to both public and private

transportation. Even though many transit systems offer reduced fares at off-peak hours, public transportation is still expensive for many older persons. Many elderly cannot afford to maintain a car with the spiraling cost of gasoline, repairs, and insurance.

7. The dominance of the automobile is at the root of many transportation problems of older people. Many destinations can only be reached by automobile. Older households have a much lower percentage of car ownership than do younger ones. Some states require a re-examination for a driver's license after a certain age is reached. Insurance companies often discriminate against older drivers by raising their rates or cancelling their policies. The dominance of the automobile has led to the decline of public transit systems. Many systems have experienced financial difficulties due to lack of patronage and have had to discontinue service. Walking is also a problem in our automobile-oriented society, where traffic devices are geared to motor vehicles and not to pedestrians.

8. The physical changes that occur with the aging process often make driving more hazardous for the older person. The growing complexities of traffic conditions compound the problem. Many older people restrict their driving to daytime hours and to less demanding traffic situations. The aging process also imposes restrictions on the utilization of public transportation. High bus steps, rapidly closing doors, poorly placed hand rails, and the like, constitute design barriers for the elderly. Many older persons are reluctant to use public transportation for fear of getting lost or of being attacked.

9. Finally, another problem of mobility is related to the place a person lives, and is particularly acute among the rural elderly because transit systems are either inaccessible or do not exist. The isolation of the rural elderly is greater and their incomes are lower than the urban elderly. Medical and social services are often difficult, if not impossible, for them to reach.

10. Beginning with the 1970 amendment to the Mass Transportation Act, the elderly were recognized for the first time as having as much right to use the public transit system as others in the population. Special efforts have been made since that time in the planning and design of public transportation facilities to help meet the special needs of the elderly and handicapped.

Notes

1. U.S. Senate, *Developments in Aging: 1976*, A Report of the Special Committee on Aging, U.S. Government Printing Office, Washington, D.C., 1977, p. 66.

2. Ibid., p. 53.

3. Herman B. Brotman, "Every Tenth American: The Problem of Aging," in *Community Planning for an Aging Society: Designing Services and Facilities*, eds. M. Powell Lawton, Robert J. Newcomer, and Thomas O. Byerts, Dowden, Hutchinson, and Ross, Stroudsburg, Pa., 1976, p. 18.

4. U.S. Department of Health, Education, and Welfare, *Facts About Older Americans 1978*, U.S. Government Printing Office, Washington, D.C., 1979.

5. U.S. Senate, *Developments in Aging: 1976*, p. 53.

6. Ibid., pp. 53–54.

7. U.S. Senate, *Developments in Aging: 1977*, A Report of the Special Committee on Aging, U.S. Goverment Printing Office, Washington, D.C., 1978, p. 42.

8. *Fact Book on Aging: A Profile of America's Older Population*, The National Council on the Aging, Washington, D.C., 1978, p. 183.

9. U.S. Senate, *Developments in Aging: 1976*, p. 53.

10. Sheila K. Johnson, *Idle Haven: Community Building Among the Workingclass Retired*, University of California Press, Berkeley, 1971, p. 172.

11. Ibid., p. 173.

12. U.S. Senate, *Single Room Occupancy: A Need for National Concern*, an Information Paper, U.S. Government Printing Office, Washington, D.C., 1978, p. 3.

13. Second Conference on the SRO Elderly, St. Louis, Mo., May 15–16, 1976.

14. U.S. Senate, *Single Room Occupancy*, p. 4.

15. Phyllis Ehrlich, "A Study: Characteristics and Needs of the St. Louis Downtown SRO Elderly," in *The Invisible Elderly*, The National Council on the Aging, Washington, D.C., 1976, p. 7.

16. U.S. Senate, *Developments in Aging: 1977*, pp. 108–109.

17. U.S. Senate, *Single Room Occupancy*, p. 6.

18. U.S. Department of Housing and Urban Development, *Statistical Year Book*, U.S. Government Printing Office, Washington, D.C., 1976.

19. Rochelle Jones, *The Other Generation: The New Power of Older People*, © 1977, p. 154. Reprinted by permission of Prentice-Hall, Inc., Englewood Cliffs, New Jersey.

20. U.S. Senate, *Developments in Aging: 1974 and January–April, 1975*, A Report of the Special Committee on Aging, U.S. Government Printing Office, Washington, D.C., 1975, p. 71.

21. U.S. Senate, *Developments in Aging: 1974 and January–April, 1975*, p. 110.

22. Joseph S. Revis, *Transportation*, 1971 White House Conference on Aging, Background and Issues, U.S. Government Printing Office, Washington, D.C., 1971, p. 1.

23. Joseph S. Revis, *Transportation for Older Americans: A State of the Art Report*, Administration on Aging, U.S. Government Printing Office, Washington, D.C., 1975, p. 143.

24. Robert N. Butler, *Why Survive? Being Old in America*, Harper & Row, New York, 1975, p. 151.

25. Marjorie B. Tiven, "Transportation and Mobility," in *Older Americans: Special Handling Required*, The National Council on the Aging, Washington, D.C., 1971.

26. *The Golden Years — A Tarnished Myth* (Project Find), The National Council on the Aging, New York, 1970, p. 86.

27. U.S. Senate, *Developments in Aging: 1977*, p. xxiii.

28. *Fact Book on Aging: A Profile of America's Older Population*, p. 217.

29. Lewis Mumford, "The Highway and the City," in *The Environmental Handbook*, ed. G. DeBell, Ballantine Books, New York, 1970.

30. Frances M. Carp. "Walking as a Means of Transportation for Retired People," *The Gerontologist*, 2, no. 2 (1971), Pt. 1, 104–111.

31. Stephen M. Golant, "Intraurban Transportation Needs and Problems of the Elderly," in *Community Planning for an Aging Society: Designing Services and Facilities*, eds. M. Powell Lawton, Robert J. Newcomer, and Thomas O. Byerts, Dowden, Hutchinson and Ross, Stroudsburg, Pa., 1976, p. 298.

32. Frances M. Carp, "The Mobility of Retired People," in *Transportation and Aging: Selected Issues*, eds. Edmund J. Cantilli and June L. Shmelzer, U.S. Government Printing Office, Washington, D.C., 1970, p. 35.

33. *Fact Book on Aging: A Profile of America's Older Population*, p. 228.

34. U.S. Senate, *Developments in Aging: 1976*, p. 95.

35. Golant, "Intraurban Transportation Needs and Problems of the Elderly," p. 299.

For Further Study

Carp, Frances M. "The Mobility of Retired People." In *Transportation and Aging: Selected Issues*, edited by Edmund J. Cantilli and June L. Shmelzer. U.S. Government Printing Office, Washington, D.C., 1970, pp. 23–41. A good synthesis of the transportation requirements and needs of older people.

———. "Housing and Living Environments of Older People." In *Handbook of Aging and the Social Sciences*, edited by Robert H. Binstock and Ethel Shanas. Van Nostrand Reinhold, New York, 1976, pp. 244–271. An excellent overview of the studies on housing for the elderly.

Donahue, Wilma T., Marie M. Thompson, and D. J. Curren. *Congregate Housing for Older People*. Administration on Aging, Washington, D.C., 1977. A selection of papers from the First National Conference on Congregate Housing for Older People.

Lawton, M. Powell, Robert J. Newcomer, and Thomas O. Byerts. *Community Planning for an Aging Society: Designing Services and Facilities*. Dowden, Hutchinson and Ross, Stroudsburg, Pa., 1976. A collection of articles that includes some issues involved in planning for housing and transportation for the elderly.

Revis, Joseph S. *Transportation*, 1971 White House Conference on Aging, Background and Issues. U.S. Government Printing Office, Washington, D.C., 1971. A good discussion of the transportation needs and problems of the elderly.

———. *Transportation for Older Americans: A State of the Art Report*. Administration on Aging, U.S. Government Printing Office, Washington, D.C., 1975. A comprehensive report of the transportation demands and needs of the elderly. It surveys the developments in public transportation, special systems, and personal transit.

Robbins, Ira S. *Housing the Elderly*. 1971 White House Conference on Aging, Background and Issues, U.S. Government Printing Office, Washington, D.C., 1971. Discusses the necessity for housing and housing programs suited to the special needs of the elderly.

Stephens, Joyce. *Loners, Losers, and Lovers*. University of Washington Press, Seattle, 1976. A participant observation study of the elderly tenants of a single-room-occupancy hotel in the slum area of a large city.

19

Crime and the Elderly

Two boys — one 12 years old and the other 15 — were held yesterday for trial in the fatal beating of an 80-year-old Brooklyn woman. The boys said that they had beaten the woman in her apartment for her money. According to a police officer, the 12-year-old said he had ransacked the apartment and found only 25 cents under the bed.[1]

An isolated incident? Hardly. Elderly persons who live in the high-crime areas of the inner city are frequently singled out by teen-age hoodlums, who live in close proximity to them, as the easiest targets around. As a result, the elderly in these areas have high victimization rates.

The Rate of Crime Against the Elderly

Surveys conducted by the Law Enforcement Assistance Administration (LEAA) on a nationwide basis reveal that, in general, persons 65 and over have lower rates of victimization than do younger persons. This is true for each of the crime categories with the exception of "personal larceny with contact" (purse-snatching and pocket-picking). In this category, the rate of crime against the elderly is the same as for the general population (Table 19.1). Overall, then, the national statistics on crime show the rate of crime against the elderly to be low. But at the same time, older persons in some inner-city areas tend to have high rates of victimization. As Carl Cunningham explains:

> Although the aging person is somewhat less often criminally victimized, considering the population of a metropolitan area as a whole, that is not a very informative comparison. The elderly living in or near certain neighborhoods of Kansas City, Missouri, for example, can be as much as eight times more vulnerable to serious crimes such as robbery, burglary, or major larcenies than a younger resident of a relatively safe suburb who works and shops in areas with low crime rates.[2]

Table 19.1   Personal and household crimes: Victimization rates for the general and elderly populations, 1973

Type of crime	Rate for the general population	Rate for the elderly population
	Based on 1,000 persons age 12 and over	Based on 1,000 persons age 65 and over
Personal crimes		
Crimes of violence	32	8
Robbery	7	5
Robbery with injury	3	2
Robbery without injury	4	3
Assault	25	3
Aggravated assault	10	1
Simple assault	15	2
Crimes of theft	91	22
Personal larceny with contact	3	3
Personal larceny without contact	88	19
	Based on 1,000 households headed by persons age 12 and over	Based on 1,000 households headed by persons age 65 and over
Household Crimes		
Burglary	91	55
Household larceny	107	47
Motor vehicle theft	19	5

SOURCE: U.S. Senate, Special Committee on Aging, *Developments in Aging: 1977*, Part 2, A Report of the Special Committee on Aging, U.S. Government Printing Office, Washington, D.C., 1978, p. 212.

Another difficulty encountered in understanding the rate of criminal victimization against the elderly is that statistics do not accurately measure the amount of crimes against older persons. At best, they offer only a very rough estimate, for several reasons. First, many police departments do not categorize victims by age, so there is no way to distinguish the elderly victims from others. Second, an estimated one-third to one-half of the crimes against older people are not reported to the police and thus do not become crime statistics. The elderly — as well as the young — often feel it is a waste of time to try to apprehend an offender or to attempt to recover stolen property. The pursuit of justice can also be expensive for an older person on a limited income. Fear of retaliation is another factor inhibiting older persons from reporting crimes. Also, some persons are ashamed to report that they have been victimized, especially when they have fallen prey to a confidence scheme or a consumer fraud.

Only recently have the elderly begun to be recognized as a group particularly vulnerable to certain types of criminal activities. The victimization of the elderly does not appear to have been discussed at the 1961 White House Conference on Aging. By the 1971 Conference, Evelle Younger found "that there was almost no attention being given nationally . . . to the problems of crimes against the elderly, and second, that there are almost no hard data extant on the incidence of such victimization."[3] Recently, crimes against the elderly have generated much interest and a proliferation of studies.

Fear of Crime, Victimization, and Its Consequences

Fear of crime pervades the lives of many older people. In fact, the elderly fear being victimized more than any other age group does. Often this fear is much greater than the actual crime rate would suggest. Surveys reveal that the elderly view fear of crime as a major social problem. For example, in two studies conducted by the National Retired Teachers Association and the National Association of Retired Persons (NRTA-AARP) in 1972 and 1973, over 80,000 persons reported that fear of crime ranked second in their lives next to the provision of food and shelter.[4] The 1975 Harris Poll found that the elderly ranked fear of crime a "very serious problem" even above poor health and lack of money.[5]

The fear of crime greatly diminishes the quality of life for large numbers of older people and restricts their mobility. Much of this fear may come from the fact that older people are acutely aware of their vulnerability to victimization. This condition is probably best summed up in the expression, "crib jobs," used by young hoodlums to refer to the crimes they commit against the elderly. In their eyes, robbing an older person is as easy as taking the proverbial candy from a baby. The special vulnerability of the elderly to crime results from several factors:

Waiting at a bus stop often makes an older person the target for criminal victimization. (Tennessee Commission on Aging)

1. Older people have diminished physical strength and are less able to defend themselves or to escape from threatening situations. They are also less likely to defend themselves for fear of being injured. Diminished hearing and vision may also contribute to their victimization.

2. Because of low income, many older people can only afford to live in the poorer sections of the city, places where crime rates are the highest. Thus they are close to the groups most likely to victimize them — the unemployed, the drug addicts, and teen-age school dropouts.

3. Many older people live alone, which further increases their chances of victimization. Also the elderly are often unaccompanied on the streets and on public transportation.

4. Many older people are without cars and depend on either walking or public transportation. This increased exposure makes them an easy target for potential criminals.[6]

How does fear of crime among the elderly vary by sex, race, income, and size of the community? Frank Clemente and Michael Kleiman explored this relationship in a study based on national surveys conducted by the National Opinion Research Center in 1973 and 1974.[7] They found that women were more likely to admit fear of crime than men: about 70 percent of elderly females expressed fear of crime, compared to 34 percent of the elderly males. Aged blacks were more fearful of crime than aged whites; Clemente and Kleiman report that nearly 70 percent of the aged blacks were afraid to walk around in their neighborhood at night alone. Forty-seven percent of the aged whites reported that they were afraid to do so. People at higher income levels reported less fear of crime than those in the lower income brackets. Presumably, those with more income live in better neighborhoods with lower crime rates and feel less threatened. Finally, fear of crime decreases as one goes from large cities to rural areas. Three-fourths of the elderly respondents in large cities (where crime rates are highest) expressed fear of crime, compared to one-fourth of those in rural areas.

Fear of crime has profoundly affected the lives of many elderly, especially those who live in the slums of large cities. There have been reports of older persons sleeping in the daytime because they were too frightened of break-ins to sleep at night.[8] Many adapt to the threat of crime by making fortresses of their homes and apartments and going out-of-doors as little as possible. Social and recreational activities are kept to the minimum. Many refuse to go out after dark, or even after 3 or 4 o'clock in the afternoon when the children begin coming home from school; others are afraid to leave their homes or apartments at any time. An 87-year-old man who had been brutally victimized by a gang of young hoodlums now rarely goes out.[9] He depends on food delivered from a delicatessen. An elderly woman was even afraid to put out her trash:

> She stuffed it in plastic bags, which she stored in a spare room. When one room would fill up, she would seal it off and start filling up another. At times she lived on candy bars, tossing coins out of a window to children who would go to the store for her.[10]

As a result of this fear, old people — black and white alike — have become virtual prisoners in their own homes or apartments, locking themselves up in "solitary confinement."

Besides fear and anxiety, crime exacts a high toll in terms of economic and physical losses from the victimized elderly. For those living on a reduced or low income, the impact of any economic loss is greater than for the younger population with higher incomes.

> Twenty dollars stolen from an elderly person represents a much greater loss than the same amount taken from a person with a job. To the elderly, that loss may represent a week's rent or half the month's food ration. To an older

person living alone, lack of a television set often means he is deprived of a major source of contact with the outside world.[11]

Older persons are frequently victims of confidence games and other types of swindles. They sometimes lose their entire life savings in these schemes.

Elderly people are more easily and more seriously injured when attacked than younger persons are. A young person knocked down during a robbery often gets up with only a few scratches and bruises. An older person getting the same treatment might suffer a broken hip or leg, which takes much longer to heal and could result in permanent disability requiring institutionalization.

Older persons are victimized by the same crimes as the general population. But the rates of their victimization vary with different types of crimes. In the following section we will discuss some of the crimes most often perpetrated against the elderly.

Crimes of Force

Robbery and Personal Larceny

Robbery refers to the stealing of property by threat of force or use of force; it involves not only property loss but the possibility of physical harm as well. A Boston study done by John Conklin found that rates of robbery victimization in both street holdups and residential robberies increased with advancing age.[12] Elderly victims were most frequently held up by young, black males working with accomplices. Even though elderly persons resisted less often than younger victims did, force was more frequently used against them, resulting in a higher rate of injury, often severe enough to require hospitalization. He concludes: "If crime, and robbery in particular, is feared more by the elderly than the young, this is not only because the elderly feel more vulnerable because they are weak or alone. Evidence indicates that the robberies they suffer are objectively more threatening than the robberies suffered by younger victims."[13]

In contrast to robbery, personal larceny refers to the stealing of property from a person without the threat or use of force. The most common type of personal larceny encountered by the elderly is the theft of a purse or wallet taken directly from their person. Surveys taken in selected American cities by the LEAA reveal that older persons have higher victimization rates for personal larceny involving body contact than the general population in the majority of cities they studied.[14]

Purse-snatching is a crime that is perpetrated primarily against older white women. Most purse-snatches occur while the victims are walking to and from stores or public transportation or waiting at a bus stop. Some snatches occur outside the victim's home or even inside public buildings and stores.

Burglary

Burglary is the most common crime committed against all age groups. It is defined as unlawful or forcible entry into a home to commit theft. A three-year study of crime against the elderly in Kansas City by the Midwest Research Institute found that burglaries accounted for the largest percentage of crimes against the elderly (56 percent), followed by robberies (25 percent) and larcenies (14 percent).[15] In the study, more than half of the elderly who were burglarized lived alone.

> About 40 percent of the burglary victims stated they had active expectations their homes would be broken into before it happened. There is also notable a deep pessimism among the victims of both races who live in the high crime areas concerning their ability to protect themselves and their property — and they express particularly adverse reactions towards youths of both races.[16]

It is not uncommon for a person to be burglarized repeatedly, and often by the same offender. One report tells of an elderly woman who slept in the foyer of her apartment fully dressed so she could run out the front door the next time someone tried to break in through her bedroom window. This invasion had happened three times.[17]

Crimes of Fraud

Confidence Games

In contrast to crimes of force, which more frequently victimize the low-income and minority elderly, confidence games are nonviolent crimes that prey upon the more affluent elderly. In California, the San Francisco and Los Angeles police departments report that 90 percent of the confidence victims are over the age of 65 and are mainly women.[18]

A popular scheme for victimizing older persons is called the "pigeon drop," believed to be the oldest confidence game in existence, originating in China over 1,000 years ago.[19] There are several variations to this scheme, but essentially it works like this. Two girls work together, usually in large shopping malls or department stores. When they spot an elderly, well-dressed woman, one girl approaches the "pigeon" and begins a conversation to try to win her confidence. The second girl then joins them, explaining that she has just found an envelope or a bag. She opens it and finds what appears to be a roll of money with no identification. The girl then offers to go to her lawyer, banker, or employer for advice on what the three of them should do with the money. On her return, she says that her lawyer will keep the money for them for a period of six months, and if no one claims it by then, they will divide the money three ways. But in the meantime to show "good faith," each of the three must match her share of the find with her own money. The elderly victim then withdraws money from her savings account and gives it to the girl to take to the lawyer for safekeeping. Of course, she never sees the money again. Sometimes these girls get away with $25,000 or more in a single incident.

Another favorite confidence game is the "bank examiner" scheme. The swindle works this way. A man calls an elderly woman on the phone, having gotten her name from the telephone book. He identifies himself as a bank examiner. He explains that he is trying to trap a dishonest teller at the bank and asks her to help in apprehending the culprit. Sometimes he offers to pay for her assistance. If she agrees, the "bank examiner" then asks her to go to the bank and withdraw all her money. Later he phones saying that the plan worked, and the culprit has been caught. He offers to send a bank messenger or an FBI agent to pick up her money and redeposit it in her account. The messenger arrives, takes the money, gives the woman a receipt. She never sees the messenger or her money again.

Another way swindlers exploit older people is by posing as social security agents. They extort money from social security beneficiaries either by claiming that they must pay a set fee to assure continuation of their benefits, or by promising that upon payment of a certain fee, their social security benefits will be increased. Another gimmick is to claim that an overpayment has been made and to ask the victim to return the money to the agent.

Two young men identifying themselves as social security agents approached two elderly citizens, aged eighty-six and eighty-four, respectively, and told them there had been an overpayment and the government demanded the excess amount immediately. The eighty-six-year-old beneficiary turned over $750 to the impersonators. The eighty-four-year-old told them he didn't have the $1,628 demanded but that he could have it for them the next day. He then called the social security office. The matter was reported to the FBI.[20]

Consumer Frauds

Consumer frauds range from land swindles involving worthless and imaginary property, to the use of high-pressure sales techniques that result in elderly people paying for thousands of dollars' worth of

Boy, 14, Arrested in Bilking of Elderly Widows

He wore sneakers with his navy blue leisure suit and briefcase and couldn't spell simple words — but he had little trouble posing as an IRS agent and bilking elderly widows of their savings by threatening to cut off their Social Security checks.

He surrendered meekly to police . . . after his latest alleged caper.

He's 14. . . .

All six victims police have identified so far are widows on Social Security, ranging from 66 to 83 in age, with their names listed in the telephone directory.

Most were contacted by phone, police said, and told their Social Security payments would be cut off because of back taxes owed by their dead husbands. The caller offered to settle with them for a lesser amount of cash.

Two were relieved to do so. An 83-year-old widow gave the youth $1,100. A 66-year-old woman said she paid him $1,600 thinking she was settling a $2,000 tax debt left by her late husband in 1961.

SOURCE: *The Miami Herald*, December 21, 1978. Reprinted with permission of the *Miami Herald*.

dancing lessons. Though consumer frauds prey on people of all ages, there are some schemes in which the elderly are the favorite targets. The elderly are frequently victimized by unscrupulous insurance agents, who rely upon their fear of illness and disability. For example, an insurance agent told an elderly couple in Ohio that the Medicare program would soon run out and sold them $787 worth of health insurance.[21] In Pennsylvania, six insurance agents teamed up to take the life savings of an 80-year-old woman. Within a three-year period, she paid over $50,000 to buy 31 different health insurance policies, all of which were permitted to lapse.[22]

To many older people, their home represents their prize possession and greatest financial asset, so they are particularly susceptible to home-repair schemes. Roving home repairmen offer to do such tasks as installing aluminum siding or painting a house at phony bargains. Their workmanship is shoddy and their materials inferior; the aluminum siding soon falls off and the paint washes off in the first rain. Sometimes older people are visited by bogus home inspectors who use scare tactics, saying their homes need repairs. One woman in Pittsburgh had a man come to her house posing as a furnace inspector. He convinced her that her furnace was dangerously faulty, although in reality it was in good condition. She paid him $14,000 in cash for a new one along with additional equipment.[23]

Real estate schemes capitalize on the dream of some older people to spend their last days in a warm, sunny climate. Operating through the mail, the brochures promise prospective buyers a retirement paradise in such states as Arizona, New Mexico, and Florida. Particularly appealing to persons on retirement incomes are those advertisements that offer homesites for a low down-payment and a low, monthly payment. Many advertisements for such lots are deceptive, persons often find they have purchased lots in remote areas without access to roads and with no provision for utilities.

> Within the past ten years, several developers, particularly in the Southwest and Florida, bilked 30,000 people — mostly residents of cold, Northeastern states — out of $350 million. Some buyers never even saw the land they were buying. When retirement day finally rolled around, many purchasers found that "the land of their dreams" was, in reality, a swamp in Florida or a Southwestern desert.[24]

Many lonely elderly women fall prey to dance studio swindles. They are high pressured and flattered into paying in advance for thousands of hours' worth of dance instructions through a scheme of "lifetime" memberships. A woman may be bilked into buying several such memberships, sometimes costing her entire life savings or her home. Butler relates how a lonely 69-year-old woman, in an effort to find companionship, paid $10,000 for dancing lessons. When she became bedridden and tried to get a refund, the studio refused.[25] One elderly widow was conned into eight "lifetime" memberships, which entitled her to 3,100 hours of instruction at a cost of $34,913.[26]

Medical Quackery

Older persons are the victims in about 7 out of 10 cases involving medical fraud coming to the attention of the criminal justice system.[27] The American Medical Association estimates that about a billion dollars a year is wasted on quack schemes. The elderly are not only victimized financially, but also by delaying needed medical attention, they are endangering their health and sometimes even their lives. The fact that they commonly suffer from chronic illnesses makes them prime targets for "guaranteed cures" and miracle medicines.

Arthritis, one of the most common chronic conditions of the elderly, is also one of the most profitable for medical frauds. Phony treatments for this disease bring in about $300 million a year. Quack medicines for this condition include alfalfa tea, sea water, and "immune" milk. The devices and methods that have been promoted to cure arthritis almost defy the imagination. One popular article has been uranium ore-lined mittens. Another is a metal disk, which is clipped to the ankle while a person immerses his or her foot in cold water. The Inducto-Scope

Older persons commonly suffer from such chronic diseases as arthritis, and are particularly vulnerable to purveyors of drugs and devices like this Inducto-Scope. (Amram Ducovny, *The Billion Dollar Swindle: Frauds Against the Elderly*, Fleet Press, New York, 1969, p. 183.

claimed to cure arthritis through magnetic induction: the arthritic places the rings of the device over the affected areas and inserts the plug into a wall socket, but this only exposes the person to electric shock. Then, there is a device which is supposed to expand all the atoms of the body through its "Z-Rays."[28]

Equally unsound medically as these arthritis "cures" are the thousands of treatments for cancer promoted by quacks. Probably one of the most creative cancer "cures" was an instrument that was called the "Sonus Film-O-Sonic." It "silently" played tape-recorded music and had electrode pads which were attached to the patient.[29]

Appliances such as dentures, eye glasses, and hearing aids are another lucrative area for quacks. Hoping to save money, many older people fall victim to mail order dentures at cut-rate prices. They receive ill-fitting dentures, which are painful and make eating regular foods impossible. Eye glasses are also sold through the mails. One mail order operator claimed to sell lenses ground in accordance with prescriptions. The Federal Trade Commission examined some of the glasses and found 10 out of 15 pairs to be improperly ground.[30] Hearing aids are often sold by unscrupulous door-to-door salesmen. The price is high and the hearing aid is generally useless. Though only one hearing aid is required, a high-pressure salesman once sold an older person two hearing aids, one for each ear.[31]

Why are the elderly so vulnerable to confidence games and fraudulent practices? First, they generally have limited incomes and are anxious to take advantage of any opportunity that they think will save them money or that promises them additional money. Second, many older people are lonely and are frequently taken in by the friendly salesperson or the attentive con artist. Also, many elderly are naive about the schemes that are designed to separate them from their money.[32] Physical impairments may further contribute to their vulnerability. Impaired hearing may prevent proper understanding of a sales explanation or the asking of questions. Many older persons suffer from poor vision, which may interfere with reading guarantees or seeing the fine print on a contract. Because of their generally low educational levels, many elderly are embarrassed and reluctant to ask questions or to have mistakes corrected. They lack the know-how and confidence to demand their rights. Finally, many older people in the face of illness, pain, and the possibility of death are desperate to try almost anything, no matter how outlandish, that promises them relief or a cure.

Summary

1. Many elderly persons view fear of crime as a major social problem. Only in recent years has the subject received any significant attention.

2. Statistics do not accurately measure the extent of crimes involving older people. Many police departments do not classify victims according to age, and many crimes against older people are never reported to the police.

3. At the national level, statistics show that older persons are the least victimized of any age group, but the rates of victimization are disproportionately high for those elderly living in inner-city areas. The elderly's vulnerability to crime is mainly due to diminished physical strength, the fact that they frequently live alone and near those who are most likely to victimize them, and their dependency on walking or public transportation.

4. Clemente and Kleiman found that those having the greatest fear of crime were women and blacks. Having a low income level and living in the larger cities were also related to an increased fear of crime. Threat of crime tended to decrease as one moved from the large cities to the rural areas. Crime and fear of crime greatly diminish the quality of life for many older people, both black and white. Some curtail their social and recreational activities and only leave their homes or apartments when absolutely necessary. Crime exacts a higher price from older victims, compared to younger victims, in terms of physical injuries and economic losses.

5. While the elderly are victimized by the same types of crimes as younger persons are, their rates of victimization tend to be higher for such crimes as robbery, burglary, and personal larceny. Older persons are particularly vulnerable to crimes of fraud. The most predominant confidence games for victimizing older people are the "pigeon drop" and "bank examiner" schemes. Some consumer crimes that bilk older people of their money are unnecessary health insurance,

and home repair and real estate frauds. Dance studios often con older women into buying thousands of dollars' worth of dancing lessons.

6. The elderly are especially susceptible to medical quackery. Arthritis treatments are one of the most lucrative medical frauds. Older persons lose thousands of dollars a year on ill-fitting dentures, useless hearing aids, and improperly ground lenses. Some factors contributing to the vulnerability of the elderly to confidence games are: the opportunity to save or to make money, loneliness, physical impairments, and desperation resulting from pain and illness.

Notes

1. *The New York Times*, March 18, 1977. © 1977 by The New York Times Company. Reprinted by permission.

2. Reprinted by permission of the publisher, from Carl L. Cunningham, "Pattern and Effect of Crime Against the Aging: The Kansas City Study," in *Crime and the Elderly: Challenge and Response* edited by Jack Goldsmith and Sharon S. Goldsmith (Lexington, Mass.: Lexington Books, D. C. Heath and Company, Copyright 1976, D. C. Heath and Company), pp. 33–34.

3. Evelle J. Younger, "The California Experience: Prevention of Criminal Victimization of the Elderly," *Police Chief*, 43 (February 1976), 13.

4. Alan Malinchak and Douglas Wright, "The Scope of Elderly Victimization," *Aging*, March–April 1978, p. 16.

5. Louis Harris and Associates, *The Myth and Reality of Aging in America*, The National Council on the Aging, Washington, D.C., 1975, p. 31.

6. Jack Goldsmith, "Police and the Older Victim: Keys to a Changing Perspective," *Police Chief*, 43 (February 1976), p. 19.

7. Frank Clemente and Michael Kleiman, "Fear of Crime Among the Aged," *The Gerontologist*, 16, no. 3 (1976), 207–210.

8. "Step-up in Fight on Crimes Against Elderly," *U.S. News and World Report*, June 13, 1977, p. 62.

9. "The Elderly: Prisoners of Fear," *Time*, November 29, 1976, pp. 21–22.

10. Ibid, p. 21.

11. "Crime and Apprehension Plagues the Elderly: Four Federal Agencies Try to Help," *Aging*, March–April 1978, p. 26.

12. John E. Conklin, "Robbery, the Elderly, and Fear: An Urban Problem in Search of a Solution," in *Crime and the Elderly*, eds. Jack Goldsmith and Sharon S. Goldsmith, Lexington Books, Lexington, Mass., 1975, p. 104.

13. Ibid.

14. Malinchak and Wright, "The Scope of Elderly Victimization," p. 13.

15. Cunningham, "Pattern and Effect of Crime Against Aging," pp. 32–33.

16. Reprinted by permission of the publisher, from Carl L. Cunningham, "Pattern and Effect of Crime Against the Aging: The Kansas City Study," in *Crime and the Elderly: Challenge and Response* edited by Jack Goldsmith and Sharon

S. Goldsmith (Lexington, Mass.: Lexington Books, D. C. Heath and Company, Copyright 1976, D. C. Heath and Company), p. 40.

17. "The Elderly: Prisoners of Fear," p. 21.

18. Younger, "The California Experience," p. 15.

19. Donna St. John, "Beware the Flimflam Man," *Dynamic Maturity*, May 1977, p. 8.

20. Amram Ducovny, *The Billion Dollar Swindle: Frauds Against the Elderly*, Fleet Press, New York, 1969, p. 183.

21. U.S. Senate, *Developments in Aging: 1978*, p. 93.

22. Patricia Fanning, "Conning the Elderly," *The National Observer*, November 16, 1974, p. 8.

23. Jerry Bennett, "They're After Your Money," *Dynamic Maturity*, January 1974, p. 15.

24. St. John, "Beware the Flimflam Man," p. 10.

25. Robert N. Butler, *Why Survive? Being Old in America*, Harper & Row, New York, 1975, p. 311.

26. Ducovny, *The Billion Dollar Swindle*, pp. 196–197.

27. Younger, "The California Experience," p. 15.

28. Ducovny, *The Billion Dollar Swindle*, pp. 37–62.

29. Ibid., p. 89.

30. Ibid., p. 130.

31. Herman J. Loether, *Problems of Aging*, Dickenson, Belmont, Calif., 1975, p. 127.

32. Ibid., p. 77.

For Further Study

Butler, Robert N. *Why Survive? Being Old in America*. Harper & Row, New York, 1975. Chapter 10 is an excellent overview of how the elderly are victimized through crimes of violence and fraud.

Ducovny, Amram. *The Billion Dollar Swindle: Frauds Against the Elderly*. Fleet Press, New York, 1969. Deals with the vulnerability of older people to a host of deceptive practices, including medical quackery, investment swindles, and nursing home frauds.

Goldsmith, Jack, and Sharon S. Goldsmith, eds. *Crime and the Elderly*. Lexington Books, Lexington, Mass., 1975. A collection of papers that focuses on the problem of society's criminal victimization of the elderly and the response to the problem.

Loether, Herman J. *Problems of Aging*. Dickenson, Belmont, Calif., 1975. Chapter 8 provides a good discussion on food and health frauds and confidence games that exploit the elderly.

Sutherland, Edwin H., and Donald R. Cressey. *Criminology* (9th ed.). Lippincott, Philadelphia, 1974. An important introductory text on criminology that provides an excellent overview of crime.

20

Death and Dying

Death is seldom discussed in American society. In fact, it has almost become a taboo subject, and has replaced sex as an "unmentionable."[1] We not only avoid the topic, but we also shun the terminally ill and are embarrassed by displays of grief. Many persons are at a loss for words when they meet a bereaved person. John Perry and Erna Perry point out that this avoidance and denial of death contribute toward making death a social problem.[2] It is a problem at the individual level, because many people do not know how to cope with impending death except possibly to fear it. Next, it is a problem for the survivors, who often do not know how to handle their feelings or how to prepare and readjust their lives before and after the death of significant others. Lastly, it poses a problem for medical personnel, who are oriented toward maintaining and prolonging life.

In many preindustrial societies, the largest number of deaths occur at the beginning of the life cycle. For instance, among the Sakai of the Malay Peninsula, about half of the babies die before the age of three. In the Kurnai tribe of Australia, 40 to 50 percent of the children die before the age of 10.[3] In contrast, in the United States and other industrialized nations, the majority of deaths are of elderly people. Death thus has become increasingly a phenomenon of the old in our society. Because of this, the problems relating to death are those related to aging.

Attitudes Toward Death

Fear of Death

Many people assume that because older people have relatively little time left and death is more imminent for them, they are more fearful of death than younger persons are. Research suggests that just the opposite is true. Death appears less frightening to the elderly than to those who are younger. In a study conducted in California, Bengtson and his associates report that middle-aged respondents (45–54) had the greatest fear of death, while the older age groups (65–74) expressed the least amount of

---

The subject of death is almost as taboo as the subject of incest: we know that it happens, but most of us are so horrified at the thought that we put it out of our minds. . . . We even refuse to use the word "dead." People "pass on" or "depart." To say "so-and-so died" is a violation of an important folkway comparable to uttering a vulgarity.

SOURCE: John Perry and Erna Perry, *Face to Face: The Individual and Social Problems,* Educational Associates, Boston, 1976, p. 511.

fear.[4] There also appears to be no increase in fear of death among older persons, even as the time of death approaches.

Richard Kalish proposes three reasons why older people are less fearful of death. First, older persons place less value on their lives and recognize that their future is limited. Also, after having lived to old age, most elderly people feel that they have received their fair share of years and that any additional years are a bonus. Thirdly, as people grow older, they frequently have to deal with the deaths of others, which helps to socialize them to accept the appropriateness of their own deaths.[5]

Although the elderly tend to view death with acceptance, not fear, most studies reveal that the elderly think and talk more about death than do those in other age groups. For most older people, death is a frequent and important topic.[6] This preoccupation may be due not only to the imminence of their own deaths, but also to their store of death-related experiences, having outlived many friends and relatives.[7]

Fear of death is associated with religious beliefs. Most studies concur that persons who are the most religious are the least fearful of death. Some studies show a curvilinear relationship between religiosity and fear of death. The very religious have the least fear of death, whereas the nonreligious — agnostics and atheists — tend to have a moderate fear and those who are intermediate in their religiousness tend to be the most fearful.[8]

Since older people are not usually disturbed by the fear of death, Kastenbaum speculates that it may be because, in most respects, they are ready for death.[9] He observes that though elderly persons face death in a number of ways, two orientations toward death tend to be predominant. The first orientation involves getting ready for death by putting one's house in order, withdrawing from social activities, and then waiting for the end. The second orientation embodies the "I'll die with my boots on" philosophy; recognizing that death can come at any

Most surveys reveal that relatively few persons indicate a fear of death, and of all age groups, the elderly tend to be least frightened by death. (Magnum. Hiroji Kubota)

moment, these individuals remain active to the end. At the same time, they are ready for death. The death of Rosie, a resident of Merrill Court, a small apartment building housing mostly elderly widows illustrates this second pattern.

> Among the widows, there was a "good" and a "bad" way to die. Rosie's death especially was the community's example of "the right way to die." She was praised as much for remaining active to the end as for "being ready" in both the practical and philosophic sense. Her will and burial were prearranged and she was on good terms with "her people." As they looked around them, some residents were said to be "living on borrowed time" while others had not "lived out their mission." But whatever the case, they were agreed that one should try to face death rather than turn one's back on it, all while living fully to the end.[10]

The widows of Merrill Court shared a collective concern for being ready for, and facing up to death. They talked freely about death among themselves and accepted it as a fact of life. Victor Marshall found a similar orientation toward death among residents of Glen Brae, a retirement community located on the eastern seaboard of the United States.[11] About 400 residents lived in Glen Brae; their ages ranged from 64 to 96, the average age being 80.

Socialization for Death

Marshall says that people in communities composed of elderly residents, such as Merrill Court and Glen Brae, socialize each other for impending death. Residents are fairly successful in accepting their approaching deaths as legitimate, that is, appropriate and nonproblematical. They look upon death as part of the natural scheme of things that characterize the social reality shared with others. By legitimating death in this way, they are able to face death — their own and that of others — with equanimity.

Marshall points to three factors that contribute to the process of legitimation of death at Glen Brae: management of grief, talking about death, and role modeling. In the first year of its existence, the residents formulated a community policy about the treatment of death, which has remained in effect. This point of view is expressed in the following excerpt from the *Glen Call*, the resident newspaper:

> It is forecast that we can expect a death amongst us as frequently as one every two weeks. . . . Our responsibility, therefore, involves a point of view, a determination. Either Glen Brae will turn into a place shrouded in a funeral parlor atmosphere of tears and perpetual sadness, or it will play its intended role — the best place to be when crises occur. It is suggested that . . . we reduce to a minimum the prolongation of sorrow, the discussion of pain, loss, and tragedy. . . .[12]

In line with this thinking, both the death event and grief are low-keyed at Glen Brae. Deaths are marked only by a discreet notice on the bulletin board and in the *Glen Call*. Funerals are held elsewhere, and the external appearances of grief are minimized. One resident in discussing the behavior of the survivors observed: "Most of the time, outside of going to funerals, they pick up and go on in a very remarkable fashion. And they do it purposefully — for the other residents. It's very obvious."[13]

At the same time, death is discussed openly and freely among the residents:

> When people begin to think about their impending deaths, they frequently talk with others about it; this proves beneficial in assisting them to come to terms with it. Glen Brae is, in a sense, organized to provide such assistance by encouraging a high level of social interaction which allows death to be dealt with informally.[14]

Glen Brae also provides the residents with role models that allow them to anticipate their own dying. These models give them a clearer idea of what their own death might be like and assist them in planning for it. Many residents feel that there is an appropriate pattern for dying.

For example, one resident stated: "I think the thing that is feared is dying, not death. You see you want to die nobly, and you're afraid you won't be able to." Another said that she would like to die gracefully. "I aim to die without yelling, 'Hey, I'm going.' "[15]

The Process of Dying

The Dying Trajectory

Dying is viewed by Barney Glaser and Anselm Strauss as a status passage in which the dying person is passing between the status of being alive to the status of being dead.[16] Earlier, we discussed other types of status passages, such as those between adolescence and adulthood or between work and retirement. These passages are regulated by rules designating when the passage should be scheduled, a sequence of prescribed steps, and the actions that must be carried out by various participants in order to accomplish the transition.[17] In contrast to most status passages, "dying is almost always unscheduled; second, the sequence of steps is not institutionally prescribed, and third, the actions of the various participants are only partly regulated."[18]

To describe the process of going from normal health to the downhill pattern of dying, Glaser and Strauss use the term, *trajectory of dying,* which has two major characteristics — duration and shape. *Duration* means that the trajectory of dying takes place over time, and *shape* refers to the fact that it can be charted. Durations of some patterns are slow, while others are quite sudden. The shape may be all downhill or it may go down and then up before going down again. Different patterns include, for example, the familiar *lingering* pattern in which the patient is expected to die sooner than he does, resulting in a slow downward trend. In the *short-reprieve* pattern, the patient receives an unexpected postponement of death. Another pattern is the *abrupt surprise* trajectory: a patient is expected to recover but suddenly dies. Then there is the *suspended sentence* in which the patient is sent home from a hospital and may live for several years. Finally, there is the *entry–re-entry* pattern, in which the patient goes slowly downhill and returns home several times between hospital stays.

Each of these trajectory of dying patterns rests on the expectations of medical personnel about how a patient's dying will proceed (duration and shape). In addition, dying trajectories also depend on the nature of the disease or the condition from which the patient suffers. A patient dying from cancer will have a different trajectory from one suffering a fatal heart attack.

A Stage Theory of Dying

From interviews with terminally ill patients, Elisabeth Kübler-Ross has proposed that persons aware of their impending death pass through five psychological stages in preparation for it: denial, anger, bargaining, depression, and acceptance.[19] In later writings she has said that not every person goes through each stage in sequence, and many individuals may move back and forth between stages.

The first stage, denial ("No, not me"), is characterized by a person's refusing to accept the reality of impending death or feeling that some mistake has been made. Some people frantically go from one doctor or treatment center to another in search of a more positive or satisfactory diagnosis.

In the second stage, denial is replaced by feelings of anger or rage ("Why me?"), which the person directs at the family, friends, and medical personnel. Much of this anger is quite justified. Kübler-Ross states that we too would be angry if all our life's activities were suddenly interrupted, "if we had put some hard-earned money aside to enjoy a few years of rest and enjoyment, for travel and pursuing hobbies, only to be confronted with the fact that 'this is not for me.' "[20]

In the third stage, bargaining ("Yes me, but . . ."), the person tries to make a deal with fate to bargain for a postponement of the event. Much of the bargaining is likely to be between God and the patient. Many patients promise "a life dedicated to God" or "a life in the service of the church" and to others in exchange for some additional time.

The next stage is depression ("Woe is me!"), characterized by a sense of great loss. Persons grieve not only for what they have but for what they are in the process of losing. It is a time for saying goodbye to family and friends. This grief helps prepare persons to make the break with those they care about and to separate themselves from this world.

The last stage is acceptance ("It's time for me to go"). The patient now feels neither depression nor anger. There is almost an absence of feelings. This is a time when the dying individual "will contemplate his [or her] coming end with a certain degree of quiet expectation."[21] One patient described it as "the final rest before the long journey."[22] Helen Whitman and Shelby Lukes relate the case of a 70-year-old widow who had reached this stage of acceptance, after having undergone surgery and treatment for cancer with no sign of success. In preparation for death, she had made her own funeral arrangements and put her estate in order. She then said goodbye to her family and friends and withdrew into herself to await her fate. But an unusual phenomenon occurred — her condition began miraculously to improve. The hospital personnel were then faced with the task of completely reversing her outlook and attitude from one of dying to one of living.[23]

Although Kübler-Ross's stage theory of dying has received considerable recognition and has done much to establish the topic of death and dying as one of general concern and study, at the present time there is little evidence available to support the theory. Some writers have proposed other stages, while others maintain that the process of dying is stageless.

> Clinical research concerning the dying process by other investigators does not clearly support the existence of the five stages or of any universal form of staging. A recent review of the literature, scant as it is, finds no evidence for five predictable stages of psychological adaptation. . . . Although this has been perhaps the most systematic exploration yet made of the stage theory of dying, much remains to be learned and discussed. It is possible that the theory, either in its present or a revised form, might eventually become established as a faithful representation of central facts in the dying process and a dependable guide to education and action.[24]

Two Important Issues

Two of the most controversial issues in death and dying are: whether or not the dying patient should be told about the medical prognosis, and how long artificial means should be used to keep a hopelessly ill or mentally disabled patient alive.

THE RIGHT TO KNOW   The situation involving patients who are terminally ill is defined by hospital personnel, their families, and themselves. Glaser and Strauss distinguish four types of awareness situations that may develop: closed awareness, suspicion awareness, mutual pretense awareness, and open awareness.[25] The first type, *closed awareness*, refers to a situation in which patients do not know that they are dying. The information is kept from them by hospital personnel and by family members. In the second situation, *suspicion awareness*, the patients suspect what their real condition is and attempt to confirm or negate these suspicions. The third situation is *mutual pretense awareness*, a situation in which patients know they are dying, and the hospital and family members know, but everyone pretends that death is not imminent. Finally, there is the situation of *open awareness*, in which all concerned are fully aware of what is happening and thus there is no need to conceal the truth from the patients.

It is often recognized that the closed awareness context is easier in some ways on the dying patient's family, especially if the patient is the kind of person who is not likely to accept death with fortitude. But it can be a very painful and difficult experience for family members to keep the truth from the dying person, especially if the dying trajectory is slow. Closed awareness is generally more comfortable for hospital personnel because an unaware patient is usually easier to handle and less disruptive to hospital routine. On the other hand, the situation may subject nurses to a great deal of strain, as they must constantly be on guard against disclosure.

In an open awareness context, the patient is now openly recognized as having the status of a dying person:

> Once a patient has indicated his awareness of dying, the most important interactional consequence is that he is now responsible for his acts as a *dying* person. He knows now that he is not merely sick but dying. He must face that fact. Sociologically, "facing" an impending death means that the patient will be judged, and will judge himself, according to certain standards of proper conduct. These standards, pertaining to the way a man handles himself during his final hours and to his behavior during the days he spends waiting to die, apply even to physically dazed patients. Similarly, certain standards apply then to the conduct of hospital personnel, who must behave properly as humans and as professionals.[26]

Glaser and Strauss make the point that the problem concerning awareness of dying is more than just a technical one; it is a moral one as well. It raises the question, Has anyone the right (including the physician) "to deny a dying person the opportunity to make peace with his conscience and with his God, to settle his affairs and provide for the future of his family, and to control his style of dying, much as he controlled his style of living?"[27] Avery Weisman feels that "to be informed about a diagnosis, especially a serious one is to be fortified, not undermined."[28] He notes that many patients realize the diagnosis for themselves long before they are told. Ineffective treatment, persistent symptoms, evasive answers to questions, and cues from relatives and family convey this information indirectly.

Most physicians do not choose to tell their patients the truth in cases of terminal illness. They are often evasive and ambiguous in discussions with their patients. In a survey of staff members of a Chicago hospital, Donald Okeon found almost 90 percent of the physicians said that they preferred to deceive terminal patients by withholding information. Their policy is to tell the patient as little as possible, using the most general terms. Most of the physicians surveyed feel that the majority of patients do not really want to know the truth, regardless of what people say.[29] Some physicians feel that informing the patient of impending death merely subjects the patient to psychological torment.

Though awareness of approaching death gives patients a chance to complete important work, to get their affairs in order, and to make plans for their families, awareness can have certain disadvantages. Other people may not approve of the way the dying persons are managing their death, and may try to change their plans. Also, for patients who are unable to face death, an awareness of dying may result in more anguish and less dignity than if they did not know.[30]

Some nurses prefer working with patients who are aware of their impending death. There is no need for pretext, and the nurse can help the patient prepare to confront death. One nurse with considerable experience in dealing with dying patients expresses these feelings about her own death:

> Personally when my time comes, please don't read me scriptures or poetry. Hold my hand and let the light come in. Don't leave me alone because I haven't been through this experience and it scares me. When my time comes I hope I can accept it. Life is sweet to its bitter end.[31]

THE RIGHT TO DIE   As the pain and suffering of a patient with a terminal illness increase, or as the dying patient's life is being prolonged by machines though the patient is comatose, the question arises, How long should life be maintained? Robert Morison cites three possibilities open to the physician attending the dying patient: (1) use all possible means to keep the patient alive; (2) discontinue artificial means or heroic measures, but continue ordinary procedures; and (3) take some steps to hasten death and the speed of the downhill trajectory of dying.[32]

Although most people admit there comes a time when it is proper to shift from heroic measures of keeping a patient alive to ordinary medical procedures, there is much less agreement about the decision to accelerate the termination of life. Permitting a patient to die naturally, rather than employing heroic measures to sustain life, is referred to as *passive euthanasia*. When a physician deliberately terminates the life of a patient who is hopelessly ill or nonfunctional, it is called *active euthanasia*.[33] The line between passive and active euthanasia is difficult to draw.

> The more one thinks of actual situations, however, the more one wonders if there is a valid distinction in allowing a person to die and hastening the downward course of life. Sometimes the words "positive" and "negative" are used, with the implication that it is all right to take away from the patient something that would help him to live but wrong to give him something that will help him to die.[34]

In discussing euthanasia, another distinction is the degree of voluntarism involved on the part of the dying patient. In cases when patients are mentally competent and conscious, they may request or consent to passive or active euthanasia — then their death can be termed *voluntary euthanasia*. When passive or active euthanasia is imposed upon a patient who is incapable of giving consent, as in the case of a comatose patient, it is referred to as *involuntary euthanasia*.[35]

To prevent the prolongation of life when death is inevitable, some persons complete documents referred to as *living wills*. These documents, distributed by the Concern for Dying, an educational council, are intended for future use in the event that persons are unable to participate fully in decisions regarding their treatment during a terminal illness. The living will, prepared while individuals are mentally competent, informs others of their wish not to prolong the inevitability of death by artificial means or heroic measures (Figure 20.1). Up to the present time, the living will has not been tested in a court case. If and when the will is tested, it is believed that it will be found to be legally binding.

Whether or not euthanasia should be regulated or legalized has been the subject of much controversy. Many cases of active euthanasia that have come to the attention of the public involve elderly persons. One of the earlier cases that received international attention occurred in 1950; it involved Dr. Herman Sanders, who injected air into the veins of an

Figure 20.1   Sample of a living will

```
TO MY FAMILY, MY PHYSICIAN, MY LAWYER, MY CLERGYMAN
TO ANY MEDICAL FACILITY IN WHOSE CARE I HAPPEN TO BE
TO ANY INDIVIDUAL WHO MAY BECOME RESPONSIBLE FOR MY HEALTH, WELFARE
   OR AFFAIRS


Death is as much a reality as birth, growth, maturity and old age -- it is
the one certainty of life. If the time comes when I, _____
_____ can no longer take part in decisions for my own future,
let this statement stand as an expression of my wishes, while I am still
of sound mind.

If the situation should arise in which there is no reasonable expectation
of my recovery from physical or mental disability, I request that I be
allowed to die and not be kept alive by artificial means or "heroic measures."
I do not fear death itself as much as the indignities of deterioration,
dependence and hopeless pain. I, therefore, ask that medication be merci-
fully administered to me to alleviate suffering even though this may hasten
the moment of death.

This request is made after careful consideration. I hope you who care for
me will feel morally bound to follow its mandate. I recognize that this
appears to place a heavy responsibility upon you, but it is with the
intention of relieving you of such responsibility and of placing it upon
myself in accordance with my strong convictions, that this statement is
made.

                           Signed_____

Date_____

Witness_____

Witness_____

Copies of this request have been given to_____
```

SOURCE: Reprinted with the permission of Concern for Dying, 250 West 57th Street, New York, N.Y. 10019.

older woman who was suffering from cancer and had only a short time to live. Ninety percent of the citizens in his home town in New Hampshire signed a petition expressing their support of his action. Dr. Sanders was later acquitted of a first-degree murder charge. In fact, to date no physician ever tried for active euthanasia has ever been convicted. More recently, there was the highly publicized court case concerning 21-year-old Karen Quinlan, in which a state supreme court ruling was required to withdraw life-sustaining machines from the comatose patient.

Public opinion polls reflect the fact that euthanasia is becoming more widely accepted. In 1973 a Gallup Poll found that 53 percent of the public supported active voluntary euthanasia in the case of terminal illness. Another poll made during that same year by Harris revealed that 62 percent of the population supported passive voluntary euthanasia.[36] Most studies show that there is little or no variation in those supporting euthanasia either by age, sex, or religion.

Erdman Palmore notes that the certain trends in our society are likely to increase the acceptance of euthanasia in the future.

1. The increasing number of persons who reach very old age when prolonged but terminal illness becomes the typical cause of death.
2. The trend toward more rational allocation of scarce and expensive medical equipment (e.g., kidney machines) and the personnel to those who can benefit most.
3. The growing belief in the right of all persons to do what they want with their own bodies, so long as it does not harm others, as reflected in the growing acceptance of contraceptives, abortion, masturbation, premarital intercourse, and cremation. The right to die under certain circumstances may become another generally accepted civil right.[37]

An innovative approach to dealing with the terminally ill in the last weeks of their lives, which perhaps both opponents and proponents of euthanasia can accept, is a *hospice*. A hospice may be a separate unit within a hospital, or it may be an independent facility. Originally, the term was used to refer to a way-station for travelers, but in modern times a hospice has come to mean a facility devoted specifically to the care of the dying. Since hospices are designed for the dying, their orientation and practice differ from that of a general hospital. They emphasize care, not cure, and schedules are designed to fit the needs of the individual patient and not the institution. The key principle of hospice care is reduction of pain, both physical and psychological, accomplished through administration of pain-killing drugs in doses large enough to keep the patient's pain always below the pain threshold and through humane environment and treatment, psychiatric care, and religious counseling.[38]

I suggest that American culture is faced with a crisis of death because the changed demographic and structural conditions do not fit the traditional concepts of appropriate death, and no new ideal has arisen to take their place. Our nineteenth-century ideal was that of the patriarch, dying in his own home in ripe old age but in the full possession of his faculties, surrounded by family, heirs and material symbols of a life of hard work and acquisition. Death was additionally appropriate because of the power of religious belief, which did not regard the event as a final ending. Today people characteristically die at an age when their physical, social, and mental powers are at an ebb, or even absent, typically in the hospital, and often separated from family and other meaningful surroundings. Thus "dying alone" is not only a symbolic theme of existential philosophers; it more and more epitomizes the inappropriateness of how people die under modern conditions.

SOURCE: Robert Blauner, "Death and the Social Structure," *Psychiatry*, 29 (November 1966), 392.

Hospices are now found in England, the United States, and Canada. The best known is St. Christopher's Hospice, a 54-bed facility outside of London. It offers meals on demand and with alcoholic beverages. Private rooms are available for relatives who wish to live with, or near the patient. Pets and children are welcome. Patients are permitted to shift back and forth between hospice and home as their strength permits.

> When physicians elsewhere finally give up on treating the disease, St. Christopher's takes over and treats the patient. Noticeably absent are the mechanical respirators, cardiovascular shock equipment, oxygen tents and intravenous feeding apparatus to which such patients are often made an appendage in hospitals. Present is a staff deftly alleviating pain. Here, many of the horrors that make euthanasia seem merciful evaporate in an atmosphere of comfort and safety.[39]

Perhaps, the essence of the hospice can best be summed up by the underlying philosophy of the hospice movement, namely that one's last days should be spent in living, not dying.

After the Death

Grief and Bereavement

The death of an elderly person in our society is generally perceived as being less disruptive and having less impact on the social structure than the death of a young or middle-aged person. This attitude is explained, in part, by the fact that very old persons are no longer actively engaged in the vital functions of society and therefore leave less of a void. Responsibilities of work have generally been passed on to others, and the tasks of socializing children and of parenthood are over.

On the other hand, when a middle-aged person dies, the social loss felt is much greater. Besides contributing to one's family, occupation, and society, the middle-aged person has time left for further contributions. Elaine Cumming and William Henry note that when middle-aged persons die they are torn from the fabric of society, but when older people die, they have already unravelled the threads of interaction so that their deaths are not as noticeable.[40] An old person's death, then, is viewed as less of a social loss because it terminates a life that society considers to have reduced value and whose potential has been largely exhausted. Weisman compares the death of a child whose potential is yet unrealized with that of an elderly person:

> The death of a child is always a tragedy. It is unforgettable and futile, because so much of a child's worth depends upon unrealized potential and its capacity to evoke tenderness. In contrast, the death of the very aged fits into an acceptable order of nature and we find reasons to explain why it is right and proper for an old patient to die when he does. "It is just as well." "He was about ready to die anyway." "I don't think he wanted to live." "He never took care of himself." "He couldn't have lived much longer." The terminally aged may be as helpless as a child, but they seldom arouse tenderness.[41]

Bereavement is generally composed of three distinct phases. The first phase is a brief period of shock, which lasts for several days. The second is a time of intense grief, characterized by physiological changes, such as the loss of sleep, appetite, and weight, as well as withdrawal from social activities. Finally, there is a period of recovery, in which there is a resumption of social activities and a reawakening of interest in life.[42]

Older persons often anticipate the death of a spouse or of their peers. As a result, they prepare themselves in advance by rehearsing and experiencing, in part, what life will be like following their anticipated loss. When death does occur, the task of mourning is eased and reconciliation is accomplished more quickly because a certain amount of the "grief work" has preceded the event.

Compared with younger persons, older persons are more likely to suffer from a succession of bereavements by having outlived many friends and relatives. Kastenbaum suggests that this can cause a "bereavement overload."

> Moreover, bereavement may follow so closely upon bereavement that the elder is never able to complete his "grief work." It is often estimated that normal mourning requires approximately a year to run its course. It is

possible that even more time is required when one is an octogenarian who is mourning for the spouse whose life has been shared for thirty, forty, fifty or more years. But other deaths may intervene before the mourning is completed. The elder can reach a point at which he feels he no longer can respond fully to a new death; he is still so closely involved with the old deaths.[43]

Reactions to multiple bereavements may take the form of increased bitterness and irritability. Older persons may direct their hostile feelings outward and become negative and distrustful of others. When grief can no longer be handled psychologically, an elderly person's grief may be manifested in the development of bodily symptoms. Karl Stern, Gwendolyn Williams and Miguel Prados found that grief in older

---

A Grandson Grieves at the Death of His Grandmother

Many times families go through hardships, but the hardest our family went through was when Ms. Ivan McCurdy (Mom's Mother) passed away. In October my grandmother went to Mayo Clinic because she was sick with lymphoma. Mom stayed with her at the clinic, until Gram could fly back to Tennessee. She was put on board the plane in a wheelchair. Mom and Dad checked her in at the University Hospital where she had an operation on her lungs. My sister Jennie and I went to see Gram after she had ten stitches across her chest and a blood machine hooked up to her. But that was the only time we saw her in University Hospital. About two weeks later she came home feeling fine.

Later on we had great times together. We took walks together and played games. Gram went in for a lot of checkups, and one day Doctor Solomon didn't recognize her because she looked so good! She still got sick, but always got better, until one night Gram dropped way down. Dad and Mom checked her back into the hospital. Next night after Mom came home from staying with Gram, Dad went to the hospital and stayed until 3:00 in the morning. Then on Monday Gram was fine. On Tuesday she was fine. On Wednesday she was fine, and they unplugged the machines. We all thought she would be well again. But on Friday we got a call from the hospital. Gram was dying. Mom and dad went to her. It was very easy for Gram. She tossed and turned a few times and found a comfortable spot on her pillow, and then in about an hour her breath just faded away.

We went to the funeral on Sunday. This would be the last time we would ever see Gram. But we knew she would watch over us. We knew how she had been a great grandmother, and how she had always helped people.

It hurts when somebody dies, but everybody knew how much Gram loved everybody and everybody loved her.

Jeffrey Porter Black, age 10

SOURCE: William E. Cole and Diana K. Harris, *The Elderly in America,* Allyn & Bacon, Boston, 1977, p. 44.

persons primarily took the form of somatic illness, while younger persons tend to display more overt mental manifestations.[44]

Funerals

The funeral is an important rite of passage in all societies dating back to prehistoric times. It fulfills many functions, including the affirmation of the fundamental meanings of the society and of group solidarity in the face of the ultimate threat of death. In nearly all societies, these fundamental meanings have been of a religious nature. In a secular society such as ours, however, there has been much difficulty in making these affirmations and in coping with death partly because of the decline in religious beliefs.[45] Death becomes especially difficult to accept when many people no longer believe that there is life after death, or that "all is for the best." There is a tendency to mask the reality of death. Expensive caskets are sold today complete with inner-spring mattresses or "Perfect Posture" beds. There are high-fashion clothes and accessories for the dead, along with special cosmetics for grooming.[46] These cosmetics not only are designed to make the deceased more presentable for viewing but even attempt to make them appear in a state of healthy repose. Foreigners are often amazed by our custom of open-casket viewing. An English woman states:

> I myself have attended only one funeral here — that of an elderly fellow worker of mine. After the service I could not understand why everyone was walking towards the coffin . . . but thought I had better follow the crowd. It shook me rigid to get there and find the casket open and poor old Oscar lying there in his brown tweed suit, wearing a suntan makeup and just the wrong shade of lipstick.[47]

In an effort to further disguise and soften the impact of death in our society, a whole new terminology involving death has evolved in the funeral business. For example, the *funeral director* or the *mortician* (not the *undertaker*) sees that *Ms. Jones* (not the *corpse*) is placed in a *casket* (not a *coffin*) in a *slumber room* (not a *laying-out room* or *display room*) before the *service* (not the *funeral*). Later the *coach* or *professional car* (not the *hearse*), will transfer her to a *memorial park* (not a *cemetery* or *graveyard*) where she will be *interred* (not *buried*).

In recent years the funeral industry has been under attack for the high costs of funerals, burials, and related expenses. Mourners are often taken advantage of at a time when they are most vulnerable and least able to judge what they can afford. Many deplete their savings or go into heavy debt in an effort to "do the right thing for the deceased," or to do what is expected of them by their family and friends.

Funeral rites serve to reaffirm the group identity of the survivors and the fundamental meanings of the society, and to help readjust the community after the loss of a member. (Magnum. Roland M. Freedman)

Summary

1. Death has become almost a taboo topic in our society. Our attitudes and behavior toward death have made it a social problem. Since the majority of those who die are older people, the problems related to death are also related to aging. The elderly are less fearful of death than younger persons. At the same time, they think about it and discuss it more often than younger persons do. Persons who are the most religious tend to be less afraid of death.

2. Residents of retirement communities like Glen Brae socialize one another for impending death. In such environments, death is legitimized because it is viewed as an appropriate and matter-of-fact aspect of life. This process of legitimation took place in Glen Brae through the management of grief, discussions about death, and role modeling.

3. Dying is viewed as a status passage in which one moves between the statuses of living and dead. The term *trajectory of dying* as used by Glaser and Strauss, denotes that dying has both duration and shape. The trajectory may be slow or sudden, and may reveal a regular or erratic downhill pattern. The pattern of the trajectory depends to a large extent on the nature of the terminal condition. Kübler-Ross has proposed that a person passes through five stages in preparation for death: denial, anger, bargaining, depression, and acceptance. As yet, there is little research that supports the existence of these five stages or that they can be universally applied.

4. Glaser and Strauss distinguish four types of awareness situations as defined

by terminally ill patients and those around them: closed awareness, suspicion awareness, mutual pretense awareness, and open awareness. There is much debate on whether or not patients should be told that their condition is terminal.

5. Most people feel that when a patient is hopelessly ill or disabled, there comes a time when it is proper to withdraw extraordinary measures to sustain life. Permitting a patient to die in this way is called "passive euthanasia." When a physician deliberately ends the life of a terminally ill patient, it is referred to as "active euthanasia." Euthanasia may also be voluntary or involuntary depending on whether or not one has the consent of the patient. To prevent the prolongation of life by artificial means when death is inevitable, some persons complete documents referred to as living wills. Palmore observes that certain trends are operating in our society that will increase the acceptance of euthanasia in the future.

6. Hospices are an innovative approach to providing care for the dying. Their goal is to furnish an optimum level of care and comfort for the dying patient. Hospices may be independent facilities or units in hospitals.

7. The death of an older person is likely to have far less impact on the social structure than that of a younger person who is actively engaged in family, work, and community affairs. Older persons often anticipate the death of a spouse or friends and prepare themselves in advance for their expected loss. In comparison with younger persons, older people are much more likely to suffer from a succession of losses resulting in "bereavement overload."

8. Funerals are important rites of passage in most societies, and they fulfill many valuable functions. Because death is becoming increasingly difficult to accept in secular societies like our own, funerals are designed to mask the reality of death.

Notes

1. Geoffrey Gorer, *Death, Grief, and Mourning*, Doubleday, Garden City, N.Y., pp. 192–199.

2. John Perry and Erna Perry, *Face to Face: The Individual and Social Problems*, Educational Associates, Boston, 1976, p. 512.

3. Robert Blauner, "Death and Social Structure," *Psychiatry*, 29 (November 1966), 380.

4. Vern L. Bengtson, José B. Cuellar, and Pauline Ragan, "Stratum Contrasts and Similarities in Attitudes Toward Death," *Journal of Gerontology*, 32, no. 1 (1977), 76–88.

5. Richard A. Kalish, "Death and Dying in a Social Context," in *Handbook of Aging and the Social Sciences*, eds. Robert H. Binstock and Ethel Shanas, Van Nostrand Reinhold, New York, 1976, p. 490.

6. Matilda W. Riley and Anne Foner, *Aging and Society, vol 1: An Inventory of Research Findings*, Russell Sage Foundation, New York, 1968, pp. 332–335.

7. Kalish, "Death and Dying in a Social Context," p. 490.

8. Ibid., pp. 491–492.

9. Robert Kastenbaum, "Death and Bereavement in Later Life" in *Death and Bereavement*, ed. Austin Kutscher, Charles C. Thomas, Springfield, Ill., 1969, pp. 28–54.

10. Arlie Russell Hochschild, *The Unexpected Community*, © 1973, p. 80. Reprinted by permission of Prentice-Hall, Inc., Englewood Cliffs, New Jersey.

11. Victor W. Marshall, "Socialization for Impending Death in a Retirement Village," *American Journal of Sociology*, 80, no. 5 (1975), 1124–1143.

12. Ibid., p. 1134.

13. Ibid., p. 1140.

14. Ibid., p. 1138.

15. Ibid., p. 1137.

16. Barney G. Glaser and Anselm L. Strauss, *Time for Dying*, Aldine, Chicago, 1968.

17. Ibid., p. 244.

18. Ibid., p. 247.

19. Elisabeth Kübler-Ross, *On Death and Dying*, Macmillan, New York, 1969, pp. 38–137.

20. Ibid., p. 51.

21. Ibid., p. 112.

22. Ibid., p. 113.

23. Helen H. Whitman and Shelby J. Lukes, "Behavior Modification for Terminally Ill Patients," *American Journal of Nursing*, 75, no. 2, (1975), 100–101.

24. Robert Kastenbaum, "Is Death a Life Crisis? On the Confrontation with Death in Theory and Practice," in *Life-Span Developmental Psychology: Normative Life Crises*, eds. Nancy Daton and Leon H. Ginsberg, Academic Press, New York, 1975, p. 45.

25. Barney G. Glaser and Anselm L. Strauss, *Awareness of Dying*, Aldine, Chicago, 1965, p. 11.

26. Ibid., p. 82.

27. Ibid., p. 6.

28. Avery D. Weisman, *On Dying and Denying: A Psychiatric Study of Terminality*, Behavioral Publications, New York, 1972, p. 17.

29. Donald Okeon, "What to Tell Cancer Patients: A Study of Medical Attitudes," in *Ethical Issues in Death and Dying*, ed. Robert F. Weir, Columbia University Press, New York, 1977, pp. 9–25.

30. Glaser and Strauss, *Awareness of Dying*, p. 103.

31. Armena Abernathy, personal communication.

32. Robert S. Morison, "Death: Process or Event?" *Science*. 173 (August 1971), 694–698.

33. Celia Berdes, *Social Services for the Aged Dying and Bereaved in International*

Perspective, The International Federation on Aging, Washington, D.C., 1978, p. 42.

34. Morison, "Death," p. 696.

35. Berdes, *Social Services for the Aged Dying and Bereaved in International Perspective*, p. 42.

36. Ibid., p. 43.

37. Erdman Palmore, "Sociological Aspects of Aging," in *Behavior and Adaptation in Late Life*, eds. Ewald W. Busse and Eric Pfeiffer, Little, Brown, Boston, 1977, p. 52.

38. Berdes, *Social Services for the Aged, Dying and Bereaved in International Perspective*, pp. 15–19.

39. Wayne Sage, "Choosing the Good Death," reprinted in *Focus: Aging*, ed. Harold Cox, Dushkin, Guildford, Conn., 1978, p. 192.

40. Elaine Cumming and William E. Henry, *Growing Old*, Basic Books, New York, 1961, p. 226.

41. Weisman, *On Dying and Denying*, p. 144.

42. Gorer, *Death, Grief and Mourning*, p. 129.

43. Kastenbaum, "Death and Bereavement in Later Life," p. 47.

44. Karl Stern, Gwendolyn Williams, and Miguel Prados, "Grief Reactions in Later Life," *American Journal of Psychiatry*, 58 (1951), 289–294.

45. Peter L. Berger and Brigitte Berger, *Sociology: A Biographical Approach*, Basic Books, New York, 1975, p. 361.

46. Jessica Mitford, *The American Way of Death*, Simon & Schuster, New York, 1963, p. 16.

47. Ibid., pp. 75–76.

For Further Study

Berdes, Celia. *Social Services for the Aged Dying and Bereaved in International Perspective*. The International Federation on Aging, Washington, D.C., 1978. Geared to the interests of the practitioner, this monograph focuses on services for the aged dying and bereaved and on some ways to help meet their needs.

Kalish, Richard A. "Death in a Social Context." In *Handbook of Aging and the Social Sciences*, edited by Robert H. Binstock and Ethel Shanas. Van Nostrand Rheinhold, New York, 1976. An excellent overview of death and dying in our society.

———, and David K. Reynolds. *Death and Ethnicity: A Psychocultural Study*. University of Southern California Press, Los Angeles, 1976. This study deals with how persons of four ethnic groups think and behave about death, dying, and grieving.

Kastenbaum, Robert. "Death and Bereavement in Later Life." In *Death and Bereavement*, edited by Austin H. Kutscher. Charles C Thomas, Springfield, Ill., 1969, pp. 28–54. Discusses how elderly persons view death and dying, as well as the orientations that young people tend to ascribe to them.

Kübler-Ross, Elisabeth. *Questions and Answers on Death and Dying.* Macmillan, New York, 1974. A sequel to her original book *On Death and Dying*, which sheds further light on the dying process.

Riley, Matilda W., and Anne Foner. *Aging and Society, vol. 1: An Inventory of Research Findings.* Russell Sage Foundation, New York, 1968. A good resource for facts and statistics about older persons and death.

Weir, Robert F. *Ethical Issues in Death and Dying.* Columbia University Press, New York, 1977. A collection of articles that treat the medical, legal, and ethical concerns involved in death and dying.

VI
Programs and Prospects for the Elderly

21

Social Services for the Elderly

Some of the earliest attempts to intervene in the social conditions of older persons can be traced back to the Byzantines, who honored old age. They established a number of homes for the elderly, which were in existence during the fifth century. These homes, known as *gerocomeia*, were supported by the church, the state, and private persons.[1] Throughout most of history, however, social problems including those of the elderly, were considered to be inevitable — nothing could be done to eradicate or ameliorate them.

Today the concept of *social intervention* — which refers to a planned attempt to change, supposedly for the better, the lives of other individuals or groups through the application of skills and knowledge — is a widely accepted attitude and practice in modern societies. Social intervention may take the form of *social services*, which may be defined as "a social mechanism for [the] distribution of resources designed to achieve and maintain a prescribed level of well-being for all members of society."[2] This definition implies that social services are not just for the poor, but that everyone is entitled to a basic level of welfare.

Some groups, such as the elderly, need more social services than others to achieve an acceptable level of well-being. Specialized social services for the elderly did not develop until recent years. This development coincided with the expansion of our knowledge of the biological, psychological, and sociological aspects of aging. Social services for older people generally focus on activities that are supportive, help protect, conserve, improve physical and social functioning, and provide opportunities for personal fulfillment.

In this chapter we will briefly review some services provided for the elderly in their homes and in community settings (Table 21.1). We will then look at the availability and utilization of social services for older people. Many of these services relate to the problems mentioned in previous chapters.

Table 21.1 Services for the elderly

Services for the homebound	Services for the ambulatory	Services for those with special problems
Homemaker services	Transportation and escort services	Protective services
Home-health aides	Congregate meals	Counseling
Home-delivered meals	Legal services	Day-care centers
Friendly visitors	Employment	
Telephone reassurance		
Information and referral		

Types of Services

Services for the Homebound Elderly

Most older people prefer to remain in their own homes and retain their independence and autonomy as long as possible. The services listed in the following sections are designed to provide some of the necessary resources that the elderly need in order to function more independently within their own homes and to prevent or delay the need for institutional care.

HOMEMAKER SERVICES Homemaker services provide professionally supervised, "trained" women who furnish housekeeping and other help to those elderly who are temporarily or permanently disabled. The homemaker usually has some training in the home care of the sick, but she is not a substitute for a nurse. She assists her client by shopping for food, preparing the meals, doing light housework, and offering companionship. She may be needed only a few hours a day several times a week, or she may come on a daily basis. Sometimes the need for the service is only temporary, such as after an illness or hospitalization. In 1976, homemaker services were provided in 49 states and served over 150,000 older persons.[3]

HOME HEALTH AIDES Home health aides provide paraprofessional nursing care and serve a variety of out-of-hospital needs. In some communities, homemaker and home-health-aide services are combined so that one person may do both jobs. Home-health-aide services are covered by Medicare, while homemaker services are not. The services of homemaker–home health aides make it possible for older people to live alone more comfortably and for a longer period of time before institutionalization. Such services also shorten or circumvent prolonged hospitalization.

An estimated 2.5 million elderly people are in need of home health services, but are doing without them largely because of the lack of their availability.[4] Possibly as many as 14 to 25 percent of the institutionalized elderly might live outside institutions if home health services were available to them.[5] Until older people reach the point where they are extremely disabled, home care is far less costly and much more desirable than nursing home care.

HOME-DELIVERED MEALS   Popularly referred to as meals-on-wheels, this service provides for the delivery of a hot noon meal to elderly persons who are homebound and unable to cook and shop, or obtain help to do so. Not only is the older person given a nutritious meal five days a week, but also he or she receives a friendly visit from the volunteer delivering the meal.

> In his garage apartment he was pretty much a prisoner. He didn't dare risk the stairs by himself, now that he was on crutches; and there wasn't another place he could move to on his little pension. His life was bounded by a dirty alley at the back and the tall brick apartment house wall from his living-bedroom. . . . There was just Mr. Wilmont and the impersonal television set. But when Meals-on-Wheels found Mr. Wilmont, Mr. Wilmont found a new way of life. With that nice Mrs. Freedman stopping in every day, he began to get himself cleaned up a little, and the apartment too. He also started listening to the news in order to have something to say to her when she came. Life was different, in a good way.[6]

The hot meal is often delivered along with a cold snack for dinner and cereal and milk for the next day's breakfast. With home delivered meals, many persons who might otherwise require institutional care can remain in their own homes.

FRIENDLY VISITORS   Sometimes referred to as "organized neighborliness,"[7] this program provides volunteers to visit isolated, homebound persons and institutionalized persons on a regularly scheduled basis. The visitor and older person may do such things as play cards, or checkers, watch television together, or just sit and talk. The visitor is usually trained and supervised by a professional person, and must have an understanding of the older person's needs and be a good listener. Visitors offer continuing companionship to elderly persons who have no relatives or friends to fill this need. Older persons themselves make especially good visitors.

Many professional workers have observed how this program relieves the loneliness of older people: "clients look better and take more interest

Lack of transportation has become an increasing problem for many elderly. The provision of a minibus like the one pictured can fill this need. (Tennessee Commission on Aging)

in things outside themselves after receiving friendly visiting. Frequently, there is improvement in actual physical condition, or at least, less absorption in illness."[8]

TELEPHONE REASSURANCE SERVICES Many elderly persons who live alone worry that they may become ill or injured without being able to contact anyone for help. The telephone reassurance program, just as the name implies, helps allay these concerns by calling persons who live alone at a certain time each day. The older person generally informs the telephone reassurance volunteer if he or she does not plan to be home at the time of the regularly scheduled call. If the phone is not answered and the volunteer has not been notified that the client will be away, then someone will immediately go to the home to check on the person. Community agencies and churches often provide space and funds for such a service. The callers may range in age from teenagers to older persons. By checking on an elderly person's health and well-being, telephone reassurance provides continuing personal contact and a feeling that someone cares.

INFORMATION AND REFERRAL SERVICES Information and referral services link the needs of older people with the resources available to them in their community. The primary function of an information and referral agency is to develop and maintain a file of all the services for the elderly in the community and to make this information easily accessible to them. Information and referral services are usually provided over the telephone. Generally organized by councils on aging or community welfare councils and their affiliated social agencies, information and referral services are now being offered in over 100 communities.[9] In addition to the initial contact, most information and referral agencies do follow-up work to evaluate whether or not the client was properly referred and received the needed service. The agency also performs a valuable function by identifying unmet needs in the community and discovering gaps and duplication in available services.

Services for the Ambulatory

Besides home-delivered services, most communities offer an array of services to those elderly who are relatively well and able to travel to them. The focal point for the delivery of many of these services is the senior citizen center. At such centers, older persons may often avail themselves of a broad range of individual and group services.

TRANSPORTATION   A number of innovative projects for meeting the transportation needs of older people have been developed in many communities across the nation. These communities provide door-to-door, flexible transportation services for the elderly in a variety of vehicles, including station wagons, 9-passenger minibuses, and 60-passenger buses. The older person generally calls a central dispatching office, usually 24 hours in advance, and specifies the trip needs. The scheduling and routing for the next day's transportation requirements are then worked out accordingly. An example of such a service is the "Seniors on the Move" project in Chicago, which serves the special transportation needs of the elderly in its service area. This project provides for free door-to-door transportation for an average of 350 to 400 elderly persons per month.[10] Passengers call the dispatcher a day in advance of their prospective trip and a two-way radio permits last-minute changes. Whenever possible, requests such as shopping or clinic visits are organized as group trips.

Some senior citizen centers provide a bus that runs between the members' homes and the center. In Menlo Park, California, center members may arrange to be picked up by having a standing reservation or by phoning in advance. The 12-passenger minibus is also used for group outings and other occasions.

Another transportation alternative is the use of volunteers driving private cars; this service is especially valuable in rural areas where no accessible public transportation exists. A volunteer driver picks up older persons at their homes and takes them to doctors' offices, clinics, stores, and other essential destinations.

In some communities, escort services are provided for older persons who may need someone to accompany them when walking or traveling either because of their physical impairments or for protection from criminal victimization. In New York City, police are using teen-age volunteers in an escort service program for the elderly. Currently, the plan involves 1,000 teen-agers and 5,000 senior citizens.[11] Besides furnishing a pedestrian escort service for the elderly in Wilmington, Delaware, volunteers have been recruited to serve as escorts on wheels. Escorts are screened and issued identification for themselves and stickers for their cars to overcome any suspiciousness that older persons might have (Figure 21.1).[12] In one Chicago slum area, the police department hires a bus and a driver the day that social security checks arrive. The driver picks up older people from two housing projects and anyone else who needs help and takes them to a bank, a grocery store, and then safely home.[13]

CONGREGATE MEALS   The federal nutrition program, under title VII of the Older Americans Act, is currently serving over a half-million meals daily to persons over 60 years of age.[14] Most meals are offered to groups of elderly at midday in central locations, such as senior citizen centers, schools, community centers, and churches. In addition to a hot, nutritious meal, each of the nation's 10,200 meal sites offers a variety of services and programs, such as consumer advice, health and nutrition counseling, and arts and crafts. During a testimony given before the Senate Subcommittee on Aging, Senator Edward Kennedy remarked:

> Title VII, though, is more than just a hot meal program for the elderly. It also provides a place for the elderly to meet and talk with others. In some cases this socialization function is more important than the meal itself. Title VII project directors have made this point emphatically. They have described the friendships, even marriages, resulting from interaction among participants. Many older Americans have become volunteers, cooks, transportation assistants, and outreach workers after becoming involved with this program.[15]

Birthdays and holidays are also celebrated in congregate meal settings. In some instances, older men and women having met at the meals program have decided to get married and have held their weddings at the meal site.

LEGAL SERVICES   It is becoming increasingly apparent that the elderly are in need of a wide variety of legal services, which range from tenant rights, consumer protection, and contracts to the preparation of wills.

Figure 21.1 This badge identifies volunteers who accompany elderly persons on errands in Wilmington, Delaware

SOURCE: Federal Bureau of Investigation.

Many older people lack access to the legal system. One reason for this is that they cannot afford to pay lawyers' fees. Also, some elderly fear involvement with lawyers and their subsequent fees.[16] Another reason is that older persons are often unaware of their legal rights or of the legal services available to them.

In recent years, there has been a growing commitment to make legal assistance more readily available to the elderly. One approach has been through the establishment of the Legal Research and Services for the Elderly program in 1968. Under the sponsorship of the National Council of Senior Citizens, this program has initiated many legal-aid services and has promoted an awareness among the aged of their legal rights. Another effort to expand legal help to older people is being made by the Legal Services Corporation, a federally funded program of legal services for the poor. In 1977 the corporation joined forces with the Administration on Aging to provide the elderly with increased access to legal services.

In some cities special programs have been designed to help meet the legal needs of the elderly. For example, in San Diego, lawyer referral services are available to the elderly through a senior center referral program. In New Orleans, a group of participating lawyers are available to provide legal services to the elderly with fees based on the client's income. Older persons who are enrolled in a legal service plan in Philadelphia receive unlimited telephone advice and consultation from a panel of lawyers.[17] Still another source of legal aid for the elderly is provided through the use of senior citizen paralegals. These paralegals, many of whom are aged themselves, work under the supervision of a lawyer. They are trained to provide legal assistance in problems that confront older people and to serve as advocates for the elderly poor.

EMPLOYMENT SERVICES   While a number of nonprofit volunteer employment agencies are specifically designed to help older people secure full-time and part-time jobs, one of the best sources for information about job opportunities is the state employment service offices. Though they offer counseling and job placement to all age groups, these agencies have been expanding their services to older workers. Many have established Older Worker Service Units, while others have personnel who specialize in securing jobs for the older worker.

A number of federal programs have been developed to make useful, paying jobs available to the low-income elderly. Two notable examples are the Foster Grandparent and Senior Companion programs. Besides providing meaningful work roles for older men and women and relieving the effects of poverty, these two programs give older people an opportunity to utilize their skills, talents, and experience to meet community needs. In addition, the elderly derive a sense of self-satisfaction and respect that comes from feeling useful and serving others.

The uniqueness of these programs lies in the fact that they are mutually beneficial to the worker and the recipient. The Foster Grandparent and Senior Companion programs employ low-income persons aged 60 and over to work four hours a day, five days a week for a modest stipend. Foster Grandparents offer support, companionship, and love to children with special needs. Modeled after the Foster Grandparent Program, the Senior Companion Program focuses not on children but on older adults who have special needs. Senior Compan-

In the Senior Companion program, older persons provide services to other older persons with special needs. This Senior Companion is reading to a homebound client who lives alone. (ACTION)

ions work with elderly persons — especially the very old and infirm — both in private homes and institutions as companions and helpers (Table 21.2).[18]

In the private sector, one of the most unique and innovative employment services is provided by Rent-A Granny and Rent-A Grandpa. Started in Albuquerque, New Mexico, in 1960, the concept has spread to other cities. Seventy-year-old Anne Beckman, founder of this nonfee service, has an ability for matching talents and jobs. She has secured over 10,000 jobs for older persons in Albuquerque, from working as domestic workers and tour directors to being private investigators.[19] Beckman finds that most people do not know the wealth that they possess in hidden assets.

They don't realize that their hobbies, avocations and special interests often can be "recycled" and sold as valuable commodities in the job market. For example, we had a woman here last week who casually mentioned that she had won many prizes in garden shows. I had no trouble getting her a job arranging flowers for a nursery. . . . A granny with a flair for whipping up tasty hors d'oeuvres was hired by a party caterer. A learned college professor,

Table 21.2 Foster Grandparent and Senior Companion programs: Data summary, 1976

	Foster Grandparents	*Senior Companions*
Year established	1965	1973
Scope of operations	50 states	26 states
Local projects	174	28
Workers	13,500	1,382
Clients served daily	32,400	6,500

SOURCE: Adapted from Elinor Bowles, "Older Persons as Providers of Services: Three Federal Programs," in *Older Persons: Unused Resources for Unmet Needs, Social Policy,* November/December 1976 Volume 7, No. 3, p. 83. Copyright © 1976 by Social Policy Corporation.

exiled into idleness by mandatory retirement policy, was offered a chair in a department store — behind its information booth.[20]

It is not unusual for Beckman to obtain jobs for persons in their seventies and eighties. In one instance, she placed a 92-year-old man with a resonant voice as a telephone solicitor.

Services for Those with Special Problems

PROTECTIVE SERVICES   Usually sponsored by legal-service centers, or voluntary or public agencies, protective services are distinguished from other social services in that there is a potential or reason for legal intervention. These services provide assistance to older persons who are too mentally or emotionally incapacitated to manage their own affairs and have no relatives or friends to act in their behalf. Protective services may take various forms including guardianship, conservatorship, or commitment. It is estimated that 10 to 15 percent, or 3 to 4 million persons aged 60 and over, may be in need of protective services.[21] However, these services are not yet widely available.

Another important aspect of protective services concerns institutionalization. Often an older person is confined to an institution involuntarily, either by a court order following commitment proceedings or because the community does not have any other option. The 1975 Supreme Court decision in *Donaldson* v. *O'Connor,* has challenged the legality of involuntary institutional treatment. The court ruled that it is unconstitutional for a state to confine persons in institutions when they are not dangerous and are capable of living alone or with the help

Employment agencies like Rent-a-Granny or Rent-a-Grandpa are helping older persons to secure full-time or part-time jobs. (*Parade*. Ben Ross)

of relatives and friends. This decision is expected to have far-reaching consequences.

COUNSELING SERVICES These services, generally offered by public or voluntary social agencies, provide assistance in many areas, including personal and family problems, retirement adjustment, finances, and living arrangements. Often the request for help comes from the older person's relatives. The referral may also come from other agencies or professionals. The following situation illustrates how uprooting a person from familiar surroundings into an institution, without careful consideration of such a move, can create problems and the need for intervention by a counseling agency:

Miss R's attorney asked the agency to plan with Miss R., a 90-year-old woman who had refused to remain in the institution for the aged where she had been placed by relatives a month previously. . . . It was found that she had a calcium deficiency of the spine which would require her to wear a body-brace and to limit going up and down stairs to once a day. Relatives then arranged for her to enter a sectarian home for the aged by mortgaging her property in order to pay her admission to the home. At the institution Miss R. was placed in the hospital section where she could not adjust to strangers coming in and out of her room at will. When it came time for Miss R. to sign the permanent contract at the institution, she rebelled and went home.[22]

After Miss R. returned home, a caseworker began visiting her and found that she felt betrayed by her relatives and friends. Her physician confirmed that she was not in need of nursing home care. In time, Miss R. developed a good relationship with the caseworker and was persuaded to employ a woman on a part-time basis to assist her. With household help and the support of the caseworker and the agency, Miss R. was able to remain in her own home where she had strong, meaningful ties and felt secure.

GERIATRIC DAY-CARE CENTERS   Day-care centers are designed to prevent premature institutionalization for those who have mental or physical impairments and are not capable of full-time independent living, but who can manage to stay in the community if professional support is provided. Day-care centers fulfill a variety of needs, including social, psychiatric and rehabilitation services, health maintenance, and recreational activities. These services are usually offered five days a week on an eight-hour basis, along with meals and transportation.[23] The centers are especially valuable for those elderly whose families work and where there is no one at home to care for them during the day. Day-care centers may be located in an independent facility, or they may be part of a senior citizen center, a neighborhood center, or hospital.

The Availability and Utilization of Services

All these social services and more are needed by the elderly. Yet, at present, most communities have only some services, and they are not available to all the elderly who need them. Three major concepts involving development and planning of social services are availability, accessibility, and utilization. Social services must not only be available when needed, but they "must be in existence and organized in a comprehensive, coordinated way on a continuous basis, so that older people can utilize them when they are required."[24] In addition, social services should be geographically accessible to where older people live. Also services should be accessible in the sense that they are easily obtainable and not blocked by elaborate procedures and red tape, which discourage their use.

But neither availability nor accessibility will assure that services will be utilized. Often older persons do not use traditional social services, and in many cases, services are not used by those who need them most. The elderly lack awareness of the services that are available and lack information concerning them. Also, the elderly often do not like to accept such services and attach a certain amount of stigma to them. These attitudes and lack of knowledge are further compounded by the problem of having to cope with complex bureaucratic structures to gain access to services. Finally, the elderly's sense of dignity and pride often stand in the way of utilizing services. Many elderly who have been self-sufficient and independent all their lives are too proud to accept free assistance readily.[25]

In order to overcome the reluctance of the aged to request help and to let them know of the opportunities for aid that are available, one useful method is through community outreach programs. These programs seek out older persons in the community to advise them about the services available and where they may be obtained. For example, when both Medicare and SSI programs were first implemented, outreach workers were used to inform older persons.

> Mrs. Julia Covington, 100 years, had never received a government check or a social agency's aid when Yazoo Community Action outreach workers discovered her living in a run-down house in their central Mississippi town. The widowed black woman, who had mothered 13 children decades ago, was in poor health, the result of a diet dependent solely on her tiny backyard garden.
>
> Now 104, Mrs. Covington is receiving regular Supplemental Security Income (SSI) checks. Her house has been repaired. On weekdays, an outreach worker comes at noon with a nutritious lunch. . . . Returned to health in spite of her age, Mrs. Covington is now active in her church and occasionally travels to visit her children.[26]

Often outreach workers are older persons themselves. In Operation Medicare Alert, about 14,500 persons — most of them elderly — went into communities across the nation to reach those eligible for the program. Within six months, they had signed up over 4 million elderly for Medicare.[27]

Probably one of the most successful and comprehensive of all outreach programs was Project FIND.[28] Conducted by the National Council on the Aging in 1967 and 1968, Project FIND (Friendless, Isolated, Needy, or Disabled) used aides ranging in age from 50 to 85 to survey 12 communities across the country. The target group was the isolated elderly of low socioeconomic levels. When the aides found elderly who needed help, they referred them to services that were available in their community. If needed services were not available, the aides tried to secure volunteer help. A significant discovery was the large number of persons who were not aware of the services that they were entitled to. Many persons eligible for social security were not receiving it.

> We helped many in receiving services that are available to them for which they knew nothing about, such as home nursing, home health aid, and in

many cases special equipment, such as hospital beds, wheelchairs, etc. Most of the agencies wait for the aging to seek them out.

Without knowing about these special services, many of our bedfast patients suffer more than is necessary. In most cases, these people have little education and are afraid to ask for help.[29]

While no community was totally without resources, according to the Project FIND report, the number and kind of services varied widely from community to community. There was no community, however, in which the available services even began to meet the documented needs.

Over a decade has passed since Project FIND was carried out. Since that time, the number of services for the nation's elderly have been greatly increased and expanded. The Post-White House Conference on Aging Reports of 1973 established the federal government's official policy toward the elderly, which committed the government to the responsibility of meeting the needs of the elderly.[30] Though great strides have been made in fulfilling this commitment, as the older population continues to grow, so will the gap between the government's policy and the programs to implement it. The challenge for the future appears to be the development and availability of a fuller range of services for the elderly, while at the same time trying to keep pace with the needs of an increasing population of older persons.

Summary

1. Specialized social services for the elderly are of recent origin. Their development has coincided with the expansion of our knowledge about aging. Social services for the elderly may be classified into services for the homebound, the ambulatory, and those elderly with special problems.

2. Many older people prefer to live independently and remain in their own homes as long as possible. Various programs have been designed to help achieve this objective, including homemaker services, home health aides, and home-delivered meals. Each of these brings services into the homes of the elderly who are incapacitated and need assistance to maintain themselves. The homemaker offers assistance by preparing food and doing light housework, whereas the home health aide provides paraprofessional nursing care. For those elderly who are unable to cook, shop, or obtain help in doing so, a hot noonday meal is delivered to them.

3. The Friendly Visitor and Telephone Reassurance programs provide a continuing personal contact for those elderly who live alone. Information and referral services, not only invaluable to the homebound elderly, but to the ambulatory elderly as well, link the needs of older people with services available to them in the community.

4. For those elderly who are relatively well and ambulatory, many communities furnish a flexible, door-to-door transportation service. Special vehicles for this

purpose range from buses of all sizes to private cars. Escort services are furnished in many places to give older people physical assistance while traveling, as well as to assure them of safety from criminal victimization. The congregate meal program provides older persons with nutritious meals at a central location in the community and an opportunity to socialize. In addition, a wide range of services and programs are provided at these meal sites.

5. The elderly need a variety of legal services, but many, especially the poor, are often denied access to the legal system. To alleviate this situation, such groups as Legal Research and Services for the Elderly have initiated a number of legal-aid services and programs. Also the federally funded Legal Services Corporation has committed itself to increasing the availability of legal services to the elderly. Another area in which the elderly need assistance is in finding full-time and part-time jobs. Nonprofit employment agencies have been designed for this purpose, and the state employment offices have been expanding their services to older workers. Two outstanding federal programs that provide useful jobs for the low-income elderly are Foster Grandparents and Senior Companions.

6. Many elderly have problems that require special services: protective services for those who are mentally or emotionally incapacitated to manage their own affairs, and counseling services for assistance on such matters as living arrangements and family problems. Day-care centers have been developed for those who have mental or physical impairments but who can live at home with professional support.

7. Availability, accessibility, and utilization are three major concepts involving the planning and development of social services. Often older persons do not use available services because they lack awareness or acceptance of the services, and experience difficulty in trying to obtain them. Outreach programs have been effective in informing older people of these services and in helping to overcome the reluctance of many elderly to ask for assistance. The federal government is committed to the responsibility of meeting the needs of the elderly, and much has been done to fulfill this commitment. With the growing population of older people, however, this policy will become increasingly difficult to implement in the future.

Notes

1. Demetrios J. Constantelos, *Byzantine Philanthropy and Social Welfare*, Rutgers University Press, New Brunswick, N.J., 1968, p. 222.

2. H. Shlonsky, quoted in Sheldon S. Tobin, Stephen M. Davidson, and Ann Sack, *Effective Social Services for Older Americans*, Institute of Gerontology, University of Michigan-Wayne State University, Ann Arbor, 1976, p. 6.

3. U.S. Senate, *Developments in Aging: 1977*, Pt. 2, A Report of the Special Committee on Aging, U.S. Government Printing Office, Washington, D.C., 1978, p. 284.

4. Frank E. Moss and Val J. Halamandaris, *Too Old, Too Sick, Too Bad*, Aspen Systems Corporation, Germantown, Md., 1977, p. 236.

5. "GAO Reports Home Health Care Cheaper Than Nursing Homes," *Aging*, March–April 1978, p. 9.

6. Bert K. Smith, *Aging in America*, Beacon Press, Boston, 1973, p. 152.

7. Administration on Aging, *Let's End Isolation*, U.S. Government Printing Office, Washington, D.C., 1972, p. 23.

8. Ibid.

9. Louis Lowy, "Social Welfare and the Aging," in *Understanding Aging: A Multidisciplinary Approach*, eds. Marian G. Spencer and Caroline J. Dorr, Appleton-Century-Crofts, New York, 1975, p. 157.

10. Joseph S. Revis, *Transportation for Older Americans: A State of the Art Report*, Administration on Aging, U.S. Government Printing Office, Washington, D.C., 1975, p. 353.

11. "Step-up in Fight on Crimes Against the Elderly," *U.S. News and World Report*, June 13, 1977, p. 62.

12. Federal Bureau of Investigation, *Crime Resistance*, U.S. Government Printing Office, Washington, D.C., 1977, pp. 45–46.

13. Ibid.

14. U.S. Senate, *Developments in Aging: 1977, A Report of the Special Committee on Aging*, U.S. Government Printing Office, Washington, D.C., 1978, p. 159.

15. Ibid., p. 123.

16. Dee Pridgen, "Legal Concerns of the Elderly," *Aging*, November–December 1977, p. 5.

17. Ibid., p. 6.

18. Elinor Bowles, "Older Persons as Providers of Services: Three Federal Programs," in *Older Persons: Unused Resources for Unmet Needs*, ed. Frank Riessman, Sage, Beverly Hills, Calif., 1977, pp. 114–127.

19. James D. Snyder and Robert M. Engleman, "Ten Social Service Programs that Really Work," *Geriatrics*, 31, no. 10 (1976), 118–125. Reprinted with permission of *Geriatrics*.

20. Mort Weisinger, "How Granny Power Gets Jobs for Old Folks," *Parade*, February 1, 1976, pp. 14, 16.

21. U.S. Senate, *Developments in Aging: 1977*, p. 204.

22. Jean M. Leach, "Counseling with Older People and Their Families," *Working with Older People: A Guide to Practice*, vol. 3, Public Health Service, U.S. Government Printing Office, Washington, D.C., 1970, pp. 59–60.

23. Walter M. Beattie, Jr., "Aging and the Social Services, *Handbook of Aging and the Social Sciences*, eds. Robert H. Binstock and Ethel Shanas, Van Nostrand Reinhold, New York, 1976, p. 624.

24. Lowy, "Social Welfare and the Aging," p. 167.

25. Ibid., pp. 167–168.

26. Snyder and Engleman, "Ten Social Service Programs That Really Work," p. 119. Reprinted with permission of *Geriatrics*.

27. Bruce J. Terris, "Legal Service for the Elderly," in *Let's Learn About Aging*,

eds. John R. Barry and C. Ray Wingrove, Schenkman, Cambridge, Mass., 1977, p. 427.

28. *The Golden Years — A Tarnished Myth* (Project Find) The National Council on the Aging, New York, 1970.

29. Ibid., p. 60.

30. See U.S. Senate, *Post-White House Conference on Aging Reports, 1973,* Committee on Labor and Public Welfare and the Special Committee on Aging, Washington, D.C., 1973.

For Further Study

Administration on Aging. *Let's End Isolation.* U.S. Government Printing Office, Washington, D.C., 1972. Describes a number of special community services designed to improve the conditions of older people.

Barry, John R., and C. Ray Wingrove, eds. *Let's Learn About Aging.* Schenkman, Cambridge, Mass., 1977. Section IV, Part B, contains a variety of readings on social services for the elderly.

Baumhover, Lorin A., and Joan D. Jones. *Handbook of American Aging Programs.* Greenwood Press, Westport, Conn., 1977. Examines a wide range of programs that are having an important impact on the lives of the elderly.

Beattie, Walter M., Jr. "Aging and the Social Services." In *Handbook of Aging and the Social Sciences,* edited by Robert H. Binstock and Ethel Shanas, Van Nostrand Reinhold, New York, 1976, pp. 619–642. Deals with a number of topics including an overview of social services for the elderly, the planning and development of social services, and models of social service systems.

Brody, Elaine M. "Aging." In *Encyclopedia of Social Work.* National Association of Social Workers, New York, 1977, pp. 55–77. Defines the needs of the aged and discusses some services and programs to meet these needs.

Harbert, Anita S., and Leon H. Ginsberg. *Human Services for Older Adults: Concepts and Skills.* Wadsworth, Belmont, Calif., 1979. Focuses on the methods needed to provide direct services to the elderly, as well as on how older persons can be helped indirectly through program planning and development.

Tobin, Sheldon S., Stephen M. Davidson, and Ann Sack. *Effective Social Services for Older Americans.* Institute of Gerontology, University of Michigan-Wayne State, Ann Arbor, 1976. Presents an approach to the structuring of effective social services for the elderly in both rural and urban settings.

22

Aging and the Aged in the Future

Our society is rapidly changing. Change is reflected in every aspect of our lives, from norms and values to science and technology. Change has become such a prevalent element that we frequently take it for granted. Throughout this book, we have examined changes that have taken place or that are expected to take place regarding the elderly. In this final chapter, we will review some of the future changes that are likely to occur in the older population, and the impact of these changes on the society at large.

Predicting future social changes on the basis of existing trends is called *extrapolation*. Such social forecasting rests on the assumption that any stable society like ours will in the future be much like it is in the present, having certain continuities that tend to persist. The possibility of unexpected events or of the intervention of unforeseen factors is largely ignored in extrapolation. Thus, making predictions based on existing trends can be risky. Nevertheless, some attempts at social forecasting are necessary in order to plan more effectively for the future and to develop appropriate solutions for problems that may arise with change.

> Many of the problems of the present-day aged can be said to be the result of cultural lag. Our social institutions were not prepared for the relatively rapid appearance of large numbers of older people since the turn of the century. If our institutions are to be more successful in the next few decades, scholarly efforts should now be undertaken to forecast, as best we can, the likely demographic and social developments, to anticipate the problems of aging and the aging society that lie ahead, then to decide what types of information are needed for formulating policies that will be future-oriented.[1]

Numerous writers and scholars have made predictions concerning aging and the aged in the twenty-first century. Some of their predictions in the areas of population, the economy, politics, education, health, and the family will now be discussed.

Population Trends

The number and proportion of older people in the population are expected to continue increasing through the first third of the next century. These rises will result from increased life expectancy and the aging of the "baby-boom" generation (following World War II). The population aged 65 and over was 3.1 million in 1900; by 1978 it had climbed to over 23 million. In recent years the number of older persons has been rising by approximately 300,000 to 400,000 per year, or 3 to 4 million per decade. With this rate of increase continuing into the next century, by the year 2000, the elderly population will be about 31.8 million, and by 2035, it should reach around 55.8 million (Table 22.1).[2]

Population projections like the above can be made with a fair amount of reliability because they are based on death rates, not birth rates, and those who will be 65 and over in 2000 and 2035 are already born. The proportion of older people in the population is more difficult to project than the actual numbers because it depends on birth rates, which are subject to wide fluctuation. If birth rates remain low, the proportion of elderly is expected to increase to around 12.2 percent by 2000, and to 18.3 percent by 2035 (Table 22.1). As a result, the median age of our population is expected to rise from its present 29.4 years to an all-time high of 38 years by 2030.[3]

While the human life span of 100 years has probably not changed since earliest times, dramatic increases in life expectancy have taken place, especially during the first half of this century. In this period life expectancy increased from 47 years in 1900 to 68 years in 1950. Since mid-century, the gain has proceeded at a much slower pace; most researchers foresee only small improvements in life expectancy between now and the beginning of the next century. By 2000, the expectation of life for both sexes will be about 74 years, with life expectancy for men being 70 years, and for women 78 years. Leonard Hayflick strongly doubts that any spectacular scientific breakthroughs will occur, even by 2025, that will significantly increase life expectancy.

. . . 18 years or so could be added to the present life expectancy by eliminating cardiovascular disease, stroke, and cancer. But even if all causes of death resulting from disease and accidents were totally eliminated, the effect on human longevity would be merely to realize the "ultimate rectangular curve," with everyone living for about 100 years.[4]

Because of the differences in life expectancy between the sexes, the ratio of females to males in the older population will continue to increase

Table 22.1 Population projections, total and 65 and over by sex, 1977–2050 (numbers in thousands)

		65 and over			
Year	Total number all ages	Both sexes (number)	Both sexes (percentage of all ages)	Males (number)	Females (number)	Females per 100 men (number)
1977	216,745	23,431	10.8%	9,545	13,885	145
1980	222,159	24,927	11.2	10,108	14,819	147
1985	232,880	27,305	11.7	11,012	16,293	148
1990	243,513	29,824	12.3	11,999	17,824	149
1995	252,750	31,401	12.4	12,602	18,799	149
2000	260,378	31,822	12.2	12,717	19,105	150
2005	267,603	32,436	12.1	12,924	19,512	151
2010	275,335	34,837	12.7	13,978	20,858	149
2015	283,164	39,519	14.0	16,063	23,456	146
2020	290,115	45,102	15.6	18,468	26,634	144
2025	295,742	50,920	17.2	20,861	30,059	144
2030	300,349	55,024	18.3	22,399	32,624	146
2035	304,486	55,805	18.3	22,434	33,371	149
2040	308,400	54,925	17.8	21,816	33,108	152
2045	312,054	54,009	17.3	21,335	32,674	153
2050	315,622	55,494	17.6	22,055	33,439	152

SOURCE: U.S. Senate, *Developments in Aging: 1978*, A Report of the Special Committee on Aging, U.S. Government Printing Office, Washington, D.C., 1979, p. xxiv.

until the beginning of the next century. At that time, there will be about 150 females to every 100 males in the population aged 65 and older. The trend will be reversed in the years between 2010 and 2025, with a ratio of 144 females to every 100 males, but later it will resume its current rise (Table 22.1).

The Future Economic Status of the Elderly

The economic status of the older population will undoubtedly continue to improve. Average incomes will increase while the number of incomes below the poverty level will decrease. In fact, Robert Havighurst predicts that "dire poverty among the elderly will be practically eliminated before the year 2000."[5] Much of this improvement will be due to the increased coverage of the elderly under public and private pension programs, the rise in social security benefit levels, and the SSI program.

Another factor that will improve the economic situation of the elderly is what James Schulz calls the "demographic turnover."[6] Every day about 4,000 persons turn 65, and about 3,000 persons over age 64 die. Those who die are usually poorer than those who have just become members of the aged population. The newer aged often retire on pension incomes that were "undreamed of not many years ago."[7]

About 2010, when the first wave of the "baby-boom" generation starts retiring, there will be a much larger retired population in relation to the size of the labor force than ever before. As the numbers of people retiring increase, the financial burden on those working will also increase. It is estimated that by 2030 there will be one social security beneficiary for every two workers paying into the social security system, instead of one beneficiary for every three workers as it is today. A. Haewarth Robertson warns that if the present structure of social security continues unchanged into the next century, taxpayers may be paying as high as 24 percent of their earnings into the social security system.[8]

Most observers predict that the mandatory retirement age will either be raised again or abolished entirely in the next few decades. The trend toward early retirement is expected to continue at least until the year 2000. By then, Bernice Neugarten predicts that the retirement age will have dropped to 55.[9] The trend may reverse itself then, because fewer younger persons will be in the labor force due to the lower birth rates since the 1960s. This situation in turn should create a demand for older workers.

Political Prospects

Despite a rapidly growing elderly population, there appears to be no evidence of a marked increase in its political power now or in the foreseeable future. The possibility of "senior power" in the sense of a politics of aging seems highly unlikely. At present, political attitudes, party affiliations, social class, ethnicity, and the interests of the elderly are far too diverse to result in a cohesive aging vote that could determine the outcome of elections. No great change is likely in the near future since those who will be 65 by the year 2020 have already demonstrated their political diversity in national elections.[10]

Neal Cutler and John Schmidhauser, while agreeing with this position, feel that the elderly will play an increasingly important role in future politics "even if all older persons do not speak with a single political voice.[11] They base their assumptions on several reasons, including the fact that the future elderly will represent a larger proportion of the total population, and that they will have more education and political experience for participation in politics.

Interest groups, such as the American Association of Retired Persons and the National Council of Senior Citizens, will continue to be active in the future. Though much of their power rests on the bluff of the aging vote, these mass-membership organizations have ready access to politicians, the mass media, and public officials who feel that the aging vote cannot be ignored.[12] As the number of older persons increases, Robert Binstock feels that it will probably have little effect upon interest-group politics, except for increasing the magnitude of the electoral bluff and thereby enhancing the capacity of aging-based interest groups to gain greater access to public officials.[13]

Educational Trends

The rapidly rising level of educational attainment of the elderly will also continue. A generation ago, only one out of five persons aged 65 and over had graduated from high school. Today, one in every three older persons is a high school graduate, and by 1990, the ratio is expected to reach one in every two.

The educational attainment of older persons is far below that of adults in general. But by the twenty-first century, the gap between the educational level of the older and younger populations will have been greatly reduced. The median number of years of school completed by those age 65 and over about a decade ago was 8.7 years; today it is about 9.7 years and is expected to exceed 12 years by 2000. At the same time, the pattern of rapidly rising educational attainment for the younger population appears to be over. This means that younger persons will have only a slightly higher educational level in the future than the elderly.[14]

Because they will be better educated and have more free time, older persons in the future will become more involved in continued learning — in programs of general education and those specifically designed for the elderly.[15] Prominent among the latter will be preparation for retirement programs, which not only will deal with such topics as finances, health, and legal problems, but also, according to Eric Pfeiffer, will include "alternative patterns of meaningful participation in community and family life . . . through continued work participation, changed occupational status, second, third, and fourth careers, or through gradual education to leisure."[16] In addition, preretirement programs will also be changed to accommodate the increasing number of women in the labor force. Past programs have primarily concerned the adjustment problems of men as they retired; in the future, such education will also be directed toward meeting the special needs of women retirees.[17]

Future Health-Care Services for the Elderly

In the future, older persons will not only live longer, but they will remain healthier to a later age. This improved state will be largely due to rising income and educational levels among the elderly and to anticipated improvements in health-care systems and services. Sheldon Tobin sees three forms of future health services that are likely to become more visible in the next decade or so.[18] First are the community-based, local or neighborhood organizations that are now developing to provide a range of services to the elderly in order to prevent or delay institutionalization. A second form of health service will be small, local institutions for those elderly who are incapacitated and need constant care. These smaller institutions will provide their residents with a more desirable and humane environment than is furnished by many large impersonal institutions today. The third trend in health care will be the establishment of hospices to care for, and help dying persons and to provide counseling for their families.

Tobin points out that while the present generation of elderly have strong feelings against being institutionalized, they are more likely to accept the situation than the elderly in the future will. "Aged persons in the future will be more inclined to see their personal problems as being remediable either by informal or by professional help from others; and to a greater extent, they will have already used professional help in meeting earlier personal problems."[19]

Though it is predicted that the future elderly will live about an additional five years and will stay healthy longer compared with today's elderly, both Tobin and Neugarten suggest that they will still be incapacitated or have failing health for about the same length of time during the last phase of life (Figure 22.1).[20] Thus, the future elderly, having much the same health needs of the present generation, will demand health services, but at a more advanced age and in greater quantities, as there will be a larger older population. The costs of meeting these needs will be correspondingly multiplied.

Future Family Patterns

Family networks are expected to increase, rather than decrease, in importance in the future. This prediction is based on the fact that persons who will be old in the year 2000 will have more children and relatives due to the "baby boom" and to lower mortality rates than the

Figure 22.1 The timing of life events, 1970 and 2000

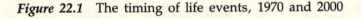

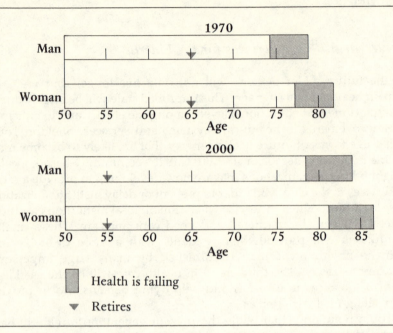

SOURCE: Bernice L. Neugarten, "The Future and the Young-Old," *The Gerontologist*, 15, No. 1 (1975), Pt. 2, 5.

elderly do today. In addition, the four- or five-generation family will be the norm by the next century because of increasing longevity and shorter gaps between generations. Children will come to know their great-grandparents and even great-great-grandparents.[21]

Many adult children now aid their aged parents and may continue to do so in the future, but there appears to be a gradual weakening in the family support system and an increasing need for resources outside the kin network.

> Just as Social Security shifted economic support of the aged from the family to a broader societal base, so do support services for the sick or senile require a societal response. Already the limitations of the family support system are spawning a service industry and a professional corps to provide regular meals, housekeeping services, and institutionalized care. This trend can be expected to continue.[22]

Today persons in their sixties and older have aged parents in their eighties and nineties. This trend should even be more pronounced in the future and may lead to more intergenerational households in which both generations are old. Such living arrangements will depend on whether a more effective network of social and home health services can be developed in the future than exists today.[23]

Summary

1. Predicting future trends within a society on the basis of present trends is called extrapolation. Social forecasting is necessary in order to develop proper responses to problems and to plan more effectively for the future.

2. The older population will continue to increase into the next century from 23 million in 1978 to about 55.8 million by 2035. At the same time, the proportion of older people in the population will increase markedly if birth rates remain low. It is estimated that by 2035, 18.3 percent of the population will be age 65 and over. Only small improvements are predicted in life expectancy in the near future.

3. The economic situation of the elderly will continue to improve mainly as a result of increased coverage under pensions, the rise in social security benefits, and the federal provisions for SSI. The number of social security beneficiaries will rise so that by 2025 there will be one beneficiary for every two workers paying into the system. The mandatory retirement age will either be raised again or eliminated altogether by 2000, and the retirement age is likely to drop to 55.

4. There appears to be no evidence to justify the possibility of "senior power" in the near future. Presently, the elderly do not constitute a cohesive voting bloc, and there is no reason to expect a change. The educational attainment of the elderly will continue to increase so that by the next century the gap between the general population and the elderly population is expected to narrow. In the future, more older persons will be involved in both general education and educational programs designed for the elderly. As educational and income levels of the elderly increase, along with improved systems of health care, older people will live longer and remain healthier to a more advanced age. Tobin sees three forms of future health services for the elderly: community-based organizations, small, local institutions, and hospices.

5. The family size of the elderly in the year 2000 will be larger than it is today because of the decline in mortality rates and the "baby boom." Four- or five-generation families will be the norm because of increasing longevity. Supportive services for the elderly will continue in the direction of collective responsibility, rather than on an individual family basis.

Notes

1. Bernice L. Neugarten, "Introduction," *The Gerontologist*, 15, no. 1 (1975), Pt. II, 3.

2. U.S. Senate, *Developments in Aging: 1977*, A Report of the Special Committee on Aging, U.S. Government Printing Office, Washington, D.C., 1978, p. xiii.

3. "End of Youth Culture," *U.S. News and World Report*, October 3, 1977, pp. 54–55.

4. Leonard Hayflick, quoted in Richard F. Graber, "Aging in 2025: Telling It Like It's Going to Be," *Geriatrics*, 31, no. 2 (1976), 113.

5. Robert J. Havighurst, "The Future Aged: The Use of Time and Money." *The Gerontologist*, 15, no. 1 (1975), Pt. II, 11.

6. James H. Schulz, *The Economics of Aging*, Wadsworth, Belmont, Calif., 1976, p. 157.

7. Ibid.

8. "Social Security Tax Bite Increasing," *Aging*, Nos. 287–288, September–October 1978, p. 49.

9. Neugarten, "The Future and the Young-Old," *The Gerontologist*, 15, no. 1 (1975), Pt. II, 7.

10. Robert H. Binstock, "Aging and the Future of American Politics," *The Annals of the American Academy*, 415 (September 1974), 203–204.

11. Neal E. Cutler and John R. Schmidhauser, "Age and Political Behavior," *Aging: Scientific Perspectives and Social Issues*, eds. Diana S. Woodruff and James E. Birren, D. Van Nostrand, New York, 1975, p. 398.

12. Robert H. Binstock, quoted in Graber, "Aging in 2025," pp. 115–116.

13. Binstock, "Aging and the Future of American Politics," p. 209.

14. Robert Clark and Joseph Spengler, "Population Aging in the Twenty-First Century," *Aging*, Nos. 279–280 (January–February 1978), p. 10.

15. Howard Y. McClusky, "Designs for Learning," in Lissy F. Jarvik, *Aging into the 21st Century*, Gardner Press, New York, 1978, p. 177.

16. Eric Pfeiffer quoted in Graber, "Aging in 2025," p. 115.

17. McClusky, "Designs for Learning," p. 179.

18. Sheldon S. Tobin, "Social and Health Services for the Future Aged," *The Gerontologist*, 15, no. 1 (1975), Pt. II, 32–37.

19. Ibid., p. 33.

20. Ibid., p. 32 and Neugarten, "The Future and the Young-Old," pp. 5–6.

21. Neugarten, "The Future and the Young-Old," p. 6.

22. Judith Treas, "Family Support Systems for the Aged: Some Demographic Considerations," *The Gerontologist*, 17, no. 6 (1977), 490.

23. Neugarten, "The Future and the Young-Old," p. 7.

For Further Study

Dakoff, Sanford A. "The Future of Social Intervention." In *Handbook of Aging and the Social Sciences*, edited by Robert H. Binstock and Ethel Shanas, Van Nostrand Reinhold, New York, 1976, pp. 643–663. Focuses on aging in postindustrial societies and discusses aging as a social concern.

Fowles, Donald G. *Some Prospects for the Future Elderly Population*. National Clearinghouse on Aging, Washington, D.C., 1978. An overview of some future trends among the elderly.

Jarvik, Lissy F., ed. *Aging into the 21st Century*. Gardner Press, New York, 1978. An excellent collection of articles that deal with the future of aging and the aged from the perspective of social science, biology, and education.

Neugarten, Bernice L,, and Robert J. Havighurst, eds. *Social Policy, Social Ethics, and the Aging Society*. U.S. Government Printing Office, Washington, D.C., 1976. Contains papers and discussions from a conference regarding the economic welfare of older persons and their health services, with an emphasis on the policy decisions that lie ahead.

Ogburn, William F. *Social Change*. Viking, New York, 1950. Ogburn presents his theory of culture lag and examines how technological change can lead to social disorganization.

Glossary

ACHIEVED STATUS: A status that is earned through individual effort.

ACTIVE EUTHANASIA: Deliberate termination of the life of a patient who is hopelessly ill or nonfunctional.

AGE COHORT: Those individuals who were born during approximately the same general time period.

AGEISM: Prejudice and discrimination directed toward people simply because they are old.

AGE NORMS: Social expectations of what is considered proper behavior at different ages.

AGE-STATUS SYSTEM: Differentially awarding rights and obligations to individuals in a society on the basis of age.

AGING: All the regular changes that take place in biologically mature individuals as they advance through the life cycle.

ANTICIPATORY SOCIALIZATION: Advance preparation for a new status and role.

ASCRIBED STATUS: A status that is assigned by society without regard to individual ability.

BURGLARY: Unlawful or forcible entry into a home to commit theft.

CASE STUDY: A detailed and in-depth analysis of a single case.

CATARACT: Opacity of the lens of the eye.

CENTENARIAN: A person over the age of 100.

COMMUNITY: People living in a limited territorial area where they have a sense of belonging and fulfill most of their daily needs and activities.

COUNTERPHOBIA: The tendency to face a dangerous situation in order to convince oneself that it can be overcome.

CROSS-SECTIONAL DESIGN: Study of the characteristics of a population at one point in time.

CRYSTALLIZED INTELLIGENCE: The skills one acquires through education and the socialization process.

CULTURAL RELATIVISM: A concept that implies that all patterns of behavior should be analyzed in the cultural context in which they are found.

CULTURAL UNIVERSALS: Certain broad characteristics and general categories that all societies have in common.

CULTURE: Social heritage of a society that is transmitted to each generation; learned behavior that is shared with others.

DEPENDENT VARIABLE: The variable that the experimenter measures during the experiment or after it is completed; a variable that is believed to be affected by the occurrence or change of one or more independent variables.

DISCRIMINATION: The unfavorable treatment of individuals or groups on the basis of their membership in a racial or ethnic group.

DISPLACEMENT: Shifting the blame from the real source of one's anxieties or difficulties onto another person, object, or situation.

EARLY RETIREMENT: Retirement before the age of 65.

ECONOMIC INSTITUTIONS: The norms and ideas controlling the production and distribution of scarce goods and services in a society.

EDUCATIONAL GERONTOLOGY: "The study and practice of instructional endeavors for and about aged and aging individuals." — David Peterson.

ELDERHOSTELS: A network of colleges and universities that offer special courses during the summer months to older people.

ETHNIC MINORITY: Persons distinguished by cultural characteristics that differ from the dominant group.

ETHNOCENTRISM: The tendency to regard one's own culture as superior to all others.

EXPERIMENT: A research method in which the investigator controls or manipulates at least one variable and then makes precise measurements or observations of the results.

EXTENDED FAMILY: A family that includes three or more generations that live together and are joined by an extension of the parent-child relationships.

EXTRAPOLATION: The predicting of future trends within a society based on the observation of present trends.

FILIAL MATURITY: A stage of development in which children are depended on by their parents and seen as being dependable.

FOLKWAYS: Norms that govern the conventions and routines of everyday life.

FORMAL ORGANIZATION: A highly organized, impersonal group that operates according to formally stated policies and procedures and is designed to pursue specific objectives.

FUNCTIONAL DISORDERS: Those disorders which have an emotional origin.

GEROCOMY: The belief and practice that an old man may absorb youth from young women.

GERONTICIDE: The killing of the old.

GERONTOCRACY: A form of government in which the old men are the rulers.

GERONTOLOGY: The scientific study of aging.

GROUP: Two or more people who interact with one another in a standardized pattern and share a sense of common identity.

HOMES FOR THE AGED: Nonprofit institutions that are usually sponsored by a church or a fraternal organization and are operated for people who are physically well, but socially dependent.

HOSPICE: A facility or a hospital unit that is devoted specifically to the care of the dying.

INDEPENDENT VARIABLE: The variable that is directly manipulated by the investigator; a variable whose occurrence or change results in the occurrence or change of another variable (the dependent variable).

INFORMAL ORGANIZATION: A small, loosely organized group whose relationships and normative expectations occur without deliberate planning.

INSTITUTION: An organized cluster of norms that surround an important social need or activity of a society.

INTERACTION: Action directed toward another person who interprets the act and responds to it.

INTERMEDIATE-CARE FACILITY: A facility that provides health-related care and services to those who need less care than a skilled nursing facility, but more than custodial care.

INVOLUNTARY EUTHANASIA: Passive or active euthanasia imposed upon a patient who is incapable of giving consent.

LAWS: Norms that are enacted by those who exert political power and that are enforced by the authority of the state.

LIFE EXPECTANCY: The average number of years of life that a person has remaining at a specified age.

LIFE SPAN: The biological age limit.

LIVING WILL: A document that is intended for future use in the event that a person is unable to participate fully in decisions regarding his or her treatment during a terminal illness.

LONGITUDINAL STUDY: Study of the same person or population over a period of time.

MINORITY GROUP: A category or group of people who in some ways differ from the dominant group of society and, because of this, are the object of prejudice and discrimination, which results in their being disadvantaged.

MONOGAMY: Marriage involving one man and one woman.

MORES: Norms that govern the moral standards of a society.

NORMS: Standards or rules for behavior.

NUCLEAR FAMILY: A husband, a wife, and their dependent children.

NURSING HOME: A facility that provides some level of nursing care.

ORGANIC DISORDERS: Those disorders that have a physical origin.

PARTICIPANT OBSERVATION: A technique used in the case study method in which the investigators join and participate in whatever group they are studying.

PASSIVE EUTHANASIA: Permitting a patient to die without the use of artificial measures to sustain life.

PERSONAL LARCENY: The stealing of property without the threat or use of force.

PERSONAL POWER: The ability to control one's own life.

POLITICAL INSTITUTION: An institution that serves to maintain social order, to protect against outside enemies, and to plan and coordinate for the general welfare.

POLITICS: A process by which people acquire and exercise power over others.

POLYANDRY: A type of marriage in which a woman has two or more husbands at the same time.

POLYGYNY: A type of marriage in which a man has two or more wives at the same time.

POPULATION: In survey research, the total number of cases that the investigator plans to study.

PORTABILITY: The transfer of pension rights from one plan to another when the worker changes jobs.

PREJUDICE: A negative, prejudged attitude toward a category or group of people.

PRESBYOPIA: The inability to focus on close objects, commonly referred to as farsightedness.

PRESTIGE: The social recognition and respect that one receives from others.

PRIMARY GROUP: A group in which members have an intimate, personal relationship.

PROGRESS: Social change that is considered desirable.

PROJECTION: The process occurring when an individual attributes to others his or her own undesirable feelings and attitudes.

    racial minority: Persons distinguished by physical characteristics that differ from the dominant group.

RANDOM SAMPLE: A sample that gives each member of the population an equal chance of being chosen.

REFERENCE GROUP: Any group or category that we use as a standard of comparison and by which we measure our accomplishments and failures.

REPRESENTATIVE SAMPLE: A sample that has the same distribution of pertinent characteristics as the population from which it was drawn.

RETIREMENT: The acquisition of an economically nonproductive role, which traditionally occurs around age 65 when one leaves his or her primary occupation.

RETIREMENT COMMUNITY: A planned, relatively self-sufficient entity that is spatially separated from the larger community and whose residents are retired or semi-retired.

RITES OF PASSAGE: Ceremonies that mark the occasion when an individual moves from one age category to the next.

ROBBERY: The stealing of property by the threat or use of force.

ROLE: The expected behavior of one who holds a certain status.

ROLE AMBIGUITY: A condition resulting when there are no clearly defined guidelines or expectations concerning the requirements of a role.

ROLE DISCONTINUITY: The lack of preparation for a role that one will take on at the next consecutive stage.

ROLE MODEL: An individual whose behavior in a certain role provides a pattern for another individual to follow in performing the same role.

ROLE REHEARSAL: The opportunity to act out behavior required in a future role.

ROLE-REVERSAL: When a child assumes the role of father or mother to his or her parent.

ROLE SET: The entire array of related roles associated with a particular status that an individual occupies.

SAMPLE: A limited number of cases selected from the population being studied.

SECONDARY GROUP: A group in which members have an impersonal, superficial, segmental relationship.

SHAMAN: A religious specialist who derives his power from supernatural forces — also referred to as a medicine man or a witch doctor.

SKILLED NURSING FACILITY: "A specially qualified facility which has the staff and equipment to provide skilled nursing care or rehabilitation services as well as other related health services." — HEW, *Your Medicare Handbook.*

SOCIAL CATEGORY: Any number of people who have some specific characteristics in common.

SOCIAL CLASS: A category of individuals and families who share relatively equal amounts of social rewards.

SOCIAL GERONTOLOGY: A branch of gerontology that studies the behavioral aspects of aging.

SOCIAL INTERVENTION: A planned attempt to change, supposedly for the better, the lives of other individuals or groups through the application of skills and knowledge.

SOCIALIZATION: A lifelong process through which individuals learn and internalize the culture and social roles of their society.

SOCIAL MOBILITY: The vertical movement of persons or groups from one social class to another.

SOCIAL POWER: The ability to control or influence the behavior of others.

SOCIAL PROBLEM: A condition that a significant number of people believe to be undesirable and feel should be corrected.

SOCIAL SERVICES: "A social mechanism for [the] distribution of resources designed to achieve and maintain a prescribed level of well-being for all members of society." — H. Shlonsky.

SOCIAL STRATIFICATION: The ranking of individuals and families into higher and lower social positions according to their share of social rewards.

SOCIOLOGY: The scientific study of human interaction.

SOCIOLOGY OF AGING: The scientific study of the interaction of older people in society.

STEREOTYPES: Oversimplified, exaggerated generalizations about a group or category of people.

SUBCULTURE: A group that is part of the larger culture of a society, but at the same time contains its own distinctive lifestyles, norms, and language.

UNRELATED INDIVIDUALS: Those persons who live alone or with nonrelatives.

URBAN FRINGE: An area beyond the established suburbs of a city.

URBANIZED AREA: An area that contains at least one city of 50,000 or more inhabitants plus the surrounding densely settled incorporated and unincorporated areas.

VALUES: Socially learned and shared conceptions of what is desirable, good, or right.

VESTING: The right of employees to receive the benefits they have accumulated in a pension plan if they leave the plan before retirement.

VOLUNTARY ASSOCIATION: A formal organization in which membership is based on choice.

VOLUNTARY EUTHANASIA: Passive or active euthanasia consented to by a mentally competent patient.

Index

86 87 88 89 9 8 7 6 5

Student Evaluation of
SOCIOLOGY OF AGING (Harris/Cole)

Your comments on this book will help us in developing other new textbooks and future editions of this book. We would appreciate it if you could take a few minutes to answer the following questions. You can then mail this page to: **College Marketing Services, Houghton Mifflin Company, One Beacon Street, Boston, MA 02107**

1. What was your overall impression of the text? _____
   _____

2. Did you find the book interesting and readable? ☐ Yes ☐ No
   If not, what problems did you have? _____
   _____
   _____

3. Did the illustrations clarify the text in a useful way? _____
   _____

4. How would you rate the following features of the text?

	Excellent	Very good	Good	Fair	Poor
Writing style	☐	☐	☐	☐	☐
Reading level	☐	☐	☐	☐	☐
Photographs	☐	☐	☐	☐	☐
Cartoons	☐	☐	☐	☐	☐
Charts and tables	☐	☐	☐	☐	☐
Chapter summaries	☐	☐	☐	☐	☐
Bibliographies	☐	☐	☐	☐	☐
Glossary	☐	☐	☐	☐	☐

   Feel free to comment on any of the above items. _____
   _____
   _____
   _____

5. Which chapters were required reading for your class? _____
   _____
   _____

6. Did you read any chapters on your own that were not required reading? _____

_____

_____

7. Are there any topics that you think should have been covered in the text, but were not? _____

_____

_____

8. Did you find the opening chapters useful in explaining the basic concepts of sociology? _____

9. Which chapters did you find the most interesting? _____

10. Do you have any suggestions that might help make this a better textbook? _____

_____

_____

NAME OF YOUR SCHOOL: _____

COURSE TITLE: _____

DEPARTMENT OFFERING THE COURSE: _____

PREREQUISITE FOR THE COURSE: _____

NUMBER OF STUDENTS IN THE CLASS: _____

YOUR AGE: _____

YOUR MAJOR: _____